Stephen Cartmell is a travel writer, dedicated racing enthusiast and one time university lecturer. In order to give his students a well rounded education, he has been known to announce the result of the 2.30 at Cheltenham in the middle of a lecture on the application of Freudian perspective to a post-modern world (whatever that is). His interest in racing has extended to the ownership of several racehorses, all of which gave him chronic indigestion and a very thin wallet. Contact can be made through his local bookmaker. He is a Lancastrian exiled in Hertfordshire.

Also by Stephen Cartmell

GOLF ON THE EDGE

and published by Bantam Books

FROM AINTREE
TO YORK

RACING AROUND BRITAIN

Stephen Cartmell

BANTAM BOOKS

LONDON · TORONTO · SYDNEY · AUCKLAND · JOHANNESBURG

TRANSWORLD PUBLISHERS
61–63 Uxbridge Road, London W5 5SA
A Random House Group Company
www.rbooks.co.uk

FROM AINTREE TO YORK
A BANTAM BOOK: 9780553817461

Originally published in Great Britain in 2002 by Aesculus Press Ltd
as *Racing Around Britain*

Bantam edition published 2006

Addresses for Random House Group Ltd companies outside the UK
can be found at: www.randomhouse.co.uk
The Random House Group Ltd Reg. No. 954009

The Random House Group Limited supports The Forest Stewardship
Council (FSC), the leading international forest certification organisation.
All our titles that are printed on Greenpeace approved FSC certified paper
carry the FSC logo. Our paper procurement policy can be found at
www.rbooks.co.uk/environment

Typeset in 12/13½pt Granjon by
Kestrel Data, Exeter, Devon.
Printed in the UK by
CPI Cox & Wyman, Reading, RG1 8EX.

4 6 8 10 9 7 5 3

For Francesca and Hans

ACKNOWLEDGEMENTS

I owe a great debt of gratitude for the completion of this book to all those drivers who managed to avoid crashing into my car as I hurtled around the motorways and country lanes of England, Scotland and Wales. For the occasional lunatic who tried to park their car in my boot at 95 mph, I am able to supply the name of an excellent psychiatrist. My real thanks, however, go to Ben Newton of the *Racing Post*, who first showed faith in this project.

Appreciation is also due to the 61 racecourses who were willing to submit themselves to my scrutiny and were kind enough to present me with complimentary badges, the unsuspecting punters who unwittingly allowed themselves to be 'interviewed', and to any horse I backed which managed to scramble past the winning post in first place.

A final thanks goes to my family, who have given me great support despite the subject of British racecourses becoming the sole topic of conversation around the dinner table for the last two years.

CONTENTS

Perth

Hamilton Musselburgh

Kelso

Ayr

Hexham Newcastle

Carlisle Sedgefield Redcar

Catterick Thirsk

Cartmel

Ripon York

Wetherby Beverley

Pontefract

Haydock

Aintree Doncaster Market Rasen

Chester Southwell

Nottingham

Bangor-on-Dee Uttoxeter Fakenham

Wolverhampton Leicester Great Yarmouth

Ludlow Huntingdon

Worcester Warwick

Hereford Newmarket

Stratford Towcester

Cheltenham Great Leighs

Ffos Las

Chepstow Newbury Windsor

Ascot Sandown

Bath Kempton Epsom Downs

Salisbury Lingfield

Taunton Goodwood Fontwell Folkestone

Wincanton Plumpton

Exeter Brighton

Newton Abbot

INTRODUCTION

I was bankrupt at the age of eighteen. I don't mean the sort of fake bankruptcy which afflicts city slickers who are down to their last million. I'm talking about being so strapped for cash that a bet of sixpence each-way involved a major life decision. This state of insolvency was mostly thanks to a smiling York bookmaker who seemed to have no hesitation in relieving me of my first-ever wage packet. Such was his willingness to take my money that 'Never give a sucker an even break' was probably his family motto.

At least it wasn't a lingering death. My advancement from calm prosperity to anxious poverty took little more than five races and about three hours. They put me down faster than a vet dispatches an old dog. From that day, I joined the worthy band of men and women who make up at least 95 per cent of racegoers – 'The Honourable Society of Small Punters'. Initially I had no choice. My fingers had been burnt so badly at York that my doctor refused to remove the bandages for more than two years. Whenever I find myself reaching for a £20 note, I need only glance down at those scarred digits.

Did it put me off horse racing? Did a steamy night with Marilyn Monroe ever put a man off sex? If anything, the tragic York experience only reinforced my enthusiasm for a pastime which has been wrongly tagged as the 'Sport of Kings'. When was the last time you saw someone wearing a crown in the Tattersalls enclosure? You may come across the occasional 'high roller' – those shady gamblers who seem to carry bigger wads of ten-pound notes than you'd find in a crooked politician's brown envelope. But royalty and hard-faced gamblers are a minority and the chances are that you belong to the less publicized majority who are the lifeblood of British racing. However tall you are, you're likely to be a small punter – a man or woman who thinks twice before wagering a fiver. You don't go racing to make your fortune. You'll probably be fairly content if your horse manages to get in the frame. You're more likely to have a few bob on a rank outsider than a 15-8 favourite.

Your delight in winning has more to do with defying the so-called experts than simply buying money on a racing certainty. Serious gamblers treat horse racing as a business. The admirable small punter treats horse racing as a hobby and with a constant enthusiasm. It's a chance to meet old friends, an opportunity to enjoy a good day out, an occasion to enjoy the company of fellow punters in one of the least threatening situations you're likely to find at almost any other social gathering. If a small punter makes a profit – heaven. If a small punter breaks even – bliss. If a small punter loses money – *c'est la vie,* no problem, there'll still be food on the table.

Like football, racing is only just catching on to the fact that of the five million people who attend racecourses in a given year, the majority want to be treated with respect, want to have a good view of the course, want to feel included with welcoming simplicity rather than stuffy pomposity. They want facilities that meet their needs rather than those of racing's small but powerful elite. This book addresses these issues and puts the product to the test.

What does he know? I can hear the clamour already. 'What does he know about racing?' 'Bet he doesn't know a stirrup from a bridle.' 'Doubt the chap even owns a brown trilby.' 'How can an "outsider" pass judgement on the racecourses of mainland Britain?' The answer is that most racegoers are outsiders and rarely have any contact with racing's tight-knit community. This book represents the view of the all-rounder, those people who enter a racecourse and take what they're given. I think you'll agree that I have a very strong pedigree.

As a *fanatic* (I shout at the television when my horse isn't winning). As a *dashing punter* (I wore a suit at Haydock Park in 1992). As a *jockey* (I fell off a rocking horse on my second birthday). As a *trainer* (I once suggested to a well beaten selection that it ought to try using all four legs). As a *journalist* (I recently had a letter published in the evening paper criticizing the limited choice of bookmakers in my local high street). As a *bookmaker* (at the age of six, I ran a book on my school's mother and toddlers three-legged race). As an *owner* (I have been insane enough to either own or take a leg in two racehorses, which drained my bank balance on a monthly basis. My last racehorse was named Pacific Run. I should have called it Direct Debit). With such a solid background in racing how could I fail to supply an informed yet objective critique of British racecourses? The problem was – how could this be achieved?

procedure

I have three passions in life – racing, writing and Mars Bars. There seemed no option but to combine these obsessions by attending every course in mainland Britain armed with a notebook and an endless supply of chocolate. This is a simple exercise if you say it quickly. In reality, visiting all sixty-one courses over an eighteen-month period saw me cover almost 16,000 miles, with only the occasional stop for a dental check-up. I developed a simple but effective strategy – i.e. entering each course as a small punter ready to be entertained and intent on keeping an open mind. Though occasionally offered the company of the great and good of racing, it was always my objective to retain a low profile and do no more than to try and put myself in the position of a racegoer visiting the course for the first time. Social anthropologists would no doubt term it 'participant observation'. I'll simply call it 'joining in'.

betting

Attending a racecourse without gambling would be akin to booking a table at a Michelin 5-star restaurant and ordering beans on toast. True to the spirit of small punting, I limited all bets to an initial float of £30. If early success was gained I would be happy to wager more than my usual £5 each-way. On no occasion, however, was I tempted to lose more than £30. By doing so, my maximum loss for the whole exercise would be no more than £1,830. For those interested, a precise record of my successes and failures can be found at the end of the book. I am happy to swear on a faded edition of the *Racing Post* that this is a true representation of my betting track record.

reports

Each of the sixty-one reports are intended to achieve two objectives. Firstly, to entertain anyone who has been or intends to be a visitor to a mainland Britain racecourse.

Secondly, to provide a critique which will help you to decide whether they are worth the effort and how you can make best use of the facilities. On occasions you will find that I have been so taken by the course that I urge you to visit as soon as possible. On the other hand you may find subtle hints that I wasn't too impressed. This may be cleverly concealed in an obscure comment such as, 'I'd rather be lying in a flea-ridden bed with two broken legs and an incontinent bladder than attend this course' – but you'll have to work on these disguised criticisms yourself. To aid your decision, at the end of each article, I have rated each racecourse with a simple-to-follow and highly unoriginal symbol.

5 symbols	Stunning. You'd be a mug to miss this experience.
4 symbols	Excellent – go there.
3 symbols	Good – but one or two drawbacks.
2 symbols	Could do better and need to get their act together.
1 symbol	They should consider turning their racecourse into a greyhound track.
0 symbols	Management should apply for planning permission to build a supermarket.

Can I trust this man's judgement? It's a gamble, I agree. But if you're reading this book, gambling is likely to be part of your life already. In almost all other sports, journalists feel free to criticize and occasionally destroy the players, coaches and management. Not so in racing. To the 'outsider' (i.e. the majority), the world of racing is a closed shop, a secret society which operates with its own codes and practices – including acceptable styles of journalism. Reporting is governed not by law but by an understood etiquette.

The following reports are not an attack on this etiquette but may occasionally stray beyond unfettered kindness. Racecourses, like strutting peacocks, sometimes develop an overblown sense of their own importance and become oblivious to criticism. Unlike a tabloid journalist, I wasn't tempted to wring the peacock's neck – but I couldn't resist ruffling its feathers.

CHAPTER ONE

AINTREE

It all started with four threepenny bits wrapped tightly in a grubby handkerchief. Hardly the crown jewels, but at the time these four coins represented my total life savings. I was desperate for a new fishing rod and certain I'd found a short cut to raising the money.

'Sixpence each-way? You sure?' asked my elder brother.

'Yes,' I answered with nervous bravado, untying the knot and spilling the coins onto the table. 'All of it.'

The rest, as they say, is history. Dick Francis was only a few hundred yards from the winning post when Devon Loch decided he would entertain his royal owner with an impression of a ballerina performing the splits.

'We are not amused,' murmured the Queen Mother as ESB gratefully took his chance and romped home to win by a distance. And I was on it, screaming at the wireless as he was declared the winner. At a starting-price of 100-7, my dreams had been answered – the new fishing rod had become a reality.

You may well think that, even as a small child, I had developed the ability to read racing form. Sadly, this was not the case. My only motive for selecting ESB was that I was incapable of reading the names of any other horse, as I had only reached the stage of recognizing separate letters. ESB fitted the bill perfectly – and so became my first 'mug's bet' winner. A small punter had been born during the magic of a Grand National.

The last time I visited Aintree on the Saturday of the big race had been in 1965, when Jay Trump made it a very profitable day. Unfortunately, despite travelling eighty miles in a road-weary Austin A40, the immense crowd meant that I saw nothing more than the bobbing head of Fred Winter's winning horse. What's more, my old banger broke down on the way home, creating a traffic jam which looked as if it stretched back to Southport. The trauma of this experience has stayed with me, and on this occasion I opted to play safe and visit the course on a Thursday, the day of the Foxhunter Chase, which runs over the National circuit. I had come to see the course, rather than spend four hours with my nose pressed hard against the neck of a Liverpudlian punter.

Get there early. Even on the first day of the National meeting, traffic begins to build up about ten miles from the course and the signposts would test a taxi driver with the nose of a bloodhound. Having followed a number of obscure directions for the Canal Turn, I eventually ended up in a Merseyside Water Board pumping station. Somewhat bemused, and with the aid of a kindly man who had slipped out for a quick smoke, I parked up in the Aintree Retail Park, which lies only a short walk from the racecourse's main entrance. Despite being stung for five pounds, it's a good spot and one to aim for if you can get there before midday.

Owing to the IRA bomb scare in the mid-nineties,

security at Aintree is so tight that it would have been easier for me to get into a pair of trousers with a 32-inch waist. There were so many men in dark glasses and discreet earpieces that I half expected to see the arrival of Bill Clinton – with a moll on his arm. As it turned out, Aintree proved to be a personality-free zone, barring a couple of second division TV actors who looked desperate to be recognized.

Having survived an intimate body search, I stepped into the arena, the entrance lying directly behind the old but still impressive County Stand. There is no gradual effect at Aintree. The impact and sense of occasion is immediate, the atmosphere almost tangible. It's a sensation I have only encountered at a British Grand Prix or the first day of a Lords test, a quality which can't be measured or analysed. I could tell you that bands were playing, clowns were performing, crowds were bustling, spring flowers were blooming and voices buzzed with excitement. But it would be inadequate. As ineffectual as telling you what ingredients went into my Aunt Nellie's old-fashioned chocolate cake. At Aintree the whole is definitely greater than the sum of its parts – and you'll just have to get out of your armchair and make the effort to pay a visit.

If you do, I'd suggest you try and arrive at least two hours before the start of the first race. This will give you chance to stretch your legs and head off on the course-walking route. Thankfully, this is not an organized tour and you are left to wander over and across the course to see the famous fences at close quarters.

After crossing the Melling Bridge, the walk cuts in to the centre course and takes you up the long back straight towards Becher's Brook and the Canal Turn. Unless you've got very high blood pressure or a nervous disposition, don't miss this opportunity. The whole walk takes about an hour at a fairly brisk pace, but you'll return to the stands with the adrenalin pumping and a certainty that jumps jockeys are either completely mad or braver than a cat turning up at Cruft's.

The Aintree fences have been described on many occasions, attracting more comment than the Mona Lisa in a Teach Yourself Painting book. But they easily qualify as works of art, their spruce construction warranting a place in any London gallery. Yet it was the two fences which follow Becher's Brook that took my eye rather than Becher's terrifying obstacle.

I'd wager my next winning betting slip that you've never heard of 'Two-Glove Johnson'. Apart from being a tailor in the docklands of a Lancashire fishing port, he was also the only man I ever knew who had a £5 bet on Foinavon in the 1967 National. At a starting-price of 100-1, this was a serious result which saw him driving a new car within days of collecting his winnings – and guaranteed he could afford to buy left- and right-handed golf gloves for the next three years.

There are two ironies attached to this tale. Firstly, Two-Glove Johnson in fact backed Foinavon by mistake, having confused its name with a well fancied 5-1 shot which fell at the second fence. Secondly, and as I witnessed, the Foinavon fence (as it is now called) turns out to be the smallest obstacle on the course and appears to be no more difficult than a hurdle at Wincanton. Yet it was here that horses fell like bar-room skittles, Foinavon taking his chance and making Two-Glove a surprised but happy man.

It's amazing that the horse got over the next fence. The Canal Turn is probably one of jump racing's great curiosities, a fence set at such an angle to the runners that jockeys must need a school protractor to work out the best line of approach. Having negotiated the jump, they are then required to turn ninety degrees and head off towards Valentine's Brook. All this must be negotiated within seconds of clearing the Canal Turn. A slightly missed calculation is likely to end by a slow horse taking tea in the front room of a house on the Melling Road estate, or a speedier mount joining traffic in the outside lane of the M57.

The course walk takes you along the old Grand Prix circuit where Stirling Moss won his title, and only a year after ESB kick-started my racing career. The winning post marks the end of the tour, which finishes appropriately at the grave of Red Rum, an Aintree legend who, between 1973 and 1977, won the race three times and came second twice. It is a truly remarkable achievement, especially his victory in 1974, when he carried 12 stone around the gigantic fences. Inscribed on his horseshoe head stone is a poetic stanza, which has probably brought a tear to many a punter's eye. Given my failure to back him on any of these occasions, I was very tempted to add the words: 'Over all the fences he has soared. But never had my cash on board'. But perhaps not.

Returning to the stands, I began my search for an early winner in a card of seven races and all high-class fields. After drawing a blank in the first, a novice hurdle, I managed to take MacGeorge at 16-1 in the Martell Cup. As any small punter knows, getting an early return sets you up for the rest of the meeting and there's no greater satisfaction than backing horses with a book-maker's money. Flush with my moderate win, I toured the main facilities, marvelling at the impressive and new

Princess Royal Stand which dominates the main concourse.

Wherever you happen to be at Aintree, you'll have little difficulty finding a drink. Bars of every description litter the site, though the majority can be very crowded. The best tip is to head for the extremes of the course, such as the Chair Pavilion or the very welcoming Glenlivet Bar, just past the paddock. Don't be put off by the 'no neck' guards, who stand menacingly at the entrance and looked as friendly as my neighbour's Rottweiler. When they're not threatening people, I'm sure they are very sweet and kind to their mothers.

Refreshed by my celebratory drink, I headed to the paddock and winner's enclosure. As hard as I tried, I couldn't find fault with the whole set-up. The paddock is perhaps surprisingly small but is decked in flowers and shaded on this breezy but warm spring day by what I think might have been English oaks, horse chestnuts and flowering cherries. (As you'll find in other reports, my identification of flora and fauna displays a complete lack of attention during my sixth-form biology lessons.)

Surrounding the paddock rails are steep grass banks, adorned with bedding plants and flowers spilling out of tastefully placed wicker baskets. Dominating as always, is a fine, life-sized bronze of Red Rum. But look to your right and you'll see something even better: Angela Connor's bust (forgive the ambiguity) – of Peter O'Sullevan – is quite stunning. She has produced a sculpture which seems to display all the emotions this commentator has enjoyed in his sporting life, every race etched into the rough bronze surface.

In its own way the winner's enclosure is equally impressive and must be unique in style. Decked in flowering baskets, the whole area is enclosed on three sides but gives a good view to the admiring public. The box for the winner is detached from the also-rans and, as I witnessed in the next race, can accommodate owners, trainers, jockeys and assorted hangers-on with consummate ease. Get a winner at Aintree and you're going to feel like royalty.

J. P. McManus, Ireland's winner of the Mel Gibson lookalike contest, is a regular visitor to this enclosure and appeared yet again when his horse, Elegant Lord, picked up the Martell Foxhunter Chase and a handy cheque for £13,000. This famous Irish big-time punter was presented with his prize by Monsieur Patrick Martell, the president of the famous drinks company. He proved to be a Frenchman of such charm that it was suggested by one wit in the crowd that when Monsieur Martell goes to work, he's probably the only thing in the office smoother than his Five Star Cognac. From what I saw I think he's probably right.

I had watched the Foxhunter Chase from the famous Mound Stand, an extraordinary concrete slope to the left of the Princess Royal Stand. The size of a football pitch and like a dry ski slope laid on its side, this facility represents racing in the raw. No steps, no seating, no cover but a wonderful view over the finishing stretch – especially the terrifying Chair fence. At a guess, it can probably hold about five thousand people and the roar that goes up as the runners head for the line provides a truly magical moment.

The start of the Foxhunter Chase was preceded by a display by the local hunt, the hounds baying as they passed the stands. As if orchestrated by a musical conductor, punters on the Mound Stand cried out 'Tally ho!' in perfect unison. Two good place bets followed my little touch on MacGeorge and the steps at the rear of the Mound Stand drop you straight into the tented village and the Aintree Pavilion. I had glanced in here on my arrival, a cavernous, canvas hall, containing at least eight bars and an equal number of betting shops.

By the time of my return the place had been turned into a giant dustbin, litter strewn in every direction. Though it had become a bit of an eyesore, the atmosphere had reached fever pitch, whipped into a frenzy by an Irish band with a fiddler whose fingers moved faster than a five-furlong sprinter. They fed the crowd with all the favourite songs, guaranteeing applause and involvement and rising to their finale with 'Sweet Molly Malone' and the surefire winner 'In My Liverpool Home'. It could have been Cheltenham on Gold Cup Day. But it wasn't. This was Aintree – and it had its own individual flavour.

There was only one other thing to experience. I'd glanced at it. Walked past it. Thought about it. Been embarrassed by my childlike desire. But I went for it. Paid my £3 and climbed the steps with the furtive look you see on men's faces as they slip into a Soho strip club. I'd walked the course but now I wanted to ride it. Two young boys and their weary mother viewed me with suspicion as I took my place on the narrow benched seats. The simulator kicked into action.

Like my last bet, it was all a bit of a let-down. The film and jolting box are intended to give you the sensation of a jockey weaving his way through the field and winning the Grand National to the tumultuous applause of the crowd. Sadly, the horse's head which bobs up and down looked more like a dead sheep in desperate need of a hairdresser and they seemed to have reduced the race to a two-mile cavalry charge. To be fair, I did feel my stomach go as I dropped over Becher's Brook but overall it was what I used to call 'a bit of a swiz'. The odd thing is that I went for another go. There was no way I was going to ride the Grand National course and only do one circuit.

Unusually, I stayed right up to the last race of the meeting. My luck was running and the atmosphere heightened with every race. It had been a fine day in every respect, only marred by the fact that, at Aintree, the amount of racing you actually see is very limited. When horses reach the far end of the course they might as well be running in another county. But the indescribable 'feel' of this course should make it a must on everyone's racing calendar.

It was late at night by the time I completed my 200-mile return trip to deepest Buckinghamshire. Pulling into the garage, my lights caught the shape of a long thin object hanging on the redbrick wall. Its brown cotton cover was draped with cobwebs yet clearly visible and scrawled in black ink were the letters ESB. If the weather picks up, I might just give that fishing rod another try.

Postscript: Following a £35 million redevelopment in 2007, overseen by the ubiquitous Charles Barnett (see Ascot chapter), Aintree now boasts five major stands and many more racing days. It has finally, and justifiably, taken its place amongst the top rank of British racing. Can anybody fulfil my dreams and persuade them to bring the British Grand Prix back to Liverpool? Probably not, but I live in hope.

CHAPTER TWO

ASCOT

My visit to Britain's self-proclaimed premier racecourse happened to coincide with a small event, which might affect (or has already affected) more than your occasional visit to the local bookmaker. Across the Atlantic pond, Barack Obama and Hillary Clinton, the two Democrat 'wannabes', were fighting for their presidential lives. As an ardent political voyeur, I'd been following their progress through the mysterious caucus elections and, as far as I could see, they were both delivering their soapbox oratory with a reliance on no more than one word. 'Change,' sings Barack with baritone evangelical zeal. 'Change,' echoes Hillary with the soprano tones of a Washington scrapper.

It made me recall a similar demand by Queen Elizabeth II not long after she had dipped her toe into the millennium. 'ER' (or 'er indoors, as Prince Philip possibly calls her) had suggested that change was needed at Royal Ascot. The various authorities doffed their plumed hats and immediately replied, 'You got it' . . . or, at least, words to that effect. But, as with Hillary and Barack's silky promises, 'change' can be a dangerously ambiguous term.

In the words of the philosophic chanteuse Joni Mitchell, 'You don't know what you've got 'till it's gone.'

Unless you've spent the last ten years in solitary confinement, you will be aware that, in 2006, change came to Ascot with more trumpeted celebration than a royal wedding. Down came the old stand; the track ripped up by its ancient roots; the glorious tree-filled paddock consigned to history and the segregating tunnels buried under glistening steel and sweeping lawns. The redevelopment was decisive and sure-footed in every respect; planners, architects and builders driven by the policy of 'out with the old and in with the new'. Had they succeeded? I was here to find out.

I'll be honest. Though I am instinctively drawn to antiquity, I never really liked the former Ascot. The divisive tunnels between paddock and stands had become an anachronism; the high-railed winners' enclosure a symbol of an outmoded 'us and them' society. In short, it was a racetrack that made its clients feel uncomfortable and terrified of breaching social conventions. I was glad to see the back of it.

Sadly, the grand opening proved to be something of a false start, the public screaming with displeasure, the press unified in tabloid condemnation and the management regime cringing in embarrassment. A morsel of faint praise was offered but at the core of the criticism was the inadequacy of the standing areas below the main grandstand. Like the horses the crowds had come to watch, some of the modernizers had become blinkered to the small fact that punters quite like to see the racing. Unfortunately, the raked stands had been built in such a manner that from the lower steps, racing could only be viewed by a visiting American basketball team. Perhaps, by an ill fate of luck, the old management were all blessed with an average height of 7 feet 6 inches and failed to notice that there may be a problem. Worst of all, and to the sweating horror of the then chief executive, it was found that Her Majesty was unable to see out of the newly constructed Royal Box. This normally placid but constantly diminutive sovereign was not best pleased and, despite Prince Charles offering to let her stand on his shoulders, she demanded that something had to be done.

To no-one's surprise, the perpetrator of these heinous errors fell on his sword just in time to avoid being sent to Tower Hill for public execution. And after much head scratching and a couple of phone calls on the 'old school' network, Ascot found its saviour in the shape of Mr Charles Barnett. A former Oxbridge man, lawyer and managerial 'Mr Fix It', he seemed ideal for the post. Not only had he earned his spurs at Haydock and Aintree, he had once been instrumental in providing floating accommodation for troops after the Falklands War. In 2007 he sailed into Ascot Sound to muster his battalions and shake up the jaded junta.

There's no doubting his pedigree. His former stewardship of Aintree saw him transform this once decrepit Liverpool course into one of the finest racetracks in Britain and, only in his Ascot post for a year, I was willing to grant him some slack. Unlike the politicians' misplaced understanding of the word 'change', I'm aware that transformation comes through evolution rather than a hurried £200 million revamp.

Enter Ascot racecourse through the main High Street gates and the new Grandstand smacks you straight in the face. Three giant, parasol rooftops sit proudly above five floors of glittering windows and four blue towering supports. The old, more austere red brick offices, which border the main road, have thankfully been left in place but seem to be bullied into insignificance by their new usurping neighbour. And though it would have been easy to be sucked in by the fluttering eyes of the Grandstand's preening opulence, I strode forward to put Mr Charles Barnett's skills to an early yet unusual test. Stepping quickly past the paddock, I hurried towards the track and the gloomy exterior of the north-facing grandstand. With a quick detour to place £2 each-way on the outsider Norman the Great, I took my place amongst the sparse, glove-clad crowd.

As the starter let the horses go, I stood on the first step, murmuring 'One' as the runners passed the winners post for the first time. With each furlong of the race completed I moved up by one step, on every occasion whispering my location with a frosted breath. By the time I had reached the sixth row I was beginning to attract some very suspicious glances from fellow punters. But to clarify my methodology, I had cleverly worked out that the two-mile hurdle would therefore allow me to ascend sixteen steps (one per furlong) before the runners reached the end of the race.

I have to report that I was only able to see the final six furlongs, the rest of the contest obscured by white plastic rails and a variety of flora and fauna which attempts to hang on to life in the centre of the course. And given this mathematical detail, you will have no difficulty in realizing that there is little point in standing anywhere below the tenth step if you want to see your selection get beaten into second place by six lengths (the fate of Norman the (not so) Great). If you want confirmation of these findings, wander down to the 'owners and trainers only' viewing area as they watch their charges fail to meet their expectations. You won't find one miserable body below the tenth step. But to be fair to Mr Charles Barnett, he's given the problem his best shot and despite spending £2 million raising the stands, he has publicly admitted that there's nothing else that can be done without knocking down the grandstand and starting again.

Whether he has managed to rectify the Queen's personal sighting problems, I have no idea. I had as much chance of getting in the Royal Box as I have of taking Cate Blanchett out to dinner. All I can report is that any race-goer who attends Ascot will become intimately familiar with Queen Elizabeth's rear end. I don't mean this in any disrespectful manner but only to offer a visual image of the Royal Box's eccentric nature. This rounded, bulbous, black and blue structure looks as though the captain of an ocean liner has rammed the main stand at 30 knots and abandoned ship with the stern of his vessel being the only evidence of his naval collision.

As far as the track is concerned, it remains as a fairly flat one-mile, six-furlongs triangle with sweeping bends and a tough two-and-a half-furlong inclined finish. To the right (from the stands) a mile-long straight course extends to the eastern boundary of the track. I know little about turf apart from cutting my grass twice a week between May and September. My only comment is therefore limited to reporting that it is very green and, despite some early teething problems, now provides enough grip to prevent most horses from falling over in the middle of a race.

Buildings are another matter – especially as I have lived in one for many years. I can therefore speak with some authority on matters concerning the Grandstand. Just after entering the course, I overheard a highly technical appraisal of the new grandstand from a clearly well-qualified fellow punter.

'Stone me! Look at the size of it!' declared the shrill, high-heeled critic. To put it in layman's terms, the new Ascot grandstand is gargantuan in every respect, pragmatic in design and a true symbol of 21st century architecture. Sadly, it also looks like one of the omnipresent shopping centres that have invaded Britain's urban sprawls. Yes, the sea swell roof is dramatic, the expansive glazed frontage reflective of a new era and the four towers (of the apocalypse?) imposing in every respect. But it is hard to avoid the feeling that you are observing Tesco's latest attempt to take over the retail world. It is only saved (or damned) by the bizarre state of its interior. You will be confronted by a convolution of corridors (they call them concourses), an entanglement of escalators and bridges, a labyrinth of levels and cores, and a ratatouille of restaurants. It is reminiscent of the futuristic world depicted by early sci-fi writers in which automatons glide between their various workstations. For those of you with a more artistic nature, think of Escher's 1953 lithograph entitled *Relativity* in which faceless bodies wander though a series of doors and staircases which have no point of destination or any sense of perspective.

Standing for a few minutes on Level 2 (unsure whether I was on a concourse, a core or a corridor) I watched the orienteering crowds attempt to find their way around the grandstand. Armies of bowler-hatted attendants tried their best to reduce the confusion, constantly restraining bewildered punters from taking an escalator which would send them onto a level way beyond their station. I could bear no more and after taking two wrong bridges and four wrong escalators found myself thrown out onto the terrace above the new paddock.

Before attempting a description of this area I must pay homage to the past. The old paddock was truly a thing of beauty, eager horses meandering through the dappled light of ancient shading trees, bending their balletic knees to the regular Royal patronage. Now, it stands discarded, the finest oak tortured into depression by a wooden number board, screwed into a proud gnarled trunk infused with memories of its faded history.

At least it can glance over to the pre-parade ring and think of better times. From here the horses are led along a rubberized track, their nervous metalled hooves dancing on the unfamiliar surface as if walking on hot coals. And once under the tunnelled entrance they are persuaded into the new paddock arena, a Romanesque amphitheatre surrounded by high-banked steps. With the grandstand as its backdrop it is a truly stunning setting which gives access to not only the premier ticket holders but also the general public. Despite my admiration for the old paddock, this is definitely a major improvement and a symbolic recognition that Ascot has made a real effort to introduce an element of egalitarianism into its once stuffy attitude to racing's true supporters.

There are, however, a number of blemishes to report. It's a pity that the weighing room is tucked out of sight and that the presentation stand is of such a mystifying design. From one position it looks like a wilting, heraldic fleur-de-lis, from another angle like a Perspex crashing wave. Perhaps I missed something but its obscure form seems a little inconsequential amongst such grandeur. And the same could be said for the new bandstand which sits adjacent to the paddock. It's a grey gunmetal affair that wouldn't encourage me to dance around its steps on a hot summer's day.

My current visit was far removed from the social bedlam of Ascot's Royal summer meeting. It's a 'must go to' event – if you like being crushed by champagne swilling drunks and women who spend thousands of pounds transforming themselves from delicate English roses into ridiculous, wide hat, wrinkled mushrooms. (OK, there are a few exceptions, but it's not my cup of tea.) I can't disguise the fact that I'm always happier on a cold January day when glowing skin is provided by nature and the dress code involves a cosy woollen muffler and a pair of stout, sober shoes.

The Victor Chandler Day provided all the necessary ingredients of winter pleasure. Despite two weeks of torrential rain, Ascot, to their credit, inspected at 8 a.m. and declared they were fit for running. The going was declared as soft/heavy in places and clearly a day when I would take money from the bookmakers. The beauty of these conditions is that form goes out of the window and high priced outsiders (favoured by small punters) have every chance of upsetting the odds. Norman the Great gave me a satisfactory place in the first, whilst Warne's Way (backed at 33-1) was beaten only one and three-quarters lengths in the second. I clearly had the measure of the track and it was only a matter of time before the book-makers felt the full force of my expertise.

As the feature race approached, I unfortunately forgot one of my golden rules of betting (see Goodwood). This is based on the scientific method of backing the first horse or trainer you encounter when entering the course and has served me well over the years. On entering Ascot, I hadn't so much as encountered a trainer as become involved in a full collision. The man in question was David Pipe, the man who had taken over the reins of one of the most successful National Hunt yards in history. What greater clue was I looking for? But, like the former management of Ascot, I had become blinkered to the obvious and I backed a donkey which clearly hated water, mud and any fence higher than a garden gnome.

It proved to be a sensational race which I viewed (as best I could) from the tenth step of the raked stand, the outsider Tamarinbleu (trainer: David Pipe – damn it) headed twice by the favourite Twist Magic, before pulling away in the home straight and battling his way to the winning post. This magnificent contest suggested that despite the National Hunt track being somewhat distant from the Grandstand, this racecourse can still provide a true thrill of the chase.

I felt a little better about the new Ascot. 'Change' may have come with indecent haste and it has certainly been a bumpy ride for the managerial jockey, Charles Barnett. But there are signs that he is beginning to trim down his charge to a racing weight and could well ride out as strong a finish as David Pipe's Tamarinbleu. What Ascot now needs to do is to drop the hollow political rhetoric of Barack Obama and Hillary Clinton. 'Change' is not enough on its own and they must now search hard for Ascot's soul. Maybe it's buried, somewhere deep below the foundations of the new Grandstand, perhaps amongst the twisted roots of that melancholic tree, which once spread its sturdy branches across the discarded old paddock. Until it's rediscovered, I'm reserving judgement.

CHAPTER THREE

AYR

Amongst my closest friends, I am known as a man who possesses the map reading skills of a blindfolded chimpanzee. The challenge of locating this Scottish racecourse from deepest Buckinghamshire was too great a test, so I took the 'knees under your chin' flight up to Glasgow, hopped on a local train and arrived in Ayr well before I'd digested my breakfast. The forty-minute rail journey is a delight, slipping along a coastline bristling with windswept golf courses. The jewel amongst them all is Royal Troon, a course whose gorse-lined fairways are so terrifyingly narrow that members have to walk in single file.

The beauty of an Englishman racing in the West of Scotland is that you feel like a truly international punter, the language being as incomprehensible as that of an Icelandic auctioneer. Most of my information comes from chatting to the locals, so I anticipated a hard day at Ayr racecourse. But this is Burns country, and you can't fail to be struck by the poetic and musical accent, the animated facial expressions and flailing arms, which make the French look wooden in comparison. Unfortunately, this immersion in Celtic culture proved to be a short-lived pleasure, as I was soon to discover that the English establishment still has a firm grip on Scottish racing.

Nowhere is this more apparent than when entering the course from the members' car park. I stood for a moment on the steps of Western House (the ancient and magnificent quarters for past clerks of the course). I was passed by various weather-beaten officials, annual tweeded members and sleek-suited businessmen, who all seemed to have less in common with Scotland than the Duke of Edinburgh. At the time of my visit, entrance through Western House was £16 – double the alternative Tattersalls enclosure, but perhaps worth it just to experience what turned out to be the only really comfortable facility on the whole of the racecourse. If you are treating yourself to a special day, the very refined (but enclosed) restaurant offered an acceptable lunch for £16, though it's so far from the paddock and course that you'll need a good meal to retain your stamina.

The majority, however, gain access through the main entrance, an ill-designed monstrosity that enjoys the style of a 1960s technical college. Scattered leaflets promote this course as 'Scotland's premier racecourse' – and within seconds of entering, I had the impression that Ayr has pretensions to join the big league. This is no small country venue and on size alone could lay claim to being taken seriously. However, you'll see from other reports that I belong to the school of 'small is beautiful'. There are exceptions such as Goodwood, Sandown and Kempton, which seem to combine large venues with a sense of intimacy. Sadly, I'm unable to include Ayr in this list.

From the glamour of Western House to the far reaches

of the Tattersalls enclosure must be at least a quarter of a mile. Within this stretch of land are a mishmash of rather unattractive buildings which appear to have been sited with the logic of a very dumb punter. The Club Stand with its impressive clock tower and canopied roof is pretty enough, but has begun to look worn and jaded; while the remaining collection of grandstands and bars enjoy the seediness of a vagrants' hostel.

Nowhere is this more apparent than the extraordinary Eglington building above the main turnstiles. Access is gained over two bridges behind the main stands, and the building offers bars and function rooms that would raise complaint at a motorway service station. Not only are they plastic paradises but they enjoy no view whatsoever, apart from the traffic on Whitletts Road and the grimy brick facade of the Ladbrokes betting office behind the Grandstand. If I ever come into money, I'll buy them a bulldozer.

I'm not sure what's happened over the years but, at a guess, they've used the darning tactic. This involves the over-optimistic belief that if you mend a sock often enough, you end up with a new sock. Not so. The result is rarely more than a multicoloured patchwork, which threatens to come undone at the seams.

In the case of Ayr, these seams are all too apparent, from the nonsense of the Eglington Bars to the myriad of grey concrete steps, which have the appeal of an entrance to a disused Victorian street lavatory. This haphazard approach to development is also highlighted by the New Craigie Stand – a building erected at the end of the main straight for the benefit of the dreaded corporate punters. I'm sure it's functional and does the job, but I've witnessed more architectural panache in an industrial warehouse –

or the new Tesco building, which looms over the two-furlong pole.

The paddock area may be Ayr's only saving grace. The oblong parade ring has retained the old white wooden rails and numerous button seats, and grassed banks allow easy viewing of the sweating contestants. Yet even here the presentation seems a bit half-hearted, the grassed centre of the paddock left totally bare, with a few potted plants reserved for the accessible winner's enclosure, which is incorporated into the arena.

At its side stands a new weighing room and the single-storey Be Friendly Bar, whose interior proved to be a clutter of plastic seats and age-worn tables. Despite having a potentially good view of the paddock, the powers-that-be had managed to allow two fast food outlets to park up outside the windows, turning the bar into a dark and dingy dungeon.

So this is the backdrop to Ayr racecourse – a disorganized and rather shambolic folly, which wastes its main resource. Without exception this is the friendliest course I have visited in mainland Britain. Everyone I encountered seemed willing to sacrifice their life to increase my pleasure, happily avoiding the 'have a nice day' insincerity. Whenever a greeting was given you felt they meant it. Perhaps my face betrayed my dissatisfaction with the racecourse and I looked like a man in need of therapy. Even ordering a cup of tea from one of the numerous fast food vans provided much-needed pleasure.

'Milk and sugar?' asked the young man.

'Please.'

'Neh problem.'

I liked that. 'Neh problem.' Nothing seemed to be a

problem. From gatemen to office staff, the sincere willingness to raise my contentment was obvious. Transport this
lot to a real premier course and they'd have to close the
gates half an hour before the first race. When I arrived,
there was some confusion about my ticket, and three times
I was shuffled between Western House and the main
turnstiles. As it turned out, while I had been running in
one direction, a member of the staff had been running in
the other.

With great apology I was finally presented with a bright
orange badge by a young woman who was obviously
taking a day off from a very successful modelling career. If
I had shown her the black notes in my little red book,
she'd probably have shown me the door.

You'll see from my other reports that the notebook
often gets me into trouble. Ayr was no exception. Like
doctors with stethoscopes, carrying anything which
smacks of authority appears to give you a false air of
unquestionable knowledge. I must have had at least ten
conversations with complete strangers, which followed a
very similar pattern.

'Fancy anything in the next?' I was asked.

'Not sure.'

'You look like you know what you're doing.'

'Not really.'

'Come on.'

'Favourites' race,' I would answer, with as much
certainty as I could muster.

'Great. Thanks.'

'Neh problem,' I'd respond, slipping into the ver-
nacular.

Whoever those ten people were, I suspect they thought
they'd just encountered the King of the Tipsters. Of the

seven races on the card, four favourites sneaked in – while six out of seven got into the frame. Needless to say, as a confirmed mug punter, I only managed to back two of them – but enough to make it a fairly cheap day out. I don't know what percentage of favourites win at Ayr but I suspect it's higher than average. The flat one-mile, four-furlong course is suited to galloping stayers; while at jumps meetings, the hurdles and fences are not dissimilar to the generous obstacles at Carlisle.

None of them seem to carry much threat, though. Their main defence is that horses take them at speed rather than at a measured stride. It's therefore fairly difficult to distinguish the hurdle races from the steeplechases – and Ayr's Scottish Grand National should be renamed as The Very Long Scottish Race With A Lot Of Big Hurdles. I know it's a long title but at least punters would know what they're in for.

What a virgin Ayr racegoer won't realize is that, like many mixed racecourses (Ascot is a prime example), the jumps course is placed on the inner circuit and gives punters such a sense of detachment that the horses could be running around the main streets of nearby Glasgow.

One way to make up for this irritation is to supply the public with a really dependable tannoy system, which if done correctly can double your sense of involvement. I suspect the public address system at Ayr was made by John Logie Baird when he was no more than a wee sprat. What made it even worse was that the commentator was a real professional. His box is located at the very top of the Grandstand – an unseated area, which provides the very best view of the course and is open to the public via another set of dreary concrete stairwells.

I placed myself next to his commentary position for the third race, in which Mighty Moss did the business and came in at a short but welcome price. As I was able to pick up his narration without the aid of loud speakers, it proved to be the only moment of real excitement I enjoyed all day. As the race ended, he stepped out of his box and I approached.

'Great commentary,' I offered.

'Thanks.'

'Tannoy's not too good. I bet only half the crowd heard a thing you said. Bit of a waste, really.'

'I know. Coming to the National tomorrow?'

'Can't, I'm afraid.'

'Don't worry. Nobody will hear a word.'

As far as I could see, any new money on offer seems to have gone into a smart new weighing room and an owners' and trainers' bar. What do the management do when a race is running? Watch the television? If they were to get out onto the course and share the experiences of the punters, they might think of investing in a 21st-century sound system. You can build as many stands as you like, but ignore the detail and your turnstiles will creak with underuse.

In 1974, Red Rum won the Scottish Grand National – the only horse to have ever won at Aintree and achieve the double in the same year. Standing proudly at the side of the paddock is a bronze statue to commemorate this unique feat. Any punter whose memory doesn't go back almost thirty years is left to work this out for themselves, as the plinth on which the sculpture stands bears two large brass plates with the inscription 'KEEP OFF' – and no other indication of the jumper's glittering career. I know it's just another detail but little things like that can be as irritating as an inaudible tannoy. If I'm ever fortunate enough to own a contender for The Very Long Scottish Race With A Lot Of Big Hurdles, I'll change its name to 'Keep Off'. That should throw them – especially when they build the statue.

The night after my return from Ayr, I whiled away a few hours watching a television adaption of *Madame Bovary,* Flaubert's wonderful tale of a woman of uncontrollable desire. She was married to a country doctor who seemed reasonably alive from the waist down but completely dead from the neck up.

'Got it!' I screamed, as yet another steamy liaison unravelled before me.

'Got what?' asked my wife, irritated by the interruption to the climactic scene.

'Madame Bovary's husband and Ayr racecourse. They've got the same problem.'

'Which is?'

'Plenty of action. No passion.'

'I bet Flaubert never thought of that.'

'Don't think he was a racing man.'

Postscript: Planned improvements are to be subjected to the nightmare of a public inquiry. Here's a tip. Treat the Chairman of the inquiry to a day at Ayr races. He or she will soon see the need to rejuvenate the ingredients of this Scotch broth of a racecourse.

CHAPTER FOUR

BANGOR-ON-DEE

As you accompany me through the racecourses of mainland Britain, you may well wonder how I managed to retain any degree of solvency during my period of detailed research. Avoidance of penury is due in part to the generosity of many courses who were kind enough to respond to pleading letters detailing my shoeless children and a wife who needs to take in ironing. More than often this has resulted in the presentation of a complimentary ticket and, on the odd occasion, a slap-up lunch. Bangor proved to be a noticeable exception.

At only £10 entry to Tattersalls, this hardly broke the bank – and wallet damage was quickly alleviated by backing the first three winners at this North Wales meeting. However, the interest lies not in the refusal of my request for a freebie but in the authorities' justification for their response.

It was Countryside Alliance Day at the time of my visit and I had dressed appropriately in my well polished brogues and an extremely fetching pair of battered green corduroys. I'd probably have enjoyed more success in a black balaclava and a pair of army combat trousers.

'Just like you, Mr Cartmell, we're here to run a business,' responded the course official. 'Would you give your books away for nothing?' he added pointedly. I spluttered my answer in what was supposed to be an assertive manner, yet ended up delivering a weak protest with the self-assurance of a patient on an operating trolley. It seemed easier to put up and shut up. I did.

It's necessary to stress at this point that the rejection of my request was discharged with immense politeness and with not a hint of hostility. But – 'We're here to run a business'? I was about to test out his claims.

Before detailing the pleasures of Bangor, it's worth issuing a word of warning. If, on your journey to the course, you happen to see signs for Anglesey or the Menai Straits, you've probably missed the racecourse by at least 80 miles. I'm told that a few horseboxes have disappeared without trace when the trainer has employed a driver who thought Bangor racecourse was on the North Wales coast. Bangor-on-Dee (or to give it its tribal title, Bangor-is-y-coed) is close to Wrexham and no more than fifteen miles over the English border.

If you approach from the south, as I did, the stresses of motorway madness are eased as you meander north through the Shropshire countryside. Hitting a major traffic jam only thirty minutes from my destination, I was forced onto minor roads which rarely see anything faster than a combine harvester. Just south of Oswestry is the delightful village of Knockin, which was to satisfy my incessant craving for chocolate. Asking for a Mars Bar in the shrewdly named Knockin Shop proved more embarrassing than my later confrontation in the Bangor secretary's office.

By the time I walked into the racecourse I was only just

regaining my composure. It proved to be only a temporary condition. At first sight, Bangor appears to be just another country National Hunt course. Yet within seconds, you'll be aware that something is missing. All the usual bits and pieces are evident – paddock, winner's enclosure, betting facilities, various bars and cafes – all housed in single-storey constructions. It's bungalow city, an area which suggests that the Welsh have yet to discover staircases. And it's this determination to stay at ground level which solves the mystery of the missing element. However hard you search, there's not one sign of a stand, not one covered area which raises you more than three feet above ground level.

To be fair to Bangor, the geography of the racecourse mitigates the disadvantages of this startling omission. The course itself is set in a natural bowl while the viewing areas are sited on high banked raised ground. The effect is to create the feel of an amphitheatre not dissimilar to Chester – without the city wall. And without grandstands. And without a river. And without a railway viaduct. And without Roman ruins. Apart from that they are very alike.

The predominantly flat one-and-a-half-mile, left-handed circuit stretches out into the distance, circling arable farm land and stark single oak trees. On the horizon stand the Minera Hills, framing what must be one of the finest views in racing – especially on a late autumn day when leaves are dying for the sake of beauty. Bangor is one of nature's gifts. Unfortunately it is wrapped in rather cheap paper. At the summit of the huge bank – possibly some thirty feet above the racecourse – stand a string of wooden buildings but at their centre two rather smart brick constructions. Set in front of these facilities is the paddock, an unusually large oval which seems to dominate the whole area. A separate winners' enclosure stands immediately in front of the stewards and weighing room, built as recently as 1997. Once again viewing of these areas is limited to flat ground and you need to get against the rail early in order gain any sort of access. The other brick construction, again with a prime sight of the course, turned out to be an owners' and trainers'/annual members' only bar and inaccessible to the average punter. This is a racecourse where the priorities are not difficult to identify.

For the vulgar rabble, such as myself (and despite brogues and cords), facilities are bare and unattractive. The cafe/restaurant at the back of the Tattersalls bar is adequate though overpriced for a country course; while, on a wet day, punters would have little chance not to get soaked if they hoped to watch the racing. Even worse is that you're unlikely ever to see an exciting contest at Bangor. Two out of my first three winners won by little more than a short-head, yet the finish was as exciting as spending my evening watching a neighbour's slide show of his recent holiday to Aberystwyth.

The problem lies in the course layout. The final two furlongs of the pear-shaped circuit are head-on to the watching crowd and destroy any sense of perspective which might be enjoyed with the more common side-on view. Only by walking 300 yards or so down to the rails of the finishing straight have you any hope of feeling involved with the race to the line. As a consequence, however, you have little chance of watching any of the developing race. What is even more peculiar is that the main standing areas look down onto a perfectly adequate three-furlong straight which could give punters an ideal view of the finish if someone in authority had the nerve to introduce a simple but revolutionary remedy– i.e. turn the damned thing round. Would the world implode if Bangor became a right-handed course? If the only justification for retaining the present layout is that 'It's always been like this', then we might as well reintroduce burning heretics at the stake – or, even worse, retain hereditary peerages.

And there seemed to be a fair number of our noble lords who had been tempted down from their Welsh estates. What was extraordinary about the day was what seemed to be a complete absence of Welsh accents. At a guess, 50 per cent of punters appeared to be race-hardened Scousers, while at least 25 per cent sported the plummy tones of Knightsbridge residents. The place felt about as Welsh as the Prince of Wales. There may be plenty of 'Jones' and 'Williams' left in the Valleys but I got the distinct impression that most of this part of Wales is still owned by landlords who are more likely to be called Blitherington-Fopworth, or some such like. Whoever these people are – they were out in force. The Countryside Alliance Day had attracted every gun-toting hunter within eighty miles – perhaps even one or two from Anglesey. Falconry displays were followed by Sir W. Wynn's foxhounds and the Cheshire Beagles, their hunting horns sending every living creature within earshot scampering for cover and locking their front doors. At the risk of alienating a number of readers, I've not got much objection to fox hunting. As a country resident myself, I've witnessed the alternative – and it ain't pretty. Shooting, however, is a different matter as there's something inherently barbaric about rearing grouse, partridge and pheasant and then giving them thirty seconds to claim their genetic birthright before filling them full of lead shot. But there we are.

Following my early success, I drew a blank in the fourth

race. Venetia Williams' Cardinal Rule went off a fairly firm favourite and with A. P. McCoy on board seemed like a good thing. Five fences from home he looked to be coasting on a tight rein only to hit the third from last with a thud you could have heard in Oswestry. Despite staying on his feet, Cardinal Rule began to fade, the course commentator excitedly informing the crowd that the horse appeared to have suddenly hit a brick wall and was beginning to tail off. Like the falcons on display, I had reached the end of my tether and headed up the steep bank towards the exit. A small huddle of disappointed men bemoaned their luck, hurling their crumpled betting slips onto the ground.

'Couldn't see it getting beaten,' murmured one of the punters ruefully.

'Me neither,' moaned another.

It was obvious they had all gone for broke on Cardinal Rule and were now chasing their losses. Another voice suddenly interrupted the bleating of these injured punters.

'Got a pair of binoculars?' he asked.

'What for?' came a reply. 'The race is over.'

'Yes, I know. I just want to see where that bloody brick wall is.'

A journey of 180 miles lay ahead, the October sun already dropping towards the horizon. It was tempting to return the way I had come but opted for the longer but quicker route towards Crewe and on to the nightmare of the M6 motorway. Besides which, I didn't feel a man of my age had the energy to visit the Knockin Shop more than once in a day, however heightened was my desire for another Mars Bar. I had made money, enjoyed the view and . . . well, enjoyed the view. But all in all, it had been a disappointment. There's no doubt it's unique and quirky.

But a tin bath in front of a coal fire is quirky and quickly loses its appeal once you've stood under the torrents of an invigorating power shower. Unless I'm passing, I'll take my baths elsewhere.

Postscript I: That same evening I retired to bed only minutes after returning home. I slept lightly and dreamt heavily, at one point finding myself taking minutes at Bangor racecourse's AGM. As is the way with these flights into the unconscious, I was dressed in a full jockey's outfit and appeared to be recording the debate with a riding crop. By way of contrast the ten-man committee were garbed in full military uniform last seen during the disastrous Charge of the Light Brigade. An irate lieutenant got to his feet and saluted the chairman.

Lieutenant: 'I wish to raise a number of points, Mr Chairman.'

Chairman: 'Mmm?'

Lieutenant: 'Are you aware that the public have nowhere to stand, often get drenched to the skin and that the incidence of punter's pneumonia is rife in north Wales? And are you aware that the course is the wrong way round? Do you realize that no-one has seen the finish of a race at Bangor for over 120 years? I demand to know what action you are going to take.'

Chairman (suddenly donning a highly feathered helmet): 'Now look here, Lieutenant, and damn your impertinence – we're trying to run a business here don't y'know.'

Lieutenant: 'That's precisely my point, Mr Chairman.'

Chairman (growing in annoyance): 'Very well. I have a suggestion. We'll take the two prime spots on the hill and build a weighing room and facilities for owners and trainers. Next to that I suggest a bar for annual members only and a nice little office for stewards and officials. In both cases no access to the general public. Now if that's not revolutionary and forward thinking, I'll eat my helmet.'

Lieutenant: 'But . . .'

Chairman: 'All those in favour say "Aye".'

Lieutenant: 'Just a . . .'

Chairman: 'Good show. Carried unanimously. Next item.'

If anyone reading this article has skills in dream interpretation, perhaps you could let me know what it all means.

Postscript II: The racecourse has been taken over by the Chester Race Company. There is hope. Don't give up on Bangor . . . especially if they adopt a couple of retired Roman legionaries onto the committee.

CHAPTER FIVE

BATH

It was a day when I was certain God was on my side. Stopping for petrol on the A46 near Cold Ashton, I spotted a copy of *Cotswold Edge,* the parish magazine for a small number of villages near to Bath racecourse. Written on the top of this uncollected pamphlet was the word 'Bett'. Was this Mrs Bett? Mr Bett? Miss Bett? Bett Minor? Whatever the case, I took this as a sure sign that fate was about to take a hand in my day's punting. Such is the mind of small-time gamblers that they clutch at even the smallest of straws. It's the same logic that drives men and women to fill in football pool coupons with birthdates of spouses, children and their pet dog, Fido. There is no sense in it, of course – but that's what makes it so appealing.

So it was that, on a warm June day, I parked up outside Bath racecourse and scanned the parish newsletter for one sign that God was about to work a miracle. The Reverend Michael Westlake wrote meaningfully about the 'goodness' of summer, the newly dead, the newly born and the newly spliced. The exclusive editorial would have been enough to rock the readership of a national tabloid. The

Gymkhana Committee of Cold Ashton and Marshfield had been forced to scrap the Saturday morning holiday breakfasts due to a lack of volunteers. As the Reverend Westlake said, 'The news has proved a great blow to so many in our villages.' Could there be anything worse lurking in this small magazine? Despite searching for over fifteen minutes, there was no sign of 'Reverend Westlake's Tip of the Day' and it was plain that the clue was going to be far more obscure. God was obviously having one of his mysterious days, though I was sure all would be revealed once I had a racecard in my hands.

It's said that Bath racecourse is the highest Flat course in Britain and I took this closeness to the heavens as yet another biblical omen. Even from the grassed car park glimpses of the Mendip Hills can be seen in the distance, while the city of Bath nestles in the valley some five miles to the south. This fine setting is unfortunately not matched by first impressions of the racecourse. The back of the dour stands give an impression of a disused factory, their grey exteriors crying out for a splash of paint. The giant radio mast which sits at the side of the course does little to add to Bath's appeal. It looked like a racecourse that had seen better days.

I had only been on the course for two minutes when these first impressions were confirmed. With over an hour to go before the first race, I got into conversation with a bookie who had volunteered to lay out the small wooden boxes on which his fellow workers ply their trade. Such was his home-spun philosophy that I could have been in the back of a London taxi. It wasn't so much a conversation as a verbal onslaught delivered by a man who was unfamiliar with the word 'pause'.

'Look at it! Look at it! I remember the days when this

place would be bloody heavin' by now. Seen the card? Not a decent animal amongst 'em. Bloody donkeys. Donkeys. Prize money? Prize money? Cost 'yer more in petrol. Surprised anyone turns up. See over there? Over there? (*He points to the centre course enclosure.*) Me old mate Charlie Faulkner used to build a bonfire over there. Serve sausage butties with one 'and and take the punters' money with the other. Good days they were. Not now. Not now. They wanna' get bloody Goebbels 'an 'immler in to run it. Ve 'ave vays of makink you come racing. Bettin'? Bettin'? Lucky if 'ah see a fiver these days. Ow you supposed to make a bloody living when the punters won't part with more than two quid? I tell you . . .'

And he did tell me. And just in case I hadn't understood, told me again. What he was really saying was that small-course racing in Britain is in danger of shooting itself in the foot. And in all truth, I'm a small-course man. But in my travels I have witnessed too many courses living on past glories and hoping that punters won't notice the run-down appearance. Nowhere was this more evident than in the paddock, a spacious area, well laid out, good view, comfortable button seats and a real sense of involvement. But they hadn't even bothered to cut the grass; they hadn't even bothered to construct a few decent flower beds. Even the obligatory bell hadn't seen a drop of polish in 10 years – and the bell pull looked like a piece of string left over from a Christmas parcel.

Quibbling? You bet I am. A few tins of paint, a jar of polish and a lawn mower could have transformed this area in thirty minutes. If they'd waived my £14 entrance fee, I'd have done it myself. The sadness is that I liked Bath racecourse. It needn't live on past success as it has a lot going for it – its biggest asset being the course itself. I had read somewhere that the mile-and-a-half circuit is reminiscent of a squashed sausage. Whoever wrote that must eat some strange sausages. The best way I can describe it is to ask you to take a rubber band, throw it on a table and see how it invariably ends up as two loops, with the middle of the band pushed close together. This is Bath.

The advantage of such a strange construction is that the finishing two furlongs, opposite the stands, are no more than 150 yards from the back straight. The effect is that you are unlikely to miss a stride of the race from any position on the main concourse. The mile start is even better, the stalls being placed only a short distance from the Silver Ring stands. Even the finishing straight is designed for optimum viewing as it contains a major kink at about the two-furlong pole. Rather than having to hang over the rail to get a sight of a head-on rush to the line, the pack can be seen quite clearly and any likely winner can be spotted manoeuvring for position from as far out as the three-furlong pole.

As a small punter, I've never really been sold on this idea that you need class horses to make a good day's racing. To take the analogy of Formula 1 racing, there's a lot more fun to be seen in a touring car event. So it is with horse racing. A race is a race – whatever the pedigree of the thoroughbreds. I've enjoyed as much excitement watching a five-furlong auction race as I have with my money on board a Derby favourite.

The first race at Bath only proves my point. Despite searching the card for any reference to the *Cotswold Edge* parish magazine, I failed to locate anything of a biblical nature. In an act of desperation I went for Umistim on the solid form guide that the dam was Simply Sooty and I used to live next to Harry Corbett's uncle. As I say – small punters grab hold of some very weak straws.

With only two strides to go Umistim looked an all over winner, only to be pipped on the line by the unraced two-year-old filly Sonbelle, at 40-1. It was as exciting a finish as I've seen in the last few years and I was able to witness every stride of the winner's progress. You wouldn't get that at Epsom, York or Ascot and the slow time of the race made no difference to the passion of the contest.

So whatever the 'standard of racing' (what does that really mean to the average punter?), Bath has got everything. The trouble is that it's a Cartier watch wrapped up in a brown paper bag and tied together with the same sort of string they use for the paddock bell. Functional is about the only adjective that could be employed for the general facilities, yet they are only a few licks of paint and a small leap of imagination away from a fine racecourse.

Perhaps the only saving grace is the members' Charles Tollier Stand, built in 1996. Here they have tried to incorporate the exquisite Cotswold stone into the newer extension. Lawns (also uncut) stretch down to the rail and are amply served by wooden benches. Yet the view to the paddock is restricted by a prefabricated monstrosity holding private boxes. Clever planning that, and a fine use of six years' architectural training.

The best kept secret at Bath (and now to be revealed) is the roof of the members' stand. On a fairly busy afternoon it rarely contained more than twenty people – yet, for those who can find it, provides the clearest view of the course. For some reason the course authorities make every effort to retain its anonymity by supplying only one directional sign on the whole of the concourse. From the members' bar, head for the toilets and turn right up a narrow stairwell, the sort of darkened passageway that would have played a major role in a Hitchcock film.

What they don't tell you is that you can also gain access from the Tattersalls enclosure. Face the members' stand with your back to the Tattersalls grandstand and you'll see a service entrance with a door marked 'private'. Ignore this completely, but before going through the door, turn sharp right, walk with shoulders back, adopt an air of confidence and head up the concrete stairwell. If you don't arrive on the roof within one minute, you've probably just walked into the stewards' room and will have a lot of explaining to do.

What all racecourses need to remember is that in any seven-race card, the actual time watching racing rarely amounts to much more than thirty minutes in a four-hour afternoon. Maybe that's fine if you've got a private box or a table booked in the restaurant. But the grass roots of racing is in the small-time punter who needs to be entertained with slightly more than a greasy hamburger.

Fortunately I was still carrying my copy of the *Cotswold Edge* newsletter and that's all the entertainment a man needs when he's looking for divine inspiration. A quick scan of the racecard revealed an unraced three-year-old in the second race. With the name Mary, how could I go wrong? If the mother of God couldn't bring home the bacon, what could? With two furlongs to go, Mary challenged for third place. At the furlong-pole she had cleverly manoeuvred into seventh place, which was obviously a cunning move to catch them all napping on the line. By the time the winning post came, ninth place was firmly secured and my betting slip had hit the bin.

'OK. Got the message!' I shouted at the nearby radio

mast, hoping the Almighty was tuned in to an FM wavelength. A few of my rooftop companions glanced warily in my direction and fled down the stairwell.

Three races later my appeal to the heavens remained unanswered, though each contest provided a truly thrilling finish as the pack struggled up the tough final furlong. I know it's not high-class racing. I know the facilities leave something to be desired. I know Bath is considered a second division course. But don't let it put you off. It's a fun course and, despite all my bickering, one I wouldn't hesitate to revisit.

Postscript: On the way home I thought of Sonbelle, that 40-1 winner of the first race, and the Reverend Westlake's missive on a 'good summer'. Sonbelle was sired by Son Pardo out of Ty With Belle. Son? Maybe Sun. Pardo? Padre? Priest? Belle? Fine? Good? Good Sun? Good Summer? Ty With Belle? The strap on the paddock bell? There were enough clues there to help Hercule Poirot solve a case in ten seconds. God certainly works in mysterious ways. I bet he plays Cluedo on his day off.

With a lick of paint; a tin of polish, a leather bell strap and a decent lawn mower

CHAPTER SIX

BEVERLEY

As far as I know, Beverley is the only racecourse in Britain which sports a girl's name. It's true that I once had an old girlfriend who was given the nickname 'Pontefract' due to her blackened teeth and inability to give up chewing liquorice. But I don't think that counts and Beverley retains its unique status. (If any male punters happen to be married to a woman called Newton Abbot, I apologize for the error.)

If you haven't visited this course before don't be fooled into thinking you should head for the town of Beverley, as the course lies some ten miles to the west, near the delightful village of Bishop Burton, a small settlement with one of the finest ponds I've so far encountered.

Go into Beverley, as I did, and you've as much chance of finding the racecourse as I have of finding a winner in a 25-runner handicap. For some reason it's been disowned, as if the good people of Beverley are ashamed of its presence. In a thirty-minute frustrating tour of the area, I found only one small sign which announced its location – bad PR if a tired punter has been on the road for over three hours on a hot summer's afternoon.

Despite arriving an hour before the first race, it was obvious that this is a popular course. The free car park, across the road from the main entrance, was already bustling with racegoers. On first appearances I was surprised that this was such a well supported course. The exterior seemed more like a Third Division football ground, the steel supports of the grandstands bulging out across the narrow pavement, the concrete-tunnelled turnstile entrance filling me with a sense of foreboding. And the obligatory steel band did nothing to raise my spirits.

Don't get me wrong, I enjoy steel bands, especially when I'm in a Caribbean beach bar with a lithe bikinied blonde in one hand and a dark rum cocktail in the other (I wish). But at an evening race meeting in the middle of Yorkshire? It's about as Caribbean as a snowball – and especially tedious when they turn the volume up to Mach 7 and the last leg of a winning Yankee has just gone down by a short-head. As any losing punter knows, there's nothing less cheering than cheerful music. The events which were to follow only confirmed my intention to make dustbin lids illegal at all public gatherings where the temperature is below 90° and rum cocktails are unavailable.

Given my tortuous journey and the cacophony of noise which greeted my entry, I was in an ill temper as I gained my first view of the course. The word 'compact' immediately sprung to mind. Beverley is no grand arena but what is instantly apparent is that the one-mile, three-furlong oval course is visible from any vantage point. The right-handed course is deceptively undulating, contains two tight bends and a sharp descent into the rising ground of the three-furlong straight. In many ways it is reminiscent of Towcester and, like the Northamptonshire course, seemed likely to favour a good front runner.

This early assessment almost paid off in the first race when Slip Of The Tongue was driven to the front and just failed to get home. The winner, Pleasant Mount, had tracked my selection all the way around the two-mile maiden and they had the race between them well over two furlongs from the finishing post.

Adopting the winner's tactics, I followed Pleasant Mount to the paddock, keen to discover the identity of the sumptuously named trainer, Julie Camacho. Having never seen her before, I could only imagine she must be a member of the Beverley Mafia or a retired Hollywood starlet. It was therefore quite a surprise to observe a young attractive blonde being greeted by her delighted owners and she looked about as horsy as a ballroom dancer.

Secreting myself behind one of the pillars which support the new weighing room, I listened with interest as Sky television went through a brief post-race interview. Miss J. A. Camacho (Malton) responded in a soft Yorkshire accent (yes, there is such a thing) and in a totally unpretentious manner. In that one moment, she provided the key to Beverley racecourse.

I had been given an earlier clue when desperately trying to hear the announcer who was continually drowned out by the incessant steel band. Beverley was the 32nd course I had visited over the past few months and yet it was the first time I had heard a voice over the tannoy which didn't sound as if it had been honed at an Eton prep school.

Beverley has an endearing simplicity and a lack of ostentation. I suppose you could say that about many of the smaller courses, though unfortunately this sometimes equates with a lack of modernization and a retention of shabby facilities. In contrast, the Beverley authorities appear to have made a real effort to upgrade without losing its former cosy appeal. Nowhere is this more obvious than in the new weighing room overlooking the paddock.

Built in 1998, there must have been a great temptation to make this a 'members only' segregated area. Whoever took the decision to make it accessible to the hoi polloi deserves a Christmas bonus. What it provides is a sense of inclusion when many courses in Britain still view exclusion as a prerequisite of traditional racing – a tactic which is about as logical as voting for a Labour candidate in Matlock.

A plaque outside the weighing room informs punters that this new facility was opened by a certain Steve Huison, who was apparently a star of the much-feted film *The Full Monty*. Well, bare my ample bottom – they got it right. The gently curved structure contains a splendid bar on the second floor with access to a sweeping balcony looking over both the paddock and finishing straight. Best of all, however, is the weighing room itself, glass fronted and fully open to the curious eyes of the public. Owners and trainers can be seen in pre-race discussion, jockeys celebrating their success or bemoaning their chance to get a run on the rail. What it provides is a real sense of involvement, successfully breaking down the barriers between supporters and the racing hierarchy.

The paddock is equally delightful, though I would be interested to know the height of the person who installed the array of button seats which surround the sparkling white rail. At a guess he or she must have been at least 6' 3" – as they are set so low in the ground that only a punter of above average height could possibly gain a view of the parade. They should either hand out miniature periscopes or provide a sign at the entrance warning punters that the paddock is unsuitable for average people.

Fortunately, I was regularly watered as a child and therefore enjoy a fairly lofty physique. Viewing the runners in the third race allowed me to spot a fine-looking, unraced filly who had such an air of enthusiasm that I couldn't resist a small wager – despite a starting-price of 25-1. What attracted me even more was that this was a claiming race with a minimum price of £3,000. The owners obviously had high hopes for this two-year-old's career as they had given up any weight advantage and set their claim at £10,000. The jockey, Ollie Pears, tucked Pyramid Princess in the middle of the pack and with two furlongs to go decided to take on the two hot favourites. The large summer crowd roared as the challenge came just too late and the Princess flashed over the line a length behind the winner. And then there was silence, a silence so marked that you could have heard a horseshoe drop in a hay-filled stable.

An instant after passing the line, Ollie Pears lay still and lifeless on the course, while Pyramid Princess flailed her broken leg in front of the numbed audience. The young horse whinnied in a pitiful manner, its eyes staring wildly like a child appealing for help. For a time it careered around in circles, bewildered by the crippled leg, which now seemed to flap grotesquely, as if taunting the rest of its perfect body. Women began to sob while many a man failed to disguise their welling tears. It may sound over-emotional, even unduly sentimental, but the crowd's reaction suggested that Beverley is a racegoers' course rather than the social beanfeast of Royal Ascot or the loutishness of Epsom.

The vets, in full view of the distressed crowd, did what they had to do and with admirable care and sensitivity.

Pyramid Princess had seen her last racecourse. Fortunately Ollie Pears began to stir and as far as I know recovered well after an obligatory lay-off. Within seconds of the horsebox leaving the course the steel band began to play. I only wish someone had told them to give it a rest for ten minutes. It was as appropriate as trying to chat up a distraught widow ten seconds after she's thrown a handful of dust onto her husband's coffin. It might be successful but it leaves a very bad taste in the mouth.

In some ways Beverley had suffered from its own success. Such is the proximity to the racecourse that there was no hiding from the demise of the promising young filly. The three main stands all enjoy equally good views over the course and even the small centre course enclosure doesn't suffer from the usual limitations and restricted sight of the course. All in all, I'm not sure it's worth paying the extra transfer fee to the members' enclosure, especially as the benches have been constructed by an ardent Puritan, who considers comfort to be a mortal sin and a sure sign of lethargy.

The cheaper Tattersalls enclosure will supply a fine day's racing. Bars are plentiful (though understaffed) and the biggest thing in its favour has to be the fish and chip shop at the base of the stand. To my great pleasure, it was here that I discovered that Yorkshire has finally entered the 20th if not the 21st century.

As a red-blooded Lancastrian, the sublime art of battering fish has always been high on my list of life's essential qualities. Apart from the shared genetic hatred between the white and red rose counties there has always been one feature by which these two northern breeds could be distinguished. In my youth, it was common knowledge that Yorkshire fish and chip shops had the revolting habit of leaving the skin on even the finest fillet of haddock. To a Lancastrian this is as abhorrent as sitting next to an American who puts marmalade on his bacon. Yet Beverley has seen the light – crisp hand-cut chips and not a sign of skin on my lightly battered cod. Try getting that at Royal Ascot.

If I'd had the nerve, I'd have told Jack Berry to sample the delights of the Tattersalls chip shop. This successful Lancastrian trainer was having a bad night and I'm sure it would have cheered him up. As chance would have it, I had never seen the famous red shirt before. For those of you unfamiliar with Jack Berry, he always wears this presumably lucky colour when he sends out a runner.

I can only guess that he happened to be wearing a red shirt when he had his first winner. All I can say is that it's a pity he wasn't wearing pale blue or white. If I ever go into racehorse ownership again, I'll make a point of never wearing anything that makes me look like something out of a 1960s Burtons window. He announced his retirement not too long after. He was probably sick of wearing red shirts that don't go with anything in his wardrobe.

Facing a three-hour journey, through what looked like a rain-filled sky, I headed for the exit, stopping briefly to collect my last winning betting slip. The ill-fated Pyramid Princess had paid handsomely for a place but I hadn't the heart to collect until I was ready to leave. Approaching the Tote window, I pushed the ticket forward.

'Wasn't that the one that died?' asked the red-coated lady, pushing my money through the window.

''Fraid so,' I muttered in response.

'Shame. She was a lovely looking horse too,' answered the woman. Even the Tote ladies cared and I liked that.

You were a fine-looking girl, Pyramid Princess. And so are you, Beverley,

Postscript: I left the course with four legs of my placepot safely secured. Number five came in as I tuned into the car radio. I had the favourite in the final six-horse field. It came in fourth. Beverley, Beverley – how could you be so cruel?

CHAPTER SEVEN

BRIGHTON

I read somewhere that Brighton racecourse was known to 'retain a slight air of raffishness'. Not having encountered such archaic language since I last read *Tom Brown's Schooldays*, I referred to my dictionary. The explanation suggested that I was about to join company with flashy blackguardly fellows who were up to no good and would probably give me a jolly beastly hiding if I so much as caught their eye. I can tell you, I was pretty apprehensive as I approached the main entrance. The delightful but creaking barrier did little to dispel my misgivings. Engraved boldly on a brass plate were the words 'Dulce's Patent Rush Preventive Turnstile'. They were obviously prepared for trouble and I was determined to keep a hand on my wallet for the remainder of the afternoon. One-armed racing can be a bit inconvenient but I didn't fancy seeing my credit cards scattered across the Sussex Downs.

If you enter the course through the (reasonably priced) club entrance, you will immediately be confronted by Brighton's revamped paddock. This was the first meeting since the start of the refurbishment, the course authorities having invested over £1.5m during the winter. There was enough fresh paint to put Dulux workers on overtime for the next five years. The stark white and green glistened in what had become a shimmering, sunny spring day.

The designers were obviously a bit pushed for space, being forced to squeeze the parade ring in between the main stands and the red-tiled stabling block. The fit is tighter than my golf grip on the first hole of the monthly medal – but all in all they've done a good job. The winner's enclosure contains four boxes neatly laid with AstroTurf – though none of them is much bigger than the average department store lift. Rows of small green bucket seats surround the paddock. However, I would suggest that you don't attempt to lean back and relax. Any attempt to do so (as I found out) will leave you in a position favoured by gynaecologists but not recommended if you wish to retain any dignity.

Wandering round to the main stand it was difficult not to be impressed by the shock of the new. Stepping back to take in the full splendour of the Grandstand, I unfortunately stepped on a bookie's toe as he began to erect his stand.

'Impressed are you?' he asked, brushing my heel mark from his brown suede shoes.

'Certainly am,' I replied and offered an apology.

'Tarted it up, that's all,' he responded.

'The racecard says it's a major refurbishment.'

'Bloody tart up. Look at the top.'

Angling my head upwards, I began to see his point. It reminded me of the days when I used to pick up old girlfriends and only clean the left-hand side of my car. The authorities had tried the same trick with the Grandstand. Set behind the glistening new crash barriers and virgin white steps was a reminder of Brighton's grubby past – a place where raffish men would sit, calling in their horse as it entered the final furlong, while dipping their hands into the pockets of the nearest naive punter. But now, even in the middle of the racing, the seats remained empty, apart from the odd retired blackguard who sat alone, bemoaning the loss of illegal income.

Having said that, I strongly advise you to make the effort and climb the steps. It's from here that you gain the best and most startling view of the unique Brighton course. It is only one of four non-circular courses in Britain (see Epsom, Newmarket and York) but of all these competitors, Brighton is probably the quirkiest of them all. From the one-mile, four-furlong start runners negotiate a continual left-hand bend until finally entering the straight about three furlongs from the finish.

In between these two points, jockeys have to manoeuvre their mount along a course with more rises and falls than a nervous stock market. If your selection isn't challenging by the time they hit the two-furlong marker, you might as well start studying the form of the next race. Put your money on a jockey who likes a spectacular late finish and you're likely to leave Brighton without your proverbial shirt. Unfortunately I came to this conclusion two hours after I left the racecourse, my bare torso getting some very odd looks when I stopped at the traffic lights in Slough.

But it's not only the course which provides a breathtaking view. Look towards the finishing post and only two miles in the distance is the vast expanse of the English Channel, the Brighton boating marina nestling in a sheltered bay. Sadly, and in order to avoid disillusionment, you must keep your eyes towards the south. Swing them 90 degrees to the left and you'll discover Brighton's carbuncle.

A drab and shaded housing estate provides the back-drop for the finishing straight, a collection of high rise, grey concrete monstrosities only adding to this conspicuous blemish. The designer probably sold his plans as 'an ergonomic and functional masterpiece, constructed with the modern family in mind'. This roughly translates as 'a pile of old junk' and it's likely that the architect now lives in a penthouse gin palace overlooking Poole harbour. Is 'do unto others as you wouldn't dream of doing to yourself' the motto of the Royal Institute of British Architects? (Answers on a badly made postcard, to . . .)

Whoever they hired at Brighton seems to have tried to bolster their image. The general layout is simple but effective, a whole range of bars and betting halls providing most of the amenities you need in a day's racing. As usual the Silver Ring is left to fend for itself and apart from its small stand opposite the furlong-pole is hardly worth a mention. Its only saving grace is an on-course car park where you can nose your car up to the rails and enjoy an alfresco picnic.

On my visit to the cheap end, I got into conversation with an elderly couple who were bemoaning the conditions.

'Treat us like dirt,' protested the aged punter.

'Any tips?' I replied in a totally inappropriate manner.

'Stay off Dettori,' answered his wife with great certainty.

'Not served his Brighton apprenticeship,' added her husband.

Four races later Richard Quinn had a treble under his belt and I began to see what they meant. There's no point in being a good jockey at this seaside course – you need to be a good Brighton jockey. Come down the hill too slowly and you'll miss the break for the line. Come down the hill too quickly and your horse will be gasping for air as he hits the finishing straight. The bends of Brighton are a series of learning curves and even the finest jockeys will need to serve their time in full. I only wish the Channel 4 representative had mentioned Richard Quinn's 25 per cent strike-rate at Brighton.

Just before racing began, punters were offered words of wisdom by a TV commentator, who gave a personal performance in the rather seedy Prince Regent Suite at the top of the main stand. This middle-aged, northern-accented, nattily dressed celebrity held court to a pre-dominantly middle-aged female audience who cooed at his every comment.

After telling a few old jokes and attempting a number of passable impressions of fellow commentators, he delivered his eight certainties for the afternoon's racing. Punters scribbled notes faster than a shorthand typist taking the minutes at the AGM of the British Speed Talking Society. Naturally, I ignored the tips completely, convinced that my ability to read form was a match for any racing pundit.

Three losers later, I stood at the side of the winner's enclosure, the black dog of depression beginning to eat at my spirit, only to be revived by a trainer's indiscretion. Keeping my tattered notebook well out of sight, I shuffled closer to the conversation.

'Two hours she spent there. Offered her everything that was breathing. Didn't seem interested. Few days later I get a call. From Canada, for God's sake. Bloody Canada. Promoting a book or something. You wouldn't believe it, would you? Half a share in this. Quarter-share in that. One leg in another. I thought she was going to buy the whole stable. Asked me if she could have a bet. You know

– set one up for a touch. Said she was an Australian and liked a bet. "Too bloody right!" I said. Good for the old PR if it comes off.'

Despite having heard the celebrity name, I can't be indiscreet about an indiscretion – that would be the act of a bounder. All I can say is that if this female (clue 1) does end up buying a horse, I'd bet my next pay packet that it's a gelding – or a eunuch (clue 2) as some writers (clue 3) have described them. She'll probably want to perform a similar operation on her trainer if she ever reads this piece.

By the time of my final race I was in desperate need of a saver. If there was any horse who was going to provide profit it was Celestial Bay in the six-furlong sprint. With form which showed a creditable fifth of ten on soft going, in a Folkestone seven-furlong handicap, how could it go wrong? In the paddock she looked keyed up and probably all set to break the course record. The jockey, S. Carson (5), jumped on board with what I thought was a look of total confidence.

Celestial Bay had unfortunately not read the script and only seconds after mounting hurled the apprentice jockey onto the turf of the paddock. Though not severely damaged by his fall, the clerk of the course called for a replacement. I was just on the point of offering my services (despite my five-stone overweight), when it was announced that A. Daly (3) had been press-ganged into duty. Things weren't looking too good. My fate was in the hands of a jockey who sounded strangely like a second-hand car salesman and a horse who would obviously prefer to be in her back garden with a cup of tea and a copy of *Hay Weekly*.

Having whipped you up into a frenzy of expectation, I presume you'll be waiting for the inevitable happy ending.

If only. If only. To be fair to my salesman jockey, he put up a good show and looked like he might take the honours as they approached the furlong-pole. Sadly, the front runners shut the door and gave him as much room as a shoal of cod in a goldfish bowl. It would have been easier to run through Dulce's Patent Rush Preventive Turnstile. Tearing up my betting slip in a fit of pique, I rushed for the exit but was already planning my next visit to Brighton – determined to see the fruits of their second stage development and to adjust my betting strategy.

Two hours later, and sat in the inevitable traffic jam on the M25, I glanced through the racecard. Halfway through the programme, my eyes caught sight of a large and surprising advertisement. 'PUSSYCATS – Sussex's Only Lapdancing Club'. A lapdancing club in Sussex? A lapdancing advert in a racing programme? They're obviously desperate to raise money for that second stage development – especially promoting a club called Pussycats. The local Conservative Association must be having kittens.

Postscript: The Channel 4 tipster managed one short-priced winner and a 14-1 place from his eight 'certainties'. I doubt his form reading is any better than mine. He probably just had a slightly sharper pin. I bet those middle-aged women won't coo the next time they see him.

CHAPTER EIGHT

CARLISLE

I was on home territory. Or at least close to it. My youth had been spent trudging up and down Lakeland fells and mountains – with a knapsack on my back. These days, however, it involves a 300-mile trip up a whole network of tired and crazed motorways. Yet, like meeting an old friend after years of absence, it takes only seconds to regain that old familiarity. If you're approaching from the south, by the time you see signs for Kendal, the Lake District has announced its presence, the M6 winding its way through the mist-shrouded Howgill Fells, the land erupting as if to inform softie Southerners that they have finally reached God's country.

A quick stop at Tebay, only half an hour from the course, confirmed this opinion. This is a service station with probably the finest views in Britain, a lake all of its own and the worst coffee I've ever felt the need to swallow. Even the walls are inscribed with Wordsworth sonnets; while the toilet graffiti is in rhyming couplets. Apart from rediscovering my roots, I have to admit that Carlisle was not high on my major event list. The two main drawbacks are that this Cumbrian town seems to have fallen between two stools, edging as it does on the northern boundaries of England and the southern borders of Scotland. It's a sort of interlude between the main performances, a rather flat and dreary plateau.

Racing aficionados tell me that Carlisle is one of the 'gaffs' – those small rural courses which are at the heart of National Hunt racing. I was also informed that, if for nothing else, Carlisle is famed for its sticky toffee pudding. Being a sucker for small courses and coma-inducing sweet trolleys, it all looked fairly promising. If only it had lived up to its billing. One of the main reasons for writing this book is that I have a sneaking suspicion that the racing press has been earning its collective living by hood-winking small punters. I often sense that they've been raised on *Pollyanna* – an American children's story whose most memorable line is 'if you can't say anything nice, don't say anything at all'. Well blow that for a game of soldiers (whatever that means).

For a start, Carlisle isn't small. The right-handed, pear-shaped course is not far off the same scale as left-handed Chepstow. Apart from the fact that both these courses start with the same letter, this is about as far as the comparison can be taken. However, the stands are fairly impressive in design – though not in presentation. At first sighting, my initial reaction was to wonder why Carlisle doesn't enjoy a higher status. It seemed, in those first few seconds, to have everything you need in a jumps course – an undulating course with at least two severe climbs, four fences in the home run-in, clear visibility from the stands and a picturesque setting. The packaging looked unbeatable.

Ever picked up the most attractive present from under the Christmas tree? It usually ends up being some awful board game that maintains a family's concentration for about as long as the Queen's annual message. And as for the promised sticky toffee pudding – it would have been easier to find a yak on a Lakeland fell. But there lies another tale.

As I often do at new courses, I planned my campaign on the basis of the course layout and conditions. The official going was soft, the back straight looked like a rollercoaster and the final two furlongs about as easy to climb as a nearby Langdale Pike. It had stamina written all over it. Carlisle is no course for two-mile flyers but more one for big-hearted animals who can grind it out over three or four miles. I tested this theory in the first race.

Unfortunately, the favourite romped home, though Clonbrook Lass landed the place money and convinced me that I should stick with the strategy. Three races later I had bagged two good-priced winners and a short-head second. With my luck running like this, you'd expect me to be blinkered to Carlisle's shortcomings. Sorry, Carlisle – it only seemed to sharpen my instincts.

As you'll see from other reports, I have a burning hatred of purely functional modern racecourses, which have as much in common with racing as city shopping malls have with community spirit. They are soulless, un-imaginative and don't suit a country course. Even though I have a preference for Victoriana, I'm no Luddite. Modern need not mean square boxes and red brick (look at the success of Goodwood, for example). But if you've got some history – at least flaunt it.

And Carlisle HAS got it. Three old stands of varying character, designed by architects who hadn't overdosed on straight lines and a setting which should be a major asset. The central problem seems to be that while the course has got stamina written all over it, the course facilities look as if they've run out of steam after the first five furlongs.

The main stand epitomizes this unconcealed criticism. A dearly missed old chum, who was ex-RAF, would have described the structure as 'a lovely bit of kit'. And he would have been right. The structure enjoys three levels, wrought iron and ornate balustrades, a half-covered standing area and a roof-top stand with a perfect view over the course and surrounding countryside. Unfortunately, some buffoon then decided to paint everything in a delightful shade of pale blue – the sort of blue that would have a doctor reaching for a death certificate. Didn't they know that blue is a notoriously difficult colour?

Carlisle's problem is that it has taken them a long time to discover this simple mistake – as it looks as if the last time the stands saw a paintbrush, America was still a British colony. Presenting a course in such a manner is akin to pasting up notices which state: Come racing at Carlisle – if you like. We're not really bothered one way or another.

The various bars and cafes again confirm this view – all of them dark, dismal and barren. If I was to really push it, the members' bar is adequate and fairly cosy, though nothing to prompt a postcard home. But there's nothing to save the Tattersalls bar – it's probably the most dreary place I've been in since I used to sneak a fag in the disused air raid shelter at the back of my old school.

If anything does save this stand, it's the restaurant on the second floor. Access is through a flight of (pale blue) stairs, past walls decorated with (pale blue) wallpaper. And don't miss the extraordinary painting by Brian Organ. It shows Lester Piggott astride a horse. With the imagination only granted to a minority, the painter has entitled this work of art 'The Jockey: L. Piggott, On A Horse.' Well blow me sideways and cancel my credit with the local bookie – I'd never have guessed. I assumed L. Piggott was sitting on a tortoise.

The (pale blue) restaurant, I have to admit, is fun and lacks the veneer of pomposity which is often found at the better-known courses. It's a bit of a free for all and thankfully without formality. If there's a real buzz of racing anywhere at Carlisle, this is where to find it. I chatted briefly with the restaurant manager, a convivial man who was obviously proud of the simple but well prepared food. He stated, with some pleasure, that everything was home cooked – including the array of tempting sweets.

'So you're the man who makes the famous sticky toffee pudding?' I queried.

'Sticky toffee pudding?' he replied, somewhat bemused.

'Yes. Sticky toffee pudding. I've been trying to find it everywhere.'

''Fraid not. We do a nice chocolate roulade. Our meringues are quite sticky. Sure you're not thinking of Cartmel?'

'Cartmel?' For obvious reasons, he now had my full attention.

'They present sticky toffee pudding as one of the prizes. Novice hurdle I think.'

'You're joking!'

'Not been there?'

'Last on my list,' I answered.

So, another nail went into Carlisle's coffin. It's not small. It's not well maintained. And it doesn't have sticky toffee pudding. It could only get better.

And to be fair, it did. Search them out and there are a few little gems to be found at Carlisle. The paddock area begins to lift the spirits. The strangely square parade ring lies at the back of a small wooden stand which faces head-on to the finishing straight. The weighing room is placed below this raked stand and is an ideal spot for jockey watching as the area is left completely open to the naturally prying eyes of any self-respecting punter. Yet this is only the hors d'oeuvre to three of Carlisle's less publicized secrets.

I encountered the first treat as horses prepared for the first race. Just to the side of the pre-parade ring lies the start for the three-mile hurdle – a small dead end chute which fires contestants onto the first bend. Being so close to the paddock, jockeys tend to arrive at the tape earlier than normal and are forced to circle round in this confined area, mesmerizing their mounts into relaxation.

Surprisingly, only a handful of punters seemed to be aware of this starting position and yet, if you ever go to Carlisle, make a point of getting against this rail. What you'll witness is the stark contrast between nervous owners, neurotic punters and the languid approach of the pilots. Here are a group of men simply going about their daily business. Another day. Another race. They have left the hype to journalists and trainers. All they wish to do is get round in one piece and, with a bit of luck, get their nag in the frame.

Of course these observations aren't the result of in-depth interviews but simply the result of a well-trained eye which responds to giveaway body language and revealing 'jockey speak'. What may surprise you is that there's little sign of tension. The banter between the riders involves little more than friendly joshing and what bookings they've managed to pick up for the next day. When the starter finally gives a one-minute warning, concentration does increase but it's not difficult to work out who thinks they're on a no-hoper. One particular jockey, struggling to keep his mount on its toes, declared: 'Come on, you thick bugger!' This was delivered to an animal whose owner probably thought they'd bought a prospective Desert Orchid. It tailed off last, proving the jockey to be a decent judge of horse flesh.

'Who's gonna make it?' came another voice from the back.

'No effing chance!' came the reply.

Miss this at Carlisle and you've missed a vital part of a punter's education. Racing is not about sanitized contests broadcast into your centrally heated homes. It's about real, tough, small men (and women) on real, tough, large animals, battling around racecourses six and seven times a week. It's a merciless way to earn a living and there aren't many driving Ferraris.

If you do make the effort to watch the three-mile start, it's only a few strides to the best viewing spot on the course and fortunately open to both Tattersalls and member's badge holders. Barring the fun restaurant, I wouldn't bother paying the extra cash for a day member's badge.

Look to the left of the weighing room and you'll see a small staircase running up to the open roof at the side of the old wooden stand. Although it's head-on, you'll enjoy a marvellous view of the pack heading up the final straight. But best of all, get yourself up there for any of the hurdle races which take place on the outer ring of the course. By standing against the rail, you'll be able to look directly over the heads of the jockeys as they approach the top bend.

You are so close, in fact, that it's quite easy to pick up the riders' polite instructions to their fellow jockeys. 'For effing hell's sake, give us some bloody room!' was only one of the many examples of light-hearted repartee I heard from this position. Once they have passed by, glance over to the far side of the course. Not only will you see flocks of sheep drifting like woollen waves across the farming landscape but you'll also see Carlisle's best kept secret and the one sign of hope in this paint-flaking venue.

The Old Tote Building stands just across from the winning post and is accessible by crossing the course between races. In contrast to its supposed betters, it retains an attractive cream and green facade. This single-storey building once housed over thirty Tote windows which are now boarded up, though the ancient guide rails to each window have thankfully been retained.

Inside is a snug little bar and a small private function room. Only twenty or so punters sat quietly reading form while a lone Tote lady manned (*personned*?) her small kiosk in the corner. In terms of facilities, it felt like the only sign of sanity on the whole course.

It was from here that I made my now obligatory efforts to get close to the final fence. It's a bit of a trek across open farmland as the authorities, understandably, are insistent that you keep clear of the ambulance course. In Carlisle's case, this is a good move as I have never seen so many cars hurtling after the runners. The cavalcade seemed to take ten minutes to pass by and it would have been easier to walk across Marble Arch in the middle of the rush hour.

'Would yer look at that now. Have yer ever seen so many effing cars?' came a voice at my side. 'I think they bring the whole bloody family wid 'em.' His tone was heavy with a strong but musical Irish accent. 'Yer an ambulance man yerself, are yer?'

Why he thought this, I've no idea. I displayed no visible

bandages or fluorescent yellow jacket. But tell someone you're a writer and it's about as useful to a conversation as announcing you're an undertaker. Instead, I mumbled something incomprehensible and responded with my own question.

'And you?' I asked.

'Jockey,' he answered simply.

Panic set in. Should I have recognized him immediately? Was he expecting to be recognized? I decided to bite the bullet.

'I'm sorry,' I stuttered. 'I hope you're not offended – but I don't know who you are.'

I won't betray the jockey's name but I can tell you he WAS well known and yet not in the slightest bit miffed by my lack of recognition. The man was a delight and spent the next ten minutes convincing me that jump jockeys deserve to double their wages. And I was convinced. In the last four days he had travelled over 1,500 miles and not made the winners' enclosure. Yet his dedication wasn't in doubt. Despite having ridden many times at Carlisle, he still thought it worthwhile to trudge down to the last fence just to get a feel of the obstacle. He had no more than two rides at the fag end of the card – and on a couple of novice chasers who were likely to dump him on the turf.

Yet, what he did tell me is that Carlisle remains a favourite spot for northern trainers to school (sorry, educate) young jumpers. The fences are considered fair, their bowed gorse and birch fences apparently invite inexperienced chasers to take them on.

'If a horse can't jump at Carlisle – they'll not jump anywhere.'

Even amateurs like myself could see what he meant, and throughout the afternoon horses tended to stay on their feet and handle the obstacles without much difficulty. Possibly as a result of this, four of the races concluded with some extremely tight finishes and there's no doubt that Carlisle is capable of supplying very exciting racing. It's just a pity that the course authorities (to date) have such a poor regard for the punters who line their pockets. Perhaps by the time you read this report, they may have discovered how to use a paint brush and that pale blue is a difficult colour. Appearance isn't everything but I bet the owners of Carlisle wouldn't dream of going out to dinner in a pair of faded jeans and a ripped T-shirt. You've got your little gems, Carlisle, but sadly they've been created by accident rather than by design. I wonder if they'll ever let me in again.

Postscript I: My new found jockey acquaintance didn't make it to the winner's enclosure. In fact he never made it to that final fence. It's a tough old game.

Postscript II: I had hoped that they'd just give the old stand a new lick of paint (not blue). Instead they've built a Jubilee Stand which is functional but lacking in all that old quirkiness. These new edifices, common to many regenerated tracks, leave me rather cold and lack that touch of imagination which breeds loyalty and affection. I hope they found a place for Brian Organ's painting 'The Jockey: L. Piggot, On A Horse'.

CHAPTER NINE

CARTMEL

Do you have any American friends? You know who I mean. Those cousins across the water with perfect teeth and an addiction to psychotherapy and history. A few centuries ago they threw the British out, only to discover that they had gained a country and lost a culture. If they ever threaten to visit, I can suggest three ways to guarantee their enjoyment. A performance of *Henry V* at the Globe theatre will reveal our heritage, a greasy spoon cafe on the A1 will establish our culinary expertise – and a day at Cartmel races will convince them that the English are congenitally mad.

If eccentricity is an art form, then this racecourse is the national gallery. With only six meetings per year, it probably has the least number of inclusions in any racing calendar and a setting that would have sent Wordsworth into a frenzy of poetic activity. Unlike most British racecourses, which borrow their name from some distant settlement, Cartmel racecourse really is in Cartmel village.

If you are ever asked for directions, inform the lost punter that the course is just at the back of the village shop. (Purveyors of excellent ice cream and the infamous artery-clogging sticky toffee pudding.) To celebrate my visits to the sixty-one courses of mainland Britain, I took up residence in Grange-over-Sands, a large retirement home masquerading as a small seaside town. Whilst it has a certain charm, there's a sense that only a minority of its residents possess a discernible pulse, as the distinction between life and death is hardly noticeable. But it did at least provide that sense of calm before the mayhem of Cartmel races.

On the morning of the May bank holiday meeting, my wife and I donned our walking boots and set off for the racecourse. I had vague recollections that it was possible to walk over the top of the nearby Hampsfell and drop into Cartmel village. 'It'll take about an hour,' I stated with total conviction.

Two hours later, we wheezed our way to the summit of Hampsfell and gained our first view of the racecourse some two miles away in the distant valley. It was only 11 a.m., yet the narrow lanes into the village were bursting with traffic and the racecourse fairground was already in full swing. From such a distant vantage point you can see the unique qualities of Cartmel races. To the south lies Morecambe Bay, to the north the Lakeland giants of the Langdale Pikes – and, at the very heart of the village, the stunning mediaeval priory. If we hadn't been going racing, I could have stayed up there all day. But after a brief stop, we began our descent.

My memory failed me again and within minutes we were hopelessly lost. In a final act of desperation we decided to head for the nearest farm, passing through fields of sheep and some very frisky-looking heifers. Having become a soft southern urban man, I was convinced that I may never make my final racecourse. Was it to end in a Lakeland field, the author impaled on the horns of an ill-humoured bullock?

Fortunately my wife is no stranger to a milking parlour and has the ability to frighten a herd of cattle with little more than a threatening glance. It was with great relief that an hour later we wandered into the cobbled square of Cartmel village with all our body parts intact and my notebook gripped tightly in my hands. We might not have reached our final destination but it was apparent that the Cartmel experience begins well before you enter the race-course.

The atmosphere is one of carnival, the two main oak-beamed pubs heaving with optimistic punters who spill out into the square and mingle happily with the more refined racegoers taking tea outside the various small cafes and shops. Horseboxes weave their way through this giant party, the only entry to the course being between the antiquarian bookshop and the village store. It's quite easy to pick out the punters who are attending this Cumbrian racecourse for the first time as they all carry a constant look of disbelief. And if you think that Epsom and Ascot have cornered the market in giant picnics, wait until you visit Cartmel.

The centre of the course is a chaos of alfresco eating, car boots disgorging wind breaks, canvas tents, tinned beers, fine wines and everything from the simple ham sandwich to a five-course gourmet meal. This isn't racing. This is a giant car park filled with almost 20,000 people intent on engaging in a spot of early summer insanity. The fact that every thirty minutes a horse race is about to flash past their picnics is purely incidental.

Apart from walking over a small section of the track as you enter the course, there's little indication of a race meeting taking place at all. To the west end of the enclosures a large and garish fairground blasts out its music, the sickly smell of candy floss drifting in the light breeze. Parents appease their bored children by subjecting themselves to the hair-raising rides, fighting hard to retain their recently consumed picnics. A giant ferris wheel proved the greatest attraction, probably because it was the only place which would give you a view of the whole racecourse.

Until now, I had always considered the figure-of-eight courses at Windsor and Fontwell to be the most difficult circuits to describe. Cartmel however wins first prize in the Track With No Logic competition. The outer circuit is little more than a mile in length, with the six fences and five hurdles split between the two short straights on either side.

The strategy in all races is to send the contestants around the outside until they get dizzy on the tight bends and then usher them up the centre of the enclosures along a one-furlong chute which doubles as a finishing straight. Confused? So are the punters – and I suspect most of the jockeys. The last fence in the steeplechases is so far from the finishing post that Cartmel enjoys the notoriety of having the longest run-in to the winning post of all British National Hunt racecourses.

Just to try and make sense of these peculiarities, I stationed myself in the packed main Grandstand for both of the first two races. To call it a grandstand is something of an overstatement, as it is the only permanent structure on the course and is made up of a raked open stand, a minuscule but friendly bar and a small slate-covered tower which looks as if it's been uprooted from a Second World War aerodrome.

Yet even from this vantage point, watching the race develop is virtually impossible as the horses keep disappearing behind various grassed hillocks, copses of mature oaks and rows of gleaming charabancs which have hugged the rails. You only have to listen to the variety of comments to have the eccentricity of Cartmel confirmed.

'Have they started?' asked a woman at my side.

'Where are they now?' asked another.

In an act of kindness, I pointed to where I thought the leaders might appear. Overhearing her question, five other punters pointed in five different directions and before we had time to reach a consensus the front runners suddenly appeared in the finishing straight. As my selection didn't seem to be in the frame, I left the Grandstand quickly, only to be stopped by another confused punter.

'Did anything win?' he asked.

That one question just about summed it up. He had managed to spend the whole race without seeing one stride and still wasn't sure if anything had passed the post. It was as nonsensical as an old friend who took up suicide as a hobby on the pretext that he wanted to try everything at least once.

The answer to the viewing problem at Cartmel is that there is no answer. (Apart from a large TV screen near to the fairground.) But the only way to enjoy the racing is to forget the clear views of places like Hexham, Sandown and Pontefract and simply join in the spirit of the occasion. Pack your sandwiches, lay an old rug on the grass, pick a patch by one of the fences and hope that the commentator calls out your horse's name when the winner flashes past the post. The trick is to find the right spot.

Despite my long hike up Hampsfell, I toured the whole circuit in search of the perfect vantage point, battling my way across the body-strewn turf. The good news is that I found it in the cheap enclosure and some distance from the bedlam of the beer tents, portable toilets and tightly packed betting ring.

On the far side of the course, opposite the entrance, lies a three-furlong straight. Within the space of one furlong stand three surprisingly stiff birch fences bordered by dry stone walls and dense woodland. This provides a perfect backdrop to the obstacles and puts you close enough to the action to tell if a jockey is suffering from halitosis. It's also the starting point for at least half the races, allowing you to pry into the secret world of jockeyship and witness their general wit and repartee.

'Who's makin' it?'

'Not my bugger, he's effin useless.'

'No sir! No sir!'

'Takin' a turn sir!'

'Stand still, ya swine!'

The conversational skill of these brave men is a treat in itself and well worth the entrance fee. However, apart from this one spot, the course enclosure can get a little claustrophobic and it's advisable to pay the extra money to enter the paddock. The facilities are made up of a large tented area offering everything from restaurants to tea rooms, and a host of market stalls selling tweedy clothes to country wannabes. The main advantage is that you can at least find the odd quiet corner when the carnival begins to wear you down. There's even a small stream meandering through this paddock enclosure and it's an ideal spot to drown your sorrows if you've just backed another loser.

The parade ring is extraordinary because it's so ordinary – a square patch of fenced grass which doesn't even possess a cinder circuit. The separate winner's enclosure is equally unpretentious. Yet both these cases sum up Cartmel's determination to retain its reputation as a venue for the fun loving sparrows rather than the proud Ascot peacocks. This lack of ostentation is probably one of its greatest strengths. You'll be just as welcome here in a pair of walking boots and cagoule as you would be in your Sunday best.

It's probably one of the reasons that the course seemed to have been invaded by Liverpudlians, the strong northern accents apparent wherever you stand. I was holding my head in despair as yet another selection hit the deck and I was forced to watch the winner canter over the line.

'Back it?' asked a Scouse voice at my side.

''Fraid not. You?'

'Got the third.'

'I thought yours was going to win at the last,' I responded. 'Did it have decent form?'

'Stays on when knackered,' he replied.

By the last race I had managed no more than a distant third place and I glanced towards the nearby priory for divine intervention. Unfortunately God had decided that he deserved a day of rest, as my selection didn't make it beyond the second hurdle.

Cartmel might be seen by professional punters as a hick country course but the sharp bends, tough fences and long run-in are no easy test, even for the warmest of favourites. I scampered for the exit and in a stroke of luck managed to grab a local taxi. Despite carrying far less weight in my wallet, I couldn't face another trek up Hampsfell.

'Do any good?' asked the driver.

'Hopeless,' I answered.

'Tricky course, Cartmel. They often 'ave to shoot one or two.'

His comment was delivered with the cold objectivity of a countryman who knows that rural living isn't all pretty stone cottages and climbing roses. The southern boundaries of Cumbria can be a rugged and uncompromising place, where the simplicity of nature is in full charge.

Yet six times a year Cartmel village enjoys its racing carnival, a social chaos amongst the hard logic of the surrounding landscape. Like my 16,000-mile journey around the courses of mainland Britain, racing at Cartmel is pure madness, an eccentric pursuit, wonderful and completely irrational. I'm proud to share its name – and maybe some of its character.

CHAPTER TEN

CATTERICK

We're all familiar with the notoriously inept joke teller who begins his tale with the words, 'This will really make you laugh!' Nothing is more guaranteed to make you listen in stony silence and to resist even offering a smile when the ill-timed punchline is delivered. Raising expectations in the British is a high risk strategy but one which the management of Catterick have decided to chance. Emblazoned across the racecard is the motto, 'Catterick Races, The Course With Character.' To a man with a notebook and a sharp pencil this seemed to be about as ingenious a plan as Charles I walking onto the scaffold and asking: 'Where would you like me to put my head?'

Inevitably, a dank January day in North Yorkshire doesn't give this racecourse a real chance to shine. It's a time of year when National Hunt fanatics wished they enjoyed Flat racing. An icy wind bit into my face as I left the car park and headed for the entrance, my body wrapped in every available item of thermal clothing I could lay my hands on. If I had an accident on the way home, my three layers of dubious underwear were going to take some explaining.

Enter through the attractive green and white wooden cabins which make up the main admission gates and you'll gain the impression that Catterick has a cosy appeal. A collection of single-storey, smartly painted huts surround the long thin paddock. A small and cheery restaurant nestles amongst these miniature buildings and great credit should be given for offering rhubarb crumble and custard for pud. The paddock rail bristles with button seating and miniature hedging, though the grassed centre is left bare and smacks of practicality rather than any real effort to please the eye. The modest winners' enclosure (and hard to find if you don't know the course) is separated from the paddock and lies at the end of the main stand. Behind this, and well concealed, is the weighing room, from which jockeys, trainers and officials scurry between races.

Flanking the course side of the paddock is a pre-fabricated cafe with fine views over the parade ring. Catterick was living up to its billing. It seemed compact, welcoming and not short on personality. Despite the early signs of frostbite, I was beginning to warm towards my task. I stepped inside the cafe.

'Tea please,' I chirruped.

'Not ready. You can 'ave coffee.'

Instead of thawing in the warmth of the cafe, my body temperature dropped another five degrees. I had suddenly encountered the waitress from hell, a woman who I doubt had offered up a smile since her late husband was knocked down by a large bus.

'Sixty-five pence,' she demanded, slopping the watery looking beverage across the counter.

'It's a rip-off,' came a whispered voice at my side.

A small group of red-coated Tote ladies had joined me

and began a collective moan about the high price of the drinks.

'At least the service is good,' I replied with heavy irony.

Any chance of negotiating a better deal on the brown dishwater diminished as my gaze caught the expression on the granite face of the waitress. She could have terrified a child at thirty paces. Catterick was beginning to lose its appeal.

My usual tactic in these first few minutes is to go through the racecard in the hope of spotting a couple of outsiders to turn over the favourite. But on this occasion I settled back to inspect a flimsy pamphlet which I had picked up at a nearby filling station.

It informed me that Catterick (as it is today) used to be a major army post, created by the Romans in AD 47 as a supply station for the legions on Hadrian's Wall. In those days it enjoyed the name of Cataractonium, presumably shortened when the native savages refused to use any words with more than three syllables. Had the racecard been printed with a spelling error? Was the motto meant to read 'Catterick Races: The Course With Cataracts'? My suspicions were rising by the second.

Finally digesting my coffee, I returned to reading the form. The gaggle of Tote ladies were deep in conversation, solving the tricky problem of choosing the best shampoo for thin, flyaway hair. Naturally, as an issue close to my heart, I was momentarily distracted and scribbled down their tips as quickly as possible.

My first attempt to take money from the bookies ended in a mixture of success and abject failure. Moorlands Spring ran out of steam over five furlongs from the finish, but I did at least discover the prime spot from which to follow the race. Still distracted by the Tote ladies' hairdressing advice, I left it rather late – and, unsure where to stand, spotted a small stairway running up to the roof of the paddock cafe. I recommend it. From here you won't miss a stride of the left-handed course, which apart from the rise after the winning post is fairly level.

Professional commentators inform me it's considered to be a sharp course – an expression which I never really understood until I came to Catterick. In layman's terms it simply means there's no point in backing a nag which has the words 'started slowly' recorded in its form. Miss the break at Catterick and you're a goner, as the final three furlongs is made up of a gradual descent which sends the field into the straight with a growing acceleration.

As results showed, the ideal National Hunt type on this course is probably an ex-Flat miler who likes to be up with the pace. If you attend a Flat meeting – they offer both codes at Catterick – go for a former sprinter who's gone up in trip. But whatever you back, try and get on that roof.

Beyond the paddock area is the main concourse and the principal (unnamed) stand which was refurbished in 1998. Whilst they have thankfully resisted over-modernization, the structure rather flatters to deceive. At first glance it looks so grand it seems certain to contain a box of delights. In reality it harbours no more than a top shelf of private boxes, an inadequate first floor cafe/bar with a few snacks, only one Tote window, and the God's Solution Bar.

This comfortable drinking hole was named after a six-furlong sprinter who landed the odds no less than nine times – his last win coming as a ten-year-old. Yet strangely, there's hardly a mention of the horse once you enter the bar – no statue, no photograph, no plaque, no painting. Maybe I missed it, but that's evidence enough to suggest that any commemoration lacks the necessary prominence.

But most disappointing of all are the stands which extend into the Tattersalls enclosure. The main problem is that the members stand and the separate Tatts stand further down the concourse have been built plumb parallel to the finishing straight. Unfortunately, just after the final bend, the course bulges out and remains obscured from view until runners reach the final furlong. Racing at Catterick involves as much leaning over as a competitor halfway down a ski jump. As I've suggested, you'll be far better placed on the roof of the paddock canteen.

The alternative is to head for the centre course, which is easily accessed between races. On the basis that a restaurant is best judged by its cheapest dish, the Silver Ring is never a bad indicator of how a course intends to treat the small punter. In the case of Catterick (and a few other courses you'll come across), it turned out to be an unpleasant revelation. A Victorian workhouse would have been more palatial.

The centre-course shack contained a would-be bar that was so barren my feet echoed across its tiled floor. Despite being perhaps twenty yards in length, only four old wooden tables furnished the room, while the motley collection of broken chairs seemed to have come direct from a local car boot sale. The advertised hot food amounted to no more than a limp sausage roll; and one heater did its best to combat the ever-dropping temperature. Toilets were provided in portaloos some forty yards away from the main building, while a small open stand only allowed views of the final furlong.

Needless to say, the four bookmakers' pitches were not doing great business, despite being given the comfort of a covering roof. Instead of calling the area 'Course Enclosure', why not put up a large sign saying 'Underclass

– No View – No Facilities'? At least it would be honest. Like a dog to his basket, I scurried back to the paddock canteen roof.

It was here that I came across Mary Reveley, the now famous trainer who plunders the racecourses of Britain from her training hideaway on the Cleveland coast. If Venetia Williams is the headmistress, Mary Reveley is your favourite granny – a woman who looks as if she's suddenly given up a life devoted to knitting and decided to take on the male-dominated world of racing.

Year after year, Mary Reveley has been stinging the more prominent trainers, buzzing around the racecourses like a wasp attacking a picnic. The difference is that no-one has ever managed to swat this particular wasp and on the day that I stood at her side she was certainly buzzing. Over the last two days her seven runners had all done the business – and by her look of determination, she had no intention of ending her winning run.

All small punters hate favourites and Mary Reveley's horses were now beginning to attract silly money, even if they'd won nothing better than a point-to-point. I was bent on ending her success with a major £5 each-way bet, which would rock the gambling world. Or at least help pay the paper bill.

Unsurprisingly, I spent the next two races watching the Saltburn granny smiling quietly as her runners passed the post and on both occasions beating my selections into second place. Her excited owners bristled with pride, raised their hats and whooped in delight. Mary Reveley looked little more than content and slightly apologetic. I just looked stunned and rang home to cancel the papers.

Leaving the canteen roof for the last time I noticed a flaking sign at the top of the stairs. 'No Shooting Sticks,

Stiletto Heels or Sharp Points On Restaurant Roof Please.'
Shooting Sticks? Stiletto Heels? I could see their motives,
as the roof was covered in soft bitumen. But somehow the
notice just missed the mark, as if it belonged to another
era, as if the racecourse hadn't quite moved with the times.

And nothing confirmed this more than my abortive
attempt to examine the corporate boxes on the top of the
main stand. A security guard stood barring my way and
protecting a door with a large sign which read 'PRIVATE
– DIRECTORS' MEETING'. I hope they were meeting
to discuss a big shake-up in public relations. Any racecourse worth its salt wouldn't hold private meetings in the
middle of a public race day and trumpet their junket on a
guarded barred door. In short, Catterick needs a shake-
up. Facilities never move beyond the ordinary; service in
the bars and cafes lies somewhere between mediocre and
appalling; the tired food hardly warrants a mention.

Creating a favourable impression is often about detail
– the demeanour of a waitress; the abolition of grease-
oozing chips; an attempt to provide clear signposting; a
racecard which includes a map of the course and shows
punters where the race is about to start; a paddock which
(even in January) tries to put on a show. It's hard to know
how to sum it all up. The course has a good setting,
produces some thrilling finishes and has the potential to
offer a great day out. Yet they've lost the magic. Something is missing. I'm not sure what it is. I think it might be
character and the need to get their cataracts fixed. Raising
expectations can be a dangerous business.

CHAPTER ELEVEN

CHELTENHAM

There are some things, like Americans' bottoms, that are just too big for their own good. But criticize Cheltenham? It would be as dangerous as denigrating the Queen's name in the officers' mess of the Household Cavalry. It's just not done. We're talking about an institution here, the spiritual home of National Hunt Racing. So I'd better be careful, at least until I've sung a few praises.

The Cotswold setting is dramatic, the quality of horses second to none. The jumps are challenging and beautifully constructed, the facilities are extensive, the staff officiate with military precision – but in a courteous and friendly manner. The whole place oozes class and you can smell the tradition. Even the most ardent opponents of the jumping game have heard of Arkle and Desert Orchid. I can think of a few animal activists who secretly wish they'd had a punt on Norton's Coin at 50-1. Claiming that you've no knowledge of Cheltenham's spring National Hunt Festival makes as much sense as suggesting that you've never heard of the Second World War. It's impossible. They are both rooted in our history.

So why visit Cheltenham on a grey stormy day in late

October? Why not wait until March? Food and space, that's why. I'll come back to the food later but what I really wanted was a good look at Cheltenham. I'd been before, in 1986, when Dawn Run won the Gold Cup. I could hardly see my brogues never mind the racing. I've never been too keen on forced intimacy with 50,000 people and '86 was no exception. October gave me the chance to see what I'd been standing on all those years ago.

A 150-mile round trip up and down the A40 in blinding rain tested my motivation. I became confused as I approached Cheltenham, but was fortunate to spot A. Turnell's horsebox which manoeuvred towards the racecourse with the confidence of a homing pigeon. The public are guided to a park-and-ride area, which made me think I must be five miles from the course. Ignore this concern – it's only a five-minute walk and you'll immediately become aware of the biggest grandstand I've ever seen, the biggest racecourse I've ever witnessed, the biggest entrance I've ever cast eyes on. If it hadn't been for the force seven gale and driving rain I'd have thought I was in Texas.

But don't miss the real attraction. As you walk towards the course, you pass the back of the enclosure toilets. Someone has built a nine-hole pitch and putt course in an area no bigger than a back yard in *Coronation Street*. Quite bizarre. The fairways looked in good condition, though the greens could have done with a cut.

I arrived very early (having forgotten to wind my watch back from the previous weekend) and wandered into the complex. And complex is the word. I had that 'where do I start?' feeling, such was the scale of the place. A large Corals sign offered refuge from uncertainty and I headed off to place an early each-way patent. As I'll reveal, this proved to be a very big mistake.

Corals, situated in the Cavern Bar, was a strange introduction to Cheltenham, a deserted concrete dungeon like an empty underground station and with an equal lack of style. I raced back onto the main concourse. There's a touch of the blarney everywhere. Whispered Irish accents met me around every corner. Guinness and Jameson whiskey signs appeared to hang on every wall. I started to feel more comfortable. Cheltenham without the Irish would be like gin without the tonic.

The rain grew in intensity and I searched for cover in the Hall of Fame. This sounds more like a shrine to American Footballers than jump racing but it's well worth a look. In the centre of the hall stands Cheltenham's answer to the bucking bronco – a rodeo-style mechanical horse which threatens to jump over a sturdy brushwood fence. I was tempted. I can't tell you how much I was tempted. But a man of my age, bobbing up and down in front of an ever-growing crowd? Not really on. You'd need an ego as thick as a carthorse's hoof to pull that one off. I turned away with a little regret at my cowardice.

The passageway to the Gold Cup and Foxhunter Restaurant provides the best treat. An array of shop windows display pictures and artefacts of great champions, fine trainers and brave jockeys. I noticed Richard Pitman, still looking enthusiastic as he showed friends along the showcases. I thought he was speaking far too loudly for common decency until I realized he was listening to his own commentary of an Old Triumph Hurdle. He sounded so excited I think he must have backed the winner. Best of all – look out for the picture of an Irish priest reaching over the rail to shake the hand of a Gold Cup winning owner. It's a precious shot.

There's far too much to mention – go and see it. You

even have the chance to stare back at a hologram of Desert Orchid, to warm your hands on an open log fire, to find out how far a bookie travels in a racing year (not far enough, I'd say) and a nice touch of having a pattern of horse hooves woven into the carpet. I passed a cleaning lady who was scrubbing furiously at the double Wilton. She looked up and said: 'I wish they wouldn't let these horses in here, it makes my job twice as hard.' Or maybe she didn't. I left her to her work and hurried out to continue my exploration.

The main stand immediately reminded me of the bridge of a gigantic ocean liner. Having recently seen the film *Titanic*, I checked on the lifeboat stations. Not one to be seen, but I pressed on regardless. The standing area provides a fairly good view of the course, though the steps are dominated by the overhanging top stand reserved for members and private boxes.

Dare I risk a criticism here? For some reason the whole of this five-storey stand faces a short turn at the west end of the course. The racecourse then tilts dramatically eastwards into the distance and, as later races revealed, you can see little of the unfolding events once they have gone out into the country. The inhabitants of Oxford might enjoy a better sight of the middle section of the racing. The overall effect of the angle of the stand is that you are forced to spend the majority of any race with your neck bent at an angle of 90 degrees. A decent physiotherapist could make a fortune at Cheltenham.

The course itself is undeniably impressive. Whoever manufactures white rails must be a wealthy man. I've never seen so many ringing a course, crossing a course, dissecting a course. It looked like a giant Scalextrix Grand Prix circuit. How the jockeys find their way round here,

I'll never know. They must all have degrees in orienteering. A certain J. Magee certainly did when he rode my selection, Explain This, in the opening maiden hurdle. The horse romped in at 16-1, which is where my earlier mistake in visiting Corals became evident. The Tote paid nearly 40-1.

Even though I had just about covered my costs for the day, I was feeling rather peeved as I approached the paddock and winner's enclosure. This is a truly striking arena, a large grassed oval which would not be out of place at Augusta National. It's so big it would probably be a par five. Sadly it was rather hard to hear details of the winning connections as the announcer sounded as if he was broadcasting from inside a goldfish bowl which contained piranhas. The giant screen which looks over the paddock offered little help. It was fine if you possessed 20-20 vision and had been reared on a diet of raw carrots but the mass of information was far too detailed for comprehension. Added to this it appeared to have been invaded by some terminal virus which managed to spell an ex-champion jockey's name as R. Dun*@+d$. All very disturbing, especially for R. Dun*@+d$.

I trekked over to the saddling enclosure. Again an impressive sight, a half moon amphitheatre with raked stands. The horses must feel as if they've hit the West End after spending a lifetime in provincial rep. But it was at this moment that I realized something slightly odd was occurring. Wherever I turned, my fellow racegoers appeared to be chewing, munching, champing, gnawing and crunching. Jaws moved faster than Norman Evans' mouth on washing day (if you remember him – if you don't, you should). I suddenly had a faint memory of the morning's racing bulletin.

It was Free Food Day at Cheltenham, a bonus to com-memorate their centenary and their selection, for the third year running, as the Racecourse of the Year. And did the crowd make use of the offer? They sure did – as large Texans might say. Not only did they have to pick winners, they had to pick meals. Pizzas to the left of them. Fish and chips to the right. Bacon sandwiches to the rear. Burgers to the fore. There was many a punter who went up two sizes by the end of the afternoon and I noticed the clothes stalls doing a brisk and profitable trade.

This leads me to the sad tale of the 'organized man'. On first entering Cheltenham racecourse, my attention was diverted by a number of raised voices. It appeared, though I only caught snatches of the exchange, that a well-heeled family had moved beyond discussion and that the husband and wife had declared war on one another. They appeared to have everything. Fine clothes, beautiful children, stunning wife, handsome husband.

But what they also had was a large hamper which contained so much food they could have opened a Sainsbury's outlet. They must have been cooking and preparing since the previous day. So busy must this preparation have been, they had obviously failed to either read a newspaper or listen to the racing bulletins. But who expects free food on a racecourse? Everyone but them it would seem.

'Do you realize how long I spent organizing this . . . ?' were the last words I heard as they disappeared towards the rain-soaked Club Lawn. There was a distinct whiff of divorce in the air.

Two losers later I'm heading off to the £5 Courage enclosure, a fairly large open area at the far west end of the course. It lived up to its name. I took courage and entered.

Toilets, a Tote building and a small cafe with a desultory raked stand which looks out onto very little. Pity really. A spot on a perfect skin, insignificant but highly noticeable. Four bookies plied their trade to thirty or forty people, while fathers and sons had a five-a-side football match on the crumbling tarmac. It felt like a run-down housing estate next to Buckingham Palace. I couldn't help shaking my head slightly and thinking that a bit of inward invest-ment wouldn't go amiss. The small crowd looked just as keen on racing as their affluent neighbours and deserving of a better deal.

Back to watch the last leg of my patent promise much and deliver little. I'd discovered a good spot earlier in the afternoon, a fairly small flat roof above the owners' and trainers' Lawn Bar. Excellent view and far less crowded than the main stand. The rain began to beat down yet again and I headed to Corals to collect on my one winner, through the complex complex and still amazed by the number of bars on offer, all apparently named after heroes of the past.

If Cheltenham creates any more star names, I suppose they'll have to open even more watering holes. They could become a prime target for the Temperance League in the next few years. Back through the gates and off to the west car park and a last chance to look at the pitch and putt course. They still hadn't managed to cut the greens.

Am I criticizing Cheltenham? Not really, especially as it's a treasonable offence and my head is quite attached to my body. I'd like it to stay that way. It's just big. It's enormous. It's gargantuan. It's just that I prefer to be intimate with the racing and not with the crowd. And I won't have a word said against the Queen, or the Pope come to that. And if you believe that . . .

Postscript: Like soap powder, Cheltenham's on the verge of offering a new, improved, bigger and brighter product. The festival meeting is to be extended to four days (excellent) and they want to spend £18 million on an all singing, all dancing Centaur complex (half man, half horse . . . Mmmm, clever that). As Americans like to say, it will soon become a 24/7, 52/12 venue. In English, that means it's going to be open a lot . . . for everything from horse racing to rally cars, concerts and festivals. They hope it will 'become the Harrogate of the South West'. Now there's an interesting aspiration.

CHAPTER TWELVE

CHEPSTOW

I've always enjoyed the old war films. You know the sort of thing. Pull together a bunch of British actors with square chins and clipped accents, stick them in a jolly dicey situation, kill off a few, ensuring they don't even look injured when they die – and then let the hero win the day. More importantly, make sure the enemy charges at you across completely open ground shouting things such as, 'Please shoot me, I'm a bad person.'

It was the Severn Bridge which prompted these reflections. I had battled down the M4, hurling my car into a solid wall of rain. I've seen less water in a brimming reservoir, and by the time I handed over my £4.20 toll fee, I was almost too exhausted to go racing. It was *A Bridge Too Far*. A bridge far too far – a good title if they ever make a sequel. If they made it a trilogy, they could call the third film *A Bridge Far Far Too Far*. A fourth film could be a bit of a problem.

Chepstow lies only a stone's throw from the new Severn Road Bridge and provides the racecourse with its own grand entrance. The impressive mile-long construction (I'm guessing the length) appears like two blue and white inverted Welsh harps. All the road signs suddenly become bilingual (Chepstow/Cass – Gwent). It's easy to spot non-Welsh-speaking drivers, as they all hesitate at the signposts, but within minutes of leaving the bridge the racecourse comes into view. I'm glad we're not still driving chariots. The real name for Chepstow according to my pocket-sized Domesday Book is *Strigruil*. Put that on the signs and you could create traffic jams as far back as Cardiff.

My usual concerns about getting stuck in a Welsh bog were soon dispelled, as I was ushered onto one of the largest hard standing, free car parks I've ever witnessed. A short walk across the road brings you to the entrance. Protected by my fully waterproofed golf suit, I dripped my way into the day member's entrance (£15).

'Just a minute!' came a voice at my side, his hand placed firmly on my arm.

Assuming he was a retired policeman, who had mistaken me for an escaped convict, I smiled a response with as much innocence as I could muster.

'You can get a ticket for a tenner if you ask the *Racing Post* woman,' answered the elderly steward with a strong Welsh lilt.

Approaching the paper seller, I made my first of many mistakes at Chepstow.

'I believe we can do business,' I suggested, waving a £10 note towards her.

The young and rather attractive woman looked somewhat startled by my ambiguous suggestion.

'You've got a ticket?' I queried, in an embarrassed mumble, realizing I had just propositioned a respectable married woman.

The deal was done and I entered the racecourse with an

extra five pounds to swell the bookies' coffers. The rain still poured down stronger than a Singapore monsoon and I headed for cover in the Persian War Bar, which lies at the back of the winners' enclosure. This proved to be my only good move of the day. The small bar offers good wholesome food and handmade sandwiches to order. Even better, the tea comes in pots and is brewed freshly with every order – always a big plus in my book.

An hour before the first race, the room was empty, apart from six or seven staff who sat chatting and chain smoking in the far corner. I settled at the opposite end to respect their privacy and began to select my five inevitable winners. After getting a result on the entrance money, I was feeling lucky and certain that I'd be driving home with a full wallet. The going had gone from soft to heavy in a matter of minutes and it was clear that it wouldn't be a favourites' day. Pick a few outsiders with the ability to stay the trip and there was money to be made.

The Persian War Bar provides a good spot to take in the startling Chepstow course. I had seen it many times on television but, like so much televised sport, the reality is far greater than the image. Chepstow is no exception. The two-mile course was as idiosyncratic as anything I had so far witnessed. The oval circuit is made up of two long straights and two tight bends but with more rises and falls than a fairground big dipper.

The drop which begins just after the winning post must convince horse and rider that they've just fallen off a precipice. I've heard it described as a steep descent. If what I witnessed is a steep descent then the Matterhorn is a small bump in the road. Any trainer hoping to win at Chepstow should always run two horses in each race and make sure they're roped together. Whilst the course offers fine views towards the Forest of Dean and the Monmouth hills, the undulating course means that the racing is sometimes obscured, especially after leaving the back straight and coming up to the final turn. Two of my first three selections were handily placed seven furlongs from home, only to have tailed off once the pack reappeared over the brow of the hill. Whatever you do, back a stayer at Chepstow. A free-galloping front-runner may as well stay wrapped up in his stable. A dour plodder is far more likely to take the spoils.

Perhaps if I'd had this prior knowledge, I'd have had more success than one placed horse in the first four races. What made it even more annoying was that it was a perfect afternoon for mug's betting – the type of gambling in which I can claim some expertise. Everyone was praying for the rain to stop, and Saint Cecilia won the first at 12-1; the stock market had crashed in the morning and Mr Dow Jones won the third race at 9-1; visibility went down to a hundred yards by the fourth race, which was won by Atlantic Mist at 11-4.

How the winner of the second race fits into this strategy of coincidence, I'm not sure. Belmorebruno is a name which is hard to associate with any occurrence. Its association with A. P. McCoy was, however, a clever tactic employed by the trainer, Martin Pipe. As I've reported on many occasions (see especially Fontwell Park), Tony McCoy just doesn't know when he's beaten.

After the first circuit of the three-mile chase, Belmorebruno looked to have about as much petrol left in the tank as my lawn mower after a hard day in the garden. Stone dead last, going into the valley at the far end of the course, McCoy obviously decided he wanted to be first in the shower and drove Belmorebruno through the field as if the jockey's changing room was short of hot water. What made it even worse was that his mount won by a comfortable six lengths at a starting-price of 12-1 – not a common occurrence on a Pipe/McCoy combination.

I raced off to the flower-decked winners' enclosure to greet the winner and to convince myself that Tony McCoy only had two legs, two arms and one head. He's certainly only got two eyes – and they're both as steely as a builder's chisel. The beauty of the Chepstow winners' enclosure is that you can get close enough to pick up these details and near enough to overhear the jockey's post-race reports to owners and trainers.

After the first race, Carl Llewellyn explained to the trainer that the reason Ballynabragget had been beaten into second place was that his horse had been 'looking for a bit of toe' but had 'travelled well and run to the line'. The connections listened with an unconvincing expression of understanding. I bumped into them half an hour later and their chosen mouthpiece was still mumbling about 'a bit of toe' but with a distinctly fraudulent expertise.

The rain eased slightly and allowed the racegoers a momentary glimpse of a sunlit Chepstow. It was like a society beauty removing her disguise at a masked ball. For just a few seconds Chepstow could be seen in her true colours – and nowhere better than the sweeping lawns which run down to the course from the pre-parade ring. This is a truly stunning area, banks of flower beds, delightful wooden benches and winding footpaths passing through the manicured grass. Mature oaks, ashes and willows took their one chance to cast lazy shadows across the turf and mellow my frustration at having just backed four straight losers.

The paddock is equally attractive and whoever does the

gardening certainly knows how to grow a good heather. I can be contacted through the publisher if they'd like to give me the secret. My own rockery looks more like a bad haircut in a force ten gale and is in real need of some professional advice. The highlight of the grassed oval paddock is the large brass bell which stands proudly at its centre. Horses seemed to circle round with one eye firmly fixed on this object, their anticipation growing as the steward reaches for the bell rope and calls them to order.

The sun finished its teasing and disappeared behind the leaden skies. As more rain began to trickle down my neck I took refuge behind the display board at the side of the paddock. Despite being a relatively modern course, the authorities have thankfully retained the old system of hand-painted boards and a series of metal chains which hoist the declarations into the air. The operator was a genial but short man who immediately made use of my extra height.

'Give us an 'and, would you?' he asked, handing me a well-weathered notice. I took the black rectangular board without question and slotted it into position, sticking my head around the corner to make sure it was the correct way up. 'GOING – HEAVY' read the sign.

'Sums up my afternoon,' I mumbled to no-one in particular and headed off towards the stands to seek solace in the nearest restaurant. There are three impressive stands at Chepstow, each giving a good view across the course. All are painted in stark black and white, which gives a clean and rather classy feel to the whole venue. There are the usual collection of private boxes occupying the best positions but generally the public is well catered for and walking distances between the paddock and stands are short and easily accessible.

However, whoever first constructed the facilities must have had a penchant for potholing. All the main eating areas are underground, entombed in the bowels of the main stands. The food (especially the Cornish pasties) is of high quality, but even the members' restaurant enjoys a view equalled only by the Black Hole of Calcutta.

But don't let me put you off. The course itself is superb and should rank high on your list of 'must see' venues. The surroundings, amenities and general feel would be hard to beat anywhere in mainland Britain. My only reservation is that Chepstow is a mixed Flat and jumps course. Despite already hosting the Welsh National, perhaps they ought to go full out and turn the course into a premier steeplechase course – which it nearly qualifies for already. By doing this, the fences could be brought closer into the stands.

At the moment the straight Flat course rather detaches the punters from the main action and robs racegoers of the necessary involvement. They'll probably never let me into Chepstow again, especially with a cut price ticket. In spite of my waterproofing, I was now soaked to the proverbial skin. My selection in the fifth race, Master Chuzzlewit, was a no-hope rank outsider in a four-horse field and I decided to cut my losses and head for home.

'Make good use of the extra fiver?' asked the gate steward as I hurried through the exit.

''Fraid not,' I replied with a look of resignation.

The Severn Bridge loomed into sight within minutes and I shuffled through my pockets for the £4.20 toll fee. To my great surprise, I was suddenly over the river and heading along the motorway. For some reason you only pay to enter Wales but can escape at no extra cost. There must be some great symbolism in this arrangement. Either the Welsh want to keep the English out or they want to tempt us to leave as soon as possible. Whatever the case, the next time the sun shines and Chepstow has a meeting, I'll be the first to make the trip. Wherever you live in Britain, Chepstow has enough to offer to prevent it being a bridge too far.

Postscript: Next day's paper revealed the winner of the fifth race – Master Chuzzlewit at 33-1. I think I've got the message, but I'll have my revenge one day.

CHAPTER THIRTEEN

CHESTER

Northern racecourses put down two main challenges to the extravagance of Royal Ascot. The August meeting at York is always well supported but the May meeting at Chester kicks off the society season. Whichever your choice, there's no point in going to any of these events if your preference is for a quiet afternoon in the garden with a good book and a bottle of chilled wine. I read somewhere that Chester racecourse is best described as intimate. Intimate? Heaving might be a better description. I've seen more space in a bookie's wallet. I spent the majority of the afternoon pressed so tightly against a variety of respectable women that I'm expecting a number of paternity suits to hit the mat at any moment.

I arrived well in time, however, to absorb the true splendour of Chester, taking the opportunity to wander through the nearby city. Such is the popularity of Chester racing that the authorities deem it unnecessary to give you any indication of its location. Having heard that the course was within walking distance of the city centre, I finally parked up in a multi-storey car park, which only demanded a week's wages for a six-hour stay.

From here it was just a short walk to the tourist haven of the 19th-century 'Rows', a collection of black and white timbered shopping arcades with prices that should carry a government health warning for anyone with an income under £50,000 a year. But it's essential not to miss this Chester curiosity. Forget the architecture and history – your main objective should be to sample the finest collection of cream cake shops I've found anywhere in Britain. (They call them patisseries in Chester society.)

Still licking my lips, I dashed around the magnificent cathedral, a building which seems to have been wedged into place by a giant crane. As I left I approached a wizened cleric whose job it is to fill visitors with guilt if they refused to pay the optional entry fee.

'Any idea where I can find the racecourse?' I asked.

'There is a racecourse far away without a city wall,' he answered.

'Do a lot of crosswords?' I enquired.

'Every day,' he smiled in response.

Despite his cryptic directions, I found the Roodee (as it's known) within five minutes. This former ancient Roman harbour sits just outside (without) the city wall, nestled between the River Dee and the city fortifications. Though racing wasn't due to start until 2 p.m., I arrived at 10.45 a.m., the queues already beginning to form outside the ornate iron gates which protect the main entrance. Though unseasonably warm, the blustery wind was trying its best to remove the bevy of wide-brimmed hats and to ruffle the highly coiffured heads of the Chester glitterati. They were people who I doubt had ever stood at a bus queue in their life and I sensed a slight note of irritation in the enforced delay. At 11 a.m. precisely, the gates swung open and, though standing still, I was carried forward in a sea of anticipation. The Chester intimacy had begun.

By the time I passed through the entrance into the County Stand, I was £27 lighter and hoping that I was going to get value for money. My first rule of Chester is – don't waste your money on the County Stand, whatever the current price. On the day of my visit, Tattersalls at £16, the Dee Stand at £5 and the centre course at £3 presented far better value. For £27 I did receive a very smart grey cardboard badge, was obliged to wear a jacket and tie on a sweltering spring day, and given the opportunity to sample the delights of the sumptuously carpeted Concourse Bar. An hour before the first race this had completely disappeared under a scrum of over-dressed punters and a haze of stale perfume.

The seating in the main stand (which I admit is top class) is all reserved in advance, apart from a few rows of plastic bucket chairs whose view is completely obscured by racegoers standing on the small raked standing area. Apart from 'being seen' in the County Stand, I could think of nothing that warranted the extra outlay. The advantages of paying a far smaller price in Tattersalls are numerous. Chester (like Ludlow), has built its paddock and winners' enclosure on the inside of the course. Access to this area is gained through a tunnel system which may be entered from both the County Stand and Tattersalls. This underpass has been tastefully decorated in salmon pink tiles from wall to ceiling. If any men reading this report happen to have a wife, partner or indiscretion who favours pink, I would advise them to persuade their companion into an alternative colour. It was noticeable that many men lost contact with their female partners as they merged into the background of the tiled walls and often reappeared from the tunnel with a completely different companion. It would be a useful move by the Chester authorities if they were to provide a 'pink lady holding ring', in order to reduce the annual rise in Cheshire divorce rates.

This shared access to the paddock provides an unusual mixture of the chic and the 'eeh by gum' – a coming together of real wealth and temporary affluence. As a setting it is hard to beat. Numerous bars and Pimms tents surround a delightful picnic area laid out with small chairs and tables. A tented village of white canvas shimmers in the sunlight, the prime private box hired by the Welsh Development Agency and packed with smart-suited punters without a miner's lamp between them.

The lawns and flower beds are more highly manicured than a Royal digit and wouldn't look out of place in a stately home. At a guess, they probably hired Louis XIV's head gardener. He must be an old man by now but he's still doing a fine job. The centre piece of the paddock possibly ranks as his *pièce de résistance* – a hedged and floral display with a running fountain, the water cascading into a small pool. It's the sort of thing that a hypnotherapist would make you think of when they're trying to make you relax. If I'm ever fortunate enough to own a horse who runs at Chester, I'll give it a blindfold and ear plugs just in case it falls asleep during the parade.

Equally impressive is the winners' enclosure, the art deco stewards' and weighing room forming a backdrop to a small grassed area bursting with spring flowers. To get a decent view it's necessary to take your position well before the race has finished, as the crowds can be as much as ten deep and so intimate they've probably got their hand in your back pocket. (I witnessed at least eight people reporting stolen wallets and purses during the afternoon.)

If you can get a place on the rails of the winners' enclosure, it's worth missing a race or two. You'll have the fun of hearing jockeys, trainers and owners in deep discussion and trying to discover why their horse managed to leave its form on the training gallops. The debonair trainer Henry Cecil didn't have this problem and was having a good afternoon. He's a man who appears to show as much pleasure in victory as I would if my daughter told me she intended to marry a scar-faced member of the Russian mafia. I doubt he gets any sympathy when he's miserable as no-one would spot the difference. But say what you like, despite billowing as much smoke as a soot-choked chimney, he's got more natural style than a Savile Row suit – and I bet he's got a few of those in his wardrobe.

As you can tell from these few reflections, the racing at Chester seems to take second place to the sense of occasion and social beanfeast. As usual I was trying to beat the book by backing outsiders with a bit of form, rather than following the money and hitting a few favourites. This proved as useful a strategy as backing a shire horse in the Derby, five favourites landing the odds in consecutive races. Bookies looked as happy as Henry Cecil, big punters drank more and more champagne, and small punters took consolation in a cup of tea. As usual I headed for the nearest sweet shop and a reviving Mars Bar.

You won't starve at Chester. The bars, cafeterias, restaurants are numerous and generally offer fairly good value with food ranging from a five-course meal to a greasy burger. But you can't buy a bag of sweets for love nor money. What's more, you can't get a sniff of a bar of chocolate or the obligatory Mars Bar. My developing love affair with Chester began to recede as the full implications of this omission began to dawn. In a quiet moment between races, I began to pen a letter to the authorities.

Dear Sir or Madam,

Re : Chocolate facilities at Chester Racecourse

Now look here . . .

Unfortunately I was disturbed by a woman in a salmon pink dress, who appeared to desire unrequested intimacy but luckily lost her in the tunnel as I headed back to the County Stand. Hurrying through the crowd I finally escaped into the Tattersalls enclosure and discovered the true atmosphere of Chester. Butted up against the old city wall are two fine stands, their black and white facade reminiscent of the 'Rows' in the city centre. Not only are they preferable to the County Stand but the view over the racecourse is unrestricted and allows you to follow the race from start to finish.

In truth, it's a small punter's natural home, the atmosphere generated by the huge crowd far more effervescent than the restraint of its more expensive neighbour. From this point the remarkable Chester course can be viewed in its true glory, a one-mile round course flanked by the River Dee and a startling Victorian railway viaduct which lies adjacent to the short two-furlong back straight. It's from here that the necessity for 'Chester experience' becomes obvious. My selection in the third race missed the break at the start, finished like a train and got beaten half a length. If the phrase 'started slowly but made good headway' appears in any horse's form, keep your hand in your pocket. Even in a mile race, if you're not up with the pace, the chance of coming with a late run on such tight bends has as much chance of success as an Arab terrorist applying for the chairmanship of Marks and Spencer.

Even if you've paid for the minimal delights of the County Stand, get into Tattersalls and then keep going. The start of a one-mile, two-furlong race is held at the far end of the short home straight. Wander through into the Dee Stand and you can get within touching distance of horses and riders. Even more spectacularly, you will enjoy two of the finest sights at the Roodee. Firstly, you can delight in the truly thrilling sight of the racing pack sweeping into the straight from one of the tightest bends in British racing. But even better is to turn away from the course and incline your head upwards to view the unique character of Chester races.

The sandstone Roman wall rises at this point and provides a perfect view for any pedestrian walking along Nun's Road. As each race unfolds, the ancient battlements are lined with bobbing heads cheering in their selections without having to pay a penny for the privilege. Go to the local bookies, place your bets for the afternoon and lay claim to a spot on the wall and you could enjoy a wonderful, freebie afternoon. If you happen to work locally you could even take in a couple of races on the pretext that you 'must get some fresh air'.

The Dee Stakes (a Derby Trial no less) appeared to generate great excitement in one particular 'wall punter'. As they hit the straight, he urged his selection on with the subtlety of a deranged gorilla with a wasp up its nose. It was then that I noticed his peculiar garb. Having recently completed jury service, I immediately recognized him as a member of Her Majesty's judiciary – his high, white, two-pronged collar wafting in the strengthening breeze.

The winner, Oath, won comfortably, K. Fallon easing him up well before the line. It wasn't only the defendant who had taken the oath that day and my learned friend must have returned to the nearby court an extremely happy man. He probably got his client off with a small fine. If Oath had lost he'd certainly have gone down for ten years. A criminal's fate can hang on a very fine thread – namely, his barrister's ability to read racing form.

Leaving my lawyer from the chambers of Punter, Gamble and Leggit to his celebrations, I headed off to the free centre-course enclosure, which lies opposite the Dee Stand. This is an area which has as much in common with the County Stand as I have with the Temperance Society. I can only describe it as Chip City, with more fast food caravans than Chester's had burgers. The nearest you'd get to a healthy meal would be a deep-fried banana fritter. But it was packed with punters, families, dogs and picnic hampers, their feast accompanied by a live jazz band and ageing chanteuse. She was no Ella Fitzgerald but she could bash out the blues as well as the notorious Gladys Winstanley – in her heyday the alcohol-soaked queen of the Pontefract jazz circuit. Believe me, that's high praise from a man who likes his blues sung 'earthy'.

The odd thing was that punters in this enclosure could see only a fleeting glimpse of the racing. Yet they seemed to be having a better time than anyone in the members enclosure with a glass of champagne in one hand, a smoked salmon sandwich in the other and a fast motor in the car park. Quickly pulling off my tie, I grabbed a bag of chips and sat down, the singer suddenly breaking into a throaty rendition of 'Nobody Loves You When You're Down And Out'. Heaven.

Chester? Wonderful. In many ways it's got everything – high class racing, good facilities, history and a sense of fun. Go there – but don't take a tie. Don't dress up in that outfit you'd only wear at an enemy's wedding – just relax and take in the intimate atmosphere.

Postscript: Two weeks later I received a letter with a Chester postmark. It remains on my desk unopened. It's either a response to my complaint about the scandalous lack of Mars Bars – or a paternity suit. As yet, I haven't had the courage to open the envelope. If it turns out to be the latter – I think I know just the right lawyer.

CHAPTER FOURTEEN

DONCASTER

I hadn't had flu for over ten years. I don't mean the counterfeit cold, which decimates industry every winter and provides shirkers with the excuse to go AWOL for three days. Two days before my Doncaster visit, I'd managed to land myself with the real McCoy. The severity of my condition was confirmed when I asked my wife why we had moved to Tibet and invested in a Himalayan yak farm.

Fortunately, by Wednesday morning, I was more or less certain which country I was in, though still harboured some nagging doubts about the yak farm. It was a blissful early autumn morning, the temperature outside the car in the high 70s and my body temperature in the low hundreds. Constant sneezing at 80mph is not to be recommended and I felt relieved to be approaching Doncaster in one piece – my survival mainly due to a reddening nose which had begun to act as a warning beacon to other motorists. Approach from the M18 and you'll immediately see that Doncaster takes its racing seriously.

Signposting is excellent and even the major round-abouts are inset with mosaics of galloping thoroughbreds as if to say, 'Yes, you're going the right way.' Sadly, they've fallen into the trap of advertising parking spaces by colour coding – very confusing if you're colour blind or haven't bought a prepaid ticket. I'd suffered a similar irritation when approaching Ascot and Aintree, and they could have lowered my boiling blood pressure by displaying a simple 'Free Public Car Park' sign. (Go past the main entrance and turn left.)

Is it just me, or is Doncaster one of those courses which sits on the fringe of British racing? I know it stages the St Leger, the Lincoln Handicap, the wonderfully named Flying Childers, and a host of top class events – but it seems to be a course that no-one ever mentions in conversation. Unlike other Yorkshire courses, such as Beverley, Pontefract or Ripon, I've never heard Doncaster described with affection. It's just there. A place where horses run. For some reason, there's a missing element and I was keen to find out why it had lost its reported former magic. Doncaster is hardly a new kid on the block, the St Leger priding itself on being the oldest Classic, having been run at this course since 1776. The place is steeped in history. Close your eyes and you can imagine J. Singleton Junior driving his mount Allabaculla to victory in the very first St Leger – a feat he would repeat twenty-eight years later on Orville. With such a long gap between victories, I'm surprised the jockey's second success wasn't marked by granting him the title J. Singleton Not-so-junior.

Given this sort of pedigree, Doncaster should be a sure-fire winner. But open your eyes and you'll soon realize that there's a chink in its historical armoury. Having arrived early, I went on a tour of inspection. Like many courses, the stands are laid out in a long strip bordering the final furlong. Everything looked fine. Ample grandstands, lawn-striped paddock, a plethora of bars, gigantic betting halls – all the prerequisites of a decent racecourse. And then I saw the course – or, in truth, I saw part of the course. Clambering up to the highest point I could find, I scanned the horizon. I had discovered Doncaster's weak spot. In fact I was standing in its weak spot. A tented village in the centre of the course obliterated at least three furlongs of the tight top bend, while the back straight appeared so distant it could have been in Scunthorpe.

Tracks of this nature are often described as pear-shaped, or at least like pears which have toppled on their side. This is fine as long as you don't build the stands at the stalk end. Guess where the stands are at Doncaster? It's almost sacrilegious to say so, but Cheltenham has the same problem – i.e. 80 per cent of the action takes place so far out in the country that the majority of races gain no real momentum until they're two furlongs from the finishing post. At least the high-raked stands of Cheltenham give you a racing chance. But not Doncaster.

The new(ish) grandstands, built in 1969, reveal how the authorities have succumbed to the corporate shilling. Private function rooms dominate the grandstands. Only a third of this facility is given over to public viewing areas, the majority of punters in the members' and Grandstand areas being limited to the lawns running down to the racecourse. From this position you'll be fortunate to see the last hundred yards and 'live' racing is limited to two giant TV screens. Come racing and watch TV? No thanks. I'd rather offer to do the ironing for a family with six children.

The irony is that I'd go back to Doncaster. At least to the St Leger festival. Don't expect to see much racing.

Don't expect to make money on this flat, galloping course. But do expect to have fun. Unless you've wangled a private box, this is no place for a punter who likes to watch thoroughbreds strain every sinew, or jockeys manoeuvre their mounts into a challenging position. Doncaster is really no more than a 'right grand day out' course where the racing is incidental to what the Irish call the 'crack'. Despite the setting (Doncaster Rovers' Belle Vue ground lurks in the background) punters were obviously having a good time without being constrained by the starchiness of Ascot or the general mayhem of Epsom.

If you want a real glimpse of history, a minimal fee will give you access to the family enclosure. You'll miss the paddock and winners' enclosure but you'll also enjoy the best view of the racecourse. The small but impressive stand, with its high-vaulted wooden roof and 19th-century clock tower, is worth denying yourself the pleasures of the more expensive enclosures. It was originally constructed in 1881 by Charles Stockil Esquire, Alderman, Chairman of the Peace Committee. This elaborate title is emblazoned along the main stone support and probably took the masons longer to carve than it took the bricklayers to erect the whole building. I suspect Mr Stockil, Alderman etc, etc, etc spent most of his life with a railway company, as the stand is so reminiscent of a Victorian station that I half expected a steam train to pull up at any moment. There was certainly no shortage of porters.

On the day of my visit, the main sponsors for the day were Great North Eastern Railways. Before and after each race, a small band of employees paraded in the paddock, all dressed in their finest GNER outfits. Grey flannels, small check navy blue jackets and military style, flat, peaked caps might give an impression of a group of men with a pride in efficiency whose main hobby is studying railway timetables. Unfortunately, it seems to be the fate of all British railway staff that they would be capable of looking scruffy in a made-to-measure Savile Row suit. Frenchmen appear to achieve model status in an old woolly jumper and a pair of faded jeans. I suppose it's just one of life's mysteries but every time an Englishman tries to look smart, the result is invariably comical – especially when railway staff are given caps which are all a size too big. If I remember Doncaster for nothing else, it will be the sight of twelve men with their ears forced into horizontal flaps, the only part of their anatomy which saved them from total blindness.

What will also stick in my memory is my inability to make money. Some courses (and Doncaster's one of them, York's another) are marked in my diary as the royal road to bankruptcy. Don't ask me why, but every punter has a course like this. It's just one of those things, a sense that whatever you do, your selection will run like a donkey with a hangover. History was repeating itself. By the time of the fourth race, I'd landed no more than a small place bet and was rummaging in my pocket for the car keys. Only the Doncaster Cup could save me.

First run in 1776, this two-mile, two-furlong marathon rarely attracts more than five or six runners, yet is treated as an honorary classic. Double Trigger – the only horse to have landed the spoils three times – was paraded in front of the swelling and sweltering crowd. The announcer – with a Geordie accent carefully disguised by Jockey Club elocution lessons – explained that Double Trigger was now at stud and had covered seventy-eight mares in its first season. There was an audible gasp of admiration from the crowd. At least eight women had an attack of the vapours while their male companions tried hard to conceal their growing sense of inadequacy.

Rushing into the vast betting hall below the main Grandstand, I managed to get a late bet on the Irish raider San Sebastian – the only five-year-old in the race. Three minutes and fifty-six seconds later, Far Cry won by a short-head and San Sebastian puffed in ten seconds behind. Depressed, yet excited by the one furlong of racing I had managed to witness from the Grandstand lawn, I rushed off to the winners' enclosure to join the celebrations. A radiant and beaming owner, Mrs Nicky Chambers, stood amongst a melee of news-hungry reporters. Notebook in hand, and risking the gateman's challenge, I joined their ranks.

'Great story,' I heard one hack mutter to a colleague. The tale which unravelled would make good copy. 'Never Say Die Cry is Real Heart-Warmer' declared the next day's *Racing Post* with tabloid eloquence. Nicky Chambers turned out to be a greyhound trainer, whose husband had recently undergone heart surgery. Patrick Chambers bought Far Cry on the Wednesday, had his operation on the Friday, and watched his horse win for him on the following Saturday.

'I know nothing about horses. But he's got a great heart,' declared Nicky Chambers with a wonderful sense of timing, if not a touch of irony. Yet they missed the real story. The winner was trained by Martin Pipe – a man who occasionally drops into Flat racing like a thief in the night and runs off with the swag. And where was he on this great day when his owners landed £40,000 in prize money? Newton Abbot, that's where. Six mediocre National Hunt races and a top prize of £3,750. My admiration knows no bounds.

What I failed to realize, as I scribbled knowledgeably in my notebook, was that the greatest contest was yet to come. As Far Cry was led out of the winners' enclosure, an officious steward at my side declared, in a rather school-masterly tone, 'You may now enter.' A gaggle of some twelve women were ushered into the enclosure and asked to stand in line. Instinctively I raised my hand in order to put a bid in for a rather delicious little 35-year-old with obviously good breeding and, at a guess, a splendid record in a tight finish. Sadly, it was no more than a beauty contest – or as the very smart racecard declared, an award for the 'Best Dressed Lady Racegoer'. Channel 4 presenters salivated through the brief interviews and called on Lanfranco Dettori to make the final decision. On the point of announcing the result, the course tannoy boomed into life.

'Will jockeys please mount,' came the refined Geordie voice – a man with even better timing than Nicky Chambers. It was quite an invitation, yet with admirable restraint and to hoots of derision, Frankie made his choice. It was the same woman I had tried to bid for only minutes before. I raised my hand once more, yet could only mumble, 'I'll go to 5,000 guineas.' In truth, it had been a one-horse contest, the lady in question having more style in her outfit than anything I'd witnessed at either Ascot or Goodwood. The fact that her bosom was probably the finest I had encountered since once buying a steroid-riddled chicken from a Portuguese supermarket, only reinforced my opinion and probably that of Frankie Dettori. If the lady in question happens to be reading this piece, please accept my unreserved apology for such a vulgar nuance. You were quite delicious in every respect.

Light of wallet and heavy of step, I rushed for the exit,

leaving Doncaster's best dressed lady to enjoy her prize. I'd won no money, seen little racing and faced a 170-mile journey back to the dark south. But I couldn't help getting wrapped up in the atmosphere and sense of fun which Doncaster provides. It will never be a favourite but it might just scrape into the frame. It's hard not to get sniffy about a racecourse when you've just had a dose of flu and your head's buried in a handkerchief. Just don't forget the lowly punter, Doncaster. Corporate punters are very fickle animals.

Postscript: I'll bid 7,500 guineas. It's my final offer.

CHAPTER FIFTEEN

EPSOM

'*Racing Post*? Sorry, mate. Sold out. Always the same on Derby Day.' It was only 8.30 a.m. and my local newsagent could only point to a space on the shelf.

'Not going are you?'

'Just on my way.'

'Rather you than me.'

It was not a good start and I began the sixty-mile trip with a feeling of impending doom. With great symbolism, black clouds were already gathering, the sky heavy with the rain that had plagued the start of blazing June. By 10.30 a.m. I had reached Epsom, a quiet and pretty town in Surrey which had now become a giant car park. Weekend shoppers glowered at the growing queue with a look of pity and annoyance, agitated by the race traffic glueing up their high street but grateful that they'd chosen to spend their morning wheeling a trolley around Sainsbury's.

But, within half an hour, I had pulled into the confusion of car parks which surround Epsom racecourse, carefully positioning my car for a rapid exit. Within seconds a toothless gypsy was tapping on my window to offer the obligatory sprig of lucky heather. Naturally, but politely, I refused, trying to explain that if everyone accepted her offer and got lucky she would bankrupt the whole of the British betting industry. My attempt to engage her in a basic discussion of the philosophy of logic fell on deaf ears and she thankfully shuffled off to accost a family who thought Plato was something you looked at through a telescope.

My initial view of Epsom made me feel that it had no sense of place. It seems as if someone in the 18th century had looked at a wild piece of heathland and thought, 'Let's stick it there.' From the entrance area there is no sign of a racecourse, the skyline being dominated by two huge white stands, which look rather like an abandoned high rise development. Despite the sun now breaking through, my sense of doom continued to cast its shadow.

It had been a last-minute decision to brave the Derby crowds but thanks to a profitable Oaks meeting on the previous day, I came armed with a bookie's money. It isn't difficult to empty your wallet before you make your first bet. Five pounds for the car park was followed by a £22 fee to get into the Grandstand, which is really no more than an upmarket Tattersalls. Club tickets (£40) had been sold out weeks before and it took some serious sweet talking and suggested threats of a bad report to fiddle myself the necessary blue badge. Two pounds for the racecard meant I was already £47 down before I'd even caught a glimpse of the famous Epsom turf. For a small punter, recouping that sort of money is as likely as the government refunding my tax bill. I entered the main concourse depressed by my anorexic wallet, the credit cards sticking out like emaciated ribs.

The whirling club hit my head with a dull thud,

sending my spectacles spinning through the air and under the feet of the advancing crowd.

'Two throws off an effing record!' squealed one of the jugglers as I scrambled to retrieve my only contact with the outside world.

'Sorry,' I mumbled, 'I'm sure you'll do it next time.'

'Try walking around us next time. That's the nearest we've got in five years!'

'Just testing your skill,' I responded jovially.

'Yeah.'

Readjusting my distorted glasses and gently rubbing my bruised cranium, I hurried off to take in the delights of Epsom. At a guess you're likely to be more confused than a severe dyslexic in a school spelling test. Despite sporting my expensive club badge it was difficult to work out which areas were open for inspection. At various points the authorities had placed roughly photocopied sheets of paper bearing blurred black and white images of the various required badges. After several failed attempts at trying to work out whether I qualified for entry I adopted the ploy of simply walking through every available gateway and waiting to be accosted by stern men in sickly brown jackets. Having acted as a guinea pig, I hope I can save you a great deal of embarrassment and supply a useful tip if you ever go to Epsom. First and foremost, stay at ground level.

The top decks of both main stands are limited to private box holders and you can forget the Queen's Stand unless you're willing to remortgage your house and spend the afternoon in the required top hat and tails or (for ladies) 'formal dress with a hat'. It becomes obvious within seconds of entering the course that segregation is a byword at Epsom racecourse. If you have any foreign friends who are having difficulty in understanding the British class system – take them for a day's racing at Epsom. They'll come away as experts and wearing a very shocked expression. Anyone familiar with the Indian caste system can visit the 'untouchables' in the middle of the course – on the famous Epsom hill.

The journey from the main enclosures to the heath involves gaining a pass out at the main entrance. You are forced to leave the main stands and wander some 200 yards before negotiating the crowd down a narrow passageway that leads to a tunnel passing under the main straight. By 1.30 p.m. the queues for the Grandstand compound had grown so big, I doubt that they had any hope of seeing the first two races.

Reaching the tunnel entrance, I stopped as the Royal Procession left its tyre prints in the Epsom turf. For those with an interest in fashion, the Queen was wearing something whiteish and she kindly waved at the milling crowds as her entourage swept past towards the Queen's Stand. Briefly I caught a glimpse of myself in the glistening windows of the royal carriage – a true moment of reflected glory. I was desperate to stop the procession and fire a difficult question at our monarch.

'Do you know what a queue is, your Royal personage?' I would have asked.

'We are not familiar with such a term,' she would have answered.

With half an hour to go to the first race, the free centre enclosure was rising to a crescendo of bedlam. Picnics and bodies were strewn in every direction; open-topped buses nestled against the rails; a fairground offered its stomach-churning rides and litter decorated every blade of grass. A refugee camp in war-torn Yugoslavia would have looked more organized. What is it about the British and litter? Why do 20 per cent of the population want to soil their own patch and turn their environment into a giant dust-bin? And why is there a high security military compound in the centre of Epsom Downs?

Smack in the middle of this mind-numbing chaos is a heavily guarded area devoted to the Household Division of the British Army. At its entrance stood two statuesque guardsmen and an NCO who would have frightened a rabid dog. Not only was he built like the proverbial public convenience but he had a haircut so short that it must have been cut from the inside.

What he was guarding was no more than what one punter described as a 'squaddies' beanfeast'. Like the majority of the public on the Epsom hill, they would see little if anything of the racing – and it was at this moment I realized that Derby Day is not a race meeting at all. It is an occasion. Henley without the water. Wimbledon without the balls. Ascot without the style. Leave the horses in their stables and I doubt more than 10 per cent of the punters would notice the difference. Epsom is no more than alcohol-induced mayhem.

Hurrying back to the course, my growing suspicions were reinforced. In order to retake my place in the club enclosure, I was forced to queue for another twenty minutes just to hand over my pass out card, before fighting my way through to the lawns in front of the main stand, eager to escape the rabble.

As luck would have it, I noticed a small walkway in front of the Queen's Stand which, as far as I could see, was not restricted to the top hat and tails brigade. Walking with as much confidence as I could muster, I sauntered through, only to arrive at the small and circular winners' enclosure. A few steps beyond lay the weighing room, its glass-fronted doorway tempting me to further valour. Notebook in hand, shoulders back and with a deep breath, I walked straight in. Officials busied themselves, apparently oblivious to my presence. Jockeys jumped on and off the scales as if receiving electric shocks – the chair itself proving a major disappointment. Instead of the expected shining mahogany, the seat was no more than plastic and wire – reminiscent of a 1950s kitchen chair you'd buy at the local bring and buy.

Expecting to be ejected at any moment, I scribbled furiously. Surprisingly, no-one seemed concerned. Sir Peter O'Sullevan smiled a greeting. Greville Starkey smoked another cigarette. Willy Carson cackled. I was in the company of the great and good of British racing and all went well until Sir Michael Stoute turned his head and looked me straight in the eye. I nodded. He nodded. We jousted our heads like two fighting cocks preparing to do battle. I felt like a man who had the word 'GATECRASHER' tattooed on his forehead. When Michael Stoute looks serious he could frighten the fleece off a sheep's back. I looked sheepish. I felt sheepish. But then he smiled. He almost beamed, suddenly transformed into a third form public schoolboy who's just been told the French *assistante* is getting ready for bed and has forgotten to close her curtains. When he's not frightening people he's probably a real softie. But taking no chances, I made my escape.

The small area around the winners' enclosure proved to be a true oasis of sanity and one which makes the £40 ticket almost worth the expense. Despite being open to day club ticket holders, the authorities keep it fairly quiet. Given the nightmare of the heath and the Grandstand, I decided to set up base camp. Views of the racing are restricted to the final dash to the line. But – unless you have a private box – the same applies to almost any position on the course.

The course itself is a one-mile, four-furlong left-handed horseshoe, the ground rising 140 feet over the first five furlongs and then swiftly dropping down to the infamous Tattenham Corner. What perhaps isn't obvious is that the course is also cambered in places, which must make riding a hyperventilating thoroughbred around Epsom as easy as running around a steeply banked cycle course on a pair of stilts. Not that you'll see any of this occur. The undulations of the course, the military compound and the fairground wheels all conspire to block all available views until they enter the four-furlong straight. Even then the noise from the crowd makes it impossible to hear the commentary. If it was announced that Muffin the Mule had taken the lead, I doubt there would be a raised eyebrow.

As you'll have guessed from my report, the racing remained incidental to the Epsom experience. Despite overhearing Joe Mercer suggest that Monsajem was a certainty in the first (it won at 13-2), notwithstanding my local trainer, Peter Harris, landing the five-furlong dash at 5-1, and heedless of my daughter's advice to back Oath in the Derby, by the end of the afternoon I had failed even to land a place bet. Epsom was taking its revenge on my criticism.

Before the Derby, I paid a quick visit to the paddock – a fine but slightly cramped arena lying behind the Queen's Stand. I have to admit that at this point you do sense the tension and anticipation of Britain's most valuable race. Intensity is etched into the face of every trainer and even the jockeys (who always say 'It's just another race . . .') fail to disguise their growing anxiety. Movements are just a little quicker; bridles and girths are checked and rechecked; last-minute instructions listened to with the concentration of a man waiting for a judge to pass sentence. And then they're off, trailing round the loop to the one-mile, four-furlong start, knowing that in under three minutes one of them will become a household name.

Knowing that I was going to escape Epsom as soon as the winner passed the post, I made a pre-emptive strike on the Gentlemen's lavatory. If you are familiar with men's urinals, you will know that we are granted about as much privacy as a goldfish in a glass bowl. Just as I was about to do what comes naturally, I was tapped on the shoulder.

'Where's the lavvies, luv?' came what seemed an unnaturally high-pitched voice. I turned warily to be met by two women in the required formal day dress and hat – and before I could answer, the assembled bladder emptiers began to harangue their unexpected companions.

'You're in the wrong place!' offered one kindly.

'Get yer knickers off!' came another in a slightly less subtle manner.

The women stood their ground and waited outside the occupied cubicles. More uproar ensued until four men, obviously given courage by John Barleycorn, turned away from the troughs to display their wares to what they assumed would be an appreciative audience.

With hardly a flicker of the eyes the two women confronted the men with a sneer. 'Seen bigger chipolatas in the butcher's,' said one cuttingly and turned towards the now empty cubicle. I could still hear the cheering as I headed for the Grandstand and the start of the race. The Epsom segregation was beginning to break down.

I would love to tell you about the race and the way that

Kieren Fallon rode Oath to victory with more style than Henry Cecil's latest suit. Unfortunately I missed most of my first Derby. At 3.50 p.m. precisely, the commentator announced, 'They're under orders. They're off!' At 3.50 p.m. and 10 seconds the man at my side decided this was an excellent moment to hit a fellow punter. The punch was returned with interest and, like a 'B' movie Western, within seconds it was a full saloon brawl. I'd had enough. Ducking and weaving my way through the crowd, I ran for the exit, determined not to get caught up in the inevitable jam of traffic.

'What won?' asked a chauffeur waiting patiently for his top-hatted boss.

'A horse,' I answered. 'It's crazy in there.'

'Rather you than me,' he smiled knowingly.

'That's what my newsagent said.'

Would I go to a Derby meeting at Epsom again? Would I admit to once buying a Des O'Connor record? Would I jump into a swimming pool wearing concrete trousers? Next year it's a morning's golf, a trip to the bookies, a cup of tea and the telly – unless the Queen can find me a spare seat in her Roller.

Postscript: If you happening to be reading this chapter, Your Majesty – forget it. I'd rather spend a wet afternoon at Fontwell Park.

Only one on Derby Day

CHAPTER SIXTEEN

EXETER

Reminiscing isn't what it used to be. But do you remember those halcyon days when pumping air into a car tyre was about as difficult as breathing? Go into a garage these days and you have to pay 10p for the privilege and then engage in a race against the clock. Invariably you have just finished pumping up the third wheel when the machine stops and forces you to search frantically for another coin – which, of course, you never have. Garages on the A38, which leaves Exeter and takes you towards the racecourse, are full of such contraptions.

Knowing I had to make a 200-mile return journey and having a few minutes to spare, I pulled into the forecourt, slotted in my only 10p and began the contest between man and technology. Within seconds I realized I had located the only air pump in Devon that had been trained to suck rather than blow. I confronted the attendant.

'Your air pump working?' I asked politely.

She sucked in air and blew out slowly.

'Your pump does that,' I added with some acidity.

'Does what?' she queried.

'Never mind.'

I left the garage, my car listing as heavily as the *Titanic* in its final death throes. Fortunately, the racecourse was only a mile down the road. Unfortunately, the sign directing you to turn off to the left gives you about a millisecond to respond and I flashed straight past, forcing me to turn into the owners' and trainers' car park a few hundred yards further down the road. Seeing the absence of an appropriate badge, the gate attendant raised his hand. Opening my window, I leaned out of the car – not a difficult manoeuvre given the acute angle of my car. As the window slid down, my head fell through the open space.

'Bit of a problem . . .' I began in explanation.

'Puncture?'

'Duff air pump.'

'We'll sort you out,' he answered kindly.

It was going to be a good day after all.

With my front tyre back to 30p.s.i., I strolled onto the course with a renewed sense of optimism. I was seeing Exeter at its best – a clear sunlit but cold October day. You'll immediately be aware that this is no Sandown or Kempton. Not a house or pylon could be seen in any direction, only the heavily wooded and gently rolling hills of Devon. This is the sort of rough and ready country racing admired by stalwart National Hunt punters. But entering from the owners' and trainers' car park, it's immediately obvious that some effort has been made to upgrade a course which has enjoyed agricultural racing since the mid 1700s. New stable blocks, a new weighing room and some fairly recently built stands suggest that there has been some serious investment over the last decade.

As a result, the major facilities are laid out in a gentle

horseshoe formation, with the paddock lying adjacent to the course. Despite its lack of pretentiousness, Exeter isn't shy in displaying some of its past high class winners. All the bars, restaurants and private boxes sport the names of legends such as Deep Sensation, Sabin du Loir, Desert Orchid – all horses who have cut their teeth on the undulating Exeter course. In the Romany King Bar, I was able to complete my in-depth, comparative study of Devonian and Somerset pasties (see Newton Abbot and Taunton). Result? Exeter came in a good second but Taunton wins by a distance, with Newton Abbot pulled up before the second mouthful.

It was during this pasty testing that I solved the great question which is hot on the lips of all punters. What do bookies talk about before racing starts? What pearls of wisdom do they offer to a man desperate for a winner? Two William Hill representatives were about to provide the answer.

'It must be two hundred quid,' said William Hill 1.

'You're joking!' responded William Hill 2.

My ears pricked up at the sound of money and I edged closer.

'I mean you work it out,' continued William Hill 1. 'One pound, twenty pence a cup, two hundred tea bags, a few bob for milk, sugar and a plastic cup – you add it up. Two hundred quid profit. Bloody rip-off.'

'I had a small one. Eighty pence,' answered William Hill 2.

'Large one's no different, is it? One cup. One tea bag. Means they charge you 40p extra for a drop of hot water!'

William Hill 1 was now incensed and I was nodding off. Hurriedly finishing my (overbaked) pasty, I returned to the course unable to keep pace with the intellectual repartee and still looking for guidance in the first race.

I'm never quite sure if small-time punters such as myself ever learn much from a paddock. Do we really know what to look for? What do you do? Count legs? Look for a shiny coat? Ask a horse how it's feeling? I've seen many lethargic looking animals land the prize by a clear ten lengths. The only thing you can really do is stand against the rail looking as knowledgeable as possible and hoping that no-one asks you any searching questions.

At Exeter, you can at least gain a good view of the contestants. Rather like Plumpton, the most favourable position is to walk onto the course between races and stand by the running rail. This area is only used by a few punters and therefore gives you an unimpeded view of the smart but rather plain paddock. (In common with Stratford, a few flower beds wouldn't go amiss.) This open access to the course should be applauded, though why they haven't adopted the same strategy for the weighing room, I've no idea.

This opening up of the traditionally secretive world of stewards and jockeys is becoming more and more common, yet at Exeter they haven't been brave enough to go the whole hog. Instead the public is teased by a partial view, only gained by peering through a distant window. I turned away, ready to cast my uneducated eye on the parading hurdlers.

Why I selected the Minder, I'll never know. This 12-year-old gelding had all its meagre form on soft ground and walked around the paddock with about as much life as a dead Cornish pasty. Even a complete novice could see that the Exeter course was firm enough to get a bounce out of a cricket ball. As with most selling handicaps this was a poor field, yet the subsequent 12-1 winner had the only decent form on firm going. Sadly this didn't strike me until Little Hooligan flashed past the winning post to the cheers of a small gaggle of punters who had the literary ability to read the racecard notes.

I had broken one of the golden rules of punting – i.e. thou shalt not enter a racecourse with a mind-set. My home county of Buckinghamshire had been turned into a quagmire in September and I assumed that Devon must be the same. All my form calculations were built on stayers who could battle through the mud rather than bounce off the drying turf. It was to prove a costly misjudgement.

Yet even on firm going, Exeter is fairly testing. The two-mile oval dips into the back straight (obscured from view) while the long bends mean a horse needs to be well balanced all the way round. From the stands the finish looks fairly innocuous but the rising ground, while not steep, is rather like those hills I used to dread when I rambled in the Lake District – a seemingly never-ending steady drag to the top. Asking the 12-year-old Minder to accelerate to the finish is about as useful as suggesting your invalid granny takes up squash.

But back to the mind-set. I've had it. You've had it. We've all had it. That awful dilemma of having made your selections and realizing all too late that you've based them on a false assumption. Neurosis kicks in. Shall I change my selection? What if it wins? What if my new selection wins and I don't back it? Is it unlucky to change? Am I a mug if I don't? You can always spot these mind-set victims. They're usually to be seen rocking backwards and forwards, smoking heavily and sweating lightly, heads cupped in their hands, faces screwed up with indecision. Pity them – they are in for a bad day.

Gently rocking backwards and forwards and with my head cupped in my hands, I returned to the Romany Bar. The racecard had suddenly become an exam paper full of questions I couldn't answer. There was only one thing to do. It was time for Plan B.

Plan B does not involve the intricacy of the well-informed Plan A. Instead, simply glance at the card and pick a name which reminds you of a distant relative, an old dog or just sounds nice. My now deceased Aunt Ethel swore by this method and had a moth-eaten fox stole to prove it.

Like all good neurotics, I spent the next three races changing every possible variable. Different stand, different bookie, different Tote window – anything to persuade fate into submission. And there was plenty of choice. The three stands offer a good view of the course, though seating is limited to a small reserved area in the members' enclosure and the back straight is always out of sight. Two races later, I took the lottery option, crossing the track into the centre course. The short walk will take you past the white judges' tower, which stands by the winning post like a giant vanilla slice which has been elbowed by a truculent baker.

This is a particularly good spot to take up at the start of the race, as horses leave the paddock and are allowed to take a short cut across the inner course. So that they don't lose their way, Exeter employ a robust and bearded man to stand with a large red wooden arrow, pointing the jockeys in the right direction. He'd be better employed at the main entrance from the A38 – but I don't want to quibble. Walk from here down to the final hurdle at the one-furlong marker and you get a decent view of the jump but are well out of range of the tannoy and on-course commentary.

This is the lottery option. Simply wait by the hurdle and wait to see if your number comes over first.

Needless to say, by the time the winner of the fourth race had cleared the final hurdle, I was still waiting for my number to come into view. Eventually he appeared, coughed his way over the obstacle and cantered slowly to the line in a magnificent fifth place. In a five-horse field this was not a great achievement.

It was time to cut my losses and head home – but not before reflecting on my time at Exeter racecourse. You may well think that my opinions will be swayed by a run of four losers – yet this isn't the case. I entered the course inflated with air and optimism – yet, as the afternoon unravelled, I realized that Exeter amounts to little more than what you see in the first five minutes. Other small courses, notably Towcester, Fontwell and Plumpton, seem to have retained nooks and crannies of surprise, a discovery of delights which maintain the interest.

Exeter, on the other hand, while neat and tidy, has gone down the road of being functional and perhaps robbed punters of some of the magic of racing. Would I go again? Well, yes, but only if I was within a 20-mile radius of the course. With a 200-mile journey ahead of me it would have taken far more than 10p in a broken air pump to remedy my deflation.

CHAPTER SEVENTEEN

FAKENHAM

I was reminded of arriving at Edinburgh and thinking it wasn't too far to Inverness. By the time I arrived at Cambridge, Fakenham seemed quite near. Wrong again. It was like climbing a mountain and finding yet another summit on the horizon. The road north from Cambridge seems interminable yet pretty. The distraction of signs for Ely made it hard to keep the car pointing on a straight line. But even in these enlightened times, it's difficult to have a bet in a cathedral and I pressed on towards the racecourse.

I had left my Buckinghamshire home a little late, having been delayed by the need to lay some poison pellets in the potting shed, recently invaded by some long-tailed vermin. It's the price you pay for living in the country. It was Armistice week, and as I hurtled through Swaffham, I was delayed by a memorial service for the Desert Rats. It seemed somewhat ironic and I was touched with a sense of guilt as I turned into Fakenham racecourse. But take this description with a pinch of salt. The racecourse is actually at Pudding Norton – though to be fair, I suppose this would be a hard name to promote when you're competing with the likes of Newmarket.

The car park, a hedged and pastured field, had three definite advantages. It was free, it wasn't a mud bath and it was close – only a minute's walk from the entrance. Even the attendant offered me a cheery 'Good luck!' Perhaps I looked like a mug punter. I had driven through wild October storms, yet Fakenham was bathed in sunshine and the going declared as good-to-soft. Entry was reasonable – on this day £6 Tattersalls, £12 members. But don't bother with Tattersalls. It has little to offer, as I'll reveal later.

First impressions? A country fair, a bustle of busy people searching for the next attraction. I was surprised there was no tombola stall, or a pink-cheeked vicar in an old straw hat. Hog roasts and hat sellers seemed to exist happily with the usual array of fish and chip trailers and hot dog stands. Perhaps the real highlight was the main bar at the back of the main stand, a converted stable block which had retained its exposed beams. They'd even managed to squeeze a one-woman Tote office in the old food store. There seemed to be a real party atmosphere and at the head of affairs a barman who looked old enough to have known Hereward the Wake. What made him so distinctive was the glint of gold chains and a shining bald head, fetchingly trimmed with an extraordinary grey ponytail. As he looked so much like an English version of Fu Manchu, I strode up to the bar and asked for a glass of rice wine. He returned a look of disbelief, turned away and simply said, 'Next!' I wasn't thirsty anyway.

'Nice ambience,' declared a fellow punter as I left the bar.

'Good crack,' I responded.

'Sorry?' We parted company quickly, as any further

conversation was going to require a translator. With a little time to spare I explored the centre course, an area so often providing the best view of the jumps. It did not meet expectations. It provided nothing more than a car park and I ducked under the rails in rapid retreat. Tattersalls offers little more reward. If you're up against the rails the view of the last jump is well worth the effort but barring that it was a major disappointment. Searching for a cup of tea seemed to have about as much chance of success as a Norfolk yeti hunt.

A paint-peeled hut at the far end of Tattersalls promised to offer relief but proved to have been hijacked by one of the race sponsors. I pressed my nose against the window, only to see about twenty men looking very depressed about having being exiled to the far reaches of the course. It doesn't always pay to have connections. Adjacent to this room was an even more decrepit area, the only sign of life an ageing ping-pong table which looked as if it had been bought third-hand from the local youth club. Perhaps the ponytailed barman used it to practise his cunning Chinese serves on his day off.

In retreat once more, I headed back towards the members enclosure, passing the Tattersalls 'Stand'. I use this term advisedly. It was no more than a rough but sturdy construction made from tubular scaffolding. The odd thing is that someone had decided to completely surround this viewing position with quick-growing conifers, commonly known as the 'neighbour's nightmare'. It struck me that there was a fair chance of racegoers seeing the opening seller, only to have their view completely obliterated by the time of the final bumper. I continued my retreat to the members' enclosure, only to be distracted by the sound of crying children. As a caring citizen, I raced to their aid only to find twelve toddlers incarcerated in the 'Fakenham Crèche Facility' cunningly disguised as a building site Portakabin. Three kind young ladies were trying to teach these abandoned children to read a *Timeform* but with an apparent lack of success. I popped my head around the door and suggested that Roald Dahl's *The Witches* might be slightly less frightening but the helpers had a real look of determination and ignored my advice completely. 'Look! One-paced over final two furlongs. No extra. Can't you understand?' were the last words I heard. The child began to scream.

The opening selling handicap hurdle was already reaching its conclusion. As usual my each-way outsider got beaten into fourth place, but only by fifteen lengths. I raced round to the winners' enclosure, slightly faster than the horse I'd just backed. Having gained a prime spot, I witnessed a long and detailed discussion between trainer and jockey. It soon became clear that this wasn't a horse they intended to give up as it had jumped well and won at a canter.

The bidding started at the advertised selling price of £2,500. A hand came from the left, signalling a counter-bid and obviously that of the current owner. There was no response from the initial bidder. The horse seemed to heave a sigh of relief as it was led around the enclosure. It obviously wanted to go back to its old box. I imagined its favourite cuddly toy in the corner and a faithful old stable Labrador wagging its tail as the horse returned home. I was almost in tears as my imagination took control of my senses. A small, almost imperceptible movement at my side brought me back to reality.

'I am bid £3,000?' came the auctioneer's voice over the microphone. I turned to look at this new bidder. It was not what I expected. He could have come straight from a queue outside a Salvation Army hostel after a long career selling the *Big Issue* at the entrance to Euston station. There was nothing to suggest that this squat, balding pensioner could afford the price of a cup of tea, even if he managed to find one in Tattersalls.

The owner's bid went to £3,250. The old man gave a slight nod of the head. The stable girl leading the horse gave him a stare. The owner bid £3,750. The stable girl hardened her stare. He nodded once more. She glowered with a look that could have killed a thoroughbred at ten paces – £4,000 from the owner. Another nod – £4,500. For a second I thought she was about to launch herself into the crowd like Eric Cantona in a fit of *folie* – £4,750 came the owner's bid. The old man waved his hands in surrender.

'Thanks for bunging him up,' came the girl's reply. The small crumpled figure merely smiled, turned on his heels and disappeared into the crowd. I wondered if he banked at Coutts. And then it struck me. The very essence of Fakenham was staring me in the face. Slightly to the right of the winners' enclosure, attached to the wall of the corrugated, ivy-clad stand, a large sign briefly shimmered in the weakening sunshine. 'Chemical and Waste Water Disposal' it declared to no-one in particular. Bemused, I glanced around the array of wooden buildings. 'Wash Up and Veg Preparation' announced another sign. 'Washing Machine and Tumble Dryer' declared another.

But it was the Gentlemen's toilet that really gave the game away. Standing as one does on these occasions, my eyes drifted to the windows above my head. They had draw curtains. Draw curtains! And not ordinary draw curtains. These were finest red and white check gingham curtains, the sort that I have been stuck behind on every British road which has no space for overtaking.

They were the symbol of the ubiquitous caravan. Fakenham is not a racecourse, but a caravan park – with an incidental racecourse. The signs began to scream at me. 'Drinking Water', 'Electrical Hook Ups'. Even the racing signs seemed to develop a certain ambiguity. Did they refer to caravanners or to racegoers? Was 'Weighing Room' a test to segregate obese holidaymakers? Was 'Trainers Only' advertising a fitness centre? God knows what these caravan junkies made of the 'Members Only' sign. I thought it best not to ask and settled for a state of confusion.

So, onto the strange events surrounding Derek Thompson. For those of you not familiar with Channel 4 racing, he's the affable presenter who for a brief time sported the worse moustache ever seen on a racecourse. I watched him for a while. Very professional but a man who should stay well away from meteorology. At the start of the third race (a nice little novice steeplechase, which are always guaranteed to strike fear into National Hunt jockeys), Thompson decided to announce how lucky we all were to be enjoying the warm October sunshine. Within seconds the crowd were scampering for cover as lightning ripped through the sky and the rain began to impersonate a monsoon in Singapore. Nothing too strange in that, not until I glanced at the racecard. 'Third race. 3.20 p.m. The Anglian Water Wateraid Novices' Steeplechase.'

I last heard Derek Thompson informing a friend that he had been offered a lucrative witch doctor's job by a well-known international charity who specialize in drought-affected parts of Africa. Sounds like a good idea given his effect on Norfolk weather.

But it was really Richard Guest's day – an experienced jockey who had apparently had a winner at every National Hunt racecourse in Britain – apart from Fakenham. Going past the stand for the first time it seemed as if his horse needed to be niggled along with a cattle prod – and Guest, with more than a mile to go, was pumping as if he was within sight of the winning post. But it came in by two lengths. Guest was on it – and so was I. We were both very happy. A horse, oddly named the Great Flood, came in third. Given Thompson's effect on the weather, I'm surprised it didn't romp home by ten lengths.

I watched this race from the main stand. An October, Friday afternoon, and the place was packed, a real fight to gain a view from the raked concrete steps. Is unemployment high in north Norfolk or is it full of retired lottery winners? I didn't get a chance to ask as I was concentrating on my investment. Every fence is visible from this point and plenty of chance for close inspection. Even in a two-mile race the horses go past the stand three times. I searched the form carefully to find one horse who had been trained on a fairground waltzer – a style of schooling which would be highly advantageous on a course as tight as Fakenham.

The form of the winner, Xaipete, revealed no such training but I did feel it had a certain Romany sound and was well worth the gamble. It paid off handsomely at 8-1 and all the also-rans looked very dizzy as they entered the unsaddling enclosure.

A quick mention for Josh Gifford, who was spotted being Josh Gifford. I've never seen a smarter man on a racecourse. He wears more checks than the whole population of Czechoslovakia. Racing oozes out of every pore. He's so horsy, I'm surprised he's not led around the paddock on a bridle. It wouldn't surprise me if he travels to the races in the back of a loose box. But maybe not.

Did I enjoy Fakenham? Despite my reservations – yes. It was hospitable and had a sense of fun. I left with a replenished wallet and a little indigestion from the hog roast. Its main problem is that it seems a long way from anywhere, cast as it is in the wilds of rural Norfolk. I left early to beat the traffic, as I always do. The Desert Rats had long since left their memorial at Swaffham, but the signs remained by the roadside. I still felt guilty about those poison pellets in the potting shed.

CHAPTER EIGHTEEN

FOLKESTONE

I have one major piece of advice about Folkestone. Don't go there. You might find lots of cheap hotels, sandy beaches and a mind-boggling one-way system. But you won't find a racecourse. The racecourse is really at Westhanger, about five miles to the west of Folkestone. I'm off for a short break in Corsica in a few weeks' time, an island which is advertised as a picturesque Mediterranean retreat. Given my Folkestone experience, I'm probably about to spend five days in the Baltic.

My misplaced trust in Folkestone being in Folkestone almost ended in a day trip to France. In a state of confusion, I became sucked into a long queue of traffic heading for the Channel Tunnel rail terminal. Luckily we came to a halt and a Frenchman, with passable English, pulled alongside my car. Winding my window down I shouted across.

'Where's the racecourse?'

'You are wanting Deauville, *n'est ce pas?*'

'Folkestone,' I responded meekly.

Fifteen minutes later I found Westhanger station, and seconds after pulled onto the course. I can offer no word of thanks to the racecourse authorities for successfully reaching my destination. Like many courses, they appear to rely on telepathy as the favoured form of direction. Why do so many small courses think that road signs should be designed like obscure clues in a treasure hunt? In fact 'Join together the opposite of East and a place where they keep aeroplanes' would have been far more explicit than the occasional, minuscule notice marked 'racecourse'.

It could only get better. It got worse. Arriving early, there was only one attendant on the gate and I asked if I could park up where I might make an early exit. He was a kindly man whose directions were about as easy to understand as a Japanese car manual.

'Along here, keep left, then first right, keep the brick building on your left, turn right, then first right again, look for a white rail, ignore this one and park by the second. You'll be fine there.'

I followed his instructions to the letter, parking my car contentedly but with a sudden attack of dizziness and desperate for a strong cup of tea. The Paddock Bar is one of the first things you'll encounter as you enter the course. Its faded paintwork and chalked-up menu gives it the feel of a Kentish greasy spoon. But don't let me put you off. Despite my now growing sense of irritation, the tattered room and the welcoming staff won me over in seconds. I asked for a cup of tea.

'Not eating?' enquired the well-padded waitress.

'Not really. But thanks anyway.'

'Pity,' beamed the girl. 'Good chef today. He does a lovely ham, egg and chips.' With a sales pitch like that she could have landed a place on the board of Saatchi & Saatchi.

Ten minutes later, a mountain of food was placed before me and it was obvious that the chef must have been a magician to produce such a feast for only £3.75. The loaded fork was only inches from my mouth when the tannoy crackled into life.

'Will the owner of Volkswagen R404 BYB please move their car as they are causing an obstruction.' I recognized the personalized registration plate immediately (Rule 404: Bankrupt Your Bookie), downed tools and sprinted from the cafe, guilt-ridden, but delighted to have been given such public recognition.

By the time I arrived at my car it was soon obvious that extracting it was going to be about as easy as making love in a two-seater sports car with the roof up. Possible – but not without a great deal of general damage. The SIS TV wagon, and its contents, had boxed me in so tightly, it was evident I was unlikely to get out of the course before it was time for pyjamas and Horlicks. One of the TV crew was kind enough to comfort me by suggesting that the positive aspect of my car's imprisonment was that it wouldn't get stolen. I wasn't consoled. I could only manufacture a forced smile and head back for my congealed lunch.

But they'd kept it warm. Swept it off the table and cooked me a fresh, double yolked egg. With gratitude, I wolfed the meal down in minutes and, aware that I could be in Folkestone after nightfall, ordered a pudding to build up my energy. As it turned out, this was probably my best move of the day. If you ever see apple and toffee pudding (with custard) on a Folkestone menu, order two portions immediately. You will not regret giving in to temptation – which is more than can be said about being tempted to back horses in large fields with an average prize of £1,500. The racecard revealed one hunter chase with a first prize of £939 – about enough to keep it in hay and horseshoes for about two months. With this sort of pittance on offer, it never fails to amaze me that courses like Folkestone manage to cobble together a race meeting at all.

The results did, however, suggest a form reading strategy for this Kent racecourse. Firstly, the selected horse should have at least four legs and preferably a tail. Secondly, it should be able to stand unaided. Thirdly, it should previously have gained a place in any of its former races – including a one-horse walkover in a minor point-to-point. If all these criteria are met, reach for your wallet. Otherwise stay in the Paddock Bar and have another pudding. As you can tell, apart from the food supply, I wasn't over-enamoured by Folkestone. The racing is generally of poor quality and the course itself is flat and unspectacular. At one point I wandered into the centre course to grab a close-up of the final fence. The area is no more than scrub with a few acres of arable farmland and a collection of disinterested sheep. The facilities amount to one Tote caravan, a crumbling lavatory and, on this occasion, five elderly men in a disused tea bar.

Notebook in hand, I wandered in to join them, only to be met with some very suspicious glances. Their main occupation seemed to be one of staring into the distance through the grime-covered windows, like children who had been left by their parents and told not to move until they returned. It struck me that they could have been there since 1937, but I didn't have the nerve to ask.

The only other occupant of the centre course was a single bookmaker, with a board that must have been painted when Toulouse Lautrec was knee high to a paint brush – a state from which he never recovered. The lonesome bookie huddled at the side of the Tote caravan, his scarf pulled high on his neck as a token protection against the bitter east wind. I gave him a greeting but no money.

'Name your own price, I'll take it,' he muttered ruefully as I walked back towards the main stands. Next time I visit Folkestone (which is unlikely), I'll hunt this man down and hit him with a £50 bet. He'll probably be grateful just to touch that amount of money, even if I do make a killing.

I suppose if anything saves Folkestone, it's the paddock area at the back of the two main stands. Here you are treated to an ornamental pond with its own plastic heron, no fish and a broken fountain. The paddock itself is very pretty and contains more trees than the New Forest. It would be a good place for a jockey to hide if he'd just fallen off a sure-fire favourite with a 20-length lead. If he managed to get back on board and make the winner's enclosure, he'd be in for a real treat. An estate agent might call it 'well appointed, laid to grass with generous borders'. Being a literary type, I'd just call it very nice.

Adequate might be a better description of the stands themselves. There are three on offer, though at the time of my visit the west stand looked more like a decaying cardboard box and was out of commission. The centre, red brick stand is a curious affair containing a betting hall in the basement and a restaurant on the floor above which would be better classified as an eating area. Punters in the adjacent bar mingle near to the tables, close enough to sneeze on the butter. It could be a dangerous place in the middle of a flu epidemic.

The view from the restaurant is, however, excellent – with large windows looking over the course. From the raked stands you can peer in at the diners (always one of my favourite pastimes) and from what I saw, the South London mafia had organized a charabanc outing. There was much evidence of expensive shiny suits and cheap dull haircuts. I retreated immediately to the east stand, weaving my way down the steps and the lines of grey steel crash barriers which cascade down the steps. Whoever designed these 'crowd controllers' either spent his apprenticeship at Millwall FC or had an obsession with the French Maginot Line.

Of the three, the east stand probably wins by a short head. It's a white wood and brick construction which has seen better days. But if you're willing to clamber to the top, you'll find a little oasis of comfort, a cosy bar with fine panoramic windows, carpeted floor, small round tables and leather armchairs. Wanting quietly to pick my next loser, I joined a very elderly but charming couple who had picked a prime spot by the window. Clouds of aromatic Dutch tobacco wafted across the table and I sniffed the air with delight. He sucked his pipe with such vigour that his chin hit his nose with every draw of breath.

Seeing my fascination with her husband's technique, his wife leaned back and our eyes met. At least my eyes met one of her eyes. Her sight was beginning to fail and she held up a magnifying glass that would have been the envy of a professional stamp collector. I found myself smiling back at an object so big that if she had burst into tears we'd have had to launch the lifeboats. I made my apologies, abandoned ship and headed for the betting ring.

Hot To Trot was a warm odds-on favourite in the two-mile six-furlong novice hurdle. But I'd gone for the outsider, Kelley's Conquest, as I had counted its legs and seen it standing in the paddock without any sign of artificial support. After two miles, Kelley's Conquest had a commanding 15-length lead and Hot To Trot was beginning to struggle. It was money in the bank.

'I'll give you even-money Hot To Trot!' came a bookie's cry.

There were no takers and Kelley's Conquest extended her lead.

'I'll give you 3-1 Hot To Trot in running!' responded the bookie, obviously convinced that I was about to collect.

It was as though he'd just offered his fellow bookies a steamy night with Kim Basinger. Abandoning their pitches, men began to thrust rolls of tenners into his grateful hands and seconds later Kelley's Conquest ran out of petrol. The generous bookie went pale and then grey, the veins in his neck inflating faster than a hot air balloon. Hot To Trot came in with at least ten lengths to spare, the betting ring roaring him home with a cheer and an obscure chant of 'short and curlies!' One moment of madness had just cost this bookie a minimum of five grand. And I loved every second.

Having tired of losing money on the donkey derby racing, I headed back to check my car. My luck suddenly changed. For some reason the TV crew had moved one of their large generators just far enough away to allow me to attempt an escape. Unfortunately, a large transmission dish was still wedged up against the driver's door. I hesitated for a second but by now my adrenalin was pumping. Keys at the ready, I grabbed the dish and pulled it to one side, jumped into my car and raced for a small gap in the fence. It was like escaping from Stalag 14, the guards racing after me with mugs of tea and raised fists.

I made the border and freedom in under three minutes and disappeared into the growing darkness. If you happened to witness a break in SIS transmission, I offer you my apologies. But a trapped punter's got to do what a trapped punter's got to do. Folkestone's OK, but there was no way I was going to stay at a course which only qualifies as a point-to-point with a restaurant. Go to Folkestone by all means, but take your passport, head for the Channel Tunnel – and have a day out in Boulogne.

CHAPTER NINETEEN

FONTWELL PARK

'Not working today?' asked my hairdresser.

'Racing,' I responded, shuffling my hands free from under the nylon sheet.

'Somewhere nice?'

'Fontwell Park,' I answered, manoeuvring my *Racing Post* into position.

'Where's that then?'

This exchange raised two questions in my mind. Why are all hairdressers trained in the techniques of the Spanish Inquisition and why does no-one seem to know the location of Fontwell Park? I can only answer the last question.

The reason established punters enjoy the obscurity of Fontwell is probably the same reason I keep quiet about my favourite skiing resort in Austria – it's mine and you can jolly well find your own. But, with apologies to Fontwell regulars, I'm about to blow your cover. And thank God I had a haircut and polished my shoes.

To enter this course looking scruffy would be as disrespectful as wearing a string vest at Royal Ascot. Not that Fontwell Park is pompous or stuffy – it's just neat. Very neat. As neat as my grandmother's parlour used to be, ten minutes before the vicar called for tea. If Fontwell had antimacassars on its wooden benches, there wouldn't be a crease in sight.

You'll be given a hint that this is no ordinary course if you approach the course from Arundel, a small West Sussex town that has the skyline of a large French village. The castle and magnificent spired church are well worth a detour – so leave home early. Yet, oddly, the first impression you'll gain of Fontwell Park comes as something of a let-down, wood and wired fences guarding what looks like a ramshackle collection of buildings which, from a distance, look nondescript and uninteresting. Buy your ticket and get in there.

Entering from the car park, look to your right and head immediately for the Lawn Bar. But don't go in. Instead peek over the hedges and you'll find the most unexpected treat. The small but highly manicured garden is Fontwell's oasis, the perfect spot to recharge your batteries after backing three losers, the ideal location to contemplate your navel – or even someone else's navel. If you fail to back a winner all afternoon it would be a fine place to retreat and consider the meaning of life – which we all know is finding four long-priced winners in a £2 each-way Yankee.

Dominating the garden is the largest collection of topiary I've ever seen. By the look of most of the exhibits, the gardener had obviously read Henry Moore's *Teach Yourself Sculpture*, just after completing a detailed study of the *Kama Sutra*. Perhaps it's just me, but there are some decidedly phallic shapes amongst this collection, the centrepiece being explicit enough to give a young chap an inferiority complex.

At each end of this garden lie two extraordinary buildings. At the furthest point is the course restaurant, shaded by hedges and mature trees. It has a look of 'you need to know the right people to get in there' and I gave this miniature Acropolis a miss. But the building at the other end of the topiary park is open to all. This rotunda, which in my ignorance I first thought was a gazebo, contains a circular stained glass window with the inscription, 'Be ye therefore followers of God as dear children.' Are there any other sort of children? By definition, children are dear and I've yet to meet a cheap one. They should change this epitaph to read, 'Be ye therefore followers of the turf as mug punters.'

Strengthened by my spiritual experience in the rotunda, I headed for the course. An old racing chum had described Fontwell as 'peculiar'. I can only describe it as breathtaking and not a place to visit if you're prone to asthma attacks. The first thing that strikes you is that the finishing straight from the last fence and hurdle is so steep I'm surprised they don't run a cable car for struggling handicappers. One look at this incline made me go back to the form book. If a horse doesn't stay, it's not going to win at Fontwell. If it's a chaser, it's also going to need a good sense of direction and an A level in geography.

Whilst the hurdles course is a standard left-handed circuit, the chase course is a figure of eight that would test a Swiss mountain guide. But unlike at Windsor – the only other British course with a similar layout – you are able to watch the race unfold at every step.

It's well worth observing a rider's tactics in a steeplechase. If your chosen horse goes out in front you can be sure that the jockey was either born in Fontwell or is a complete idiot. The only sensible thing to do is to play follow the leader until you're certain the finishing post is in sight. A. P. McCoy was obviously not raised in Fontwell and he's certainly not an idiot. There's a lot of nonsense talked about only seeing real racing at the premier courses such as Sandown, Cheltenham and Kempton. The 3.20 at Fontwell provided every thrill you'd ever want to experience on a racecourse.

The centre course allows close up access to at least two of the brush fences and, in a three-mile, two-furlong race, a chance to watch the taped start. Within seconds of the off, A. P. McCoy began to scream at his mount, Nazzaro, a 10-year-old chaser who hadn't won a race in three years. After the first circuit, he was struggling to stay with the pack. But McCoy was still screaming. Fontwell began to take its toll. The favourite went down and tired legs began to go through the fences. McCoy kept screaming.

As they approached the last, Nazzaro had at least four lengths to make up on the leaders but was obviously staying the trip. McCoy began to urge his mount for a final effort, his screaming now subdued and transferred to the best bit of hands and heels riding I've ever witnessed. His nose went in front as they crested the hill and landed the spoils by a short-head.

In the winners' enclosure the jockey was surrounded by a grateful racing syndicate and cheering punters. For his efforts, A. P. McCoy was presented with a bottle of champagne. They should have given him a vineyard.

I took my celebratory cup of tea in the Comedy of Errors Buffet Bar, a simple cafe with a Shakespearean mock Tudor frontage. Having been in Taunton only a few weeks earlier, I decided to continue my survey of racecourse Cornish pasties. Unfortunately, the delightful waitress had as much knowledge of microwave cookery as I have of spot welding. Despite her ignorance she managed to display a real talent for spinning my lunch around for two minutes, only to produce a soggy offering which was steaming hot at one end and icy cold at the other. Here endeth the survey.

With rumbling stomach I wandered back to the course. The facilities at Fontwell are extremely good, offering four stands, all with fine views over the course. The members' area contains a very smart raked stand, simply painted in black and white, which gives it immense style. Between the stand and the racecourse is a grassed area containing twenty-three wooden benches, many of which bear the initials of Old Fontwellians. Feeling very shaky after my confrontation with the Cornish pasty, I collapsed onto a seat which bore the initials HAM – a bench presumably in honour of either a Sussex pig farmer or an old theatrical luvvy. I was joined by a fellow punter, who had the sallow look of a man who had just been violently sick.

'How's it going?' he murmured.

'Unquiet meals make ill digestions,' I answered theatrically.

'*Hamlet?*' he queried.

'*Comedy of Errors*, Act V, Scene 1,' I replied.

'Me too,' he gasped.

'Cornish pasty?'

'Sausage roll.'

Fortunately, my growing sense of nausea was quelled by Miss Venetia Williams. The delightful flower-strewn paddock lies at the back of the main stand and for an early spring afternoon could not be faulted. Four large sycamores (I think) cast their shadows over the parading horses, who amble past the stark white rails and budding flower beds. In an attempt to avoid an outbreak of class warfare, even the Silver Ring punters are given their own stand to view the runners – a real credit to the Fontwell management.

As the runners left for the course, I happened to be caught up with a small group of owners excitedly discussing their horse's prospects. I tagged along to monitor their fortunes, only to be joined seconds later by the trainer. Some people are blessed with what is commonly known as 'presence' and Venetia Williams has it in spades. Only days before going for the big prize at Cheltenham with Teeton Mill, Miss Williams took her place on the stands at Fontwell, to watch a poorly bred filly in a two-mile maiden hurdle. She's a woman who, during the 1999 season, was enjoying more luck than Kate Winslet's partner. Her horse, Decent Dividend, tried to win from the front, only to be swamped by the pack in the final stages. 'A bit free,' she commented, turning to her disappointed owners.

She had watched the race with the dispassionate air of a real professional and you got the feeling that in her next race, Decent Dividend would trot up by ten lengths. If I was a horse and Venetia Williams whispered in my ear, I'd listen very carefully. She reminded me of a head girl who wins the sixth form classics prize, gains a place at Cambridge and captains the school hockey team. I might be wrong, but I bet Venetia Williams plays the piano like a concert pianist.

Whatever the case, my fascination with the delectable Miss Williams completely cured my growing nausea, my recovery aided by picking the winner of the maiden hurdle at a very generous 9-4. My last race proved a more difficult task. Two-mile, six-furlong selling hurdles are notorious for producing surprises and are never likely to produce a profit. This race was no exception and was won by a 12-year-old gelding, which the racecard described as 'needing much more'.

I raced off to watch the cut and thrust of the auction. The winners' enclosure is unfortunately a bit of a disappointment. Like the rest of Fontwell, it is beautifully presented but the public are kept so far away from the horses that it lacks a certain atmosphere. Consequently, the auctioneer needs a telescope to spot a raised hand and if it's your habit to make a bid with a wink of an eye, you're more likely to start a romantic relationship than buy a cheap horse.

It was time to go, especially as my Tote placepot had fallen at the first fence. Keen to beat the rush hour on the M25, I hurried back to my car, counted the wheels and prepared for the two-hour drive. Adjusting my mirror, I happened to catch sight of my recent haircut. Despite the strong wind, there wasn't a hair out of place. It was neat. Very neat. But it was more to do with Fontwell than my inquisitive hairdresser. Put on your best togs, polish your shoes and go to Fontwell Park. It's a small course with a big appeal – apart from those Cornish pasties.

CHAPTER TWENTY

FFOS LAS

I wasn't in the best of moods. Apart from the rain beating on my windscreen, I was also recovering from the recent 'train crash' Cheltenham Festival, which saw 95 per cent of hopeful punters (including me) reduced to tears and near bankruptcy. I'm told that the Welsh name Ffos Las translates as 'Blue Ditch'. No surprise there. I was feeling decidedly blue and ready to ditch my longstanding love affair with National Hunt racing. With any luck, the first National Hunt track to be built in Britain for over eighty years was about to deliver some restorative therapy.

A quick glance at the map suggested that access to the course would present little difficulty, as the M4 motorway drops you off about fifteen miles from the track. It's a road so full of speed cameras and unmarked police cars that by the time I turned off to Llanelli, I felt I had spent about three hours driving through a renunion of the former East German Stazi. (As I write, I'm nervously waiting for a bundle of official brown envelopes requesting my presence at a succession of Welsh magistrates' courts.)

Then I made my first mistake. Instead of following my

nose, a formidable proboscis which had successfully sniffed out every other racetrack in Britain, I reverted to my newly acquired satellite navigation system. If you enjoy weaving your way through flocks of bleating sheep, along single-track lanes attempting to avoid collisions with rusty Welsh tractors, a sat nav is highly recommended. But if you're rushing to place a large bet on a 'sure thing' in the opening maiden hurdle you'd better to trust your instincts (and you nose), and follow signs for the small town of Kidwelly.

Entering the arena that contains Ffos Las racecourse is a startling experience. Whichever way you approach, you will have dropped down from the hills to be met by a large and featureless open plain, flatter than a pancake that's been run over by a steamroller. Approaching the course in heavy mist, there was a distinct feeling of desolation, as though I had chanced upon an ancient and mystical burial site that would curse all those who disturbed its hallowed ground. It was with some foreboding that I pulled into the gigantic free car park and headed for the entrance.

On my rare visits to supermarkets, I find nothing more enjoyable than squeezing oranges, pressing my thumb into the ripe skin of a melon or inhaling the Gallic odours of a fresh bulb of garlic. This isn't the admission of some perverse shopping habit but a confirmation of my claim that you can test the quality of any product by trusting your senses. It is no different from meeting strangers for the first time, when your initial assessment of their character often proves to be on the button. (For your own safety, I would suggest that squeezing, smelling and pressing your thumb into the skin of new acquaintances should be avoided at all costs.)

As I stepped into the racetrack, my senses went to work. The horrors of Southwell immediately sprang to mind. The word 'functional' demanded to be scribbled in my ever-present red notebook. Ffos Las was clearly going to have to prove its worth, as I have a major problem with functionality. It conjures up images of neat homes where the inhabitants list 'cleaning' as a hobby and carefully arrange unread hardback travel books on their mock-antique coffee tables. In all honesty, I only feel comfortable in the presence of disorder, when my surroundings give me a clue to the character of their owners. What I need is a glimpse of their history, some evidence of their spirit and a biography of their past.

But that's unfair to Ffos Las, as its major distinction is that is has no history, no tales to tell, no roots in the traditions of racing. Opened in late 2009, it is the new kid on the block, created on the surface of a defunct open-cast coal mine which once provided the life blood for the steel works of South Wales. Perhaps, after all, this racetrack really is a burial ground, a symbolic tomb which has sadly seen the internment of its industrial past. A series of sentimental theme parks have been built in many of Britain's old coal-mining areas. In contrast, the Welsh have built a racetrack. It was this realization that had me warming to this Carmarthenshire venue.

You can't always judge a present by its wrapping, but at the risk of mixing metaphors, it is all too easy to dismiss the foot soldiers and concentrate on the generals. My entrance to Ffos Las was one of the most pleasurable I have experienced: courteous car-park attendants; cheery ticket-sellers; friendly on-course stewards and a general 'we're here to help you' attitude. I know these things aren't always high on the list of the hardened punter, but if you want people to return, it's the best possible strategy and a guaranteed winner.

Once through into the main arena, you will be met by a sight that probably has no equal on British racetracks. You may well feel you have strolled into an equine mortuary and caught two veterinary surgeons in the middle of a major horse dissection. Set between entrance and paddock is a large blackened-steel structure depicting two thoroughbreds fighting out a short-head finish, their jockeys urging every last ounce of stamina from their muscle-straining mounts. Sounds fairly normal for a race-course sculpture? Take a closer look. Normality is not a term that can be levelled at this piece of artwork. For starters, the charging horses only have two legs each and their haunches look as if they have been removed to supply a local French restaurant. As for the jockeys, they have no bodies at all, suggesting either that South Wales still indulges in cannibalism or that they spent longer in the sauna than A. P. McCoy.

As a man who has just applied to be the first art critic of the *Racing Post* (a terrible omission in their content), I give my verdict on this pile of scrap metal. It's wonderful – a sculpture that perfectly reflects the sinewy energy of race horses and their riders pushing for the finishing post. As far as I could see, there is no mention of a title or the artist's name. A real pity.

Only a few steps from 'the unnamed statue by the unknown artist' lies the pristine parade ring. It's a fine pear-shaped construction with a rubberized walkway that must make nervous pre-race runners feel that all's right with the world. Thankfully, Ffos Las has opened with a non-discriminatory ticketing policy and there is little if any segregation on the course. Punters pay a general (and very reasonable) entrance fee and are allowed access to all parts of the couse and paddock areas apart from the inevitable private hospitality tents and, regrettably, the small area around the weighing room.

The track itself is only a short distance from the parade ring, a real plus for someonewho has driven 250 miles for a day out. Anyone from East Anglia would immediately feel at home, as the flat, wide-open spaces make the extended oval circuit look like a giant Scalextric set that has just been dropped into a 600-acre field. Whilst uninspiring in design, the view is magnificent and you won't miss a stride of the racing.

Within this racing one-mile, four-furlong turfed oval (with an integral five-furlong shoot) are three concentric rings, which I'm reliably informed are 20 metres wide (that's 65.6168 feet for any anti-metric members of UKIP). Ffos Las, I'm pleased to say, offers a mix of Flat and jumps meetings with the hurdles and steeplechase circuits built within the flat track. Fortunately, this squeezed oval means that jumps fanatics like myself are close enough to retain a sense of involvement. The downside is that the two bends at each end of the course mean that runners would have to tilt at 45 degrees: I made a note only to back horses ridden by Welsh jockeys who have spent their teenage years riding pillion on a Rhonda 500.

With only twenty minutes to go before the opening maiden hurdle, I headed to the main stand which contains the Blinkers Bar and Betting Hall. Though a little sterile, and a mirror image of all modern racing bars, it had a distinctly friendly atmosphere, enhanced that day by a hen party from Swansea all decked out in miners' helmets emblazoned with, amongst others, the names 'Rhianna Rawplug' and the unfortunate 'Gorawen

Grinder'. The grey-eyed, terrified bride had been kitted out in a skirt no wider than a large rubber band embellished with a packet of Willie Gum Drops strapped to her ample waist. They certainly know how to party in Carmarthenshire. Thank God I was born in Lancashire.

It was at this point that I thought of David, or 'Dave the Milk' (son of the late 'Mick the Milk'), as all the Dylan Thomas aficionados of my village affectionately know him. He's got more tips than a bag of arrows and on hearing that I was heading for Ffos Las informed me that 'It's a favourite's track.' In order to avoid three months of sour semi-skimmed, I followed his advice to the letter, happy to see B. J. Geraghty ease his mount (Captive Audience) pat the post with three and a half lengths to spare. Despite returning odds of only evens favourite, it was a good start and it looked as if my Cheltenham curse was fading into history.

I won't burden you with the tragedies that followed, but will admit that I had the conceit to think that a chap who has spent come considerable time writing about horse racing is likely to know far more about it than a man who delivers milk and does a fine line in bread, potatoes and farmyard eggs. Wrong again. By the time I reached the sixth race of a seven-race card, I had bet against three winning favourites and seen no return on my investments. Yet as things turned out, redemption was at hand, and in a way that would lead me to an embarrassing but informative encounter later that evening.

As an observer of the quality of a racetrack, I had to put my betting miseries behind me. What struck me in both hurdles and steeplechase contests is that the three-foot-six hurdles and the four-foot-six brush fences are consistent in every respect and, whilst challenging at speed, are never treacherous on landing. Because there are no undulations in the track, there are no 'fall away' areas and all the obstacles appeared to tempt horse and rider to take their fences at an even stride. If you've just bought a 'hoof' as part of a hundred-member syndicate, tell your trainer to give your young hopeful a breeze around Ffos Las. It might not win, but it won't leave the racecourse dreading its next contest.

One of the delights of the afternoon was to have the chance of congratulating Paddy Brennan on his wonderful ride on Imperial Commander in the recent Cheltenham Gold Cup. He's a favourite jockey who always seems to give his horses every chance even in a minor maiden hurdle with meagre prize money. The very next day he was to be found at Ffos Las, guiding home Petit Margot in a low-class handicap steeplechase with all the determination he showed as he willed Imperial Commander past the winning post at Cheltenham. Jump jockeys are a rare breed and deserve every penny they make.

By the time I left Ffos Las, all I could think about was sleep. I had left home at five thirty that morning but had fortunately booked a hotel room only a few minutes from the course. I strode in looking forward to a long bath, a couple of Welsh ales and a quiet meal.

'Did you say Cartmell?' asked the receptionist.

'Yes.'

'Nothing in the book,' she replied. 'And I'm afraid we're fully booked.'

I was given the Mary and Joseph treatment. No room at the inn. After five minutes' protest, I demanded they find me another hotel. By now the owner had appeared and, full of apology, located an alternative.

'It's very nice,' he stated in a strong Welsh accent. 'But you should know that they're in liquidation.'

Why this fact was of such importance, I will never know, but within twenty minutes I was standing by the bar of my unexpected temporary rest home, sipping a very welcome single malt with a large group of boisterous Lancastrians.

Fate had clearly led me to this unexpected meeting, as I soon realized that not only had they attended Ffos Las but they owned a horse which had run as a firm favourite in the final 'bumper', only to see it hack in well behind the winner.

'Back it?' I asked.

'All of us,' one replied miserably. 'You?'

'Yes,' I answered quickly. 'Dave the Milk told me to back favourites at Ffos Las.'

After a quizzical silence, I moved the conversation on, unwilling to admit that I was lying through my teeth and had in fact backed the winner (Character Actor) at a very respectable 7-1. Profiting from their grief was hardly going to elicit the information I really wanted.

'So what do you think of Ffos Las?' I asked simply.

The reply, from their delightful self-appointed spokesman, was surprisingly insightful.

'Ffos Las?' he said. 'Got everything. Good track. Great view. Treat you well. Friendly. All the facilities you need at a decent racecourse. All it needs is a bit of atmosphere. Can't put my finger on it really, but there's something mising. No soul maybe – if you get what I mean.'

And I did get what he meant. Functional racecourses, like over-neat houses, work very efficiently, but lack the warmth that makes you want to return. But is this a criticism of Ffos Las? No, it isn't. It is nothing more than a statement of fact: new racecourses, like newborn babies, only develop character when they have walked, talked and battled their way to maturity. And my gut feeling is that Ffos Las will find its place in the history of British racing. It's an old coal mine that has cleverly begun to tap the seam of race-hungry South Wales punters. It may have no history, but this will come. History, after all, is only the present, viewed from a distance.

Postscript: As I write, two seemingly unconnected events are taking place. Some wonderful spring rhubarb is peeking out of my vegetable patch, and the racing authorities are implementing plans, through the Racing for Change taskforce, to encourage younger people into racing. They would do well to focus on Ffos Las as a template: this new, guinea-pig racecourse would be the ideal place to test out their cunning schemes. There is talk of introducing decimalized betting odds. I still haven't recovered from seeing the odds of 100-8 disappear from the bookies' boards. A better plan would be to get those young blighters to learn fractions and do their homework. Who ever used decimals to divide a delicious rhubarb pie into eight pieces?

CHAPTER TWENTY-ONE

GOODWOOD

The last time I used the word 'breathtaking' was when I'd just (unsuccessfully) run to catch a number 37 bus. But having recently visited the May meeting at Goodwood, it's hard to resist the cliché. Goodwood is breathtaking – full stop. If anyone reading this fails to enjoy a day's racing at this Sussex course, then I promise to give up all interest in small-time gambling and take up Morris dancing as my main hobby. Only a few days before, I had been crushed in the chaos of the York spring meeting. Goodwood seems to say: 'York? OK. But now, here's the real thing.' (Sorry, York, but you're just too big for your own good.)

Given my journey to the course, Goodwood needed to live up to its reputation. As a protest against rising fuel costs, a thousand lorry drivers had kindly decided to block the M25, reducing my average speed to no more than 25 mph. Just to add to the fun, local councils along the main Chichester route declared 18 May as 'Hole in the Road Day'. But, despite their joint efforts to sabotage my trip, I arrived at the course in good time, the mist rising off the Sussex Downs as the sun began to do battle with the lingering cloud.

Parking (£2) was easy, directions precise and visible, the attendants welcoming and cheerful. Feeling stressed? Meander through the Sussex countryside, roll into Goodwood and feel your pulse rate drop. It was immediately obvious that the Goodwood authorities had got public relations off to a fine art.

The initial impact once you have entered the course is that you've just happened upon a Bedouin family reunion. Sheikh Mohammed must think he's back in Dubai. There was no evidence of an oil well but enough white tents to make an Arab think he'd just entered Mecca. In reality, of course, you're still in the English countryside and you are reminded of this as soon as you catch sight of the manicured lawns which lie at the front of every enclosure. To their credit, even the Silver Ring (£5) enjoys the care and attention of its wealthier neighbours. If you want to splash out, the day member's badge for the Richmond enclosure is good value (£17), though the facilities in Tattersalls (£10 – they call it the Gordon enclosure) are as good as most members' enclosures at other courses.

In this area is probably one of the finest buildings I've so far encountered. The Sussex Stand enjoys a view over the distant downs that would have you writing poetry between races. The roof is no less spectacular, three giant canopies like bursting white petunias – and, at a guess, designed by the same architect who bravely brought Lord's cricket ground into the 20th century. Beneath this tented structure are raked stands, unreserved seating areas and on the top floor an open terrace which allows you to watch every step of the race.

Goodwood is a sunshine course, everything about it challenging the elements to deliver perfect weather on the twenty-one racing days. Terraces of tables and chairs, rows of open air benches and large plate glass windows give a light and airy feel to the whole course – a garden party on a grand scale. The March Stand in the members' enclosure is equally impressive, though older than its competitor in Tattersalls. The extravagant wiring which holds up the enormous roof make you think that someone has run off with the missing canvas top. The facilities within the stand are extremely good, however, offering bars, cafes and restaurants to meet every pocket.

To mark the opening of the season they were even giving away free beefburgers which seemed to be consumed at such a rate that I suspected there must have been an abattoir behind the kitchens. It's extraordinary how the word 'free' can create such a voracious reaction in people whose normal diet consists of smoked salmon and champagne. 'It's free, sod BSE' seemed to be the motto of the day.

I am not a superstitious man and would happily walk under thirteen ladders just to be bloody-minded. There's an old wives' tale in racing that you should back the first jockey you see at a racecourse. In this case it happened to be John Stack, who I spotted in the most peculiar circumstances. For some reason he had been persuaded to pose for a number of fashion shots with a leggy Canadian model, who looked so cold in her haute couture that I was convinced she'd just been taken out of the freezer. Balancing on her head was a straw hat, which I can only describe as resembling a giant ginger snap – without the cream. The striped red and yellow silks worn by Stack gave them the appearance of two puddings you'd find at a child's birthday party. It was obviously an omen.

As soon as Bomb Alaska won the opening mile-handicap, I realized it was going to be a food day and it suggested that Bring Sweets in the second race must be a near certainty. Unfortunately the jockey on board Bathwick had other plans and I watched in despair as the red and yellow trifle urged his mount over the winning line at a starting-price of 20-1. John Stack dismounted with a grin that would have cheered up a manic depressive. The shivering Canadian model huddled in the corner squeezing a smile though her frost-bitten lips. Whoever I see first at my next meeting will have my money riding on his back – even if he's a one-armed claiming apprentice who's never made the frame.

You can be sure the owner of Bathwick enjoyed his moment of triumph. Apart from being £25,000 richer, the whole paddock setting is exquisite, bursting with late spring flowers and neatly trimmed hedges. The best view is gained from the top of the weighing room, which looks over the winners' enclosure. Access can be gained over a small bridge which connects directly from the March Stand and from a series of steps leading up from the Sussex Stand enclosure. They have even had the foresight to build a small seated stand which looks as if it's a cast-off from an outside court at Wimbledon. From here you get an authentic feel for the hustle and bustle of the Good-wood crowd and the high-class presentation of the whole course.

At ground level and particularly in the pre-parade ring, it is quite easy to tune in to the race preparations. (Does Ray Cochrane realize that trainers refer to him as 'The Cockroach'?) Just before the first race a large syndicate group gathered together to receive the wisdom of their stable's racing manager. Their horse had more noughts in its form than a blindfolded cricketer but you could still see the excitement in their eyes. 'He's a big lad. Needs lots of work. I've told Seb (Sanders) to keep him handy. If he's up with the pace, he might just sneak in.'

The hopeful members hung on the manager's every word, unaware that they were being given a coded racing-talk message which read: Why did you bother to pay the entrance fee? This nag couldn't win a race if he had six legs and was given a four-furlong start. Ten minutes later, their horse having come in a distant seventh, they gathered once more, now desperate to hear one word of hope from the jockey's report. In turn they fussed over their expensive dream, each pat costing more than I'd spend on a four-course lunch. Owning horses can be a hard business. Back a couple of losers and you can measure your losses. Get involved in horse ownership and those bills come through the door with greater regularity than a *Reader's Digest* Prize Draw.

Leaving them to their post-race depression, I headed swiftly for the exit. My intention was not to leave the course but to take advantage of another of Goodwood's attentions to detail. Look out for this in the stylish race-card. At certain times the authorities offer racegoers the chance to be transported to the mile start and enjoy the drama of the gates bursting open and releasing their thoroughbred captives onto the course. Unfortunately, like many of the horses I backed at Goodwood, I missed the break, the small coach disappearing into the distance as I arrived. I was soon joined by an elderly lady wearing an outfit which probably cost more than the average mortgage.

'Gone? Gone?' she exclaimed. 'I am taking luncheon in the members' restaurant. I simply can't get here on time. This is quite intolerable.' Unlike John Stack she was not a person to be trifled with. The gate attendant showed admirable patience and placated her with a promise of a priority seat on the next coach. Two races later we met again, her face frostier than a Canadian model.

'Al'right, luv?' asked the amiable guide with a heavy Yorkshire brogue. 'My name's John. Backed any winners?' He was a man who could have disarmed a violent bank robber. Within seconds he had melted her icy stare.

It would be easier to explain the theory of relativity than try to give you a true picture of Goodwood's eccentric course. Briefly it's made up of a six-furlong straight to which are added two giant loops which intersect just after the seven-furlong pole. Two-mile races start anti-clockwise and then go clockwise, crossing the intersection twice as they manoeuvre round the loop. Depending on the length of the race, jockeys enter the straight on either the lower or upper bend and usually display a very confused facial expression. I hope that's quite clear.

If you're still baffled by my description, all the more reason to visit Goodwood. From the main stands you get the impression that the course simply follows the contours of the Sussex Downs. What is hard to work out is why nature provided a five-furlong plateau straight in front of the course enclosures. Take John's bus trip and it soon becomes obvious that someone gave nature a helping hand. After a great amount of research (i.e. I read the free Richmond enclosure booklet), it became apparent that in 1829 the fifth Duke of Richmond and Lord George Bentinck simply dug up a Sussex hill and delivered a racecourse to their well-heeled society friends. For two men to achieve this with a shovel and small trowel is truly extraordinary – but the result was a true product of genius.

From the one-mile start and looking back to the

enclosures, the stands appear to be sitting on the edge of a cliff and, given a strong gust of wind, ready to topple into the valley below. I was just glancing over to Richmond and Bentinck's creation when a small bearded figure appeared at my side. I recognized him immediately. 'Nice horse, Mr Mohammed?' I queried in a faltering manner.

Despite my occasional appearance on wanted posters, one glance from Sheikh Mohammed suggested that the recognition was not shared. Within seconds, beige-coated men in sharp suits surrounded their charge. He seemed a pleasant enough chap and I thought I may have used the wrong form of address. What do you call a sheikh? Mr Sheikh? Your Highness? Your Oilwellness? Whatever the case, his ten-strong coterie shuffled him away, the chic-suited Sheikh groupies intent on keeping a safe distance from my notebook.

I watched as Sheikh Mohammed followed his three-year-old filly with the dispassionate air of a wealthy man. Already well beaten by the time they reached the two-furlong pole, the owner turned away, quickly followed by his entourage. The engines of two helicopters fired into action and within minutes were no more than a dot in the distant sky. If that's style, I think I'd just witnessed a prime example. My own exit was probably a little less classy.

'All on board!' came a shout from behind. I was now the only passenger left on the hill top, the other members of our small group keen to get back to the main racecourse. I ran as hard as I could, arriving at the door of the bus in an apologetic and sweating manner. It was breath-taking – just like Goodwood.

Postscript: Within ten miles of the M25, traffic queues were reported to be over fifteen miles long and I began to plan an alternative route. Five miles from junction 10, I checked the radio once more. The lorry drivers had all stopped for a cup of tea at Chertsey and the road was clear. I've always said that you can't beat a good cup of tea.

CHAPTER TWENTY-TWO

GREAT LEIGHS

In the shadowy days of 1927, one man's tale dominated the world news. A handsome American cove by the name of Captain Charles Lindbergh had stepped out of his plane and asked a passing Frenchman, 'Ou am je?'

As you will notice, Lindbergh was not an accomplished linguist but he managed to establish that he had successfully flown the *Spirit of St Louis* across the Atlantic and landed safely in Paris. It is reported that he emerged from a darkened sky and into a blaze of flashlight photographers, jostling to snap an image of a pilot who had single-handedly steered his flying chariot over the winning line, to claim his $25,000 prize.

Unknown to Lindbergh and only a few hundred miles to the northwest, far more important events were unfolding in deepest Somerset, England. Rural folk of the West Country were already preparing themselves for a day out. Stiff collars had been starched; shoes buffed to a gleam; homemade pasties carefully wrapped in clean but moth-eaten handkerchiefs and bicycle chains oiled. They were preoccupied, not with the solo flight of a then unknown American, but with the prospect of attending the first race meeting at the newly constructed Taunton track.

Almost eighty years later, history is about to be repeated in Essex. Commuter folk of the East Country will don their Italian silk shirts, crumple their designer linen jackets, ring for a restaurant table and polish their BMWs. They will be absorbed, not by the brief stardom of some as yet unhailed iconic victor, but by the promise of an evening out at the pristine, all singing, all dancing, sparkling glamour of Great Leighs racecourse.

Whether this 60th course, and first new track in Britain since 1927, will enjoy fame or infamy, it is impossible to say. Like fragile plants, they need to bed in and have time to blossom or wilt into obscurity. What's certain is that the powers behind the Great Leighs development have no intention of nursing a shrinking violet into full bloom. Situated about five miles from Chelmsford and within easy reach of Stansted airport, it looks as though this new racecourse (and hopefully the horses) will hit the ground running.

With an investment of over £40 million (the price of three untalented footballers) the public are to be tempted by, we are told, a 'state of the art' facility which will be open 365 days a year. We are promised giant restaurants (I prefer an eight table bistro); giant betting halls (I favour a smoke-filled bookies) and giant screens (I always opt for secretive viewing on my black and white 14-inch portable). Yet these are only the hors d'oeuvres on the Great Leighs menu.

The main stand is a truly extraordinary affair. My guess is that the architects may well share an obsession with Spielberg's *Close Encounters of the Third Kind*. And, creditably, in order to allow disabled access to all floors, they have stuck a prodigious corkscrew walkway on each end of their interplanetary craft. The end result seems reminiscent of a close encounter between a futuristic spaceship and a gargantuan armadillo.

Like the film's alien flying machine, I hope it takes off and there's certainly enough on offer to keep the passengers on board. Perhaps one of the main attractions of the 750 seat 'dine and view' restaurant is that members will be able to stuff themselves with calories and then burn it all off with a visit to the 20,000 sq. ft Great Leighs Fitness Centre. Situated on the upper ground level of the grandstand, this will include a 20m swimming pool, sauna, jacuzzi, yoga studio and a gym equipped with enough iron pumping equipment to satisfy every testosterone-fuelled bonehead in Essex. I have my apprehensions. Have the racecourse authorities not realized the implications of offering such a facility? The people of Chelmsford and its environs could, at this very moment, be resurrecting their old shell suits, bobby socks and head sweatbands. It is a terrifying image best imprisoned in the murky depths of the subconscious with a rejection of any plea for bail. I hope the management don't live to lament their well-intentioned fitness strategy.

What they may well regret, however, is their contribution to the Americanization of British racing. Like their counterparts at Wolverhampton, Lingfield, Southwell and ('Gawd 'elp us, guv'ner') Kempton Park, Great Leighs has been enticed into 'dirt track' racing. Advances over the last twenty years or so have seen these synthetic tracks evolve from a sanded circuit, which managed to blind both horse and jockey, to a Polytrack rubberized surface, which makes the runners think they are travelling on black bouncy turf. All well and good. But I've still got to look at it and I don't like what I see. Polytrack might be efficient, remain frost-free and guarantee all-year-round racing, but it takes the soul out of a sport which, like cricket, needs the smell of grass to retain its authenticity. By 2010, it is estimated that nearly 50 per cent of all Flat meetings will take place on synthetic surfaces. All the more reason for me to apply for membership at Towcester or Fontwell. I want to see mud on a jockey's face, not bits of old tyres stuck on his double glazed racing goggles.

This is not meant to knock Great Leighs' ambitions. Their innovative approach to the nature and timing of fixtures should be applauded. Major amongst these is the advent of 'twilight racing', aided by the employment of a modern floodlighting system. (I remain convinced that horses instinctively want to curl up in bed with a good book once the sun goes down, but I'm no specialist in equine sleeping patterns.) These day/night fixtures are planned to start around mid afternoon and run into the early evening. Nice idea. Roads will be clearer, more punters can attend and more food will be eaten. Married bookmakers across the country may have a different view. Where they already feel they have no home life they can probably look forward to a costly divorce settlement.

Whatever the case, Great Leighs represents a brave move in an uncertain market. When it's up and running, and despite my reservations, I'll certainly go and sample the goods. If I had a pilot's licence and the courage of Lindbergh, I'd probably fly solo to the course in a plane called the *Spirit of Turf Racing*, hurtling from the black sky into the beaming floodlights and seething crowds. That would shake them up. As it is, I'll have to drive there. I may even hire a big winged Cadillac for the day. I've got a feeling it would feel at home at Great Leighs.

Rating? Only when it's landed.

CHAPTER TWENTY-THREE

GREAT YARMOUTH

It's happened to us all at some point. That dreaded dinner invitation, where the hosts want to introduce you to two new friends. You know the sort of thing. 'She's delightful. And her husband, Peter. So funny. So very, very funny. He'll have you in stitches. I can't wait for you to meet them. I just know you'll get on.'

Ten seconds after you've thanked your hosts for a wonderful evening, you're hammering the wheel of your car in frustration – certain that you'd have had more fun if the night had been spent manning a Samaritans line. In short, big billings are dangerous things. Not long before my visit to Yarmouth, I had enjoyed the experience of Glorious Goodwood, the only other course in Britain which enjoys a superlative description. 'Great' Yarmouth was about to be put to the test.

Everything was in its favour. A glorious sun-filled sky hung over the whole of East Anglia, the roads free of heavy traffic and nature putting on its finest spring show. Noël Coward once famously dismissed this part of England with the words 'Very flat, Norfolk'. I can only describe this put-down as a complete understatement. So deprived are Norfolk folk of anything resembling a hillock that pubescent children must create great excitement every time they discover a new pimple. But it's pretty in its own way.

Approaching Great Yarmouth, windmills and canals punctuate the landscape, and as you near the coast the whole area begins to feel more and more like Holland – without the thin chips and mayonnaise. Sadly, and as hard as I try, that's about as far as flattery will take me. It's all downhill from here. (For Norfolk residents, the unfamiliar term 'downhill' may be translated as the downward movement from a high to a low geographical point.)

It's hard to say what first triggered my negative response to Yarmouth racing. It could have been my aching back after a 170-mile journey, though I suspect my first sight of the low drab stands did little to excite the taste buds. There was nothing about the architecture, the dust bowl car park or the surrounding red brick bungalows to whet my appetite for a day's racing. OK, I know it's a subjective response and you should never judge a product by its packaging. But if Great Yarmouth was a birthday present, I'm not sure I'd even bother to tear off the wrapping paper.

Given an hour to spare, and sniffing the hint of sea air through the mist of frying chips, I decided to stretch my legs and head for the beach. Fortunately, this lies only a brisk ten-minute walk from the racecourse entrance. The road takes you over a small road bridge and, as I was later to discover, is the only position from which you can gain a full view of the course. At this point, you are able to look down the long mile-straight, attached to which is a one-mile, two-furlong oval with very tight bends. It appears that the course has been squashed between a large housing estate to the west and a caravan site to the east. Just below the top bend is North Dennes Middle School, where I hope the breaks are geared to coincide with the start of each race. It may have been my imagination but I'm sure I spotted an 8-year-old in a big check jacket setting up a pitch at the back of the bike sheds.

Wander a little further towards the beach and you'll come across a building which epitomises all British seaside resorts. The flat-roofed Iron Duke pub was all spruced up for the summer season, the exterior displaying a fetching sun-faded peeling paint, the doors wide open to reveal a moth-eaten dark brown carpet. It was the sort of place I used to fall out of when I was a headstrong 17-year-old and it looked about as welcoming as a 1950s landlady in a £2 a night bed and breakfast. I was beginning to get the feel of Great Yarmouth.

After a five-minute stroll along the beach, dominated by the spider-like oil rigs which lay out to sea, I returned to the course. Within seconds I had made my first error of judgement and one that could have been avoided had I bothered to glance up to the top of the members' stand. Fluttering in the strong breeze was a brightly coloured flag bearing the Great Yarmouth coat of arms. Like its namesake, the flag fluttered to deceive. The first glimpse of this pennant suggests a red and blue halved cloth bearing three golden lions rampant. A second examination reveals that each of these royal beasts appear to have an aquatic tail. There was something very fishy about this racecourse and the paying of £13 for a day member's badge was a bad decision.

For the extra three pounds (Tatts was £10), you are treated to a small members' stand, three rows of plastic seats on a small lawn and a bar in a converted prefab. If there is any advantage, it is to allow you access to an open rooftop, which allows a decent view of the home straight and a clear sight of the rather nondescript paddock.

In most respects, Tattersalls has just as much to offer – though from any position on the course, the view of the racing is highly restricted. All races up to a mile simply come straight down the main chute, which means that the contest can only be seen head-on. Without the commentator's description, you have virtually no idea what's going on until they reach the furlong-pole. In longer contests, the pack simply disappears behind the caravan site before re-emerging five furlongs from home and again coming straight at the expectant crowd. In a six-race meeting, I doubt you would really enjoy more than sixty seconds visible action.

Having assessed the course, I wandered to the back of the Tattersalls stand to make my selections. It was obviously the type of circuit that would suit a long-striding galloper who stayed with the pace. A large picnic area surrounded by the usual fast food vans occupies the majority of the ground and on this late spring day proved to be a real sun trap. There was a noticeable bustle from the holiday crowd and a fairground smell that must have depressed every goldfish in Yarmouth. The weighing room, some 100 yards from the paddock, proved to be the focal point for the sunbathing public. Famous and not so famous faces shuffled in and out, but even the normally effervescent Dettori looked subdued and bore the ominous look of someone spending another day at the office.

My selections marked in the card, I headed for the bars which lie beneath the stand. They would have given the Iron Duke a run for its money, their drab interiors and limited food doing nothing to raise the spirits. Even the clientele increased my feeling of impending doom. A woman of ambiguous age flicked her false teeth at me as soon as I entered. Was I missing some Norfolk mating gesture? In her prime, and with a full set of gnashers, I imagine she had been a bit of a stunner. I've always thought that the old school dentists have contributed to the fall of many a beauty and deserve to be publicly gnawed to death by a set of second-hand dentures.

As it happened, I was forced to come within biting distance of this ageing femme fatale. Just above her head was an extraordinary picture of the actor John Inman being driven along the straight in an open top Bentley. What was even more peculiar is that the sizeable crowd appeared to be cheering the presence of this effete product of a cheap BBC sitcom. Further down the walls were a whole array of Britain's finest thespians. The likes of Russ Abbott, Larry Grayson and Frank Carson beamed out from their frames, each one hugging a very suspicious looking jockey. It was then that the penny dropped.

Great Yarmouth only mirrors the stars who appear in their summer shows on the Britannia Pier. They share in common the cheap and brash nature of British holiday resorts who have, for years, hoodwinked the public into thinking they were getting value for money. It made me even more determined to reclaim my entrance fee from the bookies.

Certain that I had found the right type to win with ease on the Yarmouth course, I wandered over to the course enclosure at the other side of the track, only to be surprised by a small collection of private tents erected near the winning post. Here sat the Norfolk county set, the only evidence of beige linen jackets within a 10-mile radius and the sole suggestion of architectural style on the whole racecourse. The stewards' box could have graced Ascot or Goodwood. Erected on metal stilts, this stark white wooden building is designed like an enormous dovecote, waiting for some giant Norfolk bird to prepare its nest. If you ever see a white dove with a 10-foot wing span, you'll know where it's come from.

Adjacent to this area, but heavily segregated by wire fencing, is the small course enclosure. Oddly this probably enjoys the best view of racing and mercifully keeps you at a distance from the cheerless stands. A handful of course bookies take small bets and a one-man Tote box plies a small trade. It was from this enclosure that I watched my carefully chosen selections struggle up the long straight. Within an hour it was obvious that any chance of re-couping the entrance fee was as likely as enjoying a night out in the Iron Duke. I was facing a long journey home with an empty wallet and decided to risk all on the third race and then make my escape. I approached the Tote booth.

'Five pounds each-way number 13,' I asked, with as much conviction as possible.

'Sorry. Machine's broken,' answered the cashier.

A small crowd had begun to form behind me and I raced to the course side to cross over into the main enclosure.

'Sorry. Horses coming out,' responded the steward, replacing the rail and blocking my access. I had the sudden fear that fate was playing a hand. Miss All Alone looked a good thing, even at 50-1. Racing back to the enclosure, I noticed a small disturbance at the gate which led to the private boxes. Punters were demanding to be let in to use the exclusive Tote office reserved for the corporate clientele. Just as I arrived, the gateman threw up his arms in surrender. Within seconds the prams, bare-chested men and ice-cream-covered children of the hoi polloi enclosure were mingling with the linen-clad gentry. Much sniffing ensued and many an eyebrow rose in disapproval. If you ever do visit Yarmouth and you want some fun – sabotage the enclosure Tote booth.

Needless to say, Miss All Alone finished alone – at the back of the field. I don't think she was that bad a filly but maybe had a bit too much class to win at Yarmouth. Heading back to the exit, I stopped for a second by the paddock as the winner was clapped in by the sweating crowd. To be fair, the winners' enclosure is fairly well laid out – until you catch sight of the banners which form a backdrop to the presentation. The Britannia Pier had paid the course authorities to advertise their forthcoming summer season of star turns – Chubby Brown, the Chuckle Brothers and the Barron Knights. Says it all really. Big billing? Big let-down. *Great* Yarmouth? Yarmouth grates.

Postscript: A glimmer of hope. They've now improved the facilities by building the attractive Lord Nelson Grandstand. I bet that cost them an arm and an eye.

CHAPTER TWENTY-FOUR

HAMILTON PARK

Six-thirty a.m. Luton airport. Mid-May. A late dose of flu. Head banging as if I've just swallowed the church bells.

'Any luggage?' asks the check-in girl.

'Just the notebook,' I sniff.

'Going somewhere nice?'

'Sorry?'

'Where are you going?'

'Hamilton Park.'

'Where's that?'

'Somewhere near Glasgow, I hope.'

'So do I.'

'Thanks.'

I felt better already, at last encountering a member of an airline staff who hadn't bunked off from charm school. I was about to jet off to Hamilton Park for the day. It may make me sound like a fast course smoothie, but it's about half as cheap as filling up the gas guzzler and staying in some flea-ridden bed and breakfast.

Little more than two hours later, I'm coughing and spluttering my way onto the suburban train that takes you out to Hamilton West station. The journey isn't inspiring, taking you through the rather desolate urban sprawl of south-east Glasgow. Within thirty minutes, we arrived and having infected the whole of my carriage I am probably responsible for what is now known as the great Scottish flu epidemic.

The racecourse is about a mile's walk from the station, though you'll have to ask for directions. There's not one sign for the course and I was forced to employ my old paper chase scouting skills. As I wandered in what I hoped was the right direction, I kept coming across old and unsuccessful betting slips wafting on the growing breeze. There had been a meeting only a few days before and it must have been attended by some of the worst punters in Great Britain. But, thanks to their inability to pick winners, I finally saw the entrance.

Hamilton bears the name 'park' for good reason. At a guess it's been constructed in the grounds of a now defunct estate, the remains of the high granite wall still evident along the borders of the course. It's a rural oasis in the middle of the once proud manufacturing heartland of Lanarkshire, and after my depressing train journey, I was ready for some light relief.

It came from the most unexpected source. As I sat waiting for the gates to open, I was joined by two men with distinctly un-Glaswegian accents.

'Been here before?' asked the first.

'First time.'

'It's a bloody odd place,' added the second.

'Yeah. But a good crack,' retorted his companion.

It transpired that they were two long distance lorry drivers who had been delivering some very mysterious equipment to a nearby naval dockyard. They had planned their whole journey so that they could spend the afternoon at Hamilton Park and then slip down to Carlisle for the following day's meeting. I was full of admiration.

'Why's it an odd place?' I asked.

'You'll see,' they laughed in perfect two-part harmony.

They weren't wrong. Go in through the main entrance and the Grandstand hits your eyes faster than a boxer's jab. Dominating the whole area is a single stark white building that could have been lifted straight out of Disney World. A row of international flags fluttered high above the cantilevered roof – yet, strangely, the Union Jack was given height preference over the Scottish blue and white. Below this display a whole array of irregular windows peer over the huge paddock lawns, while on the ground floor a series of arched colonial windows give the building a truly classical feel.

To the left stand two magnificent towers, one topped with a three-sided clock, which unbelievably gave the correct time on all its faces; the second a rounded turret which had me immediately looking upwards for that famous Scottish princess, Moira Rapunzel.

But if you think this is odd – wait until you see the course. I couldn't describe it as unique, as it shares many of the same features as Salisbury – i.e. it has the appearance of an old darning needle lying on its side. The Grandstand is placed at the sharp end and looks down the straight six-furlong course. However, at the three-furlong pole, the course extends into a tight-bend loop which the horses have to negotiate in any race over a mile.

And it gets even more complicated. The one-mile, four-furlong races start in front of the stands going left to right, head off down the course, around what the locals call 'the whip' and charge back to the finishing post going right to left. Given these peculiarities, it's theoretically possible for a very slow horse (and I've backed a few) to meet the leaders coming up the straight in the opposite direction.

It gets even better. At the three-furlong pole the ground rises faster than a bride's nightie and the horses would be better off with a Sherpa than a lightweight jockey. The straight is a complete switchback, the first three furlongs kidding the thoroughbreds that they're in for an easy day, while the long run out of the dip must have them begging for mercy. If you're tempted to back a five-furlong specialist in a Hamilton Park sprint, put a line through its name and back something that can get at least a mile.

Overall, I felt that this Scottish course just pipped it over Salisbury, where the loop is well out of sight of the stands. Because of the huge course undulations, 'the whip' at Hamilton sits on a self-contained plateau and is therefore highly visible, though fairly distant. The course management is obviously well aware of these failings as once inside the Grandstand there are so many large television screens available that it feels as if you're in a Dixon's superstore.

It turned out that this refurbished stand had only been opened a few days before my visit and it had the sort of smell you only ever witness in a brand new car. The whole place was pristine, the staff wiping the tables down ten seconds after you'd left your seat. I hope they keep it up. The last time I bought a new car I cleaned it every evening for the first week, once a week for the next six months and after that gave it the odd wipe down if we happened to be going to a funeral. But, at the time of my visit, the whole place sparkled and there was an evident sense of pride in putting Hamilton back on the map. And they've used the space well.

There's an adequate supply of bars and restaurants, most with a clear view of the course and finishing post. The members' area is thankfully limited to a fairly small area and unless you're having a special occasion, the cheaper end gives you access to almost everything on the course. Generally the changes have maintained an egalitarian feel, though the top of the Grandstand is limited to the monstrous regiment of corporate boxes. They enjoy a balcony with the finest view of the course and this extends the full length of the Grandstand. It's all a bit in your face – and it's hard not to be aware that they've got a privileged position at the expense of the true race-goers, who stretch their necks to get a clear sight of the racing.

But it's a small complaint. Hamilton's one and only Grandstand is a fine affair which has managed to modernize the course without turning it into an over-sized glass and plastic paradise. (Shame on you, York and Newmarket.) If I had one concern it was the lack of mirrors in the Gents' lavatories. It's not that I'm vain but I do like to see how desperate I look after a couple of losers. Fortunately I'd picked up a nice 9-1 touch in the second race, and managed to survive without seeing my haggard reflection. Celebration proved more difficult, as there wasn't a sweet shop on the course. As you'll realize from other reports, this is enough to make me write an abusive letter to the Jockey Club and demand recompense for my Mars Bar withdrawal symptoms.

In the end I settled for one of those expensive squirty ice creams which win annual awards from the Dead Tastebuds Society. But it passed the time as I wandered across the paddock lawns and sauntered over to greet my winning nag. The surprising thing about Hamilton is that while the course looks as if it's been built on a small allotment, the parade ring and winners' enclosure could easily be transplanted to a Grade 1 racecourse. OK – it was a sun-filled day, but this area behind the stands is truly stunning.

At least ten mature oaks (or sycamores or something) fill the parade ring and at its centre a ring of benches girdle the trunk of an ancient timber. Look carefully and you'll even see a small wooden sculpture of wine glasses and crusted bread on the arm of one of the seats. I know it's nothing, but it's little touches like this that suggest that the management care about what they're doing. Even the pre-parade ring wouldn't be sniffed at by many courses as their main paddock and the separate winners' enclosure, tucked at the north end of the course, was pretty enough to be snapped up by Newmarket's Rowley Mile course.

However, the majority of runners at Hamilton could only dream of parading their talents at HQ. The Uddingston Selling Handicap probably summed up the standard – an 18-horse field which had been plying its trade around Southwell, Wolverhampton and Musselburgh. The winner, Hill Farm Dancer, was the sort of average nag you'd dream of owning, having won twelve races and being placed on numerous occasions. It was offered for sale at £3,000, received no bids and I doubt the auction lasted for more than three minutes. The auctioneer barely whispered that the winner was nine years old and he had as much chance of making a sale as I have of selling my golf swing to Colin Montgomerie.

It would be easy to take a cheap shot at Hamilton Park. It's on the edge of some fairly dour countryside; it has a course which isn't easy to see; it has a finishing three furlongs which destroys the form book; there's not one seat in the Grandstand; and the course looks like it's been placed in a giant vice and squeezed until it screams. This is bargain basement racing. The total prize money in six races came to little more than £20,000 and the contestants were of a fairly low standard. But who cares? Not the small punters who witnessed at least four thrilling finishes, who were treated like human beings and given the facilities to relax and enjoy the racing.

Just before I rushed off to make my return trip to the airport, I bumped into one of the lorry drivers I had met earlier.

'Making money?' I asked.

'Nightmare,' he answered with a rueful smile, 'but it's a good day out.'

Got it in one. Don't expect too much from Hamilton but it's got a certain something. Like my airport check-in girl, it's got the one thing that fat wallets can't buy – a real sense of charm.

Postscript: To the course management: Thank you for providing an information caravan at the end of the betting ring. Do you realize that it completely restricts the punters' head-on view from the Grandstand terrace? Please wheel it away or provide all racegoers with wooden stilts.

CHAPTER TWENTY-FIVE

HAYDOCK PARK

The end of the 20th century saw football being marketed as the 'sexy' game. It seems an odd description, as my own experience of standing on the terraces usually involves a woollen bobble hat, a full set of thermal underwear and a half-time pork pie. In a state like that I doubt my testosterone level would even register on a sexometer. Yet our basic instincts are now employed to sell anything from floor cleaners to pints of Irish stout. I have a sneaking suspicion that racing is about to jump on the bandwagon.

Within seconds of passing through the sumptuous entrance to Haydock Park, a fixture list for the new season had been thrust into my hand. But this was no ordinary fixture list. Instead I had been presented with a giant glossy poster, one-third of which displayed a clear guide to forthcoming meetings, while the remaining space was taken up by a pouting brunette with bitten nails and breasts the size of two Millennium Domes. Provocatively laying on a bed of straw, it looked as if she'd just been surprised by a stable lad who was about to have more on his mind than mucking out. Probably due to my having donned woolly winter combinations, I'd rather have been given a picture of a three-mile chaser flying over an open ditch. Yet strangely, this soft porn poster told me all I needed to know. Haydock intends to take the 21st century by storm and wasn't going to be left behind in the rush for modernization.

The course possibly had its biggest stroke of luck in the late 1950s when the Government planted the M6 motorway on its doorstep and made Haydock the most accessible racecourse in Britain. Two minutes from Junction 23, you'll be entering the metalled free car park and with no worries about sinking into the mud. The narrow winding road takes you along the edge of the six-furlong straight and provides a sense of involvement before you've even stepped out of your car. Even if you only go into Tattersalls, take the time to wander down towards the County enclosure entrance. A white pavilion, with six tent-like domes, welcomes the members' arrival while a small coppice of trees gives the impression of an old country estate.

But regardless of which entrance you take, it's immediately apparent that Haydock (apart from its fixture poster) has gone upmarket and is ready to take on the likes of Sandown, York and Kempton. However, unlike these better known courses, Haydock does seem to have retained a greater degree of intimacy. Instead of adhering to the maxim that big is beautiful, it appears to supply equal facilities without constructing those cavernous grandstands which resemble multi-storey car parks. Bars, stands and restaurants have to be discovered, rather than being brashly displayed, and each corner turned seems to throw up yet another surprise.

What makes it even more appealing is that the enclosures and paddock are laid out in a simple strip, which runs along the course and always keeps you in touch with the racing. Apart from moving between the enclosures there's really no need to go behind the stands once you've made your grand entrance. The only other reason might be to arrange a clandestine meeting with your racing snout. It was at the back of the Tattersalls stand that I met my informant, making contact with the coded message, 'Mars Bar, please.' Despite my passion for a good wine, I have yet to acquire a private supplier and when I'm racing I wouldn't swap a Château Lafitte '64 for a Mars Bar 2006. And this sweet vendor has been selling me these chocolate delights for years at every racecourse south of the Mersey. He has also supplied me with more racing titbits than any man I have ever known.

'Bit quiet,' I offered as an opener.

'Football,' he responded simply.

'Football?'

'Liverpool at home.'

'They're only playing Middlesbrough.'

'They're crazy. This lot would watch five kids kicking a tin can in a back alley.'

'Sexy football?'

'Sexier than racing. Never get a big crowd in the winter. In the old days I used to bring three vans down here. Come on my own these days.'

'Right.'

'What's the poster for?' he asked suddenly.

'Oh – nothing,' I answered, hurriedly rolling it tighter and trying to conceal it under my jacket.

Now I understood the management's decision to promote a classy racecourse with a smutty bit of advertising. Being so close to Liverpool and Manchester they don't simply have the job of attracting local punters, they have to persuade them to change their religion. As this has about as much chance of success as inviting a bus-load of Muslim fundamentalists to a synagogue prayer meeting, I think they need to look long and hard at the fixture list and avoid coinciding with the two Liverpool and Manchester clubs' home matches.

If you do abstain from football and go racing at Haydock, I hope you can land a few winners. Sadly, this is one of the courses which carries a warning sign in my notebook. As it happens, this Lancashire course was the first track I ever attended as a starry-eyed teenager ready to take on the world of gambling. Unfortunately it turned into a baptism of fire and is probably the main reason I ended up as a wary small punter, rather than a hard-nosed favourite backer. I doubt I have had more than ten winners at Haydock in the last twenty years – and after the first two races there was no sign of change.

In the first, Cattalus flattered over the first mile only to disappear without trace; while Effectual in the second was immediately renamed after running like a complete dog. I can vouch for the consistent poor running of both these horses, as I was able to follow their progress from start to finish. The one-mile, five-furlong oval circuit is clearly visible from all the enclosures and you won't miss a stride. Being a dual-purpose course, the jumps circuit is laid out inside the Flat course, yet remains close enough (unlike places such as Ascot and Newcastle) to maintain your involvement. For the hurdle contests you can pick a spot in any of the enclosures, but for the chases try to get on the right-hand side of the main Tattersalls stand. At this point you'll be directly opposite the water jump, which the runners tend to take early in the race and invariably fly the fence as a tightly packed group.

It was from this vantage point that I was able to cheer in my first winner, The Last Fling, hanging on in a thrilling finish to pip Bobby Grant on the line. My wanderings around the racecourses of Britain seemed to coincide with the rise of Sue Smith, who was once known as the wife of Harvey Smith, the brusque Yorkshire show jumper. So many winners have passed the post that Harvey Smith will now be known as Sue Smith's husband. If Venetia Williams is the headmistress, Sue Smith has become the head girl of an all boys' school, finally putting a nail in the coffin of the male-dominated and secretive world of racing trainers. The post-race interview only confirmed her straightforward approach and a willingness to de-mystify her profession.

'Were you confident?' asked the interviewer.

'Once Seamus gave him one slap on the bum he looked like the winner.'

'And where to next?'

'Not sure. Gold Cup. Maybe the National – or some other big race.'

Simplicity itself. No huffing and puffing about the ground being right, the handicapper being fair, or the moon in the right quarter. Just a 'slap on the bum' and 'some other big race'. It must send a shudder through the racing hierarchy when a woman like Sue Smith destroys their carefully nurtured illusion.

I was only able to witness these post-race celebrations by hanging over the wall of the Tommy Whittle Stand – a spot I would recommend highly. Apart from providing a clear view of the paddock, you are also treated to a floor-level glimpse of the members' restaurant. Whilst you can see nothing of the no doubt elegant table settings, you are given access to the secrets of under-table activity. I hadn't realized that so many diners play footsie with other people's wives and husbands; no idea that women's tights wrinkle like concertinas; or that so many men fail to polish the back of their shoes.

Unlike at many racecourses, the paddock and winners' enclosure act like a magnet for a large number of the crowd. Within seconds of the race finishing it's difficult to gain any sort of decent view of the victors. And there is a good reason for its popularity. The compact area around the parade ring is without question the finest I've witnessed, a magical setting which places Haydock in the top rank of British racecourses.

Between the main stands and the elegant cream and green saddling boxes at the far end of the course stand at least fifty mature trees. This proved to be my greatest arboreal challenge so far (see other reports for my pathetic attempts at tree identification). In mid-January there wasn't a leaf to be seen but having attended Haydock in mid-summer, I can report that on a sunny day with the branches heavy with foliage, the shimmering light in the paddock is enough to send an artist into a complete frenzy.

In the paddock alone stand fourteen giant sycamores (?), trainers, owners and horses weaving their way through the sturdy trunks and languid branches. Individual, small, raked stands surround the grassed circle, while a collection of raised earth plinths are dotted around the enclosure. There's a genuine buzz of excitement before punters race off to place their bets and it's a truly unique setting which shouldn't be missed.

But the real treat of the paddock seems not to have been discovered by many punters. For at least one of the steeplechases get down to the course-side rail, where horses enter the course from the parade ring. This will place you on the corner of the first tight bend and give you a thrilling view of the final four fences which come in quick succession in the home straight. Though you'll have difficulty identifying the winner in a photo-finish, the sight of high-class jumpers bouncing over Haydock's demanding fences is worth the sacrifice.

There is so much to offer in this area that, unusually, I would recommend saving up and spoiling yourself with a County Enclosure ticket (£8 more than Tatts on the day of my visit). This will give you quick access to the paddock, extravagantly carpeted bars, and a bench-covered lawn surrounded by a wrought-iron fence topped with golden ping-pong balls. What more could a punter ask for? Tattersalls is fine, well equipped, but does require a great deal of hiking between stands and paddock. To their credit, even the Newton Enclosure (a euphemism for the Silver Ring) is very well equipped but, just to keep the economically challenged punters in their place, offers no access to the paddock. In Haydock's case, to miss the parade ring enclosure makes about as much sense as going to the cinema wearing a blindfold – so start saving and give yourself a treat.

A final word should be given to the multi-coloured racecard, which is as fine a piece of glossy printing as I've found at any of the other premier racecourses. Even Harry Haydock's Hotshots (which I ignored) proved to tip four winners and if I had bothered to really read the comprehensive form notes, I'd be booking a holiday in the Caribbean. As it was, The Last Fling proved to be exactly that and I left Haydock, as usual, with an empty wallet. But it was exciting, vivacious, good on the eye and set my pulse racing. Some might even call it sexy.

Postscript: Liverpool drew 0-0 with Middlesbrough in a match described by the commentator as the most tedious game he had seen in twenty-five years. They'd have been better off at Haydock. Perhaps next time my private Mars Bar supplier will bring two vans.

CHAPTER TWENTY-SIX

HEREFORD

I'd always wanted to visit Hereford. The name itself has a certain rustic charm, conjuring up images of grazing cattle, wooden cider presses, cathedral spires and flowing rivers. I had saved it up as a child might retain its favourite sweet in a tightly knotted handkerchief. I could resist it no longer and drove into the sunlit city with a real sense of anticipation.

As you may now realize, it has become my habit to get a feel of a racecourse by nosing around the local churches. Despite race meetings being attended by a majority of my fellow agnostics, there's probably more collective praying goes on during the final furlong of any horse race than you'd witness in an average monastery. OK – it's a tenuous link, but I've never failed to be fascinated how a bunch of mediaeval peasants managed to get all the stones to stay in place for 800 years, or how many small punters expect to enter heaven by backing a 20-1 nag.

But Hereford Cathedral is a bit of a stunner, and apart from having a bent spire, an eerie crypt and a fireplace in the transept, it also houses the Mappa Mundi. For those of you too ignorant to know what this is (join the club), it turns out to be a 13th-century vellum map, which reflects the assumptions that Jerusalem was the centre of our universe and that the world was flat. Obviously this was no more than an illusion, though I suspect that if I had been a turnip-growing serf in AD 1290, I'd have gone along with the deluded experts. Whatever the case, the Mappa Mundi was to haunt me for the rest of the day.

The racecourse lies only a mile north of the city centre, just far enough away to lay claim to a country setting but near enough to give a strong sense of suburbia. Surprisingly, the course appears to have become lost amongst Hereford's growing industrial outskirts – and the poor signposting for the main entrance suggests that it may have become incidental to the city. Yet, despite this slight disappointment, I strode into the racecourse confident of a good day.

Minutes later I became even more optimistic. Only a few steps from the entrance stood an open iron brazier, its red hot coals glowing as the wind fired it into life. A small huddle of punters stood warming their hands in the chilled January air. Before long I had spotted another six of these outdoor heaters, all surrounded by red-faced racegoers deep in conversation. The scene had the look of Agincourt the night before battle and I half expected an appearance from Henry V, rousing his troops to fight the bookmaking foe.

Edging past the window of the main members' stand, I peered inside, only to spot an opportunity to put Hereford to the ultimate test. 'Judge a man by his shoes, a horse by its teeth and a racecourse by its Eccles cakes' has always been a favourite maxim – and two bites into the finely crumbling pastry was sufficient to place Hereford at the top of the racing mountain.

There is, of course, a drawback to this form of assessment. Reach the brow of a hill or the summit of a mountain – and there's only one way to go. If I hadn't been so bamboozled by the succulent Eccles cake, I'd have seen the omens during the fateful first race. Despite Sweet Señorita being the hot favourite at 4-11, the form seemed to suggest that Oulton Broad was really the horse to back. I missed the early price of 40-1 but managed a small wager at 33-1. The favourite set off like a headless chicken, running out of steam with five hurdles still to negotiate. In contrast, Oulton Broad bided his time and then raced into a fifteen-length lead with the race at his mercy. Sadly, his approach to the penultimate hurdle resembled an athlete wearing concrete running shoes. I groaned audibly as he hit the deck.

'Back it?' came a voice at my side.

'How did you guess?' I responded curtly.

'Flattered to deceive,' replied my companion.

'Could say that.'

I suddenly had a bad feeling about Hereford. How could it lose? It had fantastic form – a fine cathedral, six braziers and mouth-watering Eccles cakes. Yet something told me it was about to suffer the fate of Oulton Broad – crash through its next hurdle and end up on its back. I raced off to inspect the possible obstacles. For some reason, I suddenly thought of Carlisle, a course which isn't certain where it belongs in the ranks of National Hunt racing. Tracks such as Kelso, Hexham, Towcester and Fontwell know their place and retain a wonderful intimacy. A more objective glance around the enclosures of Hereford revealed that it may have lost its former identity – if indeed it ever had one.

It's never easy to pin down, but somehow Hereford

appears to have manoeuvred itself into mundane modernisation by exchanging country intimacy for suburban functionality – if you follow my pretentious drift. Three main stands border the finishing straight, each with an exceptional view of the square one-mile, four-furlong course. Unfortunately these brick-built facilities enjoy about as much character as the almost inedible Cornish pasties served up over the various bars. These culinary nightmares contained a grey slime filling, which would have been more at home on a bricklayer's trowel, while the pastry had experienced only a brief affair with a hot oven.

Like Oulton Broad, the pasties suggested that all was not well at this racecourse, acting as they were as symbols of a doom-laden afternoon. Having reached the summit, I was now well into the rapid descent. Maybe it's the little things which give the game away. My entrance into the Tattersalls bar was met by a buzzing television which had ground every conversation to an abrupt halt. An hour later nothing had been done to fix this irritation and punters could do little more than stare at its screen with frustration and try to will it into submission.

As I left the bar, we were informed over the tannoy that the chase fence in front of the main stands would be dolled off for the afternoon. No explanation was offered and it was delivered with a 'take it or leave it' pomposity. Though crowds of small punters may contain the occasional congenital idiot, the majority would prefer to be treated as semi-intelligent adults with enquiring minds.

However, it is the cheap end course enclosure which really reveals the core of Hereford's disappointment. My agitation grows almost every time I come across these archaic Silver Rings and I have it on the unquestionable authority of the Hereford Cathedral children's quiz sheet that they represent a direct assault upon the common man. In Hereford's case the cathedral close was created in order to stop the local pigs digging up the graveyard.

Given the facilities in this enclosure, the view of certain punters being little better than snout-foraging pink squealers seems a useful analogy. The authorities obviously dread them rooting around the paddock and keep them firmly imprisoned behind high rows of metal fencing. Unusually, a decent stand is provided but the cafe bar, with the inevitable lino-covered floor, is as grimy and depressing a place as I've encountered (though Catterick and Redcar come a short-head second). It at least has the distinction of being opened in 1965 by Field Marshal Lord Harding of Petherton. I wasn't there at the time but I bet he made a very short speech and rushed off to the members' stand as fast as his legs would carry him.

The sad truth, however, is that the more expensive enclosures hardly need protection from the rooting pigs. Even the owners' and trainers' bar is no more than a prefabricated cafe. But what condemns Hereford to accusations of lack of effort is the paddock. The strategic design planning seems to be one of finding a bit of sloping open ground and hurling a white rail around a patch of grass. Add a strip of tarmac for the horses to walk round and – hey presto! – you've got yourself a parade ring. To add insult to injury this strip of potholed tarmacadam looks as if it has been laid by four dubious men in a white van who demanded payment in used tenners. Any decent chaser would risk greater injury in the rutted paddock than flying over an open ditch.

The winners' enclosure only adds to the drabness and is an insult to all those connections who keep racing afloat. As fate would have it, I happened to stand next to the owners of Head Gardener in the fourth race. As usual my wallet was still firing blanks and my interest in the race had become purely academic. But two fences from home, I heard a nervous shriek at my side. Approaching the last this had become a full-blown nervous breakdown. Hands twitched, eyes were covered and prayers were being chanted.

As their horse popped over the last, the owners paled visibly and stood stock still in a state of transfixed shock. It was their moment, a result which they had probably dreamt of night after night, an occasion which would be burnt into their memories and would cloud the realities of all the training bills which had been draining their withering bank accounts. Barring a good Eccles cake, sex or a genuine Cornish pasty, this is about as good as life gets.

And how does Hereford mark this moment of triumph? How does it reward the owners who keep their course in business? You will have already guessed. The winner is treated to a minute enclosure, so indistinct it hardly merits description. A few bent white rails separate the victors while a small table is hurriedly erected in the corner to support the owner's trophy. I've seen more excitement at the end of a pony club hack and the Hereford executive obviously underestimate the importance of landing a winner. It doesn't matter where an owner lands a race – Hereford, Plumpton, Redcar, Ascot or Goodwood – it's an experience which needs recognition.

If I had been of a more sensitive nature, I'd have realized that the Mappa Mundi told me all I needed to know about Hereford. The writing was on the map the moment I wandered into that sublime cathedral. Jerusalem isn't at the centre of the universe. The earth isn't flat. If the 13th-century map is an illusion, Hereford racecourse is a full-blown deception and, like Oulton Broad, flattered to deceive. Its shaky foundations are built on no more than a flimsy country reputation, six braziers and a plate of crumbly Eccles cakes.

Postscript I: Even the braziers couldn't save this racecourse. As I slipped out to the car park it became apparent that I had actually attended the annual meeting of the British Asthmatics' Society. Anyone within twenty feet of the acrid fumes created by the open fires was beginning to wheeze and splutter uncontrollably, the meagre crowd coughing in unison as I hurried to the exit. I also enjoyed a bout of chronic indigestion as I battled my way back towards Cheltenham. I think it must have been the Eccles cakes.

Postscript II: Hot and good news for owners. Hereford are undergoing a new £2 million regeneration. They proudly boast that they are resurfacing the parade ring and moving the winners' enclosure. I wonder where they got that idea from? Best of all, they promise improvements to the lorry park. Now, if anything will get me back to Hereford, it won't be that.

CHAPTER TWENTY-SEVEN

HEXHAM

I suppose we all develop a few strange habits. Some we make public, others remain dark kept secrets. Reading books backwards is no hanging offence, so I'm happy to admit that it's become my practice to attack any form of literature in this manner. If by any chance you don't share this tendency, you won't know that following my visit to Newcastle I spent the following day in the vaults of Durham University library, unravelling the enigma of Brandling House.

If you're visiting Hexham as part of a holiday trip, stop off in Durham. It's without doubt one of the most stunning cities in Britain and probably no more than forty-five minutes from Hexham racecourse. What's more, it provides the gateway to what the locals call God's county. I doubt I've ever met anyone who has only been to Northumberland once. It's a county that's got more pulling power than an eight-man rowing crew. By the time you approach Hexham, you'll also realize why the Romans built Hadrian's Wall.

I vaguely recall being taught that this monument to Roman madness and ingenuity was constructed to mark the boundary of their northernmost colony and to keep the Scots from plundering livestock. This of course is historical bunkum. What actually occurred is that almost 2,000 years ago a bunch of centurions arrived somewhere near Hexham on a glorious summer's day and came across a wandering Geordie. 'Noo then, bonny lads!' spake the Geordie. 'Howway in for a bit 'a crack.'

The story goes that they were offered a delicious meal of pease pudding and stottie bread which so took their fancy that they remained for the next thousand years.

'It can't get better than this,' declared one legionary.

'Anybody fancy building a wall?'

The delightful market town of Hexham therefore owes its development to no more than a bowl of mashed peas and a Geordie who enjoyed the company of men in leather skirts and plumed helmets. If they had arrived, as I did, during the wild winds of mid-November, history may well have taken a different course.

Strangely, I learnt a great deal about Hexham racecourse well before I entered the course. Arriving very early and with a few hours to spare, I called in at Hexham Golf Club. Within minutes I had been invited to make up a four-ball with three retired locals who professed to playing off high handicaps, yet all seemed to hit the ball like Tiger Woods. Unfortunately my own performance would have been improved if I had been wearing a blindfold and had both arms tied behind my back. But they remained uncritical and delightful company, none more so than John Scott, a Northumbrian bear of a man, who also turned out to be the former veterinary officer for Hexham racecourse. It felt like striking gold in a coal mine. Apart from supplying some interesting detail, it also seemed likely he'd be able to guide me to a profitable afternoon. A couple of beers after our game (and £5 better off despite my poor display), I had all the armoury I needed.

Hexham, John informed me, was no course for faint hearts – and like many of these country courses it contains at least two stretches of rising ground, which test the stamina of the hardiest stayer. The fence which catches out the tiring chasers is three from home. Get over this in a good position, I was told, and you can start to count your winnings. Whilst it's not a challenging obstacle, horses meet the fence after a long climbing drag up the back straight and require every ounce of energy to clear the birch.

Half an hour after our conversation, I was 800 feet above sea level with my car being buffeted by a gale force wind. Parking up (free) outside the course, I began to search my *Racing Post* for anything which might have something left in the tank after a slog around Hexham's undulating course. Within fifteen minutes, five horses had leapt from the form guide and my optimism was rising. I stepped out from the car and headed for the entrance, my head bent against the wind while stinging rain beat into my chilled face.

Yet even in these conditions, it's obvious that Hexham lies in a truly idyllic setting. In every direction, rolling Northumberland fells dominate the landscape and despite only being five minutes from Hexham's town centre, the only signs of life are the small farms clinging to the hillsides. Unfortunately, the exterior of the racecourse buildings don't generate the same impression. From the car park, you are faced with a rag-bag of single-storey buildings dominated at the centre by what looks like a giant grey council house. But once inside, the picture changes.

If you've ever holidayed in the North Wales folly of Portmeirion, you'll feel at home in Hexham. The facilities are made up of a collection of beach huts painted in various hues of green, blue and yellow. Feel miserable in these surroundings and you've got a serious depressive illness. The whole venue invites you to come and have fun, to relax, to go with the Northumberland flow. What I had assumed was a giant council house turned out to be the Jim Ramshaw Stand built in 1998. Jim Ramshaw was (and maybe still is) chairman of Federation Brewery and I suspect the architect's senses had been dulled by a few pints of his best bitter.

Perhaps because of the exposed position of Hexham racecourse, the stand is completely enclosed and, apart from large picture windows, offers no outside viewing areas. The two bars, however, are extremely well laid out and whoever chose the magnificent 'Curlew' carpets should be headhunted by Newcastle racecourse. (I am only just recovering from the horrors of Newcastle's Gosforth Park Suite.) I just wish the exterior of the building wasn't so square and grey. The contrasting facilities at Hexham belong to the same family, yet remind me of an old friend with twin daughters. One had ambitions to be a colourful actress, whereas the other daughter devoted her whole life to becoming a grey assistant bookkeeper in the local town hall.

Does this mean I'm being critical of Hexham? Not really. If anything, I probably picked on Jim Ramshaw's stand because the rest of the place is such an undiluted pleasure. From the council house, the land drops away steeply towards the course, the bank terraced like a Tuscan vineyard with white bench seats scattered across the lawns. The landscape from here is truly breathtaking, the whole of the course clearly visible as it sits in a natural bowl, well below the viewing banks.

It was from this position that John Scott's advice began to pay dividends. In the first race, Noshinannikin tucked himself into fourth place, popped over the third last and simply waited for the leaders to run out of steam. Tony Dobbin was easing his mount as they crossed the line and I was off to a good start, with a 5-1 winner. Needless to say, it didn't last, but I felt that all my selections at least gave themselves a chance. Unfortunately, in the next race, I failed to spot the most obvious winner of the afternoon but it at least confirmed the way to read form at Hexham. Even more unfortunate is that my selection, Triggerfish, jumped the last with a four-length lead, while the winner was lying a distant third. To an audible gasp, Dook's Delight won by a clear ten lengths, eating up the ground as the others paid the price for stretching out along the stamina-sapping back straight. It had been a two-mile, four-furlong chase. Dook's Delight proved to be the only animal to have previously landed the money in a three-mile, three-furlong contest. Next time I'll get it right.

Whether you back the winner or a loser, you'll still enjoy the racing at Hexham. If one description sums it up, it's the general feeling of intimacy. The water jump is in clear view of the stands and the finishing straight is a separate spur which bypasses earlier fences but brings the horses very close to the cheering punters. If you really want to get involved, drop down to the course and walk along the rails to the end of the finishing straight, opposite the Shire Bar. At this point the course turns inward and allows the public a stunning head-on view of the contestants taking the last fence and being driven out to the line.

But if I was to suggest one spot to set up camp at Hexham, it would have to be the paddock. Even from this small sloping parade ring the course is still visible. At its back lies the Bramble Tote Bar, a building which appears to have been transported from days of Empire when a chap could hire a native to waft a fan for three rupees – and well before chicken tikka masala had become a traditional English dish. Yet this still isn't the high point.

Without doubt, Hexham's jewel in the crown is to be found at the far side of the paddock. Here you'll find the ten saddling boxes with a unique covered viewing area which backs onto the parade ring. Punters crowd into here for shelter, warmth and the transmission of racing stories. It's almost more National Hunt than Kelso's 'chicken hutch' but has the added bonus that you are able to watch the parading runners in all weather conditions. Cross over to the other side of the paddock, look back, and you'll be faced with a row of faces peering out from the darkness like an audience at Shakespeare's Globe theatre. As most races I've witnessed end up as a tragedy in one act, there's something highly appropriate about this theatrical layout.

Still trying to find another winner after my early success, I sat outside the Shire Bar, sipping tea and thumbing through my rain-soaked racecard.

'Noo then, bonny lad,' piped up a voice at my side. (Before you accuse me of fiction, that's exactly what he said.) 'Nice spot for a bit o' crack,' he added.

'I'm not a Roman,' I answered instinctively.

'Eh?'

'Backing winners?' I asked quickly to avoid further explanation.

'Just the one.'

'Noshinannikin?'

'Aye. Easy money.'

'Me too.'

One of the great attractions of racing is that bonds are so easily formed. We chatted away like long lost friends, edging around the usual mundane topics while listening carefully for any hint of some good information. He bemoaned the performance of the jockey who had (he claimed) cost him a winner in the last race.

'More life in door nail. Couldn't ride a northern bus,' he groaned, yet with good humour.

For some reason we began to talk about the price of property in the North-East. I have long considered selling my meagre hovel in the south and using the money to buy three mansions in Northumberland. My companion even offered to sell me his own house.

'Nice, is it?' I asked.

'Nah. Usual. Two up. Two down. Outside lavvy. Been tryin' to sell it fah yarrs.'

'No luck?'

'Council found out. Weren't too 'appy, like.'

And that's Hexham. Friendly, warm and always a tale to tell. Not to be outdone, I returned the man's story with my own. Two days before, I had cheered in Jim Crowley as he fired in a 16-1 winner, only to find that my celebrations were premature.

'Crowley's in the next,' said my companion.

'Why not?' I smiled in return.

Despite not having been on a racecourse for almost a year, Sister Gale strode around the paddock with ears pricked and a chest full of muscle. In a rush of blood I decided this was the one. All form considerations went out of the window. Sister Gale was out of Strong Gale and the wind was now so strong that the housewives of Hexham must have been using metal clamps to keep their washing on the line. It was a sign, an irrational pointer to fortune. I watched closely as she left the paddock, the brown sack number cloths strewn across the paddock now taking off like a flight of startled birds.

Looking back, the result was inevitable and the usual Hexham story. Sister Gale was the only horse in the race with form over three miles. Jim Crowley nosed her in front on the line at a starting-price of 5-1 and 7-1 on the Tote. I hadn't quite recouped my missed opportunity at Newcastle but had gone a long way to laying the ghost. Hexham is a must for National Hunt junkies such as myself.

Postscript: Thanks John, Bill (1) and Bill (2) for your enjoyable company at Hexham Golf Club. Special thanks to my partner, Bill 1, who played so well I might just as well have carried his bag and left my own clubs in the car boot. And a note to all members of Hexham Golf Club. Do not play any of these bandits for money. You'll love their company but you'll make more profit with a day at the races.

CHAPTER TWENTY-EIGHT

HUNTINGDON

'It's off!' were the first words which greeted me as I pulled onto the rain-sodden car park.

'It's what?' I replied.

'Off, mate. Not a chance of them running on this ground.'

He was the sort of know-all you dread being teamed up with at a pub quiz night – full of certainty and invariably wrong. I could feel my car sinking into the mud as we spoke and carefully manoeuvred my vehicle as close to a shingle path as possible, desperately trying to remember whether it was front or rear wheel drive. Too embarrassed to ask my advisor if he happened to know the answer, I tossed a coin. It came down tails. Rear wheel drive.

I reversed so that my back wheels were on the path and then headed for the nearest course official.

'Any chance?' I asked in a pleading tone.

'Bit wet, but we're running,' he answered cheerily.

My relief must have been obvious. I had driven for almost two hours through torrential rain and had picked four certain winners from the morning paper. If you're driving from the south up the A1, don't expect too much guidance. In a 50-mile stretch, the genius who organizes signposts offers you only two indications that you're heading for Huntingdon. Perhaps there was more help for motorists when John Major was in power, but they now seem to bathe the town in the same obscurity as their ex-prime minister. The great fear was that I was going to end up in Peterborough, which seemed to have a signpost every 500 yards. I've nothing against the town, but if Slough hadn't existed, John Betjeman would probably have devoted his literary life to Peterborough's demolition.

On the advice of an article in a recent edition of *Rambler's Weekly*, I attempted to avoid the flooded areas by heading for the high ground. This proved to be a fruitless task. Huntingdon has about as many contours as a Test match strip at the Oval and it would be easier to find a hill in the middle of a pancake. And talking of food, if you're a fast food junkie, head for Huntingdon. You could arrive as an anorexic and leave with a weight problem. Pizza, crusty sandwiches, hog roast, a delightfully named Mr Dombey's Baked Potato, a deli bar, seafood and champagne bar – and even a cheese stall. To top it all, a noodle and stir fry bar – its aromatic delights served by an authentic eastern beauty. In a state of complete confusion, I bought my usual Mars Bar and promised myself a good tuck in once my first winner had romped home.

There proved to be two weaknesses in this strategy. Firstly (and as the afternoon proved), I was incapable of winning a prize in a one-ticket raffle, my racing certainties (will I ever learn?) handling the heavy going about as well as a ballerina in hobnailed boots. Secondly, I appeared to suffer a rapid loss of appetite as soon as I opened the racecard. Someone had thoughtfully named the opening two-mile hurdle 'The Pussy Pie Birthday Novices' Hurdle

Race'. Depending on the nature of your imagination, you can take this however you like and I've no intention of dredging the various possibilities. As far as I was concerned it meant only one thing. Cats.

As someone who sneezes even when I see a tin of cat food, this was not a good omen and I'd no intention of treating myself to one of Mr Dombey's baked potatoes or a crusty sandwich, only to find a feline paw waving back at me. Pussy Pie may well be some sort of Cambridgeshire delicacy, but I was having none of it. I retreated quickly and headed for the main stand. This in itself can prove to be a dangerous action. As you move from the parade ring area onto the front of the course, you're shepherded under a fairly narrow tunnel. Perhaps the nervousness of the possible cat cuisine had put a spring in my step but I must have missed the iron girder by about a millimetre. If you're over six foot, find an alternative route or you risk, at worst, decapitation or, at best, an involuntary lobotomy.

Whoever designed the collection of buildings at Huntingdon must never have encountered the words 'acute angle' in their school mathematics. Everything is either rectangular or square and appears to have been built by a four-year-old who's just been given a Lego set. The colour scheme doesn't help either – a mixture of pallid greys, which gives the impression that the main stand was built in five stages by ten different builders. And I thought this was bad enough until I saw the hospitality suite, which contains eight private boxes. If I fork out for a private box, I expect a bit more than plastic seats and acres of chipboard painted in a dingy blue. The racecard was advertising these boxes at half-price for the next two meetings, which seemed to be as useful an idea as selling cut price statues of the Madonna and Child on a Beirut high street.

Undeterred, I wandered off to have another bet on my next sure thing. I had spotted a bookie who uses the pseudonym 'The Asparagus Kid' and felt that this culinary reference might be something of an omen. Why he chose this odd name, I'll never know, as he appeared to have as much in common with the delicacy of asparagus as tungsten steel does with a pink blancmange. But he kindly took my money on a 50-1, ex-point-to-pointer, who sadly struggled in third in a seven-horse field.

At least I had the pleasure of seeing Collier Bay romp home without my money on board. A wet January afternoon and the chance to see an ex-champion hurdler, who I remember giving Alderbrook a good seeing to in 1996. And that's the thing about Huntingdon. For all my misgivings, it always seems to give the occasional punter the opportunity to see at least one class act making its competitors look inferior. Head up the stairs to the Gifford Bar and you'll find many pictures of old heroes such as One Man, Dublin Flyer and Remittance Man. But don't look out for Molsum, my third good thing, which disappeared without trace after one circuit of a two-mile, five-furlong hurdle. It wasn't going well.

I immediately sought solace in the Steve Smith-Eccles Bar which sits on the ground floor of the main stand. Like its namesake it didn't quite live up to expectations. What do you expect from a bar that's named after a jockey with a double-barrelled name, who I always thought would have gained more success as a permanently tanned, ski slope gigolo? Having said that, I was always a great fan, but convinced that to become so smooth he must have been sandpapered at birth. Sadly the bar itself doesn't share these characteristics and is more reminiscent of a run-down New York jazz club, with velveteen booths and shady corners. Woody Herman might have liked it but I didn't and I returned to the steps of the Gifford Bar.

Look out for a sign at the base of the stairwell which shows the depth of flooding when the Alconbury Brook burst its banks in April 1998. Huntingdon must qualify as the only course in the country which once boasted an indoor swimming pool. As I hadn't brought my trunks and given the way the water was beginning to rise, I hurried up the steps to find a good single malt.

The Gifford Bar has everything the Steve Smith-Eccles Bar fails to deliver. A deep pile carpet. Comfortable seats. A view. And what a view. The panoramic window looks out over the whole course, giving you a sight of almost every fence and hurdle. It's a truly spectacular position to view the racing – but not really my cup of tea. Watching any sport from behind a sheet of glass can sanitize the whole experience. I watched the fourth race from here, a truly thrilling three-mile chase, in which Graham Bradley came to the last with a five-length lead. Sadly his mount, Selatan, hadn't read the script and decided to try to jump the fence without bothering to let its legs leave the ground. Bad decision.

But I saw it all and felt nothing. No roar. No thudding hooves. No smell of mud. Not a single shriek from a suicidal punter who'd just remortgaged their house and had been one fence away from parking a new Mercedes in the drive. Forget the cosy bars and plate glass windows. If you go to Huntingdon, get out onto the course and lean on those rails. You're so close to the turf that if you were to sneak a riding crop onto the course and your selection was in a tight finish, you could probably give it a quick smack and persuade it to find half a length.

And it's this aspect which (despite my earlier bitching) made me warm towards this flat Cambridgeshire course. There's a real chance to get a true feel of racing, on a fast galloping course which rewards brave jumpers and jockeys who are one hedge short of a fence. This feel even extends to the paddock, a surprisingly large oval which sits at the back of the main Grandstand. Unfortunately there's no tree in the middle, which robbed me of the chance to make yet another failed identification. If the authorities get in touch, I'll bring my spade and a sapling oak to the next meeting and make a very short speech about my arboreal knowledge.

The real treat in the paddock is to watch the horses leave for the course. They are funnelled down a narrow course straight past the entrance to an outside lavvy. At the risk of arrest, I spent a considerable time observing a number of women entering this facility. On at least two occasions I witnessed them exit the toilet oblivious to the approach of three tons of thoroughbred horse flesh, all primed to jump fences but unable to handle the obstacle of a woman acting like a suffragette at the 1913 Derby.

Time was against me by now and I hadn't yet enjoyed the delights of the centre course. It was closed, flooded by the broken banks of the Alconbury Brook. I could just see the small collection of inevitably square and rectangular buildings peeking above the surface like a shy whale. I never got a close look, but was informed by the gate man that the cafeteria sells nice sandwiches, good strong tea and life jackets for women and children.

My usual £30 total stake was already gone and I prepared to beat the retreat. Passing by the rail bookies, I suddenly noticed that at least half of them were sporting sun tans. Sun tans in the middle of January! If you're ever unsure who's making the real money in racing, check your bookie's skin tone between October and April. It's a dead giveaway. My friend, the Asparagus Kid, was actually peeling – and you don't get that from a bargain weekend in Bognor. Instead, I was tempted by a very pale-faced Tote lady, who looked like she hadn't seen a sunbeam since 1976. A saving bet on Yankee Lord in the fifth race would at least add some spice to my journey home.

By the time I returned to my car the water was lapping at the tyre walls. I gave a slightly superior smile to the man parked next to me, who looked like he could be stuck in the ground until the next frost. With my rear wheels firmly planted on the shingled path, I began to reverse. The front wheels spun like a yo-yo on speed, going into the ground faster than a squaddie digging a trench.

'Front wheel drive,' I said sheepishly to my neighbour, who looked on with obvious satisfaction.

My wheels finally gripped the pathway and released me from further embarrassment, but I was caught in a queue of traffic negotiating the flooded road. Reaching across to the glove compartment I located the coin that had decided my fate. I tossed it in the air five times. It came down tails every time. I opened the window and hurled it into Alconbury Brook. Who needs unlucky money?

Postscript: Halfway down the A1, I tuned into the sports bulletin just in time to catch the latest racing results. 'Huntingdon 3.30. First, number two, Yankee Lord, 8-1.' Funny old game, racing.

CHAPTER TWENTY-NINE

KELSO

I owe a great deal to that aggressive little Austrian painter with the theatrical square moustache. It was he who first introduced the people's car, a more refined version of which now acts as my means of transport. I have no moral reservations about driving a German car and if anybody from the company would like to sponsor my next book with wheelbarrows full of euros – please don't hesitate.

Forty-eight hours before my visit to Kelso, I had left Carlisle racecourse high on profit but low in spirits. Fortunately, I chose to cross into Scotland via the A7, a fast but winding road which takes you through the Teviots, a journey with scenery so stunning it could renew optimism in a man who hasn't backed a winner for six months. Unfortunately my trip also coincided with the decision by a deranged shepherd to drive his flock across the A7 at the precise moment I exited a blind corner. Without some fine German technology there would have been no report from Kelso and a sudden decrease in the Scottish sheep population.

With appropriate symbolism, I dined on lamb chops that evening in the delightful town of Berwick-upon-Tweed, which is only half an hour's drive from Kelso. The next morning I approached the racecourse with some trepidation, fearing that Kelso may well be another small agricultural course which, like Carlisle, had seen better days. I pulled into the free car park, sniffed the sharp Scottish air and headed through the turnstiles.

My usual method of attack is to wander aimlessly around the course and facilities, just to get a feel of what's on offer. Normally, within a few minutes, you become aware of a structure to the racecourse, a sense of order, an understanding of the course's logic. Half an hour after entering Kelso, I was approached by a member of staff who kindly offered me help. I was obviously displaying signs of confusion, standing by the paddock rail with a bewildered expression and an empty notebook. I had concluded that to characterize Kelso was going to be about as easy as describing a bowl of spaghetti. (It's a round dish with squiggly bits of wheat – or something like that.) The fact is that I love spaghetti and as it turned out, Kelso proved to be just as appetizing.

A number of signs around the course display the message 'Kelso – The Friendly Course'. I've seen such notices at other courses, though more than often they amount to no more than a platitude, laying claim to a promise which isn't kept. Kelso, on the other hand, fulfils its promise from the moment you step onto the course. Having at this stage covered more than three-quarters of my around Britain visits, I probably hadn't encountered such a cheerful bunch of people, everyone of whom seemed pleased to welcome me like a long lost son.

Still standing by the paddock rail, I caught the end of a nearby conversation.

'Clerk's happy,' said the anonymous official. 'Sun's gone

in.' This raised two interesting questions. Why was the clerk happy? Most clerks of the course I've run into usually look highly stressed and carry a look of impending doom. And how many people do you know who are more content when the sun goes in than when it comes out? Not willing to shirk my investigative responsibilities, I stepped forward and posed the questions. I received a response which matched the affable treatment I had received at the main gate.

'First time at Kelso?'

'First time,' I affirmed.

'Come on. I'll show you the home straight. Then you'll know why the clerk's happy.'

My short guided tour soon led to an understanding of the clerk's contentment. The course is essentially an eleven-furlong oval but with some fairly tight bends, the hurdles course cutting inside the chase course about half a furlong from the stands. There are no major ascents on the course, though the run-in from both the last hurdle and testing final fence is an energy-sapping two furlongs on steadily rising ground. After completing a circuit, horses are asked to jink out to the right and head for the winning line via a one-and-a-half-furlong elbow. If this is confusing, think of the Grand National finish. Many a horse popping over the last has been caught on that Aintree elbow and Kelso proved to be no different. But here the comparison ends, as the clerk of Aintree doesn't mind the sun shining. Get that big orange globe low in a winter sky at Kelso and some tricky decisions have to be made.

My tour guide went on to tell me that if there's no cloud cover, jumping any of the obstacles in the straight is rather like coming around the bend of a road and meeting a lorry with its headlights on full beam. If there was a flock of sheep in your way, you'd never see them. On more than one occasion the Kelso officials have been forced to omit all hurdles and fences facing west and turn a National Hunt contest into a predominantly Flat race. If you're a student of form, it's advisable to check the Kelso weather forecast very carefully.

I had spent my time over breakfast working out my betting strategy for the meeting. Given the condition of Carlisle, I had assumed that while the going was officially good, the ground was bound to be testing. Wrong again. This Scottish border town didn't look as if it had seen a drop of rain in a fortnight and I had no idea how taxing the two-furlong finish might be. I filed my *Racing Post* in the bin and decided to let fate decide my success.

Two days previously, I had engaged in a long discussion with a well-known jockey and decided that this must be an omen. I was also convinced that God was on my side. The sash window in my Berwick hotel bedroom had a broken cord and every time I attempted to slide it open, the heavy frame threatened to guillotine my fingers. Happily, I still have use of all ten digits thanks to my discovery of why every hotel supplies its clients with a Gideon Bible. Don't read it, just wedge it under the window and pray that it will hold.

Following the rides of my jockey acquaintance unfortunately proved fruitless – though he did ride brilliantly to land a couple of place bets. On both occasions he led over the last but found his horse unable to stay those two furlongs up the rising finishing stretch. If I was to visit Kelso again (which I will), I think I'd be looking for a real stayer – even on good going.

By the end of the third race, I was beginning to make sense of Kelso's facilities. Perhaps the easiest way to clarify the confusing mishmash of buildings is to think of the main stand as the hub of Kelso's wheel. This 19th-century stand is unique, a grey stone construction which contains a winding staircase up to the wonderful viewing position on the roof.

To raise you even higher, the management supply a roughly constructed removable wooden stand with five tiers, and even in early November it was already scattered with grit and sand. The night before my visit, the temperature had fallen to minus three degrees. Scottish winters start early and a biting easterly wind was already tempting punters into scarves and gloves.

Halfway up the fifty-nine-step staircase (I'm sad enough to have counted them), you'll find the Doody Room with a coal fire big enough to heat a Scottish laird's country seat. The fireplace was on such a scale that a line of eight punters could quite happily engage in communal bottom-warming exercises. Once the blood is flowing in your veins, step out into the paddock area at the back of the stands and you'll find that Kelso has a lot more to offer. There's no shortage of watering holes, and while one or two could do with being spruced up there are one or two offerings which shouldn't be missed.

The rather bare and small sloping paddock is sited at the back of the stands. Viewing is excellent, though the area is so restricted in size that stable staff have to queue to enter the traffic jam which occurs in any field with more than ten runners. Tucked away in the corner is a tiny shack of a restaurant, run by the redoubtable Marje and Rosemary Bennet. I hope they're still there, as for under a tenner you can get a three-course lunch, including a starter of cheesy haggis balls with redcurrant jelly. And if you think that's attractive, wait until you see the waitresses.

Marje and Rosemary appeared to have dressed them up for a Hattie Jacques lookalike contest. If you recall the matron in *Carry on Doctor*, you'll know what I mean. I'd have my temperature taken in Marje and Rosemary's diner any day.

Look towards the course from this position and you'll catch sight of another Kelso treat. I won't call it a hutch because they've beaten me to it. If I was to advise you to take a drink anywhere at Kelso it would be in the Chicken Hutch, a tiny hut tucked between a small stand and the modern corporate boxes. Hot toddies seemed to be the order of the day and even the Scottish pies with dubious contents proved to have no after-effects. The beauty of this place, however, is that it feels like it's got National Hunt racing oozing through its timbered frame – and the buzz is the equal of an Irish bar at Cheltenham.

Although Kelso is a minor course, the layout is so illogical that each corner turned seems to reveal a fresh view and a new experience. All right, it has got one or two sections I'd take a bulldozer to (e.g. the 'new' Younger Stand is out of keeping) but it would be nit-picking not to sing its praises. Old hippies might call it good vibes – and this is no more evident than in the winners' enclosure at the back of the old stone stand.

Its probably one of the most rustic settings I've witnessed, the winner and placed horses squeezed into small stalls hewn out of rough timber. But this adds to, rather than detracts from, the sense of fun and dismissal of formality which is all too often evident on many race-courses. Owners, trainers and officials really seemed to be enjoying uninhibited pleasure – none more so than the announcer and master of ceremonies. On two occasions, and midway through his congratulatory speech to the connections, this trilbied man collapsed in a fit of giggles. And the crowd loved it. If the Kelso Players are looking for a lead in their next Christmas panto – here's your man. Courses south of the border could learn a great deal from this natural performer and the Jockey Club should invite him to don his fighting kilt and invade England.

What's certain is that the English trainers are happy to plunder the Borders. Only two of the six races went to Scottish trainers and the Kelso regulars must tire of marauding Englishmen. The late Gordon Richards spent years pillaging Kelso from his Greystoke hideaway in Cumbria – and, on the evidence of my visit, his son, Nicky Richards, intends to follow the family tradition.

I have only one major complaint about Kelso racecourse. Three days before my visit my old watch ticked its last tick and I hadn't had the chance to replace it. Next time I visit Kelso could the authorities put a large clock on the top of the Duke of Roxburgh's old stone stand? I had to make my son's parents' evening at 8.45 and only made it with a minute to spare. I would have held the racecourse management totally responsible if I'd missed it. My son would also have been denied the severe beating he received later that evening.

Postscript: The 300-mile journey home was entirely sheep free.

CHAPTER THIRTY

KEMPTON PARK

Leaf your way through the pages of this guide to British racecourses and you'll soon become aware that many of my observations have been inspired by various idiosyncratic aunts. Some still tread the boards of Women's Institute whist drives but most have long since gone, leaving only a memory and the lingering smell of lavender. But who is Aunty Sue? This woman who, two days before my visit to Kempton, was seen wandering around Tattersalls with a notebook, sharp pencil and a stern expression? The quest to discover her identity dominated my whole day at this West London course.

Kempton Park forms part of a racing triumvirate, which includes Epsom and Sandown. These three premier courses lie within easy reach of the M25 and, though all managed by United Racecourses, compete for a similar catchment area of punters. As you may already be aware, I have as much interest in Epsom as I do in knitting, though Sandown still remains high on my 'A' list.

Of the three, Kempton is probably the most accessible as it's no more than a stone's throw away from the eastern end of the M3. Train services also run from Waterloo and almost drop you at the front entrance. Whichever way you travel, the approach to the gates will take you through the car park, a large tarmac area attended by rather over-officious men in orange jackets emblazoned with the words 'Traffic Marshall'. Obviously recruited from retired railway staff, they order cars into position using the shrill and rather aggressive sound of metal whistles.

The first thing you will notice is that Kempton is no dinosaur. There's a fresh and lively feel about the whole place, none more so than the main stand built in 1997, its giant tubular supports angled sharply against the skyline. Go round to the course side and you'll see a roof with a sweeping curve like a surfer's dream wave. If you've ever visited Wolverhampton's Dunstall Park, you're in for an attack of the déjà views. If the restaurant at Wolverhampton looks like a giant edition of *University Challenge*, Kempton's Jubilee restaurant seems to be a lunchtime sitting of the European parliament.

Whoever designed Wolverhampton must have been on to a good thing. All they had to do was grab the original blueprint, cross out the words Dunstall Park, substitute Kempton Park – and then flog the plans to United Race-courses. Nice work if you can get it.

But similarities stop at the architecture, as Kempton's really in a different class. As yet (but see sad Postscript) no all-weather course here, no floodlights, no AstroTurf, dusky paddock. Instead you will be offered a turf course which throughout the year hosts a full jumps and Flat programme. The course is pear-shaped (three bends), right-handed and without any noticeable inclines. Chatting to a fellow punter before my visit, he suggested that Kempton's circuit was rarely testing and any horse who could get two miles round somewhere like Chepstow or Towcester would probably stay three miles around Kempton. It proved to be very profitable advice.

Who wins in the Sandown v Kempton contest, it's hard to say. It's certainly a short-head finish. Maybe Sandown's got a little more style, though it is built on a much grander scale. Kempton, on the other hand, feels more compact and the parade ring and saddling enclosure is hard to fault. The paddock and horsebox areas cover an immense patch of ground, with lawns that would have had Capability Brown drooling over their presentation.

Mature trees litter the otherwise flat arena; whilst at the southern end of the paddock, Philip Blacker's admirable life-sized statue of Desert Orchid holds court over the lesser mortals who parade the ring. Unusually, the statue bears no plaque. We are expected to know what it is, who it is and what he achieved. That really is star quality.

I was fortunate to witness Desert Orchid win his third King George VI Chase on a cold December day in 1989. I doubt any other horse has ever made Kempton's sturdy fences look so much like pony club hurdles. On that occasion, I was part of a heaving Christmas crowd, each punter carrying at least 10 lbs overweight from their holiday excesses. Ten years later, on an unusually warm November day, the crowd was probably little more than 2,000 and racing was devoted to a new crop of hurdlers and chasers. So early in the jumps season, trainers have yet to declare their hands, leaving their big guns muzzled until the winter rain softens the turf.

But the beauty of such meetings is that you'll always see at least one future star tucked quietly away amongst a group of no-hope novices. The trick is to find them before they start to appear on the top of the bill carrying an odds-on starting-price. After drawing a blank in the first race (I changed my mind – don't do it! – and missed a 10-1 winner), I crossed the course to get a close-up view of the finishing fence. It's quite a trek, as Kempton has three distinct circuits. Unfortunately the Flat course has prime position on the outer rail, which rather detaches punters from the action. There are no facilities in the centre course, though it's worth the effort if only for one race.

From this position it's possible to take in the panorama of the whole venue. Kempton operates a three-tier ticket system – premier enclosure for diners and the top deck of the main stand; paddock enclosure for general access; and a Silver Ring ticket with access to an old stand, a plastic cafeteria and a snug little bar called the Kempton Arms, which boasts old wooden beams and a mock coal fire. Seen from the centre of the course it soon becomes plain that Kempton is imploding, all the facilities being sucked into the northern end of the course with the power of a black hole swallowing up a dying star. The old Tattersalls area and Silver Ring is falling into disrepair, numerous old Tote windows shedding their paint like a snake changing its skin. The new stand has become the centre of Kempton's universe.

Just before the race began, I got into conversation with a small bunch of workers who repair the fences and heel in the turf after the hooves have dug into the ground.

'Bit of a mess over there,' I observed, pointing towards the crumbling Silver Ring.

'Aunty Sue will sort it out,' offered one of the workers.

'Aye. Aunty Sue will fix it,' confirmed another.

'Aunty who?' I asked.

Before I could gain an answer, I was ordered away from the rail to make way for the convoy of speeding cars and ambulances which follow every race. By the time I returned, the three men had gone onto the course and were out of earshot. The mystery of Aunt Sue had begun – as had my change of fortune.

Hang 'Em Out To Dry (3-1) cleared the last fence with ease and strolled in by almost ten lengths. Was this a star in the making? Maybe so. Neither by breeding nor cost should this eight-year-old enjoy any claim to fame. It had originally been bought for £300, had been off the course for nearly a year, had needed oxygen after two of its races and yet had already produced over £9,000 in prize money. Given some dry winters, I felt he might treble this money in the next three years. Flat racing breaks hearts and bank balances, while National Hunt always gives a small owner a chance of living out their dreams.

No Language Please (second at 40-1), River Bay (7-4) and Fours Are Wild (10-1) followed in quick succession. What they all had in common was reasonable form over shorter distances at more testing courses. Such information may prove my undoing, as I'm never likely to get a decent price on a Kempton winner until this book has hit the remainder list.

Flush with winnings after Hang 'Em Out To Dry, I made my way back to the main enclosures. The crossing point lies near an enormous blue dovecote in which stewards lay eggs or watch the five-furlong chute which acts as Kempton's straight five furlongs. As usual, celebrations amounted to a Mars Bar and a cup of weak tea, though Kempton offers anything from the three-course Jubilee restaurant to plain old fish and chips in the bowels of the spacious paddock betting hall.

Alternatively, simple fast food caravans are discreetly parked out of sight by the Silver Ring transfer gate. At the time of my visit there was no more than a £4 difference between premier enclosure tickets and those for the paddock. On balance I think the extra is worth paying. The second-floor bar is deep pile carpeted, classy but unpretentious and gives you access to a wonderful balcony looking directly over the paddock.

It was from here that I scanned the crowd, searching for anyone who had the look of an Aunty Sue. There were plenty of stern expressions but no notebooks. For an instant, I thought I had solved the riddle, as I caught sight of a figure with all the right criteria. I was just about to step forward and scream '*J'accuse!*' when I realized I was staring at my own reflection in a nearby window. I had the stern face. I had the notebook. I also had the wrong gender. No-one has ever called me Aunty and got away with it.

I had almost given up my quest as a lost cause when I glanced down to the tree-lined parade which separates the stand and paddock. It was a time in our history when the BSE war had just been declared on France, when posters were appearing on street corners with pictures of General Kitchener demanding 'Your Country Needs You To Eat Beef'. National tension had been rising for weeks with much face slapping and challenges of duels at the entrance to the Channel Tunnel. It was strings of garlic or Yorkshire puddings. Choose your weapon.

A deluded entrepreneur, in a corrugated Citroën van, had decided that he could bridge this diplomatic crisis by attempting to sell French baguettes filled with slices of British beef. If nothing else, I admired the effort. But business was poor. Punters approached nervously, torn between patriotism for the beef and their aversion to the baguettes. Unable to square the circle, they passed by, satisfied that they had not betrayed their country and unified in their rejection of the enemy.

The beef baguette seller looked depressed but was being given solace by a rather smart lady who seemed to be commiserating with his plight. She had a stern look. She carried a notebook. And a sharp pencil.

'Aunty Sue!' I shouted over the balcony. 'Is it you?'

A fellow punter edged away as if he'd just encountered Kempton's village idiot. I rushed for the stairs.

The next ten minutes made me feel like the frustrated hero of an Alfred Hitchcock movie, vainly searching for the villain in a crowded city. At every turn I caught a glimpse, a shadowy figure turning into a doorway, familiar shoes climbing a half-covered stairway, a flash of a skirt disappearing around a nearby tree. But Hitchcock heroes don't have to give up because their wife's at work and they've got to get home and cook dinner. I headed for the exit.

'Goodnight,' offered the gateman. 'Had a good day?'

I turned to thank him when over his shoulder but in the far distance, I caught my last sight of Aunty Sue.

'Who's that woman?' I asked urgently, pointing over to the paddock.

'Who?'

'There. There,' I pleaded urgently and pointing once more.

'You mean Aunty Sue?' he responded with a smile.

'It is her! Who *is* that woman?' I demanded.

'Mrs Ellen,' he replied. 'Mrs Susan Ellen. We all call her Aunty Sue.'

'Why for God's sake?'

'She fixes things. Fixes everything really. Just like all good aunties.'

'But who the hell is she?'

'You don't know?'

'Tell me. *Please* tell me.'

'The MD, that's who. Managing Director of United Racecourses. Got her finger on more pulses than a heart surgeon.'

The mystery was solved. The tension drained from my body as I engaged in yet another battle with the M25. I suppose if I'd really managed to speak to Mrs Susan Ellen, I'd probably have stuttered like a man with his mouth full of a beef baguette. But if I'd summoned up some courage, I think I may have told her that she's doing a good job and that Kempton is a fine racecourse, which might get onto my 'A' list – that's if she introduces a simple two-enclosure system or gives Silver Ring punters access to the paddock. But Aunty Sue fixes things. Aunty Sue sorts things out. She'll make all us little punters happy – 'cos that's what real aunties do.

Postscript I:

Dear Aunty Sue,

Sorry I missed you at Kempton. Stick with it. Hang on to Sandown. But ditch Epsom. It's an overgrown white elephant.

Regards,

One of your many nephews – Stephen.

Postscript II: There are some nasty rumours flying about that Kempton is being tempted into all-weather racing and the ditching of National Hunt racing. Are they completely mad? Have they lost the plot? My Boxing Days are very precious to me. Cold turkey sandwiches; crumbly mince pies and screaming at the television as the field battles through the King George VI chase. Adopt this polytrack nonsense and I'll never forgive you. If the rumours turn out to be true, please consider the words 'bananas' and Kempton to be completely synonymous.

Postscript III: Rumours partially confirmed. In 2006 Kempton (aka 'Bananas') became 'Europe's premier Floodlit All-Weather Track'. Is there something they know about the effects of global warming on Sunbury-on-Thames, Middlesex, that the rest of us have missed? The adoption of all-weather racing is as good a strategy as Napoleon's decision to take his winter holidays in Moscow. The people who backed this crazy scheme should be banished to St Helena and imprisoned in a room with arsenic-laced wallpaper.

At least some members of the decision-making body agreed to retain the turf track on the outside of the all-weather. My Boxing Days are safe. Cry crumbly mince pies and King George VI chase! I hereby reduce their sentence to five years in any open prison close to Redcar, Yarmouth or Southwell. But I'm still not happy. A surfeit of polytrack and bright lights? I may be proved wrong, but it sounds like an expensive flash in the pan.

The jury's still out

CHAPTER THIRTY-ONE

LEICESTER

The core of my observations on Leicester racecourse revolve around the two central factors of men's toilet activities and the former trainer Jenny Pitman. I hasten to add that, apart from the county of Leicestershire, these two elements have absolutely no connection other than the role they both played in my visit to this Midlands course.

You know when you're nearing the course as all the houses start to indulge in twee, half-timbered facades. Leave the M1 at Junction 21 and then head straight down the A563. This road contains so many houses that it solves the eternal puzzle of where all those people on the motorway find somewhere to sleep at night.

The signposting is good and I drove through the rather grand entrance to be faced with a timber and brick stockade which fronts the north end of the course. Within seconds of parking I was joined by a pair of cars, each containing what I assumed to be a man and his wife. Despite the rain, the women began to busy themselves unloading two large hampers, which wouldn't have disgraced Royal Ascot. The men's one contribution to this impending feast was to relieve themselves against the rear wheel of their respective vehicles.

To be confronted with two Leicestershire members so early in the day came as a bit of a shock, and until I heard them speak, I naturally assumed they were a pair of visiting Belgians. (Emptying the bladder against rear wheels is a national pastime in Belgium.) Worst of all, having completed their task, both men took it on themselves to hand around the sandwiches. You've got to be close friends or have an iron stomach to take lunch in such circumstances.

My appetite now in tatters, I collected my usual club ticket (£13) which included a free racecard. Although a nice touch, this unfortunately contained no plan of the course, which is a must for an occasional punter. Not having been to Leicester before, I had half expected a rather second-class set-up and third-rate facilities. But I was pleasantly surprised. Like many courses, Leicester is trying to improve its image by constructing new grandstands which blend in with the now tired post-war buildings.

I had arrived later than intended and just caught a glimpse of the horses leaving the paddock for the first race. This is a fine grassed oval, with two sycamores (I'm guessing) at its centre and only a short walk from the main stand. Having missed the parade, all that remained was a scattering of number cloths, hastily thrown to the ground as the jockeys mounted. Now deserted, the paddock seemed to be strewn with thirteen dead white doves that had mysteriously fallen out of the trees. It was so poetic, I almost wrote this piece in rhyming couplets.

It's then that I spotted Jenny Pitman, the most famous face in Leicestershire. She was being interviewed by SIS and looked about as tense as my wife's yoga teacher. What is it about this woman that makes middle-aged men want to give her a big cuddle and ask her out for a cup of tea and a round of Marmite toast? If you don't know the answer, I can help. There's a touch of magic, that's all. It's as simple as that. Any woman who looks like everybody's favourite Aunt Gladys and has forgotten more about race-horses than most trainers learn in a lifetime, has got to have something special.

There are four 'must sees' at Leicester and Jenny Pitman's one of them. The first is the weighing room, clearly visible behind the rail which surrounds the small but attractive winners' enclosure. But the best view is gained from the small bar which forms part of the new club building. From the back of this bar you are given a direct sight into the weighing room and a real sense of involvement. You feel like you've reached the inner sanctum instead of being confronted with the secrecy which is more common on most British courses.

From this vantage point you can see the likes of Fitzgerald, McCoy and Llewellyn preparing for racing, their silks hanging loose and dishevelled. Best of all you can see them return, mud-spattered, exhausted, elated, disappointed and drop onto the bouncing metal seat under the intimidating eye of the clerk of the scales. Trainers pace the floor checking the weights and whispering criticism and encouragement. I don't know about you but David Elsworth frightens me to death even through a plate glass window. If you go to Leicester, treat yourself to a day club ticket. It feels like you're really getting something for your money.

The club bar is also worth a look. A plaque greets you as you enter, informing the reader that Leicester racecourse housed the US 80th Airborne Battalion in 1944.

The inscription reads: 'In memory of friendship we shared while preparing to meet our common foe.' They ought to have a replica made for punters to read just before they enter the betting ring below the new Grandstand. This new edifice was opened in 1997 by Frankie Dettori, who had taken a few minutes' break from his day job of jumping off winning Flat horses.

Like most new racecourse buildings I have encountered on my travels, it looks highly reminiscent of the Starship *Enterprise* – apart from being permanently stationary. The interior is a bit of a let-down, both the ground floor betting section and the sitting area above being rather cavernous and indistinct. The restaurant is no more than a cordoned-off space, which suggests it was a bit of a second thought and not really aimed at the serious gourmet. For a man who gets excited by a Mars Bar, this isn't a problem – but there's room for improvement. The view of the course is extremely good, though it shares with Towcester a design which allows the diner's sight to be blocked by people standing against the windows.

What they can all see, however, is my second Leicester 'must'. The finishing straight at this course is one of the best in the country – especially on the chase course. The final fence is truly extraordinary. Constructed about one furlong from the finishing post, this brushwood fence is built in what you could mistake for a disused railway cutting and nestles some ten feet below the level of the hurdles course. It's like watching the Light Brigade charge into the Valley of Death. If you like taking the odd snap, it's definitely worth packing your Box Brownie. You'll rarely get a better chance, as you can get right up to the side of the jump. But if it's blowing a gale and raining, you'll feel very exposed. And it was.

Wet, cold and windswept, I hurried back to the old wooden Grandstand, a blue-painted structure which fits perfectly with the stockade surround. It has the appearance of an old colonial cotton house in *Gone with the Wind*. I'd had two losers so far and, unlike Clark Gable, I did give a damn. In order to give my full attention to the form guide, I popped into the Gentlemen's lavatory. (Not easy to locate at Leicester so plan ahead.) I had just begun to say hello to Armitage Shanks when a voice came from one of the closed cubicles.

'Simon? It's Tom. Yeah. Sarah there?'

There was a pause and the giveaway sounds of a man in mid-flow.

'Sarah? Yeah. No. Yeah. Fontwell. Twenty pounds each-way patent. Nah. Yeah. Yeah.'

I'm no major league punter but even I can work out that this chap was talking what I consider serious money – at my reckoning a sum total of £280. I watched him come out. He was a young man who looked as if he'd have to raid his sister's piggy bank to buy a hamburger. I'll never understand it.

Ten minutes later I'm watching Jenny Pitman greet her latest winner and one which, yet again, hadn't been carrying my £1 each-way. She looked happy. I don't mean happy happy. I mean genuinely excited and content. You get the sense that this woman always got as much fun out of winning a three-mile chase as she did when she won her first gymkhana. And if you wanted to know how to celebrate, you only had to watch this former trainer.

At the back of the old stand lies the Buffet – a quiet cosy little bar, which seems relatively undiscovered. I had retreated here in a desperate search to find a winner in my soggy *Racing Post*. I was closely followed by Mrs Pitman and a small gaggle of friends. Expecting to hear the pop of champagne corks, I glanced round to see the trainer propped on a bar stool with a cigarette in one hand and a cup of tea in the other. That's what I call style.

It must have been some sort of omen, as my luck seemed to change immediately. The next race provided a nice 8-1 winner (thank you, Mick Fitzgerald) and the realization that my cover bet on the Tote placepot was still in the hunt. For my last race, and despite the now torrential rain, I went in search of the course enclosure. It was closed. But don't let this put you off. A quiet word with the gateman proved successful and I shuffled across the heavy mud towards the now disused buildings in the centre of the course. I was told that this area was once packed with racegoers but had gradually become unpopular and been allowed to fall into disrepair. It did however provide my third Leicester 'must'.

Standing proud, yet dishevelled, is a wonderful old brick building fronted by an enormous display board. The black flaking paint waves across the course to the new club stand, almost defying its modern neighbour. In faded lettering you can see the jockeys' names and numbers and an approximate odds contraption, which chunks loudly as the prices change. There was no sign of a human presence, the display changing as if by magic. And best of all was the bell, oddly painted in mustard yellow, which rang out with a shrill peal as each race came under orders. It was as eerie as it must have been when they first discovered the deserted *Mary Celeste*, its bell still ringing as it bobbed up and down on the swell of the tide.

Pitman won again. I'm not going to use her first name as she kept beating my selection. But I was still in the placepot as I strode out of the course to retrieve my car and head off back down the M1. After only thirty minutes, I realized I was running out of petrol and pulled into the first service station. As a precautionary measure I popped into the Gents only to be joined by two businessmen in well-cut suits. We stood silently staring at the wall as nature took its course. A phone began to ring.

'Shit. I knew this would happen!' exclaimed one of the men. He fumbled in his pocket and took the call.

'Hello? Yes. Mrs Fairburn. Good of you to call. Yes. Yes. Friday at the latest.'

His colleague stifled his laughter as he watched his friend maintain his patter with a phone in one hand and . . . you can guess the rest. From what I picked up, he had managed to close the deal on a brand new fitted kitchen before completing his bodily functions. I looked on in admiration. For a second I thought this chap had more style than Jenny Pitman. But really he wasn't even in the same league.

CHAPTER THIRTY-TWO

LINGFIELD

There was a time when bargain hunting in the sales was closely linked to the seasons. An overcoat in the winter sale, a jacket in the spring sale, a shirt in the summer sale, a scarf in the autumn. Life was simple, structured and you always felt you were getting a good deal. Now that sales seem to run for thirteen months of the year, I hardly bother glancing in the shop window. Take a look at the racing page of your daily newspaper and what do you see? Lingfield, Lingfield and more Lingfield. If you take Sundays out of the equation, there's a race meeting at this Surrey course every four days – winter, spring, summer and autumn. I chose the spring for my visit and, like a fool, 1 April.

I only had vague memories of Lingfield, having last visited the course over twenty years ago. I recall a bustle of activity, roaring crowds and sharp-suited city gents with big cars and fat wallets. Maybe it's similar to only remembering sunny days on family holidays but my return shattered all those fragile illusions. The fences have gone and Lingfield now offers only Flat racing – but on two surfaces. The outer ring of this galloping course is traditional turf, though only really used during the summer months.

Sixty per cent of racing at Lingfield is on the all-weather course, a sanded one-mile, two-furlong circuit, which roughly follows the line of the outer grassed course. The effect of this arrangement is that punters are detached from the racing by about 80 yards, robbing them of any sense of involvement. And it was one of those all-weather days.

The first race of the afternoon – a one-mile, two-furlong seller – seemed to sum up this Americanized form of racing. The commentator kindly informed those present (and they were few in number) that for your horse to have a squeak, it must be handily placed at the first tight turn and then hold its position. My selection, Van Gurp, did exactly as instructed, hugging the rail as if it had just fallen in love with white plastic. By the final bend he was in a perfect position to dominate his rivals and push on to the winning line. Fifteen seconds later the chasing pack went past him like a Ferrari overtaking a Reliant Robin, the winner coming from well off the pace and passing at least seven horses in the short straight. So much for local knowledge.

As far as I could see, the only reason for a jockey to make it all from the front is to avoid getting sand kicked in his face. If you'd transferred the race to Sandown or Kempton, punters would have roared the winner in, marvelling at its acceleration and turn of foot. At Lingfield this doesn't happen and Gary Bardwell, the diminutive jockey, would have heard little more than a subdued clapping as he went past the post. The race seemed to produce about as much excitement as a party political broadcast – whatever your political allegiance.

Things may improve with the advent of the recently introduced polytrack. Whilst it's a product which you might expect to find on the shelf of your local DIY store it turns out to be a revolutionary new all-weather surface made up of sand, shredded telephone wire and crushed car tyres, with just a pinch of worn-out windscreen wipers. I doubt it will do much for the atmosphere but the punters' view is certain to improve as horses bounce above the rails like a pack of thoroughbred kangaroos. If you ever spot a Lingfield runner with a name such as Skippy or G'Day Sport, back it immediately – whatever the price.

As it happened, this was my first Flat meeting of the new season and over the winter I'd become accustomed to the normal physique of a jumps jockey. I was now back in the elfin world of the little people, grown men who can walk under a horse without bending over. I've had a theory for some time that the reason most Flat race owners are vertically challenged is that they can at least guarantee that their jockey will look up to them. We all need our egos boosting and I suppose £20,000 per year training fees is money well spent if you've always wanted to be 6' 2".

The winner of the opener was offered for sale at a minimum of 2,500 guineas. The lack of bids came as little surprise, as Saseedo was a poorly bred nine-year-old gelding who had just won his first race in two years. There was also the slight problem that there was no-one present to raise a bidder's finger. The auctioneer talked to himself for two or three minutes without creating any interest whatsoever and his voice seemed about as enthusiastic as a speaking clock.

This low-key atmosphere appears to permeate the whole of the all-weather experience. There were six races, fairly good fields, top-class jockeys and all the betting opportunities you'd expect. But the afternoon had no soul, no edge, no adventure. I had the feeling that the officials were running on automatic, that the jockeys were going through the motions, and that the owners and trainers were treating the racing as no more than another day at the office.

So what's it all for? What is the point of continually running average horses along a synthetic beach for mediocre prize money? If you want the answer, pop into your nearest smoked-filled bookmakers in the middle of the week, a time when inveterate gamblers shuffle through the door, furtively checking the pavement for anyone who might raise an eyebrow and destroy their reputation as a pillar of local society. The Lingfield authorities have long since realized that if the casino is closed there's many a punter who'll happily bet on the proverbial two flies climbing up a wall.

All-weather racing provides the flies, and breeds races faster than your average bluebottle. Who needs a live crowd when TV can supply continuous racing to every bookies in Britain? Perhaps this is the way ahead, the ever growing incidence of absentee supporters, which has become prevalent in all major sports. But if this is an image of the future, I think I'll take up knitting and start attending whist drives.

In a desperate attempt to find excitement, I left the almost empty Lingfield village and crossed the track to watch the next race from the centre course. The one-mile, two-furlong start is just opposite the stands, giving you the chance to watch the runners being loaded up into the stalls and see them flash past the winning post only minutes later.

Due to late withdrawals the field had been reduced to a mind-numbing four runners. The favourite, Gracious Plenty, was being offered at 1-14, despite being ridden by K. Sked, a 5 lb claiming apprentice. This seemed to give the stall handlers a green light for barracking the young jockey as his horse was led into the stalls.

'Never win on this donkey!' quipped one of the handlers. K. Sked (5) smiled a nervous response.

'We've tied his tail to the gates!' announced another. K. Sked (5) let out a child-like giggle but checked for sabotage, just in case it was a serious threat. As the last horse was led in, it kicked out and caught one of the men in a region of great male delicacy.

'I'm perfect for this job,' winced the handler.

'Why's that?' asked the jockey.

'My eyes don't water,' he replied.

Gracious Plenty shot out of the stalls and by the first bend had established a four-length lead. Entering the final straight, this had been extended to almost fifteen lengths and K. Sked (5) was sweating far more than his mount. If they'd done another circuit, I'm sure he'd have lapped the back runners. Needless to say, I had adopted the old ploy of backing the outsider in a four-horse field, a tactic which in the past has produced some rich rewards. On this occasion it turned out to be as sensible as investing my life savings in ostrich farming.

To gain solace, I wandered back onto the main course in search of a reviving beverage. There was plenty of choice. The Lingfield site is made up of a sprawl of buildings offering bars, tea rooms, brasserie, betting halls and private boxes. I headed for the User Friendly Bar which was so user-friendly it was closed. I tried the Marley Stand. Closed. The Champagne Bar wasn't really my cup of tea, though I finally gained success in the Ebor Bar, close to the paddock. The crowd was so small I was served in less time than it takes a course bookie to take your money.

It was a beautiful sunlit spring day, the sort of afternoon you dream about in the wintry depths of February. A small collection of plastic chairs and tables had been placed outside and I grabbed the chance to kick off my summer tan. Two minutes after I had immersed myself in the *Racing Post*, I was joined by a middle-aged woman who showed equal interest in a copy of *Cosmopolitan* magazine. Glancing over, I happened to notice that she was riveted by an article entitled 'Meet a Stranger and Spice Up Your Sex Life'. I shuffled uncomfortably and avoided all eye contact. As fortune would have it she was soon joined by her husband.

'Hello, stranger,' she said with a slight leer.

'What?' answered her bemused husband.

'Never mind.'

'Want some chips?' he added, shattering her romantic moment.

Even though the paddock was only yards away, my new-found companions showed little interest. Like many of the small crowd, their only motivation for being at Lingfield seemed to be that they couldn't think of anywhere else to go. The general feeling of apathy was confirmed in the next race, where I sat next to a couple who hardly lifted an eye towards the course, despite a very tight finish. The most noticeable thing about an all-weather course is that the sand muffles the thunder of galloping hooves – a sound which on turf demands attention and sets the pulse racing. If you've never attended an all-weather course, turn your television on but switch off the sound. The effect is that you know something's happening but you've no idea what it is.

The sadness is that Lingfield has obviously got a classy pedigree. Named reception rooms such as the Blakeney Box and the Slip Anchor Box remind the punter that Lingfield annually holds a major Derby trial in May, a race which has produced many Epsom winners. The turf course mimics the Derby course, the final five furlongs dropping steeply into the short straight in a long arc which is very similar to the famous Tattenham Corner. But to take the parallel any further would suggest an over-active imagination. Lingfield has sold out to mass market racing, TV money and expensive corporate entertaining, a strategy which cheapens the whole experience.

Disillusioned, I decided to abandon ship, but not before having one final crack at unearthing a winner. Searching for clues in the surprisingly pretty paddock, I spotted the delectable trainer Gay Kellaway, who not only has a good record at Lingfield but also trains her horses on the course. Her pre-race instructions were delivered with an arm around the jockey Seb Saunders and a great deal of whispering.

This combination of secrecy and affection suggested that Miss Kellaway was taking this seven-furlong dash more seriously than most. To my amateurish eye, her runner looked as if it had enjoyed too many free lunches but decided it would have the honour of carrying my money.

Ten minutes later, after another silent movie race, Miss Kellaway led Aljaz into the third-place box of the winners' enclosure and, like myself, seemed fairly pleased with the place money. The winner was a progressive four-year-old filly, which, if I hadn't been blinded by Miss Kellaway's whispering, had the obvious form of a good thing.

The prize giving finally put the cap on Lingfield. The announcer, whose name I shall protect, had a voice as smooth as melted butter and hair of a certain length – unacceptable around most dinner tables, unless you've got breeding or money. The rather rotund owner giggled nervously – like K. Sked (5) – and, as the small silver goblet was presented, seemed blissfully unaware of a huge ladder in her black tights. It provoked much nodding and winking amongst the ten people who watched her moment of triumph.

Unfortunately this memorable episode raised about as much interest as winning fourth place in the primary school egg and spoon race, the whole episode (like the racing) passing in total silence. The announcer and proud owner stood in silence for what seemed an eternity as they both vainly searched for a press photographer to record the celebration.

Finally, in an act of desperation, the silky presenter grabbed the microphone.

'Would the course photographer please come to the winners' enclosure.'

Another two minutes of sheer embarrassment followed, the bodies of presenter and winning owner still firmly attached in a frozen handshake. The microphone crackled into life once more, the elegant tones now beginning to reveal a noticeable inner tension.

'Will the course photographer PLEASE come to the winners' enclosure.'

He paused, but only for a second.

'Does anyone have a Box Brownie?' he pleaded.

Need I say more? Even on April Fool's Day, I'd have been better off at the spring sales.

Postscript: The Lingfield authorities have either had a sneak preview of this book or (more likely) finally plugged back into public opinion. The reintroduction of National Hunt racing and greater use of the superb turf track may yet return this racecourse to its former glories.

CHAPTER THIRTY-THREE

LUDLOW

My milkman's a bit of a racing man. As I packed my car, ready for the trip to Shropshire, 'Mick the Milk' whistled his way up my drive. I sought his advice.

'How far's Ludlow, Mick?'

'Depends where you start from,' he grinned.

'Thanks a lot.'

'I don't know,' laughed Mick in response. 'About two hours, I'd guess. Any tips?'

'Avoid my selections,' I answered, keen to maintain the quality of the repartee.

Three and a half hours later, I pulled onto Ludlow racecourse and made a note to cancel the milk for the next two months. I don't care where you start from, this isn't a course which you could ever describe as accessible. The M5 is almost 30 miles away, and you are forced onto minor roads strewn with lumbering tractors decked in go-slower racing stripes.

Fortunately I had left home very early, waking up the neighbour's cockerel as I fired up my engine. It left me just enough time to visit the market town of Ludlow. Unfortunately this was a very bad decision. If you enter from the A49 bypass, the town authorities tease you with a road which takes you within sniffing distance of the centre, only to block every possible route with numerous no-entry signs. Within minutes you are bounced back onto the A49 like a pinball that's just missed a 500-point bonus. I had no time for a replay.

The usual gathering of course bookmakers were exchanging stories in the car park, their accents heavy with a Birmingham brogue. I can't be sure, but I think they spoke in English.

'Catterick, John? See Barry? Goowin' seven to four on, nine to one bar. One mug laid four to six. Posted up broke, he was.' I have no idea what all this meant but raised an eyebrow in a look of knowledgeable disbelief, before shuffling off towards the entrance.

To call the layout of Ludlow interesting would be akin to suggesting that Joan of Arc was fairly religious. Whoever first arranged the facilities probably ended their days in a Shrewsbury mental institution, as the course is designed to reflect a chronically divided personality. On one side of the finishing straight you are treated to the delights of the paddock, the pre-parade ring, the winners' enclosure and a centre-course stand which is built inside a wire-meshed stockade. However, the main stands, course bookmakers and eating areas are cunningly situated on the other side of the course.

As a result, punters at Ludlow probably spend more time on the racecourse than a runner in a three-mile chase. To add to the confusion, the paddock area is open to all racegoers apart from those who are incarcerated in the car park compound. The crossings to the stands, however, are segregated and the authorities operate a system of Shropshire apartheid, depending on the colour of your badge – one crossing giving you access to the club enclosure, the other to Tattersalls. I doubt if it would be Nelson Mandela's favourite venue.

At the time of my visit, a day member's badge could be bought for only an extra £4, though sneaking past the sentries would not be difficult. Access to the red brick food hall at the northern end of the stands would present greater difficulty, as badges seemed to be inspected with unusual vigour. But if you restrict yourself to Tattersalls, you would deny yourself a real treat.

Many racing journalists over the years have made great play over the sumptuous curried prawns available from a small caravan adjacent to the winners' enclosure. A bad experience with a mussel, while holidaying in Amsterdam, meant I gave the seafood a very wide berth. An attack of loose bowel syndrome halfway up the M5 wasn't high on my wish list. Instead, I opted for a cup of tea and an Eccles cake.

Having spent a misplaced youth munching Lancastrian pastry dishes, I have gradually developed the palate of a connoisseur. I'd give the Ludlow Eccles cake about 11 out of 10. Don't miss it. The couple whose table I joined seemed astonished by my sighs of satisfaction and my insistence on clearing the plate of every visible crumb. It led to a very deep conversation.

'Good?' asked the ruddy-faced punter.

'Excellent,' I affirmed, licking the sugar from my lips.

I spotted the couple later in the afternoon, devouring Eccles cakes with a look of sublime delirium. Curried prawns could be in for a rough time after this revelation.

Apart from the wafted odour of spiced seafood, the other fragrance to attack the senses was the smell of Shropshire money. The crowded food hall swelled with men who revealed working-class hands and upper-class jackets. The farmers were out in force and they didn't look as if they were dependent on EU subsidies. If they weren't farmers they could only have been retired army officers. There were enough military moustaches on show to make a re-invasion of India a realistic proposition. By the sound of their accents, they'd already engineered a successful local coup and had turned Shropshire into a West Country colony. I escaped before the battalion was called to arms.

I spent the first two races on the roof of the main stand. This was not an act of protest or an attempted suicide bid. The very best view of Ludlow is from this position and it's open to members and day badge holders. From this vantage point you have a wonderful view of the course, especially the five fences and three hurdles in the main straight. They must come as quite a shock to tired horses running for the line, who think all the hard work is over. Best of all, the water jump sits right in front of this stand and you are provided with a close and thrilling sight of the fence.

Beyond the course, there is a fine view of what I was informed were the Clee Hills. The man who gave me this information claimed that they were the highest point between Ludlow and Chernobyl, and was the reason why my nose had begun to turn a strange shade of blue and why local sheep had an average of 2.5 heads and 6.3 legs. The stand itself has been described as 'quaint', a portrayal which does this brick and wood construction a real disservice. Apparently built in 1904, it is more reminiscent of a grand Victorian railway station, waiting in vain for the next blast of a whistle and a puff of billowing, soot-filled smoke. The main line actually runs just behind the main stand, though the local station, which can be seen from the back of the flat roof, fell foul of Dr Beeching in the 1960s. If the good doctor had been a racing man, it might still be there.

After the second race and another loser, I had become so embroiled in surveying the old station that by the time I turned back towards the course, there was only one other punter left on the roof. I headed for the old wooden staircase, which drops you down into the betting ring. As I passed my sole companion, and perhaps not aware of my presence, he emitted the loudest passing of wind since John Simpson interviewed Colonel Gaddafi.

'Good job I wasn't the vicar's wife,' I offered cheerily, to save his embarrassment.

'Pity you weren't,' he replied, without the slightest tinge of humour or remorse. 'I can't stand the old cow.'

Being stuck on a roof with a po-faced flatulent atheist was not my idea of fun and I headed off to view the rest of the course. Passing through the betting ring, it was refreshing to see at least five bookies who were willing to take small each-way bets. On my travels around the racecourses, it's become obvious that these are something of a dying breed.

For the small punter (which I am), seeing the sign '£10 Minimum, Win Only' is as tempting as being offered tickets to watch a German comedian in a Margate night-club. As far as I can see, most bookies have the marketing acumen of a salesman trying to sell thermal underwear in a Caribbean nudist colony. But what do I know? I'm only a member of the public, who gets nervous if I stand to lose more than £5. But there's lots of us out there and even an innumerate idiot, such as myself, can work out that a hundred £5 bets is a nice little earner for the average bookie. I headed for the centre course and the comfort of the red-coated Tote ladies.

The paddock at Ludlow is awful, a drab rectangular patch of grass where no effort has been made to add a little colour and atmosphere to the parade. The winners' enclosure is little better, and if I was a horse, I'd make damned sure I had a nice soft fall at the second last, just to avoid being seen in such barren surroundings. It's not as if Ludlow attracts really poor racing – the card offering, on this day, a total of over £30,000 in prize money. It just needs a shake-up.

Knowing I had a long journey ahead of me, the fourth race was to be my last. I listened out for a whisper, hoping to gain a little inside knowledge and recoup my losses. Sadly I was treated to no more than the graphic details of a woman's gynaecological difficulties. Her words were delivered with such power that I was convinced she must have been a former town crier. To be fair, it soon became obvious that her companion was profoundly deaf and kept asking for the story of the recent hysterectomy to be repeated at a higher volume. A small crowd began to gather and I'm sure I spotted a few medical types making rough notes on their racecards. I left for the Tote and my final bet of the day.

Picking second favourites in a four-horse race is never a bad move and Symbol of Success duly obliged, easing up well before the line. I was back in credit – just. But enough to breath a sigh of relief and hurry to the car park. The attendant kindly gave me detailed instructions of how to find the M5 and I raced away from the circuit. Ten minutes later I began to see signs for Shrewsbury and knew I was in trouble. Quickly reversing, I headed back towards Ludlow, re-entering the racecourse along the main road which crosses the course.

Reaching the other side, I could only watch in horror as

the fence was replaced, cutting me off from the road south. I reversed once again and raced for the exit which I had passed through only seconds earlier. It had been enough time to allow the course officials to block my exit. I was trapped. Caught like a rat in a cage and forced to watch the fifth race through my windscreen and with no access to a bookmaker, I remained as calm as an alcoholic with an empty bottle.

Just before withdrawal symptoms took hold, the gates were raised and I sped off towards Ludlow and home. For some unknown reason (I missed a sign), I ended up on the top of Clee Hill. The road is mountainous and peppered with cattle grids. But the view is extraordinary and on this clear evening gave me the chance to look over the panorama of South Wales and way beyond. Far, far in the distance, I could just make out the smoking stacks of industrial chimneys. I'd never seen Chernobyl before. It looked pretty miserable. Even from that distance.

Postscript I: It took me four hours to get home. I rang the milkman, cancelled the milk for three months and went late night shopping at Tesco's. That'll teach him.

Postscript II: A new Jubilee Stand has now been added to Ludlow's delights and opened by no less a person than HRH The Prince of Wales. Where would racing facilities be without his mother's constant anniversaries?

CHAPTER THIRTY-FOUR

MARKET RASEN

As my cleric brother is often keen to inform me, we are all searching for something in life. My deceased ex-neighbour, Miss Crystal de Monte (don't ask), would have been fulfilled had she discovered an alternative recipe for her inedible cherry sponge cake. The ex-trainer David Nicholson was looking for 1,500 winners. Others may be more demanding and spend a lifetime searching for the meaning of life (the answer's 2.5). For myself, I'd be happy to find out how to pick three 20-1 winners at a wet evening meeting in Wolverhampton. I know a few less ambitious small punters who might be content to discover the location of Market Rasen.

I challenge any reader outside Lincolnshire to submit themselves to a small test. Take two blank maps, one of Africa and one of Great Britain. On the first put a mark where you think Nairobi is situated. On the second place a cross where you think you might find Market Rasen. I guarantee that in 85 per cent of all cases, punters would get closer to Nairobi. Just to settle the matter, Market Rasen is a small market town, sort of north-east of Nottingham, a bit down from Grimsby, west-ish of

Skegness – and a very long way from Newton Abbot. I'm eternally grateful to a man who once refused to give me a job in Grantham. Life without contours would undoubtedly have led to my early committal in an institution.

My brief stop in Market Rasen's cobbled square didn't bode well for the day ahead. Charles Dickens apparently referred to the town as the sleepiest place in England. Was Dickens not familiar with the word coma? As far as I could see, the main industry seems to be the opening and closing of charity shops and the local pastime involves staring at sets of screwdrivers in the local hardware shop. After a brief search for a *Racing Post*, I headed for the racecourse, which lies only minutes away from the town centre.

In search of a complimentary ticket, I entered through the day members' gate. The sight which greets you is not promising. A grey, prefabricated block of corporate boxes made me recoil as I trudged across the grassed free car park. Yet I urge you to remember that the best presents don't always come in the finest wrapping paper. I had been expecting a small country course in the nature of Kelso, Sedgefield or Plumpton. Enter Market Rasen's enclosure and you may feel it has more in common with Kempton, Sandown and Haydock. It may not be on the same scale as these premier courses, but the initial feel is that Market Rasen has pretensions of grandeur. Taken as a whole, it's probably the most highly manicured National Hunt racecourse I've witnessed. I suspect the gardener also shares some of my weaknesses.

A few strides after gaining entrance, you'll spot a rather impressive lawn which runs down to the paddock. Placed at intervals are a number of topiary shrubs. Despite lacking the ornate detail of the display at Fontwell Park, they are fine specimens. Rather than the usual dog or chicken, the public is treated to a group of bushes which strongly resemble those upturned individual treacle sponges which I am incapable of walking past when I'm on supermarket duty. I was to spend the rest of the afternoon desperate to smother them in custard.

Yet this is only the start of Market Rasen's visual feast. The attention to detail is stunning – even on a bitter winter's day. The unusually shaped 'pear drop' paddock is decked in flowers and bordered by neatly trimmed hedging. At every turn a flower bed bursts into life, while the tree-lined pre-parade ring and nearby winners' enclosure look as if they've been painstakingly trimmed with a pair of nail scissors. If Market Rasen ever starts to lose money, sack everyone else apart from the gardener.

Perhaps the real giveaway clue to this course's ambitions is that they feel it necessary to put an enclosure plan on the back of the racecard. At the majority of small National Hunt courses this is deemed unnecessary, yet the enclosure at Market Rasen spreads across so much land that you'll probably spend more time walking than you would at Newbury. Having said that, the intimacy has been retained, possibly because they have resisted building any really big stands in either the members' or Tattersalls enclosure. Even stranger is that the largest stand on the course is to be found in the Silver Ring – which, if for nothing else, gives Market Rasen a unique quality. Like a lot of courses, this feature is probably an historical throwback and failed to muster more than about eighty punters in a crowd of 2,000 or so. The major factor in favour of this area is, however, that cheap end punters still have access to a paddock rail and have the closest view of the final fence from anywhere on the course. Normally the members' enclosure is treated to a perfect sight of the nearby water jump. Sadly, this had been railed off due to the landing area having subsided during the summer – the empty pit now the closest thing you'll find to a Lincoln-shire valley.

I was fortunate to cheer in my first winner from the Silver Ring Grandstand, and given the course layout, you won't miss a stride of the race. Maremma won comfort-ably from the hot favourite, guided home in style by Jason Maguire, the nephew of his illustrious uncle. A course steward huddled in the corner as my fist punched the air in delight. The bitter north-easterly wind whistled across the Lincolnshire flat lands with not a break in its progress from the Ukraine.

'You could do with a hat,' I offered amiably.

'Got a big furry one at home,' he responded.

'Forgotten it?'

'They won't let me wear it. It's black baseball caps or nothing.'

He went on to explain his aversion to being transformed into a New York rap singer and felt that, at the age of 67, he'd feel much happier in a tweed flat cap. Give him a break, Market Rasen.

Drawing a blank in the second race, I went off for a sniff around the main stands. Essentially, there's not a bad view of the Flat galloping course in the house, and never a feeling that you have to race back from wherever you are to catch a decent glimpse of the runners. If I have a favourite spot, it would be the open roof on the top of the Tattersalls bar, which is busy enough to make you feel involved but never seemed to be crowded. An added bonus here is that you can drop down the steps and straight into the racecourse shop.

The previous evening I had managed to break my one and only corkscrew. Not being a beer or spirits man, this amounted to a major family crisis, only resolved by the desperate use of a rusting bent nail, a large hammer and a pair of pliers. Fearing that my guests for the ever-nearing Christmas lunch wouldn't be too impressed, I entered the shop in the faint hope of solving the problem. Ten minutes later I was the proud owner of two pens, one tea towel, three mugs and a corkscrew emblazoned with Market Rasen's telephone number. I don't know who those shop ladies were but they were so persuasive they ought to set up a rock climbing shop in Grantham.

The flagship facility at Market Rasen is the Brocklesby Suite in the members' enclosure. Generally, I'd suggest that Tattersalls is quite sufficient for a good day out, though the Brocklesby does provide a friendly bar with direct access out onto a spacious balcony overlooking the course. The restaurant (rather like Stratford's) is badly placed and offers no view of either the paddock or racecourse. What you will find – and you've got to look carefully – is Market Rasen's secret passageway. An unmarked door (I can never resist them) takes you to the back of the bar and kitchens. For some peculiar reason, the management has decided to conceal the racecourse's proud history in this obscure corridor. Along one wall are a series of photographs, which I doubt had been straightened in the last ten years. Unfortunately I had left home without my pocket spirit level but I left the display in a much better state than I had found it.

There have been some class acts at Market Rasen over the years. Amongst others, Silver Buck and Night Nurse are shown flying the fences and hurdles; while dusty old frames reveal racecards from 1923 and a poster for the

1859 Market Rasen Steeplechase. I wouldn't be ashamed of a heritage like that and it needs to be given a lot more prominence. Sadly, Castle Owen won't be joining this hall of fame. This seven-year-old chaser was David Nicholson's last chance of reaching the magical 1,500 winners. The training licence of this much-admired yet acerbic magician was about to expire at midnight and the clock was ticking. It looked to be a good thing – a fine jockey in Richard Johnson, a recent easy win at Hereford, and a 15-8 favourite's price tag – which suggested the money was in the bank. It was also the fifth-leg of my placepot bet with Tote.

I felt uneasy as soon as I watched the chasers striding around the paddock. Two young pretenders, Storm of Gold and Inch Champion, had the look of young boxers who are determined to put the champion on the canvas. Another glance at the racecard also suggested that there was trouble ahead. Castle Owen carried top weight, his ears were pricked as sharply as a piece of wet lettuce – and, as far as I could see, David Nicholson hadn't even turned up to watch.

There are two lessons to be learned from this experience. Firstly, don't get mugged by sentimentality. Castle Owen had no idea he was a prospective 1,500th winner and had more interest in getting round in one piece than in supplying the next day's headlines. Secondly, if in doubt, back a horse with the smartest name. It's a disturbing, but statistically proven, fact that picking horses because you like the name is as likely to produce profit over a season as three hours hunched over a *Racing Post* form guide. This will be bad news for those punters (and we all know them) who boast of their ability to predict winners on the basis of a horse's course record. Most thoroughbreds can hardly remember what they did yesterday, never mind what happened at Hereford fifteen days ago.

And horses with names like Storm of Gold tend to win races. He certainly won the 2.55 at Market Rasen and left Castle Owen floundering in third place. He also confined my placepot bet to the wastepaper bin. Ask me in ten years' time how many winners David Nicholson trained and it will take me no more than half a second to supply the right answer. In a scientific test of my name theory, I glanced through the results section of the following day's racing paper. The winners from four different courses included Captain Miller, Royal Hand, Coole Spirit, October Mist, Take Control, Vain Minstrel, Storm Ten, and Heart of Armor. Need I say more? If you're ever fortunate (or mad) enough to buy a leg in a racehorse make sure it's called something like Lightning Strike or Valiant Trooper. Name it Griznie, Pantaloon or Onelegshorter and you're just asking for trouble.

The most convincing evidence for this revolutionary approach to successful punting occurred in the third race. Carmel's Joy was on offer at an attractive 5-1 and was the nearest I was ever likely to get to having a horse carrying my family name. It hadn't won a race in three years, carried a heavy weight, was trained by an unfashionable stable, and its racing colours would have been rejected by a Salvation Army fashion show. In short, it didn't have much going for it. Inevitably it romped in, beating the two joint-favourites by at least twenty lengths.

There's a slight but relevant weakness in my argument. For it to really hold up, all 2,000 or so punters at Market Rasen on a cold December afternoon needed to share my surname. I soon dismissed this chance occurrence by approaching a number of startled strangers and demanding to know their monicker. I came up with two Willoughbys, five Smiths, a couple of Johnsons – and, strangely, one Murgatroyd. But their turn will come. They must wait their chance and continue their search for the inevitable coincidence. I am certain they will have more luck than David Nicholson's search for 1,500 winners. They may even enjoy more success than those of us who search for Market Rasen on a blank map of Britain. If you ever do find it, make the effort and attend a jumps meeting. You won't be disappointed.

Postscript: Should you manage to pinpoint Market Rasen with greater accuracy than Nairobi, please contact the publishers for two free tickets to Goodwood's next festival of National Hunt racing.

CHAPTER THIRTY-FIVE

MUSSELBURGH

It went so quiet in the plane, you could have heard a tear drop. One glance out of the windows was enough to confirm that we'd been caught in a blizzard and as the runway loomed into view there was an audible intake of breath – the passengers' final attempt at self-preservation. You can never be sure what people are thinking in these circumstances. At a guess they're probably wondering if they'll ever see their families again. Call me selfish, but all I could think of was whether the Musselburgh meeting would be abandoned.

I can only describe our landing as rather similar to my last crack at ice skating. Despite a complete lack of control over the direction I was taking, I managed to remain on my feet. The chaotic attempts resulted in gaining one extra friend and twenty new enemies. I have never skated since.

'That was fun,' said the stewardess as we taxied to a halt.

'Loved it. What time are you going back?'

'Half an hour.'

'I may be on it,' I replied as the freezing Edinburgh air bit into my face.

Small punters like myself don't have a great deal of contact with racing's hierarchy. The previous evening, and with the weather closing in, I had managed to get through to Bill Farnsworth, Musselburgh's clerk of the course, who suggested that things weren't looking too good.

This helpful and affable man even supplied me with his personal mobile number and suggested I ring him before leaving home at 6.30 a.m. and again before I boarded the plane. With public relations like that, they'd won me over before I'd even seen the course.

Once in the terminal, I called the racecourse office once more, convinced that my journey had been wasted. I began with characteristic negativity.

'I suppose you've cancelled?'

'Cancelled?'

'It's going ahead?'

'Aye. Why not? It'll be fine.'

The Scots are a hardy lot. I'm convinced that at any other course in Britain they'd have abandoned the meeting well before their first bowl of porridge. The men and women of Edinburgh are made of sterner stuff.

If you're without a car, jump on the small suburban railway which runs out to Musselburgh from Waverley station. Should you do this, make sure you enter a carriage which contains Kirkcaldy Bill (for the uneducated English, this is pronounced *Kurcoddy* Bill). This delightful man will entertain you with racing stories, offer you a lift in his friend's car and save you a two-mile walk to the racecourse. As I was now as cold as the carcass of an Aberdeen Angus in a butcher's freezer, he probably saved me from hypothermia and I arrived at the course still aware of a slight movement in my aching fingers.

Like many small racecourses, the exterior of Musselburgh

doesn't quicken the pulse. Country courses at least have the benefit of a rural setting, whereas Musselburgh looks more like an extension of the town's housing estate. Wooden fencing and rails separate it from the nearby road and access is gained through rather ancient turnstiles. This wasn't helped by the building site which lay behind the Grandstand and a number of Portakabins dotted about the main enclosure. But don't let me put you off. Musselburgh's on the move and the local provost, Pat O'Brien, has promised great things to come.

Ever been house hunting and walked into a property which doesn't look too promising but has got a great 'feel'? It's a quality which is hard to pin down but is almost tangible. Musselburgh possesses this feel. Perhaps the staff have been on a Bill Farnsworth public relations course, as there's a welcoming hospitality in every corner of the racecourse.

Rushing into the Pinkie Bar on the ground floor of the Grandstand, I had to do no more than shiver and a steaming mug of tea was thrust across the counter. This was my first chance to sample the facilities and while the walls of the bar appear to have been painted in deep nicotine, it's a comfortable first stop, which supplies an excellent Scottish pie and chips, plus a fine variety of whiskies.

At the time of my visit, the course layout was fairly simple, though the promised addition of a new weighing room, new admission boxes, new public bar and betting room is likely to be a real bonus. Looking from the entrance, the three-storey oblong Grandstand lies straight ahead. To the left, the well laid out paddock and saddling boxes are within easy reach, and only a stride or two from the course. The brown and racing-green Grandstand is split between Tattersalls and members, and with – thankfully – no unnecessary Silver Ring. A long and ornate glass canopy provides shelter for the racegoers and allows a totally unrestricted view of the complete course.

In the distance you can just catch a glimpse of the raging Firth of Forth and the horizon is framed by the hills of Fife. I can't be sure, but on a clear day I reckon you could see as far as Auchtermuchty. If you can't – I'd rather not know. I just have a thing about the sound of Auchtermuchty.

As far as I could see, Musselburgh supplied everything I needed from a small racecourse. It was only as the first race approached that I realized that something was missing. And it was a serious omission. With only twenty minutes to go before the off, there wasn't a horse to be seen and I became convinced that I had become the victim of some cruel practical joke.

After a brief interlude to answer nature's call (the Armitage Shanks washbasins in Le Garcon D'Or Bar are a must) I returned to the paddock only to see it crammed with fifteen hurdlers. It was rather like watching a magician pull six doves and a white rabbit from a silk top hat. The ability to produce fifteen thoroughbreds from nowhere is enough to give Musselburgh life membership of the magic circle and I was determined to find out how they'd pulled off such an impressive illusion.

My investigations had to wait until the end of the first race – a two-mile selling hurdle, with some fairly ordinary looking animals, their heads bent against the strengthening northerly winds and snow gathering on their dull winter coats. The favourite had no better form than a second place in a Catterick seller and, given the conditions, it seemed certain that he'd be turned over. Having watched Navan Project at Carlisle, I thought he might have a bit of a chance and headed for the stands.

Musselburgh's course isn't exactly pretty but the view of the track is faultless and allows you to watch your money through every stride. The twelve-furlong oval circuit is virtually flat, with two sharp bends and four obstacles on both the back and home straights. The turn into the finishing four furlongs is particularly hazardous and any horse not up with the pace might as well throw in the towel and canter to the line. Navan Project got caught cold by the favourite, who romped in by at least five lengths, leaving my own selection a distant third.

My interest, however, was in the horse which landed second place, as it finally confirmed the revolutionary betting technique first mentioned in my description of Market Rasen. If there's no form, back a horse whose name fits the occasion – e.g. if it's a sweltering hot day – back Suntanoil; or if it's a wet spring day – back Umbrella Man. And if it's a freezing day in the Lothians of Scotland? The answer's simple – back Arctic Star, whose previous form read 00-F0 and was ridden by an amateur jockey.

It's extraordinary how often this strategy pays off – and in the case of Arctic Star it could have paid for my air fare, a slap-up meal in the members' restaurant and a new hot water bottle. Despite struggling into second place, Arctic Star paid £86.90 on the Tote and had me cursing the rejection of my master plan. All the clues had been obvious – the snow, the frost, the ice and 800 punters all dressed like Scott of the Antarctic.

Fortunately, the place money on Navan Project proved quite generous and I slipped into the Paddock Bar to defrost with a cup of tea and a single malt. I'm not sure if modernizing this bar is part of the Provost's master plan but it needs to be. A ramshackle collection of white plastic seating covers the carpet-tiled floor, while the windows are so low down and narrow that you are forced to bend double to gain any view out onto the enclosure. From the outside it was reminiscent of a Second World War pillbox. I noticed a couple of ex-servicemen approach the door in a very nervous manner.

By the time I had raised my body temperature to just above zero, I had hatched a plan to discover the paddock illusion. I drew a blank in the second race but followed the horses back to the unsaddling enclosure, determined to follow their every movement. Within minutes the puzzle had been solved. Washed down and snug in their blankets, each of the runners was led to a small gateway at the side of the paddock. I followed behind, waving my limp notebook to confirm my status as an authorized person. Assuming me to be a trainer, the gateman nodded me through and I began to follow the string of sweating horses.

With my hat pulled down and my collar turned up, I felt like a private eye from a Raymond Chandler novel. If a taxi had been passing, I'd have jumped in and told the driver to 'follow that horse'! As it was, I found myself outside the course, on Ballcarres Road, and still intent on avoiding detection, fell back by about fifty yards. To avoid suspicion, I occasionally stopped and read my racecard or, as there were no shop doorways available, stared into the windows of the nearby houses.

Five minutes later, I turned into Goosegreen Crescent, the line of horse droppings leading me straight to an unmarked set of stables from which runners for the next race were just beginning to appear. At a rough estimate I was now at least a quarter of a mile from the paddock and almost had my feet in the Firth of Forth. As I turned back, the sea wind rose to such a fury that my entry badge was ripped from my jacket and was last seen heading for Edinburgh at a height of 200 feet.

I found myself outside the course with no badge and no means of entry. Sticking closely to the line of horses, I adopted my horsiest looking face and strode back in, scribbling wildly in my notebook and not risking a glance towards the gateman. Moments later I had slipped quietly back into the crowd, content that I had revealed the magician's secret. If I was a horse and had to walk so far to hurl myself over fences – I'd be looking for a raise.

Yet this wasn't the only mystery which needed solving at Musselburgh. The majority of meetings at this Scottish course are still on the Flat, the jumps course forming the inner ring of the tight circuit. Oddly, the unused Flat course finishing straight had been marked with an athletics running track. Even stranger, the first three punters I approached to explain this peculiar set-up had no idea why it was there. My fourth attempt proved fruitful.

Musselburgh, it turns out, now hosts the famous and infamous New Year Powderhall Sprint – at one time the only professional athletics meeting in Britain. I had always imagined it took place in a large smoke-filled aircraft hanger, with large wads of money being passed between whisky-breathed punters. Maybe it used to be like this, but now it's a Powderhall Sprint without the hall – an outdoor meeting in the depths of winter.

It was more confirmation that the Scots are from rugged stock, yet perhaps no more robust than the band of National Hunt jockeys who ply their trade in weather that would have a polar bear diving for cover. The same applies to the hardy punters who turn up week after week regardless of the biting winds and storm-filled skies. If you're not sure what an enthusiast is – go to a December meeting at Musselburgh. It will tell you all you want to know about the heart and soul of racing.

All in all it had been a good day and, like most small punters, I was content to leave Musselburgh with a small profit, a frozen body and a warm impression. I've seen better racecourses, watched better racing but rarely been met with such hospitality. And you can't build that with a lottery grant. Just to prove their point, Musselburgh laid on a courtesy bus to transport punters back to the station, where a train was waiting to whisk us into Edinburgh. With two hours to spare before my flight, I wandered down the snow-covered Princes Street, stopping briefly at Scott's Memorial. The light was already going and in the brightly lit park below the street, crowds of scarf-clad skaters slid gracefully across the outdoor ice rink like figures in the landscape painting of an old Dutch master. I wasn't looking forward to my plane hurtling down that snow-packed runway. But if a day at Musselburgh races was to be the last thing I did, it would have been time well spent.

Postscript: Development now complete. A slight loss of the old quaintness but they have doubled their average crowd since 2004. They've clearly done a fine job and Scottish pies are still freely available. Thank God they weren't tempted to adopt the baguette culture. There is no greater praise I can offer.

CHAPTER THIRTY-SIX

NEWBURY

There are signs for Greenham Common as you approach Newbury. They make you feel radical, critical and intent on protest. I felt Newbury racecourse could be in for a hard day as I entered with an extra-sharp pencil.

I also had a touch of déjà vu – again (as Americans might say). It brought back memories of Cheltenham. The very scale of Newbury is initially overpowering, faced as you are with the rear view of three immense stands. If you enter from the free car park end (don't be duped into paying £2 for the field near the main road), the paint-crumbling edifice of the Tattersalls stand gives you your first impression of Newbury – and it's not a good one. It stands four storeys high, clad in a fetching grey-cream stipple effect that wouldn't pass a planning application in a run-down East London housing estate.

Nothing about Tattersalls makes it worth the £8 entry. OK, there's a surfeit of drinking holes – the Snaffle Bar, the Punter's Return (who thought of that one?), the Stirrup Bar and the Furlong Bar, which is more like two furlongs from the finishing post. The Café Normandy offers light refreshments, though it feels about as French as a Bath bun. All these areas appear to have been taste-fully decorated by Steptoe & Son. The carpets and furniture have got 'job lot' written all over them. Like many of these big courses transfer to members' is essential. Maybe it's a plot by the management to force another £6 out of your wallet, but it's a poor way to treat a punter. On the initial showing, this punter's return seemed unlikely. I hurried off to see what I'd get for the extra donation.

I felt a little like an East German trying to get over to the West before the wall came down. I've never seen so many border guards, all togged out in fluorescent yellow jackets and steely eyes. Curiously a small number of them brandished megaphones, perhaps publicly to inform gentlemen leaving the lavatories that their flies were undone – though I'm not certain this was their purpose. And beware the dress code at Newbury. Transfer is only possible when sporting a shirt and tie, or a polo neck. Despite it being a bright November day, I was fortunate to be suffering from my first winter cold and had donned a pale yellow-collared sweater, which peeked out from the top of my jacket. I looked so ecclesiastical, I could have got into the annual Church Synod and was given entrance with a polite, though misplaced reverence. Others behind me were not so fortunate and were condemned to an afternoon in the wilderness.

The difference to Tattersalls was so marked that I can only liken this experience to a homeless beggar being invited to spend a weekend at the Dorchester. Having crept into Newbury through the tradesman's entrance, I had missed the main gate, an ornate stable-like structure, which must have cost more than the whole of the Tattersalls stand. But by coming through the main entrance, you start to get the real feel of Newbury.

The very first building you witness is a champagne bar, which adjoins six Bedouin tents flanking the paddock. Though empty at the time of my visit, these tents of the Paddock Pavilions, which look like a collapsed Mound Stand at Lord's Cricket Ground, are designed for corporate entertaining. They should perhaps rename them the Far Pavilions – as, like most things at Newbury, you need a strong pair of legs to discover its offered delights. But delights there are. The main Berkshire Stand, constructed as recently as 1992, is truly magnificent. It dominates the whole racecourse and has a freshness and character which suggests that there's still some imagination in modern architecture. I don't know if Prince Charles has ever visited Newbury but I suspect that if he ever did, he might well give it the Royal nod.

Admittedly, the entrance to the stand is rather over-ornate and reminded me of a rejected design for a glass conservatory sent to me by a national double glazing company only last year. Generally, however, the building has got real style, a labyrinth of surprises and sumptuous decor. This is no Tattersalls. I can't go into detail here but the Minstrels' Gallery, which looks down onto the Long Room Bar, is a real highlight. So too is the Tote Viewing Deck on the first floor, with no less than thirteen TV monitors and a wonderful view over the course. One other highlight is the little shop adjacent to the glazed entrance. The stock is a little limited but there are so many free brochure handouts that you could restock a depleted library.

There is, however, a problem. There's something about the atmosphere that just doesn't invite participation. It's a building that seems to demand veneration rather than involvement. Perhaps it's the ambiguous signs, which don't really make it clear which areas are for public use and which are for the sole purpose of private box holders and corporate visitors. Despite brandishing my day member's badge, I stepped carefully around the building, primed to apologize at the first challenge. Not really a good way to spend a relaxed day at the races and the management need to find ways of putting racegoers at their ease. The highly visible presence of numerous security staff isn't really the most sensitive PR. Greater clarity of signs would be equally effective.

If you really want some entertainment at Newbury, I suggest you engage in some free voyeurism. More than any other course so far visited, you are treated to a total social mix. Ruddy-faced gentry in classic country garb ease their way through the fog of Essex man aftershave; trilby-hatted, tweedy ladies of a certain age cast glances at young women on the arms of shiny-suited sugar daddies. It's a delight and worth the entrance fee alone. The whole of Newbury members' enclosure is a style contest but with only one real winner. I'm seriously thinking of buying a hacking jacket tomorrow, given the ease of victory. And to top it all, the Long Room serves a full English breakfast at a pricey £5.10. But even the food has passed the style test. This is an English breakfast with kedgeree. Kedgeree! I haven't seen that served up since I was a girl's third substitute for a Cambridge summer ball.

I was so taken by this fashion battle that I almost missed the fourth race. Having already bagged two winners, the kedgeree was beginning to look a distinct possibility. Unfortunately the chance to watch horseflesh was severely limited. Only thirty-three runners took part in the six advertised races, with a total prize fund of £30,000. It seems to be a common occurrence at many of these midweek meetings at premier courses. What's the point of grand facilities if there are no horses to follow? In contrast, on this same day, Huntingdon managed to attract eighty runners for a total prize fund of £20,000. It suggests someone's cage needs a good rattle.

My selection for the fourth race must have had a late night and heaved in last in a five-horse field. Still in profit and not too distressed, I wandered down to the winners' enclosure. Though attractive, it turned out to be reminiscent of a galley kitchen in a seven-bedroomed mansion – far too small for its setting. An odds-on favourite was being cooed over by grateful connections, while a small crowd looked on silently. It wasn't really a day for serious punters and the gathered admirers were obviously followers of each-way outsiders. On Hennessy Day, I doubt you could catch a glimpse of anything at all but on a cold November afternoon, access was not a problem. As far as I could see the greatest excitement appeared to be watching Miriam Francome applying a coat of 'lippy' ready for her next interview.

But then the main attraction entered the winners' enclosure. It was sleek, beautifully groomed, a steady stride and carried an air of confidence. It was Peter O'Sullevan, the doyen of racing commentators with a voice that should have manned a Samaritans' phone line. I could only catch the odd word but within seconds I felt so relaxed I almost nodded off against the rail. And he's not a man who hurries. He drifted through the concourse with such ease and familiarity that Newbury could have been his favourite pair of slippers. Wonderful.

With the light beginning to go, I headed off to explore the outer limits. The Silver Ring enclosure is so far away, I'm surprised I didn't need a passport. Not much to say really. If you can afford a few extra pounds at least go to Tattersalls, back a couple of winners and transfer to members' – but don't forget your tie. The facilities in the Silver Ring are about as attractive as my dentist offering me a root filling without anaesthetic. The bar is no more than a glorified tent with a floor of suspect green material held together with grey gaffer tape.

It raises a number of questions. Why bother? Why insult your clientele with such atrocious conditions? I counted no more than twenty people occupying this vast area. They were so lonely one of them asked me to stay a little longer, just to make up the numbers. It wouldn't take much imagination to close this section on quiet race days and offer entry to Tattersalls for an extra couple of quid. Maybe the powers that be are intent on maintaining the 'us and them' atmosphere that tends to pervade Newbury.

If you enjoy limbo dancing, it's definitely worth heading for the centre of the course. This necessitates ducking under a series of rails but is well worth the effort. A small scaffolded construction sits by the last chase fence and provides a real contrast to the view from the distant stands. I was joined by three bored photographers and a young journalist whose hands had turned so blue he could hardly hold his pencil. By the time he had thawed out, I doubt he could decipher a word he'd written. His report was probably an act of imagination rather than a detail of events – not an uncommon event in form books. The course itself is a real galloping course, so flat you could be in Norfolk. From this centre course position it's possible to see almost every stride of the race and to watch the battle up the straight. Highly recommended.

As luck would have it, Mick Fitzgerald steered my selection over the hurdles and won at a canter. Without hesitation I rushed back to the Berkshire Stand to grab my promised kedgeree, waving my member's badge at security staff as I passed through enemy lines. Breathless and hungry, I finally battled through to the counter. A single grain of rice leered at me from the large serving dish which had once brimmed over. 'Sorry, dear,' came the friendly reply. 'I can offer you a bit of bacon if that's any good.'

Crestfallen and defeated, I headed out towards the car park, making a brief stop (as has become my habit) to examine the toilet facilities. Don't miss it. The Gentlemen's lavatory on the first floor of the Berkshire Stand has more stalls than they use in the Cambridgeshire. It's enough to confuse the most single-minded man. I presume the Ladies' powder room is equally well equipped, though verification would have been a poor career move.

Still suffering from kedgeree withdrawal symptoms, I headed for the car park. The whiff of frying fish and chips alerted my senses as I strolled through Tattersalls, and I couldn't resist. I was pleasantly surprised, not so much by the food but by the fact that the vinegar was dispensed through the pierced cap of an old Pimms bottle. At last, a hint of style outside the confines of the members' enclosure. Somehow Newbury had managed to dilute my Greenham Common protest. Perhaps it was the genial crowd, perhaps the three winners. I don't know. More than likely it was all a result of that small snatched moment in the paddock, when Peter O'Sullevan's voice lulled me into a relaxed contentment.

Postscript I: Good news – they've built a new Tattersalls Stand. More good news – it's big and it's got a great view. Bad news – it appears to have been designed by an unimaginative manic depressive, who thinks that rectangles are exciting and that grey is a cheerful colour. At least it will keep the riff-raff out of the members' enclosure and save them from the delights of the old Punter's Return.

Postscript II: Made my own punter's return to sample the new facilities. Totally unbiased by the fact that I landed a 50-1 winner and my football team won a play-off final at Cardiff's Millenium Stadium . . . Newbury, like my occasional, dated designer stubble is beginning to grow on me.

CHAPTER THIRTY-SEVEN

NEWCASTLE

It may be a sign of a disturbed childhood but, for many of my formative years, I would search the heavens with my grandfather's old ship's telescope. It was a difficult task, as the lenses had more chips in them than you'd find in a Harry Ramsden's fish restaurant. But even through the blurred image, I hoped to catch a glimpse of heaven and the angels who, I presumed, were hiding on the dark side of the moon. Needless to say, it never happened. The telescope remains with me and on the occasional clear evening, when no-one's there to witness my madness, I'll sneak out into the back garden just for a final check.

The A1 motorway through Gateshead will relieve all those grown-up punters who at one time shared my fantasies. The giant Angel of the North tells you that you're within fifteen minutes of Newcastle racecourse. The crazed sculptor who erected this wonderful rusting edifice probably has the same grip on reality as most small-time gamblers who refuse to back any horse with a starting-price less than 10-1. It's impractical, improbable, absurd but a whole lot of fun.

It had been almost twenty-five years since I last visited

Newcastle racecourse. The only memory which had survived a quarter of a century of subscribing to book-maker holiday funds was a vague image of rhododendrons. Go to this course in the spring and early summer, and you'll enjoy one of the finest entrances to any British racecourse. Even in late November, the banks of shrubbery give an impression of grandeur, a feel that you are entering a private country estate. The first sight of Brandling House only confirms this view.

The austere sandstone mansion forms the main access to the racecourse and I'd advise paying the extra for a day member's badge just to sneak a look at its interior. A stairway fit for a Scarlett O'Hara entrance rises from the main hallway and takes you into a labyrinth of stately rooms. Plaques on the wall proudly announce that the Racegoers' Club voted Newcastle the Racecourse of the Year in 1998, yet there was no soap in those irritating squeezy things which hang over the sinks in the Gentle-men's lavatory. Nothing turns me against a racecourse more than a non-functioning soap dispenser.

But I persevered and climbed to the top floor past a host of bars and cafes. Whatever you do, make an effort to visit the Gosforth Park Suite. Whoever chose the carpet in here must have been mid-marriage crisis or suffering a nervous breakdown, as the pattern is enough to send a meditating Indian mystic into a state of frenzy. The Brandling restaurant, on the other hand, looked exquisite, though the Beaujolais Villages '97 seemed a bit steep at £13.50 and there wasn't a bottle of rosé to be seen on the menu. (A heinous omission in my book.) At £19.50, the lunch seemed fairly good value apart from being about £17.50 outside my price bracket.

If you do treat yourself to a day member's badge, don't

be afraid to head for the summit of the stand. At first sight, the final staircase appears to lead only to private boxes, yet the balcony is open to all and you can enjoy the pleasures of standing directly in front of the corporate boxes full of beer-swilling businessmen on a day's subsidized junket. From this position, I gained my first view of the racecourse and immediately recalled my grandfather's old ship's telescope. The circuit appeared to be so far away that it could have been in Hexham – a course I was to visit two days later. Settling for a cup of tea from a nearby bar, I remained on the balcony to view the first race, which the commentator (with binoculars the size of Jodrell Bank) announced had been won by a 33-1 shot called Spartan Royale.

My own selection had apparently pulled up three fences from home. Glancing back at its form it probably had as much chance of success as an ice cube on a Jamaican beach, while Spartan Royale had the form of a racing certainty. As any small punter will realize, form becomes crystal clear only seconds after an unbacked winner has passed the post. It's just one of the unwritten laws of racing and something all racegoers have to live with.

In the case of Newcastle, just make sure you back galloping stayers. At first glance, the one-mile, six-furlong triangular course looks fairly flat, yet the five furlongs in the back straight have an energy-sapping steady incline and brings horses into the straight with a leg-weary stride. If the ground's dead, this could be similar to climbing in the Himalayas; yet if they're bouncing off the top, it may be no more than a minor inconvenience. As my first bet proved, it's often best to simply watch the opener and then work on your strategy from there. But even if you're having a good day, don't expect to get excited. Maybe a cold November afternoon isn't the best time to judge the atmosphere and it's possible that Flat racing on the outer ring of the course provides a greater thrill. Yet somehow I doubt it. The whole geography of Newcastle is probably its biggest drawback. The stands are separated from the course by huge sweeping lawns and you are left feeling more detached from the racing than a man feels attached to a loose-fitting set of dentures. You know they're there but contact is minimal.

Following my opening failure, even two decent-priced winners failed to produce any sign of adrenalin and I went in search of something to save Newcastle's reputation. If I was to select one major attribute it would be the paddock in front of the Brandling House Stand. The attention to detail is superb, particularly in the design of the curved steps, which provide a viewing platform into the winners' enclosure. It is constructed in such a way that the designers have created a miniature amphitheatre, which is unique on British racecourses – or at least on the forty-eight I had so far visited.

Unfortunately, glance back at the stands and you'll also spot Newcastle's carbuncle. Instead of retaining the grandeur of Brandling House, recent modernization plans have sandwiched this beautiful facade between adjoining buildings designed by architects who appear to have about as much imagination as a soap opera junkie. I'm told that the majestic frontage of the old country house incorporates columns of late 19th century quasi-Ionic cast iron (ugh?). Whilst these ornate supports are still intact, the modern members' stand and Tattersalls Grandstand rob the ancient house of all its former glory.

The only concession to style has been to cover everything in green paint, presumably to introduce some old-world charm. Such is the frenzy of green paint that standing still at Newcastle could be a hazardous risk, as you are likely to be attacked by a brush-wielding decorator. Yet it's not all bad news. If you're feeling peckish and don't fancy lashing out £19.50, head for the family food hall which lies at the far end of Tattersalls Stand. Unlike many racecourses, Newcastle supplies a restaurant ideal for the small punter. A meagre £2.90 landed me two eggs, bacon, chips, a mug of fresh tea and enough friendly service to put a smile on the face of man with no winners. And from here, it's only a stride into the Silver Ring. Without doubt, Newcastle can boast one of the best Silver Ring facilities in the country. An enormous stand, Tote boxes, a cafe-bar – even a well laid out picnic area for a warm day, provides everything you could wish for. Unfortunately, it lacked two major factors – bookmakers and people. Amazingly, by mid-afternoon, I was able to count no more than fifteen punters in the whole of this area. Even more astonishing was that a lone and deranged course bookmaker had set up a single pitch below the stand. By the third race he looked so depressed, I offered him the local Samaritans' number. Sadly, I doubt he had enough money to make the call.

Are the course authorities completely mad? Are they as self-deluded as that demented bookmaker? Who do they think wants to stand on their own in an ice box grandstand which could house 600 punters? As you'll see from other reports, I would happily scrap every Silver Ring in the country and simply reduce the Tattersalls entrance fee. Or at least have the nous to be flexible with entry on a bitter November afternoon, when many a punter is trying to save up for a Christmas tree and a dead turkey. Silver Rings are built on exclusion – keep them away from the paddock in case they pollute the members. It's a strategy which fits with the 21st century about as well as I fit into a pair of 32-inch trousers.

Sporting my Grandstand badge, I returned to the main course to infect the membership and find out a little more about Brandling House. Marching into the racecourse office, I delivered one of my well-prepared probing questions.

'What's the history behind Brandling House?' I enquired. The reaction suggested I had just asked the final million-pound question in a TV quiz show.

'Er . . . Er . . .' stammered the man behind the counter.

'Ten seconds,' I urged.

'Er . . . Er . . .' he repeated.

Pursing my lips, I made a noise like a buzzer and counted him out.

'Sorry. No-one knows,' he finally responded.

'We've been trying to produce a pamphlet for years. We even asked the university but they didn't come up with anything.'

'Nothing?'

'Nothing.'

Promising to solve the mystery of Brandling House, I left for my last inspection of the course and a final wager on a nine-year-old staying chaser. Two fences from home, Tashreef was held on the bridle while his rivals were flat out and going nowhere. J. Crowley – a 3 lb claimer and future star of National Hunt – eased his mount over the line. Despite a fairly short price on the course, the Tote paid £15.80 to a pound stake and I was due a night in a four-star hotel. I pushed my ticket under the window and opened my wallet ready to fill its depleted coffers.

'Nothing on here, love,' smiled the red-coated lady.

'What?'

'You haven't won anything.'

'Haven't won anything? I backed the winner!'

'Number ten won.'

'That's right. Number ten. Tashreef.'

'Check your ticket, love?'

'Eh?'

'Says number one on here,' she replied, gently pushing the betting slip back under the window.

'Bugger. Oops, sorry.'

'I'd swear as well,' she smiled kindly.

I am unfortunate in possessing eyesight which is only capable of spotting a London bus seconds before it runs me over. In a rush to place the bet, I had discarded my reading glasses, glanced down at the card and backed a complete donkey. It was not a good moment. Fighting back the tears, I headed for the exit, sensing the thinness of the wallet which nestled in my back pocket without causing any discernible bulge. Slamming the car door, I hurled my copy of *Britain's Best Country Hotels* onto the back seat and reached for a battered edition of *Cheap Bed & Breakfasts*. It was time to go bed hunting.

Just as I was about to weave my way through the dormant rhododendrons a policeman halted my exit. A rope was passed over the road and from the left emerged a string of sweating chasers, being led back to their horse-boxes by their lads. I recognized Tashreef immediately, not by its coat but by the jaunty stride which only winners possess. I glared hard in its direction, finally throwing up my hands as a sign of desperation. Have you ever seen a horse wink? It may have been a trick of the light but I'm damned sure Tashreef flicked an eyelid in my direction. Next time I read a racecard, I'll change my glasses. I might even use my grandfather's telescope – just to be sure.

Postscript: Having a day spare to kick my heels before visiting Hexham, I decided to camp out in Durham – my old alma mater. For those of you not familiar with this expression, it's an elitist term for the place attended by students for three years while they engage in a bit of reading, heavy drinking and as much debauchery as they can handle.

Still determined to solve the mystery of Brandling House, I called into the university library the following morning. Unfamiliar with the highly computerized catalogue system, I threw myself on the mercy of the librarians.

'Research?' they queried.

'Research.'

Ten minutes later I found myself in a locked and air-conditioned vault. The shelves heaved with leather-bound volumes, which looked as if they hadn't been opened since Roman legions stopped off in Durham for a quick pint and a bit of pillaging. I was drawing a blank until a bearded face appeared at the door.

'Brandling House?' he asked.

'Yes. Any luck?'

'*Bien sur*,' he responded. 'Pevsner's your best bet.'

'Pevsner?'

'*Certainement*. It's bound to be in there.'

'You've got a copy?'

'*Mais oui. Un moment*.'

Two minutes later this Franglais-ridden librarian reappeared. He was about as French as a redundant Geordie miner but seemed unable to utter a word without employing at least one Gallic phrase. *Mais – sans doute –* he did supply the answer.

Pevsner's *The Buildings of England* informed me that Brandling House had been built in 1764 by MP Charles Brandling. Amongst much detail, Pevsner suggests that, 'The exterior has suffered greatly from being the back premises of the Grandstand . . . and that the North Entrance Front is of three storeys and seven bays, the central three bays projecting slightly under a dentelled open pediment.' As I couldn't understand a word he was talking about, I moved on rapidly, only to unearth the most revealing section.

In 1914, the suffragettes had set fire to Brandling House in an attempt to persuade coal owner and MP Charles Brandling that they were tired of always getting landed with the housework. (As you'll know, this culminated in the infamous Washing Up Bill of 1918.) I end my report with a plea to any living suffragettes. Could you have a crack at Newcastle's new stands and give the Silver Ring punters a bit of equality? Thanks.

CHAPTER THIRTY-EIGHT

NEWMARKET

Schizophrenia isn't the sort of thing you would normally associate with a racecourse – but if Sigmund Freud was still earning an Austrian schilling, he'd probably open a consulting room in Newmarket. Had he been told the name of William of Orange's 17th century winning stallion (see Postscript I – it's far too embarrassing to mention here), this sexually repressed psychologist would surely have found his spiritual home.

Newmarket's personality is split into two distinct race-courses. I had always imagined that there are simply two courses sharing the same facilities but whoever designed the racecourse (I'm told it was Charles I) was not familiar with economies of scale. Such was the past affluence of this venue that racing was obviously treated as no more than a fashion item – the Rowley Mile for the spring and autumn outfits, and the July Course for summer wear.

This sudden realization that two completely separate courses existed led me to an immense bout of depression and a thumbing through *Yellow Pages* for a local psychiatrist. I had decided to celebrate passing the halfway mark of my investigations by visiting what is commonly referred to as 'HQ'. The awareness that there are in fact sixty-one racecourses in mainland Britain, rather than the assumed sixty was enough to destabilize even the most well-balanced personality. The added fact that the Rowley Course is in Suffolk and the July Course in Cambridgeshire makes you very concerned about the state of your marbles.

It wasn't surprising to see the eccentric, ex-world champion boxer Chris Eubank hovering around the paddock – but more of him later. As it was midsummer, I was on the July course; and, as it happened, on one of the hottest days of the season. Knowing that it was a bit of a society do, I had donned the requisite jacket and tie, leading to a bad attack of sweating up before racing and giving a whole new meaning to the expression high summer. What I needed most was the shade of an old oak tree. As I was to discover, this is no problem at Newmarket – at least on the July course.

Dominating the whole area are trees of many varieties (apart from the leaves all being green, that's as explicit as it gets). The effect is that in every section of the course enclosure, dappled light flickers like an old silent movie. The beauty of it is enhanced by the fact that there is no sense of order, mature trees sprouting where nature has randomly dropped its seeds.

Even in the main concourse behind the stands, punters are forced to weave their way between the towering trunks. If the Newmarket authorities ever take on new staff and see the words 'handy with an axe' in the skills section of the applicant's CV, they should reject them immediately. The July course at Newmarket looks as if it's matured like a fine wine and should be left in history's cellar.

In contrast, the Rowley Mile course has decided to go modern – all red brick, clean-cut lines and a Millennium Stand, which will probably rival York and Goodwood. But leave the July course alone. The last thing that's needed here is modernization, as its strength lies in the quirky and quaint setting and a sense of being quintessentially English.

The four main stands confirm this view. They are timber-roofed, lacking in seats, difficult to access and have as much in common with the 21st century as I do with any man capable of ironing a shirt. Just to see the intricate steel girdering almost makes the trip worthwhile and the head-on stand (open to both members and Tattersalls punters) makes you feel as if someone's just given you admission to the Royal Box. It would, however, be sensible to rip up the whole thing and start again – but only if you were a raving lunatic in need of Freudian architectural therapy.

It was from this position that I viewed the first of my four consecutive losers – the advantage of the head-on stand being that you can look your selection smack in the eyes and threaten it with a severe cut in its hay ration. I can only guess that my four horses were overfed lardies who couldn't care less whether they ate for another fortnight. Unfortunately this small grandstand also confirms that Newmarket is not really a racing venue but more of a laid-back garden party. I suppose it depends what you're looking for but when I go racing I like to see prolonged combat and not a one-furlong sprint finish.

I suppose it's not the thing to have a go at Newmarket – but why not? The problem is that having two intersecting courses, laid out in two inverted 'L' shapes and split by a mediaeval dyke, there's not much that can be done about the restricted view – especially as it's been this way since

1799. In a one-mile, two-furlong race the only evidence you have that a race is occurring is that the course commentator becomes slightly more frenetic in his delivery. There is no sight of the race until they enter the main straight round about the four-furlong pole and, given the situation of the stands, the field comes at you head-on and therefore allows no impression of a contest.

The one compensation is that the final furlong takes place over testing, rising ground, making the rush for the line look as if someone has pressed the slow motion button. In a six-race meeting, you're unlikely to witness more than two minutes of live action. Jockeyship has more in common with chess than almost any other sport and I like to see a race develop, watch the opening gambits and observe the tactical sacrifices. If you share my preferences, you may well be better off with an afternoon at Fontwell Park or a wet November day at Towcester. You certainly won't see much action at HQ.

But if the course is Newmarket's Achilles heel, the paddock area is surely the Golden Fleece. Of all the premier courses, Newmarket must take the awards. Whoever manages this area probably has more eye for detail than my Aunt Enid. She was a woman of limited intelligence but was famed for completing a 10,000-piece jigsaw in under four hours. Like Aunt Enid, the New-market authorities have got all the bits in the right places.

The exquisite winners' enclosure stands in front of the even more exquisite weighing room – a combination of thatched roof, newly cut lawns and more flowers than you'd find at my local garden centre. If you have any American friends in search of the elusive English character, tell them to forget the crowded streets of London and head instead for the Newmarket July meeting. Even for a confirmed internationalist such as myself, it is impossible not to sense a twinge of nostalgia for bygone days of Empire, tennis garden parties and young girls in floral print frocks.

This wistful theme is continued in the flower-strewn paddock, enhanced by a central gazebo bursting with climbing roses. Surrounding the white wooden rail are the traditional button seats, yet it is these, perhaps more than any other factor, which confirm Newmarket's meticulous approach. Not only is each button made from highly polished wood but they are also set at a variety of heights in order to accommodate even the most vertically challenged punter. All in all, it's a perfect place for a holidaying American dwarf who thinks that the USA should still be a colony. If you happen to fit the bill, make sure Newmarket's first on your itinerary.

Access to the course from the paddock is no more than a few strides and there's little point in heading for the course until the commentator announces that the field is approaching the furlong-pole. This will give you the chance to make use of the numerous bars and eating facilities dotted behind the main stand. Not surprisingly at Newmarket, you can even enjoy traditional bangers and mash with a very thick onion gravy. It was somewhat odd to find that the first aid room didn't have a 'matron' sign over the door or that the clerk of the course wasn't offering beatings to anyone who hadn't spent sufficient time doing their racing form homework. There were enough men with faces that seem to terminate at their noses to suggest that at £2 per caning, this could provide a highly lucrative income.

By the time of the fourth race, it was becoming obvious that betting was a complete waste of time. I was likely to have more success applying for a job as Julia Roberts' bathroom mirror. Forced, yet again, to watch the victor being led into the winners' enclosure, I appeared to be the only punter on the small stand who had failed to take Ronda at 8-1. The announcer described the three-year-old filly as 'a French raider', his voice containing so much chagrin that I thought the Napoleonic Wars had restarted. As I'm now past the age of conscription this was of no real concern, though I was a little unnerved by the sight of a religious figure having his picture taken with the winner.

It appeared that the Establishment and the Church were about to gang up on the French. The sponsors of the feature Falmouth Stakes were the brewers Greene King. They had come up with the bright idea of donning a fat, rosy-cheeked man in full abbot's outfit – as in Abbot's Ale. The poor chap sweated so heavily in the blistering heat that he must have needed an intravenous drip of Greene King ale to replace his loss of fluid. From this point it was all downhill, the winners' enclosure resembling a Christmas panto, as a number of minor celebrities took the stage and smiled celebrity smiles.

'Look at us!' hissed the woman at my side. 'What are we doing?'

'Doing?' I responded.

'Plebs watching celebs. Why DO we do it?'

'God knows,' I answered meekly.

Yet we all maintained our vigil, riveted by being so close to fantasy.

'Isn't that Sheikh Mohammed?' came another voice.

Nasser Hussein, the one-time English cricket captain, overheard the comment, and to his credit responded with a wry smile as he waited to be interviewed by the *Channel 4 Racing* team. Derek Thompson, employing his well-honed 'I'm interested and I'm listening' face, began to fire questions. Hussein played two forward defensives and a fine cut – and by the end of the interview was beginning to hit cover drives as if he'd been in the job for ten years. If he changes his name to Nathan Hussar, he could become very popular.

And then there was the ex-world champion boxer Chris Eubank. I wouldn't call him barking mad because he is likely to sue – or hit me very hard. It's perhaps better to call him eccentric, as this is a man who, like Newmarket racecourse, has made eccentricity an art form. Apart from looking as fit as a butcher's dog, he was resplendent in yellow suit, brown and white brogues, with monocle and walking cane accessories. He looked like a man who could outblimp Colonel Blimp and would probably have a seizure if England ever declared itself a republic.

In many ways Chris Eubank seemed to epitomize Newmarket – idiosyncratic, unconventional, quirky and a fine counter-puncher to an opponent's attack. I've still got great reservations about this course, as I really can't see a good reason to go racing when most of the track is out of sight. But that's only one side of its split personality and it's impossible not to warm to all it has to offer. Go there – but turn a blind eye to the course. There's little point in looking at it with anything else.

Postscript I: The name of William of Orange's stallion? Stiff Dick. If that's not Freudian, then I'm Chris Eubank and you'd better ring my therapist.

Postscript II: Nine months later, I attended the first meeting which unveiled the new and highly criticized Millennium Stand on the Rowley Mile. There had been much rumbling in the press at a possible uprising by the annual members. As Oliver Cromwell was born just down the road, I was on the lookout for a pitched battle.

And the verdict? I don't know what all the fuss is about. This new facility simply expresses Britain's rejigged class hierarchy – nouveau riche Porsche-driving corporate rowdies on the top layer, old-money members in the middle, and the Tattersalls underclass in their usual place. At least they've built this giant white wedding cake at an angle to the course, and you can see as far as the seven-furlong pole.

But don't bother with a day member's badge. Uniquely, Newmarket's Rowley Mile course offers more to the Tatts punters than it does to the members. There's ample access to the stunning paddock, plenty of bars, cafes and restaurants and the view from the terrace balcony can't be bettered. But if you do brave a wander through the Millennium Stand – take a compass. Most of the crowd seemed to be milling around like lost children looking for their mothers. The racecard does provide a map, with grid references, though you'd need a degree in cartography to make any sense of it.

Sadly there was no pitched battle but the murmuring membership looked like they were preparing for war. Final preference? The July Course – a three-length winner on style alone.

If they ever build a new course!

CHAPTER THIRTY-NINE

NEWTON ABBOT

Newton Abbot has only one thing in common with Tipperary. It's a long way. If you live in the heart of England, as I do, you're talking about an overnight stop. Having visited Taunton racecourse the day before, I arrived in Newton Abbot in the early but dark evening. It looked confusing and sprawled over a much wider area than I had expected. As I entered the town, crossing the Teign river, the distinctive scent of sea air drifted into my car. It whetted my appetite and I turned back towards the coast.

Teignmouth is only ten minutes away and proved to be a delightful old seaside town, with plenty of cheap, cheerful, yet clean small hotels. In the middle of winter, it looks rather seedy, as most resorts do, and the average age of the population appears to be about 153. But it's got real charm, a place where you can hear the sea lapping on the shore, where wives are still called Connie and old women scrub their front steps – 'just in case'. In case of what, I've no idea, but that's always the reason given.

Refreshed by a tasty fish supper and a good night's sleep I returned to Newton Abbot with a few hours to spare.

You can't miss the racecourse, as it sits on the main route into the town and enjoys a lovely view of Tesco on the other side of the road. And you'll know when you've entered this Devon town. There are more ambulances than you'd find on the set of *Casualty*. Drive into the main car park and the first thing you see is a Chapel of Rest. It's a market town that has cornered the market in retirement and all the nasty things that go with it. Every conversation I overheard seemed to revolve around someone's troublesome prostate or an impending hip replacement. To tell you the truth, I think I'd rather get to seventy-five and have a terminal heart attack in a Las Vegas casino with a moll on my arm. But each to their own.

If you get a chance, drop into the cattle market and treat yourself to some real Devon accents. It's like something out of a Thomas Hardy novel, the auctioneer employing the technique of screaming a list of unintelligible words for two minutes, before selling young heifers at about the same price they were fetching in 1850. Carrying my notebook, as I always do, the ruddy-faced farmers viewed me with suspicion. I ground my teeth together to convince them of my commitment to meat eating and all carnivorous activities. It didn't work. They still glared at me as if I was a vegetarian anarchist. It was time to go racing.

I was lucky to find the gates open. Newton Abbot had lost the last four meetings to heavy rainfall and I could hear my feet squelching in the sodden turf as soon as I left my car. It felt like a small punter's day. Only mugs back favourites when the ground's like an Irish peatbog. Pick an outsider who can stay on its feet and looks to have a bit of stamina, and you'll be in with a chance. Well, that's the theory.

At least I wasn't confronted with the pop music I'd encountered at Taunton. Instead, I was entertained by the sort of orchestral music they used to play in my local Odeon before the start of the black and white 'B' movie. The stuttering and grainy music suggested the course authorities had done a deal with a run-down flea-pit just before it was demolished.

Like the town, the course is bigger than you'd expect, the car parks more spacious than you'd even find at Sandown. Not surprisingly, I parked next to an ambulance. It was a fiver to get in and only an extra £6 to gain access to the members'. Given the rather barren nature of the public stand, paying for a member's badge is a good move. The management, however, had decided to paint everything the same colour as Teignmouth beach, giving the facilities a rather dowdy feel. The main Grandstand is starting to look a little frail but does offer some of the most comfortable seats I've experienced on a racecourse.

The stand and its swing-back, cushioned, leatherette seats were apparently opened by the late Queen Mother in 1969. I chose a position which looked as if it might have supported the royal posterior and waved graciously at the growing crowd. The complete lack of response was probably due to me being the wrong sex, wrong age and having the wrong breeding. But I thought it was worth a crack.

'Can I help you?' asked a rather bemused steward.

'Send for an ambulance,' I muttered.

'Sorry?'

'Nothing.'

The first race of the day was a two-mile chase, with only five runners. Venetia Williams was the new goddess of jump racing and it soon became apparent that the punters thought that she, and her horses, could walk on water. Unbelievably, Jack Tanner was backed down to 1-6 favourite. There were two hitches in this plan. Firstly, the horse had never competed over fences in its life and, secondly, hadn't seen a racecourse in over two years. A lot of people with too much money had left their brains in the car park. It had as much chance of winning as William Hague will ever have of becoming a sex symbol. Fighting Times (with my money on board) came in easily by a good six lengths.

My usual celebratory cup of tea was taken in the Manicou Carvery, positioned at the back of the main stand. It's an unpretentious setting, with plastic seating and tiled floors, yet surprisingly comfortable. There's also a fine view down into the paddock and a large outdoor balcony, which must witness some serious drinking during the summer meetings. With winnings jingling in my pocket, I was tempted by the carvery, which served a substantial meal for only £6.75. Unfortunately, my Teignmouth landlady decided I needed building up and had served me with a cooked breakfast of such proportions that my cholesterol level went off the scale. Her husband worked for a private ambulance service. When I left the hotel that morning, I noticed him parked up in a side street, engine purring and ready to go. They worked as a team, those two.

Hidden below the stand, but well worth searching out, is the Red Rum Bar. I sense the architect must have trained in a Swedish timber yard. There was more yellow pine in here than you'd find in an IKEA boardroom. But don't let me put you off, because there's a surprise in store. The walls of this rather antiseptic bar are dripping with pictures of previous winners, owners and jockeys who have landed a race at Newton Abbot. Best of all are the faded black and white photos, some of them dating back to 1959.

Here you can see the pre-silk days, when a jockey's mother would knit him a nice striped woolly jumper to keep out the cold. The prints taken in the sixties and seventies reveal why charity shops are never short of second-hand clothes. Even later snaps suggest John Francome could only have created his hairstyle by spending a great deal of time sticking his fingers in a live three-pin socket. So consumed was I by this display of history that I almost missed the second race. I wouldn't have missed much. My selection might have had a good chance if the authorities had made it a five-furlong sprint. I turned away before the race ended and took up a position in the paddock. It's not the prettiest place I've ever seen and is functional rather than appealing. The view, however, is extremely good, especially from the raked (brown) concrete steps on the eastern side of the grassed oval. Also provided are a large number of button seats, which edge up to the (brown) rails. Avoid these at all costs. It is now three days since I rested my anatomy on these sharp-edged bar stools, yet the marks are still evident and require constant medical attention.

As with many of these smaller courses, the winners' enclosure forms part of the main paddock area. Like Wetherby, they do make a small concession by marking the winning posts with small hanging baskets filled with frost-bitten winter pansies and pre-pubescent hyacinths. I suppose you could say they were trying – but perhaps not hard enough. It was time to go walkabout.

You won't miss a stride at Newton Abbot. The totally flat course is rather uninspiring but visible at every point. Long, easy bends ensure a true gallop and unless you get the conditions I witnessed, it isn't a course for the dogged stayer. Perhaps the most remarkable aspect of the course is the shortest run-in from the final hurdle and fence that I've ever encountered. Get over the last in pole position and you're almost guaranteed to win. With a good effort you could almost persuade your mount to jump straight over the winning line.

This unfortunately did not apply to Jimmy Tizzard who, in the third race, brought his even-money favourite, Rock Force, to the final obstacle with at least six lengths to spare. Perhaps this horse just hates the Newton Abbot winners' enclosure or had fallen out with his owner. As Rock Force hit the deck, Northern Saddler offered a word of thanks and strolled in by ten lengths. It was proving to be a lucky day.

It was then that I heard the crying child. Having wandered into the centre course, which offers no more than an overspill car park, I was quietly inspecting the greyhound course (open Tuesday and Friday evenings), which has been constructed by the side of the last fence. The child cried out again, this time in what seemed to be real distress. Aware of my public duty, I rushed back along the rail, only to hear a woman's voice responding to her daughter's call from the far side of the course.

'Two minutes, Victoria!' she called.

'Mummy!' replied the child.

'When the horseys have gone!' shouted the mother. 'You must be patient, darling.'

'Mummy! Mummy! Mummy!' came the impatient reply.

The also-rans struggled over the final fence and puffed their way to the line, the fourth horse straining every sinew to pick up the princely sum of £253.75. The cross-course gates opened and a yellow Volvo estate raced across towards the crying child. The mother gave me a rather withering look as she strapped her daughter into the safety seat. Little did she realize that only seconds earlier I had been primed like an Olympic athlete, ready to come to her daughter's rescue and be hailed the hero. If someone had bothered to tell me there's a daily crèche in the middle of Newton Abbot racecourse, I might not have been so eager to offer a helping hand. Pick-up time was obviously 3.15, but the 3.10 had been delayed by five minutes, leaving the distraught child on one side of the course and a manic Volvo driver on the other. By all means go into the centre course for a close-up view of the last fence. But don't go at 3.15.

It was time to go. I had a four-hour journey ahead of me and wanted to make good use of the last hour of remaining light. Rushing through the Hill Breeze Bar towards the exit, my eye caught a sign for beef and pork baps. Just what I needed to build up my protein levels for the tough drive ahead. There was only one other person in the queue and, unlike the crying child, I waited patiently to be served. The vendor and customer seemed to be exchanging prostate stories, but I was willing to wait.

Until I saw the Marigolds. One bright yellow Marigold to be exact. This rubber appliance hung loosely on the chef's hand and was being used to extract a slice of over-cooked beef from a deep pool of thin, pale gravy. With as much delicacy as a man could manage wearing a yellow Marigold, he slid this bit of haute cuisine between the two pieces of a dry, white bap. His customer, and fellow prostate sufferer, looked quite unconcerned and handed over his £3.75.

'Yes, sir?' asked Mr Marigold.

'I'll give it a miss,' I answered quickly and headed off to buy a Cornish pasty. Who wants to go home in a Newton Abbot ambulance when you've got a perfectly good car waiting outside?

Postscript: Late result – Cornish pasty comparative study. Newton Abbot 0 (cold, soggy) Taunton 3 (hot, crispy, tasty).

CHAPTER FORTY

NOTTINGHAM

There was a major record broken during my visit to Nottingham racecourse. It was the first time I have ever attended a Flat meeting in my sporty country cap. I've never been too keen on this racing uniform, as it ruins what's left of a once magnificent quiff and on removal leaves me looking as if someone's just ironed my head with a warm steamroller. But this was Nottingham in October, rain lashing down and a Siberian wind that was sharper than a cut-throat razor.

I must warn you against going to Nottingham. Attending Nottingham is a different matter. It's the 'going to' bit that causes the problems. Whether you come off the A1 or leave the M1, there seems no easy access, as Nottingham lies in a fork between the two major routes. Despite my careful planning and with only one hour to go before the start of the first race, I had become hopelessly lost. Signposting in this area was about as useful as Prince John using a map of Regent's Park to hunt for Robin Hood in Sherwood Forest.

Trapped in the city centre and reaching a point of desperation, I stopped at a small hostelry which looked about as hygienic as my garden cesspit. Forgoing a drink, I rushed in and asked for directions. 'Racecourse? Eeh, I don't know,' answered the diminutive landlady, strangely garbed in overcoat and scarf. 'Arthur!' she shouted. Arthur turned out to be her husband and a man who obviously didn't know that soap had been invented. 'Racecourse? Up 'ill. Turn right. Follow signs for Trent Bridge. Can't miss it.'

Arthur was right. At least for thirty seconds he was right. A small sign for Trent Bridge soon came into view but was the last sighting I had for the next five miles. Any indication of a racecourse was conspicuously absent and I was in danger of missing the first race. I was very close to giving up when, by chance, I spotted an old red and flaking board peeking out from behind a tree, the only discernible letters announcing 'OURSE'. I took a gamble and won, arriving at the course with five minutes to spare and about as relaxed as a bungee jumper who's afraid of heights.

'You look lost,' smiled the attendant, responding to the manic face which now squinted at him through the rain-smeared windscreen. 'I'll sort you out,' he added. It was a small moment of calm in a raging sea of irritation. It's not often you encounter a therapist guiding you into a car park space, yet this genial man had a more beneficial effect on my blood pressure than a boxful of Valium. He proved to be a sign of things to come.

I only detail my mental state in order to make it plain that I entered Nottingham racecourse in ill-humour and ready to wield my pen in an act of retribution. I was cold, agitated, irascible and if 'course rage' is a recognized affliction, it was well underway. Yet two hours later, I was the calmest and most contented man in England.

Once through the small and unassuming turnstiles, and even on a bleak October day, Nottingham manages to present you with a welcoming face. It's immediately apparent that many of the offered facilities lie at the back of the stands rather than on the racecourse side. Large lawns, flower beds and scattered trees greet your entry and suggest that the authorities take great care to manicure this expansive area.

The paddock and pre-parade ring are beautifully presented, a maze of stark white railings surrounding a grassed oval which wouldn't look out of place at Goodwood. Banked terraces circle the parade ring, giving punters an unhindered view of the runners. A magnificent 20-foot hedge provides a stunning backdrop to the horses' glistening coats and jockeys' racing colours. The therapy had begun. Arriving as I did, it was only minutes before the starter called the first race to order. Having no time to study form, I selected Quito – simply because it reminded me of my mood as I circled the centre of the city. (I was ready to quit.)

The mile-start lies on the far side of this flat, left-handed, one-mile, four-furlong circuit. What you'll notice in an instant is that visibility of the course is excellent and you're unlikely to miss a stride. Despite being fairly close into the city, there's a country feel to the arena, heavily wooded areas in every direction and a small church nestled amongst the trees which border the back straight. Quito led at the furlong-pole but was headed at the line. At 13-2 it at least provided some comforting place money and was a good result for a hurriedly chosen mug's bet. What it did teach me is that, though fairly flat, the long four-furlong finish from the final turn is a real tester and the winning post must feel as if it will never come into view.

Stamina seemed to be the key, especially as the ground was now absorbing the rain and thoroughbred sinewy legs were being tested on an increasingly heavy surface. It looked like a day when favourites would be turned over and some big-priced winners might just need searching out. Taking a seat at the top of the Tattersalls stand, I buried my head in the *Racing Post*, hunting for soft ground specialists who'd had some minor success at one mile, two furlongs. It was plain that the mile-course around Nottingham was going to take some getting.

In a brief interlude, I glanced back over the track. Inside the main Flat circuit lies the now redundant jumps course, National Hunt racing having been abandoned in 1996. Normally this would turn me against the racecourse authorities but given the style of this venue it was perhaps a sound idea. Ironically the two new stands were both opened by jump racing legends. Following a fire in 1986, the Tattersalls stand was reopened by Jonjo O'Neill in 1987. Whilst it has the look of a modern railway station, the facility works well and the giant banked steps give a fine angled view over the wide finishing straight.

Similarly, the members' 1992 Centenary Stand was opened by Desert Orchid. I am led to believe he had great trouble chewing through the ribbon but gave a short indiscernible speech about the need to retain National Hunt racing. At the time of writing, access to members' was a reasonable £15 (as against £6 Tatts) and well worth the extra money. Given that it was built many years before my visit, the designers were well ahead of their time. Apart from a very comfortable bar and spacious balcony overlooking the course, its greatest feature is the weighing room on the ground floor. Not only do you have a clear sight into the front of this normally secretive inner sanctum, but go around to the course side window and you'll feel you're almost sitting on the weighing scales.

By sheer chance I happened to visit Nottingham on the very day that Kieron Fallon joined the greats of racing by becoming only the third jockey ever to ride 200 winners in consecutive seasons. (He joins Fred Archer and Sir Gordon Richards in gaining this accolade.) Apart from my wearing of a flat cap this was the second record to be broken at Nottingham. K. Fallon will obviously remember his winner, Alva Glen, until he takes his last breath, though his day will undoubtedly be marked by sitting on the weighing scales, only to see a lone and still slightly manic, bespectacled punter (in cap, scarf and gloves) peering at him through the large plate-glass window. I raised a thumb by way of congratulation. He thumbed back. I doubt I shall lower my thumb for many years.

Oddly, the record-breaking jockey looked no more elated than someone who has just won a pot of homemade jam in a church tombola. Another day, another winner. What may well be forgotten is that, in 1999, Fallon not only had more than 200 victories but also rode three classic winners in one season – Derby, Oaks and 1,000 Guineas. He's a classic rider in every sense.

Unfortunately, Fallon's achievements rather overshadowed John Carroll's great day. This rather less fashionable jockey rode three of the best driving finishes I've ever seen on a racecourse and landed three consecutive races at cumulative odds of 747-1 – a truly jumbo performance. Sadly, I missed out on two of his mounts but did land the spoils on Zanay at 14-1. Following my rule of always backing 'lesser' jockeys on the Tote (small punters

tend to go for big names), I scooped odds of 32-1 on a
£5 each-way bet. This led to the third record-breaking
moment of my visit.

Lying to the side of the paddock is a small and friendly
bar with one Tote box and the cheapest tea on the course.
Presenting my winning ticket at the payout window, I was
informed that I would have to go elsewhere, as there
was only £73.20 in the till.

'You mean I've broken the bank?' I enquired.

'Completely,' answered the red-jacketed lady. 'How did
you pick that one?' she asked cheerily.

'Had a bit of form,' I mumbled in response.

But success or failure is not the measuring stick for my
assessment. It is not Kieron Fallon, the success of Zanay,
or the splendid Centenary Stand which will leave a lasting
impression. What marked my visit is the evidence at
Nottingham that racing may well be entering a period of
enlightenment and a casting-off of tradition for tradition's
sake. I don't deny that I'm quite conservative about racing.
I enjoy good behaviour from punters. I have no objection
to the maintenance of casually smart dress standards. I
don't even mind the odd chap touting an Etonian accent
and a battered brown trilby. What I do object to is the still
common enforced segregation, which is about as archaic as
a third-class railway carriage. Someone at Nottingham
shares my opinions.

Normally, and in order to visit the Silver Ring or centre
course, I am obliged to be issued with a pass out, which
permits me re-entry to either Tattersalls or members'. At
Nottingham, I had virtually free movement without a sign
of any border guards. There were restrictions for the odd
area in these facilities but Silver Ring 'untouchables' (five
men, three women, one child and a dog) had full access to

the paddock and were made to feel they were taking a full part in the day's racing.

The racecard delivered even better news. Nottingham were about to embark on a two-enclosure system, scrapping the Silver Ring and reducing the price of Tattersalls to make it open to the majority of small punters and their families – a policy you will see I have advocated in many other articles. I am not of a religious persuasion but I'll wear a dog collar and cassock and sing hallelujah! if the racing establishment supports such a progressive and long overdue strategy.

By the fourth race I was wet, cold yet more relaxed than Delia Smith's Christmas turkey. I had seen Nottingham at its worst, shrouded by leaden skies with its trees bending against a fierce north-easterly wind. On a sunlit summer's day I'd guess it's a delight – if you can find it. The course strikes me as being the equivalent of a male adolescent whose strategy for finding a girlfriend is to lock himself in his bedroom and take the phone off the hook.

Get on to your city council, Nottingham, and tell them to put up a few visible signs. Half your prospective customers are probably on their third circuit of the ring road or stranded in a decrepit city centre pub without the slightest idea of how to find you. You've got a great deal to offer. At least let the punters know where you are. I'm just glad I wasn't going to see a Test match at Trent Bridge. I'd have been lucky to make the tea interval.

Postscript: S. J. Carroll's third winner came in at a starting-price of 20-1. It paid £39.60 on the Tote. I rest my case.

CHAPTER FORTY-ONE

PERTH

You may never have heard of the Craigvinean Novice Hurdle, yet I can assure you it's one of the finest races ever run in the last twenty years. The winning filly strolled over the line with some ease, her victory a testament to the inept display of every other horse in the field, who either fell over or weren't prepared to work at weekends. Lady Windmill never won another penny, but on that day in 1987 she was the star of her stable and the pride of her owner. I was that owner. I was also the man who had decided that Perth was simply a racecourse too far and had to settle for hearing the result on a crackling transistor radio, while digging up my crop of first earlys. Almost eighteen years later and I was at last able to pay homage to the scene of Lady Windmill's legendary victory.

If you think that Newton Abbot's a long way from anywhere, try Perth. It's the most northerly course in Britain and lies on about the same latitude as Moscow, as well as sharing its sub-zero winter temperatures. But they're a cunning lot, these Scots, and they sensibly run their National Hunt meetings between April and September.

Like most ex-trainspotters (I make no apology), I was brought up on steam and have developed a passionate dislike of modern railways. But if you get the chance, board the train from Edinburgh to Perth, a journey which takes you over the Forth Bridge and meanders towards the Highlands past the shimmering Loch Leven. Yet I almost missed it, my head buried in the *Racing Post*, searching for a few winners that might cover the cost of my long journey. Fortunately, I was alerted to Loch Leven by another passenger.

'She's a real beauty,' said my companion.

'Stunning,' I replied, suddenly looking up.

The comment had been delivered by a middle-aged woman who sported fishnet tights, a skimpy lace dress and a pair of earrings that were so long she could hardly lift her head. Unfortunately she also had a voice about five octaves lower than Paul Robeson's and a three-day growth of beard. I was journeying to the racecourse with a full-blown transvestite – who, while amiable enough, would not have inspired Sir Walter Scott to pen *The Fair Maid of Perth*.

It was with some relief that we arrived at Perth's fine old station. Desperate to stretch my legs and with half an hour to spare, I headed off to the city, stopping briefly at the Lower City Mill to buy a gift of real porridge oats for my obsessively organic family. Minutes later I hailed a cab.

'Racecourse please,' I asked.

'Off te' the Scoon, are yeh?'

'No. The racecourse.'

'Aye. The Scoon.'

Perth racecourse lies about ten minutes from the centre of Perth and, as I was informed, was built in the grounds of Scone Palace almost 100 years before. It was a tricky conversation with my taxi driver and proved about as easy as a chat with a Muscovite in Red Square. Yet, within a few minutes, I had learnt to pronounce Perth as 'Peyrth' and Scone as 'Scoon'. I was picking up the language faster than a Linguaphone student.

Because of its setting, Perth enjoys one of the great entrances in British racing, a scenic winding road through the grand estates of the Earl and Countess of Mansfield. (As far as I could make out from my taxi driver, this noble couple run a portable burger stall near the main stand – though I could have misunderstood him.) However, the first sight of the racecourse comes as quite a disappointment after such a palatial introduction. All that can be seen are a row of dilapidated wooden huts, a hardcore car park and a few blue-coated security men who had no idea where I could find the entrance. Yet Perth isn't a book to be judged by its dowdy cover.

The main gates (once I found them) deliver you straight onto the paddock, and from this moment Perth starts to win you over. The parade ring is far from spectacular, yet its simplicity is its greatest virtue. It has the shape of a triangle with all the pointy angles rounded off. There's not a sign of a flower to be seen, barring a few appropriate hardy winter heathers peeking through the shingle surround. The winners' enclosure is placed in the apex of this triangle, shielded from the main ring by a trellised partition and a large advertisement for Isle of Skye Whisky (which I recommend in large quantities). Dotted about near the edge of the ring are a series of small wooden stands giving a clear view over the heads of the rail punters. It's not pretty, but as holidaying Americans might say – it's pretty neat.

In fact the whole place is neat and compact, giving the

punters a feeling that they can relax and enjoy the racing. The day member's badge is priced almost double that of the standard paddock ticket – but overall I think it's worth it. There's no stuffiness at Perth and they've created an atmosphere that would have the laird and his gillie gaining an equal amount of pleasure. Even the three stands are of identical height and thankfully the newish Dewhurst Stand for the private boxes is placed fifty yards beyond the winning post. Neither the paddock nor the members' Grandstand have any outdoor seating, though the members' enclosure wins by a couple of lengths, as it's placed much nearer the winning post and directly opposite the water jump. It's also got the two best watering holes on the whole course.

The club bar is reached by clambering up the wooden raked steps of the Grandstand – a Victorian-looking building – with a large glass canopy. The effect is to turn the bar into a giant greenhouse and the local pastime is to try and drink your whisky before the ice melts. Displayed around the oddly painted yellow, orange and white walls are a series of photos dating back to the early 1900s. Men with dubious moustaches can be seen cavorting around the winners' enclosure in very suspicious check skirts. Thankfully they all seemed to be wearing tartan and there was no sign of make-up, skimpy lace numbers or heavily weighted earrings.

Like a lot of punters, I always look out for a base camp when I go racing – a safe haven, somewhere that comforts you when you know you've just paid for the bookie's next box of Havanas. The Club Dining Room proved to be just the place. At first sight, it's a bit of a dungeon, hidden away under the stand, has no view of the course, a limited menu and a tiled floor. Yet the place is a delight. For some reason it was like discovering a rustic French restaurant – basic but full of what the eating set call *porte-bonheur*. Someone's been on an interior design course as they've smartened up this large basement room with a pale and dark green paint job, while floral drapes hang from the pillars and the ceiling is scattered with three ball chandeliers, as if it's been taken over by a bunch of pawnbrokers.

I had found a darkened corner and was quietly sipping my favourite Bowmore single malt, when I was approached by a young man brandishing a clipboard.

'Could you spare me a couple of minutes for a survey?' he asked.

'Not washing powder, is it?'

'No. No. Perth racecourse.'

'Fire away.'

Five minutes later and following the usual grilling about facilities, he edged towards his final question.

'How does Perth compare to other racecourses?'

'For its size – extremely well.'

'How many other courses have you attended?'

'Fifty-seven,' I responded with total precision.

'How many?!'

'Fifty-seven.'

'You sure? I thought there were only fifty-six.'

'Sixty-one.'

'Positive?'

'Absolutely.'

'You must be good for a tip,' he answered, now certain he was in the company of a true professional.

'Beaver Run in the next,' I responded, with as much self-assurance as I could muster. 'Get on it.'

Why I said this, I'll never know. If I'd backed all the

tips I'd been given over the years, I'd now be living in a cardboard box under Waterloo Bridge.

Fearing that I may have to avoid this man and his clipboard for the rest of the meeting, I rushed off into the stands to watch the two-mile novice hurdle – the same race which had given me five seconds of stardom so many years before. I was in for a very nervous ten minutes as this was my banker of the day, a horse which seemed to fill all the requirements at Perth.

I'd done a little research before leaving home and unearthed the fact that Perth was a flat one-mile, two-furlong course with tight bends and not the type of track for a horse who likes to come off the pace. Come round those bends too quickly and you were likely to end up in the Earl of Mansfield's sitting room. Beaver Run had all the credentials – a recent win at Kelso over the same distance, same firm going and a horse who liked to bowl along in front.

In a sense, the course is Perth's best and worst feature. The fact that it's totally flat with little to obstruct your view, apart from a small copse of mature oaks, means that you can follow the field quite easily as it approaches each fence or hurdle. The drawback, however, is that, like Stratford, the lack of contours rather dulls the spectacle, while the undemanding fences are almost incidental to the contest.

I caught sight of the man with the clipboard as the leading contenders approached the three-furlong pole. Beaver Run was not amongst them and knowing that coming late at Perth was as useful as a paper kilt in a monsoon, I prepared to go into hiding. At the last hurdle things didn't look much better until Tony Dobbin gave his mount a stern look and suggested she might like to join in.

She came late, gobbled up the leaders and sailed in by about four lengths. So much for my insightful theories. Beaver Run had broken every rule in the book and still cantered in.

'Thanks for the tip!' came a beaming face at my side. 'Had fifty on it.'

'How much?!'

'Fifty. Took 3-1. Nice touch.'

'Stone me,' I responded. 'You must be mad.'

'You sounded so certain.'

'Used to do a bit of amateur dramatics.'

I couldn't bear to tell him that I'd only had a fiver on it at 9-4 and left him to assume that I'd just become a wealthy man. Instead, I sidled off to the course enclosure in search of a cup of tea and an ice cream.

Only a few cars had bothered to take advantage of the cheap entry into the centre of the course, probably because the view from here is very limited. But it's worth a look, especially as it has two very unusual features. Firstly, the small bar in this enclosure is as neat and tidy as the rest of the course, and is surprisingly run by a local Indian restaurant. And it's an Asian theme which continues if you fancy a walk across the course. Tucked away in the central copse of trees is the Dundee and Perth Polo Club, who were hard into training, slogging their chukkas with a mallet or whatever they do. It's also the only place on the course where you can catch a glimpse of Scone Palace, its creeper-covered turrets just visible above the forest of parkland trees.

A single flag fluttered in the breeze and I assumed that the Earl and Countess must have been in residence. So much for them running a hamburger stall, though I've heard the nobility is a bit strapped for cash these days.

They should take up gambling – then they'd know the real meaning of poverty.

I had chance to watch only a couple more races before heading back to the station and on to the airport. It was going to be a close thing. For the final race I had to find a spot near the exit for a fast getaway and by chance found myself on the small roof of the lavatories just beyond the Dewhurst Stand. If you enjoy head-on racing and have a poor sense of smell, this is the place to be. It gives you the best view of the last two fences, a clear sight of the back straight and a chance to grab a taxi before anyone else.

Two and a half hours later I was back at the airport, rushing through the security check for a flight that was about to leave.

'Can I check your bag, sir?'

'My plane's about to leave.'

'Won't take a second,' he answered, dipping into my holdall. 'What's this?' he asked.

'Bag of flour,' I answered mistakenly.

'It says oats on the front.'

'Well, oats, flour, same thing.'

'One second, sir.'

Having run all the way through the airport, I was now sweating heavily and would have looked less guilty had I been a Perthshire transvestite holding a parcel marked 'Bomb – Handle With Care'. The resulting body search fortunately avoided my more sensitive orifices and I was sent on my way, guilty of no more than trying to smuggle porridge out of Scotland.

It had been a strange day, filled with a cross-dressing Scotsman, a grateful punter with a clipboard and a security officer who couldn't tell a bag of innocent oats from enough cocaine to buy a string of thoroughbreds. As the plane burst through the clouds, I sat back and began to read the surprisingly smart racecard. It told me that Perth had won the prize for the best small course in Scotland and Northern England no less than five times during the 1990s. I wasn't surprised at all and I bet Lady Windmill would have given it her vote. And so would I.

CHAPTER FORTY-TWO

PLUMPTON

Odd word, Plumpton. It always sounds like somewhere in Cornwall. Don't know why. Just sounds that way. It could be an ingredient that jumps off the page of Delia Smith's cookbooks, or what Billy Bunter might do to his chums after eating one of her pies. But it's in Sussex – not far from Brighton. They told me I might even smell the sea, a real bonus for a man who lives in the heart of rural England.

I approached from the north. Only Brightonians and Frenchmen approach Plumpton from the south. Is it difficult to find? Not if you have the driving instincts of a rally driver it isn't. Signposts for Plumpton come only seconds before the necessary turn. The garage at Cooksbridge probably spends most of the day watching frustrated racegoers doing three-point turns in their forecourt. The sign for Plumpton must be a relic from the Second World War, designed to confuse and dis-orientate invading Germans. *Gott in Himmel,* it nearly worked.

Even when you've located the correct road, you begin to doubt your decision as it turns out to be no more than a leafy lane, giving no indication that you're about to engage in the excitement of National Hunt racing. Usually there are clues. Not large signs or horseboxes, but simply the fact that as you approach a racecourse the cars often become more expensive and all you have to do is tag along behind. Not at Plumpton you don't. As far as I could see there wasn't evidence of anything more exciting than an old Volvo estate.

The road into the car park (I use the term road loosely) was obviously designed before tarmac was invented. All entrants are funnelled along this narrow strip, into a field which lies adjacent to the two-furlong marker. It was a fairly crowded event for a Monday afternoon in mid-October – and all I could think about was how on earth I was ever going to get out.

For those of you familiar with deep sea fishnets (which in my youth, I was) the arrangement reminded me of the notorious 'cod end' – a net designed to let fish in but make it impossible for them to escape. I felt there was a danger of being discovered by a racing archaeologist in a thousand years' time, stuck behind the wheel, my *Racing Post* still clutched in my hand. Like many punters, I decided I would have to leave the course early, missing the last race – the inevitable novice hurdle.

Course managers should always include a completely fictitious final race on the card, in order to encourage the public to stay on the course. The real final race would then become the penultimate race, after which the public would leave, deluded into thinking that they had missed the traffic. Revenue would increase enormously, bookmakers' bags would bulge even more, and jockeys would have the pleasure of racing in front of more than six or seven exhausted catering staff and a bewildered man whose only reason for staying was that his watch had stopped after the third race.

There's no grand entrance at Plumpton. No sense of grandeur. It's plain, simple and probably all the better for it. You drift into the course through a collection of little wooden boxes in which faceless but cheerful men behind wire shuffle your badge towards you. 'Morning,' came a rustic Sussex voice. 'Fine day for it.' It was like creeping into a ramshackle farmyard.

On the day of my visit it was £9 for Tattersalls, £14 for the members' enclosure. And it showed. The Tatts badge resembles an old piece of brown cardboard and leaves you with no choice but to pay the transfer fee into members', if only to get hold of the smart yellow badge. This can be bought from what appears to be a converted chicken shack at the back of the Lewes Stand (pronounced Lewis not Loos – a mistake which can, and did, lead to some very confusing conversations).

But once onto the course, I thought I'd walked into Twickenham. There's a rugby pitch smack in the middle, its posts sticking upwards like four giant javelins thrown from the heavens. I half expected the considerable crowd to break into 'Swing Low Sweet Chariot' at the end of every race. Mercifully they resisted the temptation. Yet I liked Plumpton. I liked it as soon as I saw it. Small, compact, intimate and everything you need within a few strides. Admittedly, the new stands look as if they were designed by a Lego consultant; but like Danish plastic bricks, they work well, they fit together and don't look as if they're about to fall over. And some smart cookie pointed the main stand in the right direction.

Each tier gives a wonderful view of the tight undulating course, allowing an almost unrestricted view of every jump, a great advantage to the average punter. If your horse is going to fall, you want to see it fall. There's nothing worse than seeing your money two lengths in front, disappear from sight and vanish altogether once the pack comes back into view. If you want your investment to dissolve in a black hole, you might as well stay at home, ring a stockbroker and buy some shares. Any punter worth his salt wants to see that money hit the deck – not an unusual occurrence on the steep back straight, which must be like falling down a set of stairs.

But even better is the restaurant, its large windows looking out onto the course and into the paddock. Given the money, it's the way to go racing. Aromatic duck, smoked salmon, beef castillane, lamb shank, prune and Armagnac tart and treacle suet pudding. Yes, treacle suet. It appeared to be a restaurant full of wealthy, naughty schoolchildren. It looked wonderful. The wine list was fairly impressive, even including a '93 Beaune Teurons, at a mere £35 a bottle. I know how good this is as I once asked a wine waiter if I could smell a cork he'd just removed at an adjacent table. Needless to say, I slipped downstairs for a bag of chips, a Mars Bar and a cup of sweet tea. But I'd have killed for that suet pudding.

The paddock is delightful – in its centre, two large leafy oaks. Horseboxes stand close by, giving outsiders the chance to see the frenetic activity which precedes each race. Nervous owners are placated and reassured by equally nervous trainers, both parties masking their concerns with false bravado. Like the whole of Plumpton, the racing is accessible and you feel part of the show. With any luck you can listen in to the pre- and post-race analysis.

The first race of the day proved to be the most exciting, which was surprising considering it was a dog meat two-mile claiming hurdle. By chance I stood close to an owner and his entourage as his horse walked round the paddock. He was effervescent, as excited as a man with a favourite's chance in the Champion Hurdle. As it happened his horse (no names, no pack drill) ran well and was involved in the shake-up. I stuck to him like a piece of chewing gum on the sole of his shoe. He hugged. He kissed. He patted his sweating five-year-old horse and his four-year-old daughter. It was time for champagne. But not after the tannoy crackled into life. 'Horse number five is subject to a claim,' the cultured voice announced. Deflation came quicker than an air balloon that's just run out of gas. Conversations were intense, huddles became tighter as the minutes ticked by. In the end it was too late. He who hesitates is lost, and he hesitated.

I'd seen it before. Well-meaning owners advised to enter claiming races and not aware of the implications. In short you can arrive at a racecourse with a horse you love, dreaming of glory, and go home with an empty horsebox and a meagre cheque in your back pocket. Seems archaic somehow, if not a little cruel.

Then there was the tale of the first hurdle. Well-known trainer, well-known jockey, well-bred horse – but first time over hurdles. It was all too apparent. The horse in question appeared to be blindfolded as it approached the fence in first place, only to deposit its rider under the hooves of the following cavalry charge. Fortunately both horse and jockey survived but the stewards weren't happy and called an inquiry. As usual this took place *in camera,* as wealthy lawyers would say, but we were informed that the horse had 'schooled well at home'. This proved a surprising conclusion, as I overheard one trainer in a deep and whispered conversation with his owner.

'I tell you. He couldn't jump over a box of effing matches. I'd stick to the Flat if I were you.' Even to my uncultured eye, it seemed obvious that the horse had been playing truant from school. I was surprised he didn't trip up on the grass as he went to post. But what do I know?

I wandered into the centre course area (roughly translated as a place from which nothing can be seen), which contained seven or eight bookies trying to eke out a living from £2 bets. There seemed to be no more than 200 racegoers willing to forgo the pleasure of the Tattersall and members' stand. The Centre Course Bar is little more than a converted Nissen hut, though the tea was no less palatable than they were serving in the Lewes Restaurant – and in its own way felt more friendly.

Yet this area contained its own contribution to grandeur, a hexagonal ice cream hut which disguises itself as a Tote building. The staff were about as busy as a family of hibernating hedgehogs. There was such a gap between customers, I was surprised they could remember how to operate the machines. I only gave them my five pounds to make them feel wanted and, to give them credit, they seemed extremely grateful.

There's one particularly nice touch at Plumpton. Punters who have been cast out into the wilderness of the centre course are allowed, between races, to congregate on the racecourse and peer over into the paddock. What's more, they have a fine view. Only at the sound of a bugle, which heralds every race, are they mustered back into the middle. This military call to arms, as the horses leave the paddock, appeared to have some interesting effects. I swear that I noticed ex-servicemen spontaneously adjusting their dress and checking the polish on their shoes. Old habits die hard.

By the time the last race was approaching, I had wandered back into Tattersalls in order to make my escape from the fishnet. The main thoroughfare at the back of the stands is well supplied with caravans, whose main purpose in life is to sell pure cholesterol to already overweight punters. One even had the audacity to advertise itself as a 'Gourmet Diner'. Whoever came up with that slogan has got an overactive imagination and should apply for a job in advertising. The overall effect of this gastronomic feast is that the whole area smells of chips and curry sauce. It was enough to make a man plead for exile to the centre course.

My final bet of the day went the same way as the rest – promising but only for one furlong. It must be that finishing straight, a climb to the post that would terrify Chris Bonington. My betting slip hit the bin and I raced to the car like an old driver at Le Mans. But a pit stop came first, a need to answer nature's call. There are no services on the M23 and you've got to plan ahead. And if you need a toilet, Plumpton's the place to be. I've never seen so many splendid cloakrooms concentrated in such a small area. They should advertise Plumpton racecourse as an incontinent's paradise. Perhaps it's a necessity in this part of the country. Is there such a thing as Sussex bladder? I suppose there must be.

I never did smell the sea. Lots of curry and chips – but no sea. Perhaps the wind was in the wrong direction. Maybe next time, as I'll be back. It's a fine racecourse.

CHAPTER FORTY-THREE

PONTEFRACT

I suppose we all recall certain smells which evoke our youth and instantly trigger memories of childhood days. That hint of lavender favoured by wrinkled aunts; the musty coal fire which can have you dreaming once again of a majestic steam train billowing its way through the night; or perhaps a waft of perfume that takes you back to adolescent love-torn madness. Hurtling up the M1 towards Pontefract, I was suddenly aware of the faint yet pungent aroma of tar. Immediately I thought of George.

It was a strange name for a female budgie, and as a protest George decided to shed all its feathers only two weeks after entering its cage. A bald budgie was not an attractive proposition and I sought advice from my local pet store, who provided me with an ointment with the same odour which was now seeping through my car's air conditioning. Unfortunately the medication proved about as successful as giving an aspirin to Anne Boleyn just after the axe had given her a severe headache – well intentioned but all too late. George died as he had lived – bald and unflappable.

It may seem a tenuous link between a day's racing in Yorkshire and the demise of my pet budgie – but that's how long-forgotten odours can conjure up the past. In order to console myself over the loss of my non-feathered friend, I had raced off on my tricycle to Mrs Ogden's corner shop and spent my total savings on an extremely large bag of Pontefract cakes. They contained enough liquorice to make me shed black tears for nearly a fortnight. By the time I drove into Pontefract racecourse, I was wallowing in sentiment and still grieving over the loss of what my brother had cruelly termed Slapper George.

You'll know when you're in Pontefract as the smell of liquorice pervades the air and the vowel sounds are flatter than an Oval cricket strip. As a man who also says 'laf' rather than 'larf', this isn't a problem – but, as often happens, I can't resist having a dig at the complete lack of signposts guiding you to the course. Going round in circles for half an hour never endears me to a racecourse, though on this occasion it did allow me sight of the posh environs of Pontefract, a fine collection of Edwardian houses along the Barnsley Road. There's some serious brass tucked away in this dark satanic region of Yorkshire.

The racecourse is best located by heading for the town park, just a short distance north-west of the centre. Car parking is free, spacious and dotted with mature English oaks. At first glance it's hard to make sense of the layout, a small section of the course immediately apparent and bordered by a children's playground and large boating lake. Tempted as I was to head for the swings, I resisted my Peter Pan instincts and strode out towards the rather ornate stone-clad entrance. Reaching into my wallet for the required cash, I discovered nothing more than two old betting slips, a scribbled note to remind myself to make a dentist's appointment and a scrap of paper containing three tips to improve my golf swing – none of which have ever worked.

'Where's the nearest bank?' I asked the gateman.

'Just up the road. Ten-minute walk,' he replied.

Despite offering him my swing tips for a meagre £20 he declined my generosity.

'Left out of the car park. Up the hill. Left into Liquorice Way,' he continued.

'Liquorice Way!' I exclaimed, certain that I had become the butt of Pontefract humour.

'Liquorice Way,' he repeated with some gravity.

Thirty minutes later I was back on the course, five crisp £20 notes in my back pocket and ready to do battle with Pontefract. Entrance to the members' enclosure was a reasonable £14, plus a free racecard, and at only £4 more than Tattersalls, well worth the investment. Like Beverley, Pontefract is compact, with easy access to all the main facilities. What is lacking is any sign of the well-appointed, concrete, glass-fronted buildings which are beginning to proliferate amongst British racecourses.

Instead you are presented with a long strip of old Georgian stands, which stretch for almost a furlong from the club enclosure to the £4 Silver Ring. It felt as if I had stepped back at least sixty years and I half expected to encounter women in ankle-length skirts and men in starched collars. It left me with two questions. What is the clerk of the course playing at? Has he not heard of the 21st century? The answers are plainly obvious. The clerk of the course is a smart cookie who realizes that modernization doesn't have to be achieved by a complete destruction of the past. Quick-fix strategies are all too apparent on many racecourses, who seem to have adopted the formula of knocking everything down and hiring a pea-brained architect with the refined imagination of a three-year-old capable of drawing nothing but straight lines. Thankfully, the course authorities at Pontefract have resisted the temptation by making a policy decision to leave the beautiful facades of the old stands and revamp the interiors in a truly delightful manner.

But it gets better. Despite the clerk of the course driving a very swish car with a personalized number plate (sorry, I couldn't help but notice), he hasn't lost touch with the grass roots of racing. Instead of going down the well-worn road of private boxes, private boxes and more private boxes (known as 'sod the small punter strategic planning') the authorities began their reconstruction by enhancing the facilities in the public enclosures. Even the visitors in the 'Butts' (£5 for four people and a car) and Silver Ring (£4) have access to a fine grandstand with an unrestricted view over most of the course. They have even carpeted the simple but attractive bar and cafe on the top floor – a pleasant change from the usual public and humiliating ghettos I have witnessed on many other courses.

What is perhaps even more impressive is that there is little to distinguish the cheaper stands from the usually more opulent facilities of the Club enclosure. If there is a marked difference, it's possibly in the views which can be gained from the members' section. This not only looks over the course and winning post, but also allows close access to the winners' enclosure from a white-railed balcony at the back of the members' restaurant (£15 for an excellent four-course spread). My visit occurred during the height of summer but on a previous visit many years ago, on a cold and rainswept autumn day, I had been equally impressed by the paddock area.

Unusually, for a course of this size, the parade ring and winners' enclosure are separated by a short walk and provide an added bonus to owners who are competing for some fairly meagre prize money. What makes this area so distinct is that the lie of the land rather mimics the course in that they are both built on a steep incline. Runners in the parade ring will be battle hardened by the time they start their race, though horses who make it into the frame need to enter the winners' enclosure with great care. Any over-excitement would inevitably lead to the horse sliding head first into the back of the Grandstand and joining the jockey on the weighing scales.

Bolstered by some excellent skinless fish and chips (see Beverley) and a large cone of delicious homemade ice cream (a small but spotless van at the back of the Tatts stand), I was confident of making money. As my various reports confirm, reading Flat racing form isn't really my forte. But my first inspection of the course suggested I could be in for a profitable afternoon. Pontefract only masquerades as a course for Flat racing thoroughbreds. Its undulating circuit, tight bends and short two-furlong finish is more like a jumping course without the fences. And it's all thanks to the Ministry of Transport.

Until 1983, Pontefract was an uncompleted oval but the construction of the M62 (visible from the stands) forced a reconstruction. What they've ended up with, I was informed, is the longest continuous Flat circuit in Europe – a two-mile, 125-yard full oval course surrounding a large public park. Even more remarkable is that apart from a small stretch to the east of the stands, the extended course is visible from all the various enclosures.

'Bookies love Ponte,' said an amiable steward. 'Favourites always get turned over. Can't handle the finish.' It sounded like my sort of course and a chance to beat the form book. For the first of my certainties, I shuffled into the small seated area in the Club enclosure Grandstand. As far as I could tell these were the only seats on the whole of the course – and all the better for it. The half-covered stands are quite adequate and take you back to the days when football grounds were built for genuine supporters rather than corporate johnny-come-latelys with one eye on the pitch and the other eye on the FT index.

At my side stood the local mayor and mayoress puffing out more smoke than the giant cooling towers in the far distance. They had observed all the correct protocols of formal dress and highly polished chains of office. With the temperature now in the high seventies, they became increasingly flushed in their state of overheated dehydration. But it was an obvious omen. I had backed Protocol, a five-year-old stallion with decent form over one mile, four furlongs – ideal preparation for the one-mile, two-furlong trip over the testing Pontefract course.

It looked fairly promising as they hit the two-furlong pole, only for Protocol to run out of steam and finish a distant seventh. The only form which held up was my continued inability to read Flat racing form. The favourite did get turned over, but by the 13-2 River's Source, who had no apparent history of recent success yet seemed to have been backed by half the local population. My tip for Pontefract is to throw away your *Racing Post*, sneak up on a number of unsuspecting Pontefractians and try to see what they've marked on their card. It seemed to go on all afternoon, horse after horse being cheered in by flat-vowelled hard Yorkshiremen, while Lancastrians and 'nacely spoken' soft Southerners looked on with bewildered expressions.

You may feel that any objectivity in these racecourse tales is likely to be affected by the degree of success I attained with the bookies. If proof is needed that I am able to maintain a journalist's hard nose, then look no further than Pontefract. Like my old pal George, I was being plucked, defeathered and by the fourth race had fallen from my perch. However, unlike the sexually confused George, I was still alive and kicking and enjoying the delights of Pontefract – no more so than in the one-mile maiden stakes.

If anything sums up Pontefract it was this contest for some very average three-year-old contenders. The race was exciting, hard fought and in doubt until the last stride, with my own selection, Solfeggi, not getting within ten lengths of the winner. Yet I enjoyed every moment and every highly visible stride. What made the whole experience so worthwhile was that the management had given the race the grand title of 'The Matty Brown Memorial Maiden Stakes'. So who's Matty Brown?

After a few enquiries I discovered that Matty Brown was one of the original workers who had constructed those wonderful red-turreted Georgian stands back in 1919. Now that's what I call a real loyalty to a worthwhile history and it's as far removed from the encroaching corporate entertainment as I am from sleek-haired city slickers. Keep it up, Pontefract, you're doing a fine job. If you're ever tempted to ring an ambitious pea-brained architect for advice – count to ten, put the phone down and trust your instincts.

Postscript: If you happen to be a chicken farmer with falling profits, I have a very sound piece of business advice. Call all your chickens 'George' and supply the market with ready-plucked birds. You could probably retire within five years.

CHAPTER FORTY-FOUR

REDCAR

Dracula was an odd chap. Poor complexion, strange dentures and an even more peculiar diet. Not long before pulling into Redcar racecourse, I had been getting my teeth into a short biography of Bram Stoker, the creator of this Transylvanian blood sucker.

Having visited Sedgefield the previous day, I had taken lodgings (as Stoker might say) in a Whitby bed and breakfast, only a few miles down the coast from Redcar. It was the sort of place frequented by elderly folk who Morse code their conversations by scraping knives and forks across plates in the crypt-like silence of a dingy breakfast room. As those of you with a literary bent will realize, a large section of Count Dracula's tale is set in Whitby. It's an idyllic Yorkshire resort, yet there is a hint of menace in the air – mostly conjured up by a jutting-jawed male population, who have become devotees of aggressively tight-cropped hair and golden earrings.

I had slept badly, the garlic necklace and large wooden cross digging into my neck every time I tossed and turned under the nylon sheets. But, unlike the idiot solicitor in Stoker's novel, I escaped Whitby as soon as possible and headed up the coast, freeing myself from a sense of impending doom. I should have known it wouldn't be quite that simple. Entering Redcar, I soon realized that Stoker had got it wrong. Even on a sunlit crisp October morning, the town seems bathed in darkness and a much better spot than Whitby for a Transylvanian count who dissolves in the light. To make matters worse the small road into the racecourse's main car park takes you through the town graveyard. If Dracula had been a racing man he'd have had a ball in Redcar.

But like this villain's teeth, the racecourse is far bigger than you'd expect, the main stands stretching down almost as far as the furlong-pole. Escalators ferry punters up to the members' and Tattersalls stand in the style of its near neighbour at York. And the first impressions are promising. Entering through the main gate, a large grassed winners' enclosure is situated to the right, above the entrance to the weighing room a large sign informing you that, 'RACING IS FUN AT REDCAR.' How could I argue with such certainty? I went off in search of the promised entertainment.

With only twenty minutes to go before the first race, a small number of horses were already circling the paddock. Again the scale of this area took me by surprise. It's a parade ring which could easily be transported to a Grade 1 course – circled and decorated by heathers, a separate covered viewing stand and even (unusually) its own Gentlemen's lavatory – with no wash basin. I made a mental note not to shake hands with anybody within fifty yards of the paddock and sauntered over to the pre-parade ring. Unlike the main paddock, this is a very minor affair and contains only nine saddling boxes. Given that I was attending on a day when the average field contained more than twenty runners, it became a continuing fascination to see how the management would handle the crush.

It immediately became apparent that the solution is to condemn the runners to 'hot bedding' – a device employed by the Royal Navy when they have a crew of 150 and only seventy available bunks. Seconds after a horse left its box, another would be led in, while the already prepared runners milled round the paddock, linked so tightly they looked like a string of thoroughbred sausages. I was quietly watching this organized chaos and jotting a few comments in my notebook when I was approached by a young woman in high heels and jeans but thankfully with a small silver crucifix around her prematurely wrinkled neck.

'Can I 'ave yer autograph, please?' she asked politely.

'My what?' I responded, startled by this sudden promotion to fame. 'Why's that?'

'Seen you on the telly,' she laughed nervously, now unsure whether she'd got the right man.

'Of course,' I answered genially and reassuring her with a knowing smile.

To be honest, the only time I had ever been 'on the telly' was when my late parents ran out of chairs at a Christmas tea party. Turning to the first available page in her smart leather-bound autograph book, I scribbled 'Best Wishes, Bram Stoker'.

'Great!' she said, showing her friend her latest trophy.

She was happy. I was happy. There seemed something appropriate in signing the name of a ghoulish writer, who had drawn his last breath in 1912. As a now paid-up member of the living dead, I wandered off to sample the further delights of the racecourse.

Unfortunately, Redcar had flattered to deceive. The

sheer scale of the racecourse suggests that Redcar has, or once had, pretensions of grandeur. Yet, as they say, size isn't everything. Go round to the front of the stands and you are faced with a dying star, a course which has seen better days, a course whose light is fading. The new annual members' facility overlooking the paddock may be an attempt to breathe some life into a corpse which is already in a state of advanced rigor mortis.

Guarded by peak-capped security guards it does little more than confirm that Redcar has perhaps forgotten the real punters, who are left to stare through the plate glass windows at a privileged and affluent minority. A similar construction at Windsor has managed to incorporate a public area, with an equally good view into the paddock for both members and general public. If Redcar wants to embark on refurbishment, the maintenance of exclusivity is not the way to go at the end of the 20th century.

The facilities offered to day members and Tattersalls punters only confirms this opinion. The grey stands, with grey pebbledash walls and grey floors, have begun to resemble a deserted army barracks; while their interiors do little to lift the spirits. The escalators lift you up to a Formica paradise, which reminded me of the seedy Whitby bed and breakfast I had left only hours before. Carpets are threadbare, the tables and chairs like exhibits in a museum of 1950s memorabilia. Apart from a few seats in the stand outside the members' bar, there is no discernible difference between Tattersalls and its more expensive counterpart. The two adjacent bars are featureless mirror images and I could see no point in punters dipping their hands into their wallets for the privilege of becoming a day member.

Ironically, the most comfortable bar is to be found in the basement of the Tattersalls stand. At least here, the carpet didn't appear to have been trampled on by a herd of crazed wildebeest and it's a good spot to find a quiet corner and study form. The self-service restaurant is cheap and cheerful, with very friendly staff. Unfortunately there wasn't a Cornish pasty in sight, the only alternative being a chip buttie or a corned beef pie. (Do they *know* the war's over?)

It was in this area that I began my search for a winner. As I hinted at earlier, this was going to be no easy task. Like the entrance to the racecourse, October is a graveyard for punters trying to find a winner on the Flat. It's the time of year when every owner in the country tries to persuade their trainer that despite having lost its last ten races their horse is a potential classic winner. They will have been paying training fees since April and probably seen no return. Their dreams will have been shattered. October meetings provide the last throw of the dice before Flat racing goes into hibernation. What alternative do they have but to give it one more go – or send their once promising thoroughbred to an all-weather evening meeting at Wolverhampton?

Obviously the blame cannot be directed at Redcar. On the day of my visit there were two Flat meetings, which together had attracted nearly 300 runners. Two hundred of these entries probably had as much chance of winning as I have of being bitten by a vampire in a garlic-oozing French restaurant.

Unfortunately, Redcar had compounded the problem by offering seven races, five of which were cavalry charge sprints under a mile in distance. In many ways the course lends itself to this sort of contest. Although the circuit is an adequate one-mile, five-furlong oval, the course is dominated by a six-furlong straight. Walk over to the centre course, look down this stretch of turf and you'll be astonished by the narrowness of the track. At a guess it would be impossible for more than eight horses to span across its surface. Any horse coming off the pace in the last furlong would inevitably be met with a wall of equine rumps and have no chance of winning without disqualification for barging. Given that there were over twenty runners in most of the races, the form book looked redundant and the proverbial pin back in employment.

Needless to say, my pin proved to be as sharp as a rubber chisel, though I enjoyed the consistency of selecting horses who all failed to get within ten lengths of the winner. I tried all the tactics known to the panicking small punter: different Tote window, different bookie, different viewing position – and all to no avail. The nearest I got to recouping my losses came in the second race when Carambo finished a valiant fourth in a 26-horse field. Not being a handicap there was no place money on offer – despite my nag having beaten twenty-two other runners. If racing wants to attract more customers it's time they ditched this archaic policy and paid out on the first four in any field over sixteen runners – whether it's a handicap or a level-weights contest.

I had watched this race from the centre course, a pleasant enough area with another Formica cafe and a large grass bank giving a decent view of the final three furlongs. Sadly, wherever you stand at Redcar, all the sprint races come at you head-on and there's little chance of real involvement until the leaders are within 200 yards of the finish. Two races later, I decided it was time to cut and run – and save my wallet any further damage. Leaning against the paddock rail, I suddenly heard the sound of children playing. Glancing to my right I realized that the pre-parade ring sits alongside the local junior school. Further round the corner and bordering the course is a giant housing estate.

My eyes wandered further, catching sight of the smoking pillars of heavy industry set against the distant hills of the East Yorkshire moors which descend back towards the racecourse and end at the cemetery that had greeted my entrance. It was a circuit of life, from childhood to work, to domesticity, to retirement and the racing certainty of the graveyard. My impression of Redcar is that it may well have completed the full circuit and its only hope may be an outside chance that there's some truth in the theory of reincarnation.

As I was about to step into my car, I felt a sharp pain in my neck. Instinctively reaching towards my collar I swatted a wasp who was taking its final revenge before winter guaranteed its end. At least I thought it was a wasp. Given my experiences in Whitby, I left with a simmering doubt, wondering if Bram Stoker was about to retaliate for my taking his name in vain.

Night was beginning to fall and for some strange reason I felt more comfortable as the sun dropped below the horizon. My only certainty was that Redcar had already succumbed to Dracula's kiss. Was I about to join it as a member of the living dead? Only tomorrow's sunrise would give me the answer.

CHAPTER FORTY-FIVE

RIPON

There are some very strange surviving customs in the Yorkshire city of Ripon. Since AD 886 they've employed an eccentric local to stand in the town square at 9 p.m. and blow a gigantic ram's horn. Originally this was repeated on the hour until 4 a.m. but curtailed a few centuries later when the inhabitants suffered severe sleep deprivation and found they were too tired to go picking fights with Lancastrians. These were steely men with large bags under their eyes and something had to change. The Wakeman, as he was known, was told to shut up and transform himself into a very quiet mayor.

I only gathered these facts by arriving so early in the area that I had a couple of hours to spare. It gave me a chance to grab a stunning fry-up in a local greasy spoon, snatch fifteen minutes with the *Racing Post* on a pew in the spectacular cathedral, fend off a few disapproving looks, and then head for the market square. If you're pushed for time, forget the history and head for Appleton's butchers who make the finest pork pies I've seen since Reggie, our donor card carrying pet pig, turned up his trotters.

From the market square to the racecourse is only a

matter of minutes by car. Parking is free and I was ushered into position with a smiling welcome, the attendants immediately putting me on Ripon's side. It's a lesson that many other courses would be wise to take note of. If you're trying to sell a beautiful house, why stick a rusting gate at the entrance?

But Ripon knows something about the value of first impressions. Even on a cold early April day and with snow still lingering on the nearby moors, I was confronted with a barrage of colour. Amongst the nine Yorkshire courses, Ripon has become known as the Garden Racecourse. If you happen to live in a large city and are visiting Ripon for the first time, you'll probably think you've just walked into Kew Gardens. There's such a variety of trees, shrubs and flowering plants that the management should consider entering a competition in *Country Life*. 'It's like going to a village cricket match,' came a voice at my side.

She couldn't have put it better. There's something unmistakably English about Ripon, something that makes you want to march into a cafeteria and demand cucumber sandwiches with the crusts cut off. The white cricket flannels had been transformed into the sparkling white rails surrounding the paddock; the pitch into the manicured lawns; the pavilion into a quaint five-pillared weighing room; the sound of leather on willow replaced by the clatter of hoofed feet on grass. To a man who has a built-in aversion to Flat racing, Ripon were doing their best to win me over.

However, dig a little deeper and there are signs of a few fraying edges. Fresh from my wandering around the delights of the market square, I went in search of the obligatory cup of tea. The rather plain but adequate black and white racecard contains a section devoted to 'Where to eat and drink'. The fact that there are thirteen outlets proved to be an unlucky number as plastic appears to dominate almost all the cafes and bars. There's the occasional thin threadbare carpet to be found here and there and some extraordinarily gaudy fruit wallpaper in the Paddock Room of the members' enclosure.

But apart from these few distractions, the warmth of Ripon racecourse lies outside rather than inside its rather cold facilities. Nowhere is this more true than the Fountains Cafe in Tattersalls which advertises itself, somewhat optimistically, as a self-service restaurant. If this is a restaurant, then I'm chairman of the Jockey Club. For some bizarre reason it contains a number of fixed chairs and tables that you're more likely to find in a fast food outlet, while the flooring looks as if it's suffered death at the hands of a thousand sharpened stilettos.

So here's the first tip for Ripon. Even if it requires two jumpers and a bobble hat, stay outdoors. And it has plenty to offer. Even the normally desolate Silver Ring sports a magnificent children's play area with grass fit for a bowling green. The central piece is a very odd climbing frame that looks like a cage which has just been vacated by a pack of wild animals. You can draw your own conclusions.

Yet the main attribute of the cheapest enclosure is, without doubt, the Gentlemen's lavatory. This sparkling edifice was enough to make me wish I had a weak bladder and it was in here that one punter got lucky. As I was leaving I chanced to pull out my handkerchief to suppress a constantly dripping nose. As I did so, a two-pound coin slipped from my pocket and began to roll across the floor. I chased. It gathered speed and turned to the left. I changed direction. It turned right. Now almost running across the slippery tiled floor I made a final lunge for the money as the golden coin disappeared under the locked door of the only occupied stall. By this time I was completely out of control and hit the floor with a dull thud, my only view being a pair of unpolished shoes draped with crumpled trousers. Seconds later, the fingertips of a single hand appeared, swept up the coin and the unseen body offered up a loudly forced cough. I must have waited for over five minutes, yet no-one appeared and I doubt I'll ever know how he got out of that lavatory. But consoled by the fact that he must have really needed the money, I raced back to the Tattersalls enclosure.

Enter from the Silver Ring gate and you gain a clear view of all the enclosures. The back of the Tattersalls stand is dominated by a large decorative bandstand surrounded by yet more pristine lawns and a collection of benched seats. But be careful where you sit. Look closely and you'll see that the bench ends are constructed with fiery dragons, their tails at your arm and their fanged mouth concealed under the seat, ready to attack your delicate bits. It's not a place to linger unless you happen to be carrying a machete.

Further down, the paddock and winners' enclosure are delightful and really raise the spirits, even when you've just had your last three selections beaten into second place by no more than a short-head. The parade ring has so many mature trees that someone from the more select parts of Gloucestershire would probably call it an arboretum. If it's crowded (which I'm told it is during the summer) and you've got a day member's badge (it's worth it) head for the small Tote window at the side of the Champagne Bar. It was here that I queued to collect my measly place money for yet another unfortunate short-head loser. The man in front of me looked delighted, clutching his ticket as if he was waiting to be mugged. My own head, in contrast, was bowed in dejection and could only stare towards the floor. I recognized those shoes. I recognized those once crumpled trousers. I recognized those sinewy fingers clutching the winning ticket.

'Good win?' I asked as he turned away from the window in triumph.

'Big price,' he answered gleefully.

'Much on it?' I enquired with restraint.

'Just the two pounds.'

'Thought so,' was all I could muster.

Halfway through the afternoon's card and I was still to land a gamble, mostly due to my occasional habit of adopting the strategy of a mug punter. Real gamblers study the form, find the likely winner and then look at the price. Amateurs look at the price and then study the form, desperate to justify backing a donkey. Needless to say, this is illogical – but that's what makes it so appealing. The reality, of course, is that if your employer offered to treble your wages you'd bite their hand off. Yet suggest to a mug punter that odds of 3-1 are good value and they'll find every excuse to pick an outsider. The occasional lucky hit makes it seem like a good plan (it isn't really) and small punters never change. The trouble is that even when you let your head do the talking, there's often a surprise in store.

The fifth race, a six-furlong straight sprint, seemed to suggest only two possible winners, despite a large field. I backed them both and grabbed a spot in the cosy members' stand, the only place on the course that offers raked seating. With expectation high, I settled back to watch one of my selections flash past the winning post. Thirty seconds later I was screwing up my betting slip. Despite starting perfectly, it was soon obvious that within three furlongs both my selections were at least ten lengths adrift, the pack having split into two groups, with the bunch on the far rail so far ahead, it looked as if they'd taken a short cut.

Chatting to a gateman a few minutes later, it soon became clear that I was the only person on the course who didn't know that in Ripon's five- and six-furlong sprints there's no point in backing anything with a draw number lower than ten. If I was an owner and got a draw in stall number one, I'd demand a vet's certificate and shove the animal back in the horsebox.

Races over six furlongs don't seem to suffer the same problems, though, with two sharp bends to negotiate, any jockey losing position as they enter the straight has got a real battle on his hands. The sharp, right-handed one-mile, five-furlong course is fairly flat, apart from a very strange dip just opposite the furlong-pole which seems to break the stride of the leaders as they charge for the line. From the head-on position in the main stand, it looks more like a tank trap than a minor dip. I'm certain that if they'd levelled it out I'd have landed at least three winners. Or maybe not.

If you enjoy seeing the stall starts, Ripon provides one of the best views I've found on my travels. All the twelve-furlong races begin close to the enclosures and you can gain easy access to the centre course between races. But don't stand side on. Walk along the course another thirty yards or so and you'll find that the stall is set at an angle for the first bend, with the effect that when the starter's flag goes down the pack seems to be heading straight at you. You're also close enough to hear the jockeys' comments as they battle for position.

'Get going, you effing brute,' seemed to be a favoured encouragement – even from the senior jockeys. It's an eloquence and skill that could only come from years of dedication and a five-year apprenticeship. I should have guessed that Ripon was going to be a punters' graveyard. Early season Flat meetings are notorious for large fields of untested horses. It's a period when the only people on the course with a suntan are the bookies, having scooped so much money in the first few weeks that they head off to the Algarve for a couple of nights on the local brandy. By the time of the sixth race I felt like I was paying for their next holiday.

After watching the start of a one-mile, four-furlong race, I stayed in the centre course, only to discover that, despite the usual lack of amenities, it probably provides the best view of racing on the whole course. Together with a small concrete stand, there's also a large grassed mound and the only spot on the course where you can see all of the circuit. Even the tea bar was a pleasant surprise, despite reminding me of a giant scout hut. The standard tiled carpet floor and scattering of fold-up chairs and tables was unexpectedly cosy and far preferable to many of the drinking holes in the main enclosures.

The sixth race produced yet another blank and I headed for the car park with an emaciated wallet but a feeling that Ripon is a course to mark in the diary. The buildings aren't pretty, the course nothing special – but it does have that undefinable appeal that you only find at the smaller country courses. Of the nine Yorkshire courses, it's definitely up there with Pontefract and Beverley, and is well worth visiting.

With a long journey ahead, I had no time to stay for the last race, which was a cavalry charge for 25 three-year-olds with no worthwhile form. The A1 beckoned and I treated myself to an old tape, *Carly Simon's Greatest Hits* – remember her? My car radio was broken and I'd bribed my daughter to lend me her Sony Walkman, which was now firmly planted in my ears. By the time I reached York, I had achieved a lifetime's ambition as I was beginning to fall asleep with Carly Simon. I flicked the switch and managed to find Radio 5 and the late racing results. Boss Tweed won the last at 20-1 and in a final desperate attempt to save the day I had put £5 on its nose. There was a God after all. My eyes lost their heaviness and sparkled into life. Who needs a Ripon Wakeman when you've got your daughter's Walkman?

CHAPTER FORTY-SIX

SALISBURY

Cincinnati is the only place I've ever wanted to visit in America. I know nothing of its history, nothing of its climate, nothing of its scenery. What I do know is that it sounds brash, cosmopolitan and attractively vulgar. I bet Americans feel the same about Nether Wallop. No other name could reflect such archetypical Englishness. Approaching Salisbury from the east, along the Andover road, takes you through not only Nether Wallop but also Middle and Old Wallop. There's enough wallop along this road to make you think you're driving on the Cincinnati racecourse.

Running short of fuel, I stopped briefly at a filling station which also boasted a Little Chef restaurant. If you're not familiar with these culinary establishments, you'll see them tucked alongside most British trunk roads. On entering, signs request that you must wait to be seated – despite the fact that there are rarely more than two tables occupied in the whole of the restaurant.

I was placed next to a small group of American tourists whom I suspect had been told that the Nether Wallop Little Chef was an Olde English tea room. Following the delivery of some toasted tea cakes, much discussion ensued on the appropriate way these should be consumed and whether the lurking currants might be a health hazard. It also became obvious that their next port of call would be Stonehenge, a pile of old stones just north of Salisbury and assumed to be close to the heart of every Englishman.

'Going there?' asked one of the group, spotting my prying eye.

'Racing,' I answered, with the embarrassed look of a child who's just been discovered with his ear to the keyhole.

'Stonehenge?'

'Salisbury. You should try it.'

'Not on the itinerary,' prompted his wife, picking another currant out of her disintegrating tea cake.

Within half an hour I was pulling into Salisbury racecourse. Signposts in the city are limited and the trick is to follow directions for Wilton (as in carpet) and then keep your eyes peeled for one or two tricky turns. Only five days before, I had battled my way through the chaos of Derby Day. Salisbury felt like a return to civilization and had about as much in common with Epsom as the affinity between a city stockbroker and an Armenian pig farmer.

In a state of PDT (post-Derby trauma), the entrance to Salisbury relaxed me faster than a king-sized bottle of Valium. The fairway of a local golf course acts as the main free parking area and is surrounded by enough mature oaks to make an Englishman dewy-eyed. There isn't a hint of frenetic activity and you're immediately aware of being enveloped by Wiltshire's easy-going pace. Even the usually manic course bookies seemed to amble towards the entrance as if it was a privilege to be working on such a perfect summer's day. Wicker hampers creaked open, while radio cricket commentaries drifted through the air. It was just a straw boater kind of day.

The majority of courses in Britain welcome you with their worst features – often the back of their main stands. Salisbury (like Ludlow) gives you an immediate full frontal, as once having passed through the small garden shed entrances, the Grandstands are in full view. Access is gained by crossing over the course and entering the various enclosures by striding over the main straight.

Apart from giving you a jockey's-eye view of the course, you can also dig your heel into the turf and make your own decision about the going. If nothing else, it gives you the chance to linger for a few seconds and give the impression of being a knowledgeable punter. The morning paper had declared 'good, good-to-soft in places'. Even to my uncultured heel, the course was about as soft as a steel girder and any horse with form solely in testing ground was going to have a line put through its name.

My advice on entering the main concourse is to slow down as quickly as possible. Stride out too quickly and there's a fair chance you'll have walked straight through the course and out the other side. Salisbury is no more than a narrow strip of land, a one-mile straight onto which is tacked a collection of buildings at one end and a small loop at the other. I can only describe it as reminiscent of my mother's old darning needle, which saved many a terminal sock and delayed the growth of Marks and Spencer for almost a decade. The effect of this design is to make all races up to a mile no more than a straight dash for the line, giving better horses time to tuck themselves in and wait for the right moment to hit the accelerator. Anything over one mile and Salisbury becomes far more interesting. Over a distance of one mile, six furlongs the field starts almost in front of the main stand, with the added bonus of giving punters the chance to witness a taped start – usually reserved for jumps meetings.

It's rather like being taken back twenty years and the horses must spend the initial two furlongs looking for the first hurdle. At this point, the racing pack passes the stands left to right, heads up the straight to the loop and re-emerges onto the course going right to left. It was noticeable that most winners came back with a look of elation mixed with a distinct expression of déjà vu.

In the second race, I was certain that Turtle Valley looked a good thing, despite being ridden by a 3 lb claiming apprentice. My major reservation was that it was trained by Simon Dow – a man with whom I have had some dealings in my short spell as an owner. This is not meant as a slur on Simon's ability, as he does a fine job with the horses in his charge. The main drawback is that I have almost a 100 per cent failure rate whenever I back one of his entries. It's catch-22. Back it – it loses. Don't back it – it wins. It's what's commonly known as a lose-lose situation. And I lost. Frankie Dettori (on Knockholt) did his best to run for the line from the mile post but lost by an eyelash. Does Simon Dow train his horses to wink in a tight finish? I'll ask him next time we meet. Perhaps he'll put me on a retainer if I promise never to back his horses.

Whatever the case, Turtle Valley was led into the winner's enclosure by a large syndicate of owners with bigger smiles than a pianist with twelve fingers. The paddock is surprisingly big for a course of this size. Whilst its tree-lined surroundings are exquisite, it's all rather plain and a shame they haven't made more effort with the old flora and fauna. Even a bunch of daisies stuck in a vase would have helped; and why do the button seats, familiar to all racegoers, only extend around a quarter of the rail?

But there are some noticeable highlights. The pre-parade ring near the one-mile, six-furlong start is delight-ful, while the paddock rail is an unusual construction. Instead of the normal single white barrier, someone with a bit of flair decided to present the public with a metal rail made up of three white strips. Apart from giving the appearance that Salisbury is sponsored by Adidas, it's an ideal place to collapse against when your banker has just gone down – by an eyelash.

All punters look for scapegoats and I found mine only seconds later. Sky TV had set up their interview camera outside the weighing room, a glass-fronted single-storey building at the side of the paddock. It's an open access design, which seems to suggest that racing authorities are at last catching on to the fact that running the industry like a secret society is not popular with your average punter. Forget lobbying for a Bill of Rights – what we need is a Freedom of Racing Information Act.

As I peered into the weighing room, Miriam Francome was attempting to present her thoughts on the first race. Her delivery to camera seemed unusually disjointed and lacking its usual chatty style. The producer was probably turning grey by the second. Had he stood in my position, all would have been revealed. Hanging out of the jockeys' changing room (and behind the camera) was one Lanfranco Dettori, pulling more faces than a PG Tips monkey with a five-year contract. It seemed quite logical to blame Miss Francome for distracting my jockey and his failure to get Knockholt over the line.

But that's the beauty of small courses such as Salisbury. Only days before, I had watched Dettori leave the Epsom paddock ashen-faced, his legs astride a Derby favourite who was sweating up more than a Spanish bricklayer in the middle of July. Courses like Salisbury dissolve this tension, the small crowds eased into relaxation. In many ways this Wiltshire course shares some of the disadvantages of places like Great Yarmouth. Much of the action is seen head-on and the field in longer races disappears from view. But here the comparison ends as the whole course enclosure, despite its rather worn looking stands, does maintain a sense of style and friendliness.

The main Grandstand is made up of three levels, each with its own character. Best of all, though not offering an ideal view, is the lower tier. Long bench seats are covered in strips of cushioned covers and give you direct access to the restaurant. Like the rest of the course, the interior is something of an oddity and more like a Trust House Forte reception area than a country racecourse. Whether this is a plus or a minus depends on your taste in hotels but the carvery restaurant offered great value (£24) for a reserved seat, lunch and cream tea thrown in. Naturally, I wandered into the main bar for a Cornish pasty (8 out of 10) and a weak cup of tea (9 out of 10). The brown and faded carpet tiles needed a revamp but the atmosphere was again welcoming and the staff keen to make losing punters feel more optimistic.

I sat at a table by the window, next to a rather elderly lady who seemed to own more form books than a *Racing Post* hack. We exchanged glances and bad tips. It transpired that she had also been on Knockholt and I felt obliged to explain my theory of the Miriam Francome distraction. She looked somewhat bemused and returned to her *Timeform* bible. Seconds later, peering down at the course, I noticed Nifty Norman being taken down to the start five minutes before the rest of the field. Unfortunately no-one had informed the shoulder-hunched man who now wandered down the straight replacing the loose divots. What was even stranger was that he was also called Norman.

Much flag waving ensued, but Norman, keen to attend to his duties, had his eyes firmly on the ground. 'Norman! Norman!' came the shout from the stewards. Naturally, Nifty Norman looked around. Even the jockey, J. D. Smith (3), turned his head. Norman continued, oblivious to the fact that he was about to be mown down by a five-year-old thoroughbred. 'A multi-million pound industry and they can't even let the poor chap know . . .' My elderly companion's words were cut short as Norman suddenly looked up and sidestepped his fate with a move that would have flattered a Welsh fly-half. 'Typical Salisbury!' she added before returning to her books.

And that was it. It was typical Salisbury – and all the better for it. The layout of the course is eccentric, the facilities idiosyncratic, the racing quirky, the punters typical of an English country course. If you happen to be American and reading this report in a Little Chef near Nether Wallop, you should change your itinerary. Hijack your coach, forget Stonehenge and head for Salisbury racecourse. You'll learn a lot more about England and the English than you ever would by standing around an old pile of stones.

Postscript: My elderly friend in the Grandstand bar had left her *Timeform* open on the runners in the fourth race. Heavily underlined was the four-year-old filly Imani. It won comfortably at 4-1. Toasted tea cakes were definitely on the agenda as I pulled out of the car park and headed for home.

CHAPTER FORTY-SEVEN

SANDOWN

'You want to be buried *where*?' asked my solicitor.

'Sandown Park,' I replied, without hesitation.

'Are you serious?'

'Believe me, Charles. I'm absolutely certain.'

It's some years since I had this conversation about the disposal of my mortal remains. Planning your own funeral is never a comfortable experience. I've always been squeamish about providing worms with a month's supply of food and have no intention of ending my life as an underground supermarket. Like cricket devotees, I'm more of an ashes man. Give me a good roasting, pour me into a little urn, wrap me in an old copy of the *Racing Post*, then bury me under the last fence at Sandown.

My solicitor, more of a rugby man, suggested Twickenham might provide a more elegant resting place. I was having none of it. It was Sandown or nothing. You'll guess from these brief comments on my funeral arrangements that, despite the odd reservation, I rather like this racecourse. Maybe it's just good memories. If I got food poisoning at my local restaurant on the same day that I won the lottery, I'd probably never eat anywhere else.

The day started well. I'd just dropped off four friends at Heathrow, heading for the sunshine of the Costa del Sol, leaving me with the cold winds of a February morning.

As the plane took off, God switched on the central heating. By 1 p.m., the temperature at Sandown was nearly 60 degrees, the sun was shining and the forecast for Marbella was 58 degrees and cloudy. If anyone happened to see me lurking around the course on this particular day, I apologize for the constant and irritating smirk.

Like many of the bigger racecourses, it takes quite a time to find your bearings. However many signs the authorities display, the first half-hour is a total confusion. This is even worse when (as I always do) you arrive early. You are placed in the position of the pioneer, unable to latch onto a sure-footed group of punters.

The size of the main Surrey Hall only strengthens your bewilderment. It's a truly cavernous area, which could double as an aircraft hangar. The snaking network of pipes, air ducts and stairways gives the place a rather sterile feel and it lacks any of the cosy appeal you'll find at the smaller courses. But give it a chance. Once the crowds begin to swell (and you never get a small crowd at Sandown), the place comes to life.

In the first fifteen minutes, I scurried about the area like an illogical child trying to find its way out of a one exit maze. Don't get me wrong. I love children – as long as they're my own. Present me with the fruit of other loins and you might as well offer me a summer holiday in Grimsby. I chose the wrong day.

It was school half-term and by the time of the first race the Surrey Hall seemed to have become a giant crèche. Inveterate punters hadn't been put off by this minor irritation and had dragged their offspring to the racecourse. Hundreds of no-neck fathers dragged their obviously bored children with a white knuckled grip. Their free hand was employed to make a constant series of calls on their mobile phones. Just who do these people speak to? I can only guess they were ringing the Sandown helpline and asking for information about how to get out of the Surrey Hall.

Seeking refuge, I headed down some inviting steps, which were signposted for the Esher Hall, a place which carries my highest recommendation. If you want to get away from children, go here immediately. This, like a bar with no beer, is a crèche with no children. On offer in this barren warehouse is a dumping ground for the under tens. Punch and Judy, face painting, bouncy castle – and, best of all, a life-sized racehorse simulator. Unfortunately the children of Surrey had other ideas and other temptations.

The Americans have Thanksgiving Day, the French Bastille Day, and the Russians probably have a Let's Get Rotten on Vodka (Again) Day. The English, on the other hand, celebrate National Chip Day. In February. On Friday, 19 February, to be precise. The life expectancy of a potato had gone down to about three minutes, given the fact that the Sandown authorities had decided to celebrate this event by giving away free chips. Unless you're a Belgian, avoid this meeting at all costs. I made one abortive attempt to claim this free meal, only to be set upon by a bunch of adolescents who were obviously studying *Lord of the Flies* for their GCSE. Scary is not the word.

As a change of policy I decided to watch the first race from the centre course. An elegant six-year-old stallion named Lordberniebouffant had attracted my money, due to the fact that I'd recently watched a remake of *The*

Scarlet Pimpernel. This isn't form reading of the highest quality, but the coincidence of something French and something slightly effeminate suggested fate was on my side. As my sexually ambiguous selection came to the last, it was going well and threatening to pip the 13-8 favourite. Unfortunately it spotted a mirror on a car parked close to the course and seemed unable to resist checking that its hair wasn't looking a mess. Vanity can be very costly at times.

I abandoned the centre course immediately. If you limit yourself to this cheap compound, you'd probably never visit Sandown again. They've made a slight effort in providing two raised concrete standing areas; two open-sided tents which appear to serve no purpose whatsoever and a raked grandstand for a hundred people or so, which oddly faces away from the racecourse. The Park Bar (as usual, no more than a shed *à la mode*) had the distinction of containing more TV monitors than clients.

The whole place can be summed up by witnessing the collapse of Arthur Nicholas. He and three battle-weary bookies were trying their best to earn a meagre wage, when a sudden gust of wind swept Arthur and his stand onto the litter-strewn turf. The contents of his bag emptied at the punters' feet, who responded by instantly claiming rights of treasure trove.

Not wanting to miss the bedlam created by the four people who constituted the total crowd, I jumped in immediately. The highest denomination I found in a ten-minute search was a 50 pence piece. Says it all about centre rings really. I handed back the small handful of change and tried to hide my expression of sympathy. I was almost tempted to stick a fiver in just to make Arthur feel better. If Lordbertiebouffant had obliged, I might have felt more charitable but I turned quickly away, wallet still intact.

It was then that I realized the schizophrenic nature of Sandown. Looking across to the main stand, you are faced with a grey, drab edifice which has all the attractiveness of the old *Ark Royal* in the middle of a refit. Yet behind this facade lies the true Sandown, the elegant areas which have punters returning year after year. It's an accepted fact that the course is magnificent, presents wonderful jumps to high-class hurdlers and chasers, gives one of the best views on any British racecourse, and has one of the two finest finishing fences you would find anywhere. But Sandown scores most points behind the scenes. If the course Grandstands give you the feel of a seat at the Royal Opera House, the area looking onto the paddock gives you La Scala, Milan.

Whether you stand on the terraces above the Eclipse Bar, or sit on the wrought iron benches above the Sandown Diner, the sight is breathtaking. Even in February, the striped lawns of the huge heather-rimmed paddock make it plain that this is a class act. Amongst the big league courses, Ascot is truly pretty and pompous, Cheltenham manicured and functional, but Sandown has it all and looks as if it means business.

Even the horses' access to the course, along a wood-chipped Rhododendron Way, gives the punter a magnificent view of horse and rider right up to the course. Don't stop as they pass the Cavalry Bar but follow them all the way. If you're lucky, you'll hear the jockeys declaring, 'He's got no chance' or 'If I had a mortgage, I'd put it on this nag.' I tried this trick with Djeddah in the Stag Handicap Chase. The trainer and jockey cunningly spoke in French to avoid giving me any inside information. The phrases *'pas de chance'* or *'la mortgage sur cette nag'* were not evident and my money went elsewhere. But it was worth it, just to hear the voice of the sumptuous Madame Françoise Doumen, who's enough to make a man take three sugars in his tea.

At the far end of the paddock lies the unsaddling enclosure, which Djeddah returned to ten minutes before the rest, having pulled up at the fifteenth. (I may have been mistaken but I'm sure I heard a woman's voice screaming some strange word called *'merde'*.) Adjacent to this enclosure is a pre-parade ring that could match the main paddock at most courses. Look out for a large board that displays previous winners of the Whitbread: Mill House, Titus Oates, Royal Mail, Special Cargo, Mr Frisk and Desert Orchid to name but a few – or at least the ones who were carrying a percentage of my wages.

But the real stars in this area are the ten maples which cast their shadow over the pre-parade ring. Such is my arboreal knowledge that I am certain they are maples, this expertise being confirmed by a plaque which tells you that the maples were planted by the late Queen Mother on her 80th birthday in 1980. She must have had some stamina to plant ten maples in one afternoon. It could even have been the day I took my daughter to Sandown in her new pushchair.

An elegant, elderly lady suddenly approached, leaned over the pram and declared, 'What an absolute dear!' Somewhat stuck for words, I mumbled my thanks and my daughter, with her usual confidence, did her famous impersonation of a highly efficient whoopee cushion. I think her Royal Highness was very impressed, but the invite to the garden party never came.

But if you're ever lucky enough to bag a winner at

Sandown, make sure you welcome it into the winners' enclosure. Despite Lordbertiebouffant being the nearest I'd got to any success, I paid my usual visit. When you're depressed, it's nice standing next to people with winning betting slips, fat wallets and smug faces. This is the Rolls-Royce of enclosures, a white-railed oval, the winning horse enjoying a flower-strewn private box that was probably designed by Capability Brown.

Fronting this grassed area is a tasteful, single-storey brick building, its fascia covered in a laurel hedge that is so well behaved, it must have been trained by Mary Chipperfield – before she was arrested. Can you beat a hedge into submission? I've never seen anyone try it on *Gardeners' World*. Perhaps I'll write and suggest it.

It was time to sound the retreat. I was having a bad day. Wandering through the Esher Hall, which had now amassed about five children, I stopped briefly to watch the Punch and Judy show. Punch seemed to be shouting, 'Throw the bookie down the stairs! Throw the bookie down the stairs!' I wasn't the only one having a bad day and I scurried up the steps into the confusion of the Surrey Hall, stopping briefly to flick through the offerings on the bookstand.

'Pass me the stats book, would you?' came a voice at my side.

'Of course.'

'Thanks.'

One glance told me it was Jamie Osborne, a once favourite jockey and still in full riding gear. He's smoother than my wife's legs after two hours in a waxing parlour. Resisting asking for a meaningless autograph, I watched his finger trace through the lists, saw him stop briefly at the letter 'L' and then close the book quickly before hurrying away. What he was doing I've no idea.

With steps as fast as Osborne's, I raced to the exit, halting at a litter bin to deposit a fistful of losing betting slips. I'd been buried by the bookies. Buried at Sandown. Even been forced to attend my own funeral. I reached for the mobile and rang a familiar number. The response was immediate and I spoke without hesitation.

'Charles?'

'Yes?'

'It's about my will . . .'

Postscript I: The following day Jamie Osborne won the first race at Ascot on a horse named Lord Of The River. I'm told he rode a very clever race and came in with fifteen lengths to spare. He retired from the saddle only a few months later.

Postscript II: 2002 saw a £23 million redevelopment including a new state of the art Eclipse Stand, canopies over the grandstand and, best of all, improved car parking. If you're tempted to go don't resist. Sandown provides one of the finest views of racing in Britain.

CHAPTER FORTY-EIGHT

SEDGEFIELD

I'd never heard of a Piesporter Michelsberg Mozel QbA Prinz Rupprecht '96. Just to put you in the picture, at £10.95, it's the cheapest bottle of wine you can buy at Sedgefield and not what I had expected in the industrial heartland of North-East England. I'm no wine connoisseur, but given Sedgefield's political roots, I'd assumed their wine cellar would contain nothing but large vats of chianti.

It's an ugly name, Sedgefield. I don't know why but it seems to be imbued with darkness and depression – not a title that lifts the spirits. What can be done about it I don't know – perhaps take a lead from their former MP, the ex-prime minister, and call it New Sedgefield, or Brighter Sedgefield – possibly even New Improved Sedgefield. Maybe they should leave well alone. Both the small town of Sedgefield and its nearby racecourse probably take pleasure in springing a few surprises. Tony Blair's former constituency is no pit village but a leafy and attractive suburb of grime-ridden Middlesbrough. There's enough Virginia creeper on the picturesque high street to suggest that there's a few bob in this part of England. New Labour? New middle class?

The course itself is only a few minutes from the village centre – so this really is Sedgefield and not a course which hijacks a name from a nearby town (see Folkestone). Given its dour name, I approached the course with some foreboding and must immediately issue a warning to prospective punters. The car park stewards, while polite and helpful, had obviously never driven anything bigger than a Reliant Robin. Unless you protest, they will line the cars up in such a way that retrieving your vehicle will be akin to removing your legs from a pair of shrunken jeans.

Once you've persuaded the attendants that your car has not got a turning circle of two and a half feet, enter the course and prepare for the mish-mash. This may sound a derogatory criticism but in my book it's exactly how things ought to be. Nothing kills a course more than uniformity (see Southwell), yet Sedgefield has created a fine blend of the ancient and modern. Great changes have been made here during the 1990s. The Pavilion, built in 1991, was opened by A. Blair Esq. (then just a jobbing MP); and the Fosters Stand, built in 1998, contains a new weighing room – regrettably still guarded and secretive and out of bounds to Joe Public. The old weighing room has been retained but this delightful old wooden structure behind the Pavilion looks as if it is falling into disrepair. Sedgefield stalwarts should start a 'Save Our Old Weighing Room Campaign' – before it's too late.

All in all, there are four stands, all with excellent views over Sedgefield's greatest asset. Has anyone ever described this course as magnificent? I doubt it. Am I completely mad? It's possible. But I'll go for it anyway. It's magnificent. OK, it's no Sandown or Kempton, but like Fontwell and Towcester, it has a certain unique quality which will guarantee a punter's return. From any of the stands, you will be provided with a panoramic sight of the local countryside. On the far side of the course, a working farm nestles amongst well-tended fields and even the centre of the course is split into three areas of arable pasture, neatly divided by trimmed hedges and coppice fencing.

The course itself is highly visible from all points, rising and falling at least four times in its one-mile, two-furlong circuit. Two tight bends and oxygen-sapping inclines demand that the horses have real staying quality. At first sight, I guessed that any winner was going to need a good three-mile course record to get a two-mile, five-furlong race around Sedgefield. The 200 yards from the final fence only confirmed this view – a rise to the finishing post that must be like going the wrong way up an escalator.

And for a change, my strategy worked. In the first, Nocatchim lived up to his name and landed the spoils at 5-1 (7-1 on the Tote). Things looked promising. There's nothing like backing the winner of the first race and spending the rest of the afternoon playing with a bookie's money. I raced off from the winners' enclosure to see what Sedgefield had to offer my stomach. It provided yet another surprise.

This racecourse bristles with cafes and restaurants, and yet (thankfully) only one fast food caravan. Although this latter meals on wheels tempted me with 'all-day stottie' (a North-East delicacy of dubious content), I looked for something more substantial. Having left home at 5.30 a.m., there were mumblings of protest from below and demands for more than my customary Mars Bar.

Resisting the delights of the rather theatrically named Sedgefield Pavilion Mezzanine Restaurant (lunch £16.95), I sought out something more appropriate for a man who had so far only landed one winner. The Durham Edition

Bar provided the answer – a whole array of simple food for not much more than £3.50. My £1.50 bacon and mushroom sandwich contained enough pork to depress the most optimistic squealer, and did the job perfectly. To be honest, the cafe and bar is a bit of a dungeon, with no windows; but it's run well and the staff seemed to recognize that I was a human being – a rarity in Britain's food service industries.

Around the walls are proudly displayed small silver plates engraved with the winners of Sedgefield's more prestigious races, each one mounted on a collection of what looked like old hymn boards. A horse called Meeting Abandoned seemed to have won at least 25 per cent of all the races run at the course since the mid-1970s – a testament to the hard climate in this part of the world. But amongst the names were some old favourites such as Boreen Owen and High Padre – both having provided rich pickings in the past.

Needing to book a room in Whitby for the following night, I tried in vain to kick my mobile phone into life. 'No service' flashed back at me from the small grey screen.

'What do you mean, "no service"?' I shouted back at the phone. A young woman glanced at me nervously.

'Don't you shout at me!' flashed the screen.

In a fit of pique I switched off its life support and went hunting for a public phone. Following a brief search I unearthed an old red phone box tucked at the side of the main stand. A small sign informed me that it had been donated to the course by British Telecom in 1991 and at a guess must have been over fifty years old. Stepping inside (something I highly recommend) I found it retained the atmosphere and smell of my youth, the venue for my sex education evening classes in the mid-1960s, evocative of adolescent fumblings and the certainty that I had discovered heaven. This was of course before discovering the real facts of life – that heaven is a successful £1 each-way Yankee. My call made, and with some regret, I returned to the racing.

Sleeting almost did it for me in the second race – going well until two out but suddenly running out of puff as he hit the rising ground. But what I did discover during this race is the best place to watch the racing at Sedgefield. Immediately in front of the Fosters Stand is the paddock and winners' enclosure. This small oval parade ring is probably the smallest I've seen on any racecourse and if they ever have big fields running, it must be like the M25 on a Friday afternoon. The winners' and placed horses' stalls are incorporated into this meagre acreage but you can get close up and enjoy the celebrations, where you can hear trainers deliver such memorable professional lines as, 'He just needs further. He'll do four miles in the shit, no bother.'

What isn't immediately obvious is that behind the paddock lies a small strip of grass, which puts you right up against the rail and provides a perfect view of the back straight, top bend, final fence and hurdle plus an excellent view of the hill-climb finish. From here you can follow your selection from well over four furlongs from home, using telepathic transmission to inform your horse, 'If you don't jump clear over the last, you're dog meat.'

Yet it's the access to this area which provides as much interest as anything at Sedgefield. During my travels I have encountered numerous deserted pre-parade rings. It's almost as if they don't exist – punters ignoring one of the great pleasures of racing. Maybe it's because these preparatory areas are so often detached from the main facilities – yet you can learn a great deal by making the effort.

Unusually, the Sedgefield saddling boxes and pre-parade ring are immediately adjacent to the main paddock, and entice punters to view the early preparations. As an old student of body language, it's amazing what you can pick up from watching this procedure – i.e. never back a horse when the owners show little interest and the trainer walks with hunched shoulders. Never mind looking for a spring in the horse's step – look instead for the connections carrying their heads high and walking with a jaunty stride. Results and analysis sections of the *Racing Post* should include a new section with reports such as, 'Owners went to paddock with poor action' or 'Trainer looked depressed while saddling chaser'.

Employing this new-found form guide (patent applied for), Young Tomo hit the deck three fences from home and immediately seemed to disprove my theory. However, un-deterred by this setback, I watched carefully as preparations were made for the fourth race. The trainer of the even-money favourite looked like he'd just heard his dog had died while the owners of the two outsiders strode about as if they'd just been given the next day's results from Haydock. I rarely back two horses in a seven-horse field but given this display of unbridled confidence, I was unable to resist.

To cut a long story short, the favourite was gasping from three furlongs out and my two selections battled it out to the line in a thrilling short-head finish – the winner at 5-1 and second at 10-1. Not being a dual-forecast man (picking just the winner seems hard enough), I failed to pick up the £43.50 on offer but did come away with a handsome profit. And guess what happened next? Same tactic, same result – Charnwood Jack (4-1) beating the odds-on favourite Eskleybrook by at least twelve lengths.

Having now let the cat out of the bag, I may have done

racing a great service and my bank balance some mortal damage. In a few years' time you may well see owners, trainers and jockeys putting on an exaggerated display of confidence just to throw the betting market and having a nice touch on an even bigger-priced outsider. Hopefully, by the time this happens, I'll have patented yet another method. (I have been considering a detailed study of a horse's nostril shape as an indicator of success.)

As I point out in other reports, there's always the slight danger of having one's opinions coloured by the degree of success you enjoy at the course under scrutiny. Yet I liked Sedgefield from the moment I saw it and before I had crossed a bookie's palm with silver. The later discovery that the Racegoers' Club had voted Sedgefield the best small course in Scotland and northern England four times in the '90s came as little surprise. The racing isn't particularly high class (who cares?), it's not easy to gain access to the fences, and the stands and paddock have no seating – yet it was as much fun as I'd had at a racecourse during the previous six months.

To employ a modern cliché – Sedgefield is user-friendly – a clever mixture of the traditional and contemporary, with amenable non-officious staff and a racecourse that really involves the amateur punter. In my introduction, I expressed foreboding about Sedgefield. It may well have been a dreary place twenty years ago but they've really got their act together. Piesporter Michelsberg '96? New Sedgefield? New Improved Sedgefield? New opinion. Go there – you won't be disappointed.

CHAPTER FORTY-NINE

SOUTHWELL

Twelve hours before parking my car at Southwell racecourse, I had waited patiently in the departure lounge of Deurne airport. Deurne? Who's ever heard of Deurne? Do you know where it is? Do you know where Southwell is? After a recent straw poll of racing pals, it was apparent that if Southwell suffers from anything, it's a bad case of anonymity. Of all sixty-one courses in Britain, it's the only course which isn't actually anywhere. As it's pronounced 'Suthul' I'd always presumed it was somewhere in North-West London. Wrong again.

Southwell is sort of near Doncaster, sort of near Nottingham, sort of near nowhere. And yet they've been racing here for over a hundred years. I've no idea which Victorian first built the course but whoever it was must have been wandering through the wilds of the Notting-hamshire countryside and declared, 'Oh look! There's a big flat field in the middle of nowhere. Let's build a racecourse.'

But back to Deurne. If it ever comes up in a pub quiz, this is the main airport for Antwerp. It's best described as a small shack with a short piece of tarmac, so short in fact, that the tails of the aeroplanes stick out over the main road prior to take-off. It's a delight – unless ten drunken football hooligans attempt to board a forty-seat aeroplane.

'Where's the effing duty free, Terry?' were the first words I heard as they staggered into the departure lounge. An equally eloquent but brain-dead companion demanded attention from the increasingly nervous travellers.

'Who's a Belgian then? We 'ate Belgians!'

Whoever this man's grandfather might have been, he was probably now lying in his grave wishing Churchill had surrendered in 1940.

Fortunately, eight policemen, three Alsatians and two scary, cigarette-smoking men in dark glasses made it very obvious that these representatives of British manhood had about as much chance of boarding the plane as Muffin the Mule winning a Cheltenham Gold Cup. 'Zey are a baard adivert for your country, I zink,' smiled the stewardess as we taxied onto the runway. I could only shrug an embarrassed apology and spent the rest of the journey trying to look like a Belgian.

This may seem like a digression from Southwell racecourse. Maybe not. Southwell certainly isn't loutish. Not in any way aggressive. Not really embarrassing. But a good 'adivert' for British racing? Well . . .

The approach to the course from the Newark Road didn't fill me with optimism. The free, grassed parking area lies at the end of a straight, mile-long country road that must have been built by a bunch of Roman navvies practising for the real thing. The local sewage works greet your arrival, while a series of humps shake your car so badly that I expected the car park attendants to be dishing out complimentary aspirins.

First impressions often flavour your response and

Southwell is no exception. The main gate for the general public seemed to be no more than a small gap cut into a prefabricated factory unit, decorated in rather dour cream and grey hues. Shaken but not stirred, I shuffled in with low expectations.

As it transpired, this mass of sheet metal turned out to be the back of the main stand, built as recently as 1991. I can only describe the whole facilities as practical, functional but lacking in any discernible character. I can't deny it's all there. Bars, betting halls, cafes and restaurants – all offering good value for money. In the main eating area you could feast on a full English breakfast for as little as £2.50, and a strange combination of Cornish pasty and mushy peas for only £1.50. And, to be fair, there was quite a buzz amongst a surprisingly sizeable crowd for an October afternoon.

But I like soul in a racecourse – a sense of history, of old tales being whispered in dark corners, of walls that have overheard a thousand poor tips. If Southwell ever had any history it has been bulldozed into oblivion and replaced by practical modern facilities. I'd seen a similar approach at Beverley. Yet for some reason Beverley succeeds where Southwell fails. I went in search of the reason. It didn't take much finding.

In 1989, Southwell went all-weather, allowing them a fixture list longer than the index in my children's *Encyclopaedia Britannica*. With a mixture of National Hunt and Flat, this enables people who live in the middle of nowhere to enjoy fifty meetings per season – possibly more than any other course in the country. As you'll now have discovered, I find all-weather racing about as attractive as a drunken football supporter who's trying to get on my plane. What's the satisfaction in watching thoroughbreds race on a beach, where the tide never comes in? What's the fun in knowing that the going will inevitably be declared as 'standard'? And what's the point in Southwell retaining a grass jumps course inside the all-weather course, which is so far from the punter's gaze that it might as well be in Shropshire? Prejudiced? You bet I'm prejudiced. If I go racing, I want wall-to-wall green – not miles of insipid, standard grey sand.

Fresh from a hard summer's Flat racing, I was suffering from that little known ailment *jumponus miserabilis* – the withdrawal symptoms suffered by punters who haven't seen a decent steeplechaser in over three months. Luck was on my side and by sheer chance I had chosen one of the infrequent National Hunt days at Southwell. It felt like coming home after an over-long vacation, the certainty and comfort of familiar territory. I returned to the Southwell parade ring like a prodigal son, who had invested badly. It was time to start back on the path of profit.

There are two factors which perhaps save Southwell from undiluted criticism – the paddock and The Pantry. Tucked way at the back of the main stands, the well-tended and shrub-lined paddock has a real rustic charm, plus some rather incongruous palm trees. A high grass bank at its rear gives a fine view of the twitching contestants; while three tall ash trees (I think they were ash) bend in the wind, snowing their autumnal leaves across the tight-trimmed turf.

I spotted Inch Champion within seconds. The complete outsider in a thirteen-horse field. He looked in prime condition – heavily muscled, ears pricked and a slight swagger in the step. Rushing off to the betting ring, I took a small each-way wager at 33-1. By the off he had come in to 20-1 and I felt certain of a result. Positioning myself at the highest point in the stand, I waited to watch Inch Champion bring home the bacon.

Sadly, even from this vantage point, the race remained somewhat remote and I would advise taking binoculars. In my case this would be a telescope, as I have been blessed with the genetic inability to focus both eyes in anything approximating unison. Yet, far in the distance, Inch Champion was looking promising, coursing the two front runners on a tight rein. The money was in the bank.

For a flat, sharp course, Southwell proved to be very testing. The grass is lush but the hooves go right into the ground, even after a small amount of rainfall. Inch Champion found it all too much and by the second last was struggling to keep his place. By the last fence, however, he had secured a spot in the frame and my place money was safe. W. Marston almost carried his mount over the final obstacle but he plodded on to the finishing post. I was back National Hunt racing – and in raptures.

I must have been the only person clapping Inch Champion into the winners' enclosure – a rather small and cramped area, with an unappealing synthetic lawn. Unless you're against the rail, close viewing isn't easy, though a raised bank does allow punters to watch the celebrations. Unfortunately a boxed hedge rather pushes the public away from the proceedings and denies you the fun of listening in to the post-race whispering.

It was then that I discovered The Pantry – an oasis of history at Southwell racecourse. This single-storey, yellowing wooden building sits facing the course at the back of the pre-parade ring. In here are tranquillity, good food and a comfort found nowhere else on the course. Dress appropriately and walk with confidence (as I did) – and you'll probably manage to sneak into the owners' and trainers' bar which adjoins The Pantry. In here you can relax on floral-patterned chairs and sofas, with a glowing fire crackling in the corner. Unlike the rest of the facilities this area is delightful, impractical and dysfunctional – just how a real racecourse ought to be. But don't blame me if you get turfed out by one of the green-jacketed stewards.

Back in The Pantry, I was joined by an elderly couple, who turned out to be Southwell stalwarts. (Yes, there is such a thing.)

'How's your luck?' I queried.

'She had seven winners last week,' answered the husband. 'It was her 75th birthday and I didn't get a touch,' he added.

'Any good tips?' I asked his wife, suddenly interested in this obvious professional.

'Red Emperor in the fourth,' she replied, without hesitation. 'It's a certainty.'

'Thanks. Hope you're right.'

'She's never been wrong,' laughed the husband.

Two races later, and having failed to find a winner, I glanced at the runners in the fourth race and put a thick line through Red Emperor. Any woman who has just picked seven winners was the last person to ask for a decent tip. As any punter knows, the best thing to do after a good day is to prepare for a bad day. It's as certain to come as your next tax demand. Instead I took Pertemps at 11-2 to beat the odds-on favourite Derra Glen.

There proved to be a long delay before the three-mile hurdle started. Sadly an aged punter had suffered a heart attack during the third race at the same time as two jockeys had been catapulted from their mounts. Three ambulances were now hurtling through the Nottingham countryside with sirens blazing, leaving the course authorities with a serious problem. But at least it gave me time to head for the centre of the course and position myself to watch Pertemps clear the last with a ten-length lead – or so I hoped.

I noticed something odd about the racecourse as soon as I arrived at the final (plastic) hurdle. On all other National Hunt courses, the chase and hurdle courses are placed side by side in a staggered formation, yet all I could now see were a whole line of hurdles. Southwell's got a quirky side.

'Where have the fences gone?' I asked a fluorescent-jacketed workman leaning on his tractor.

'Took 'em off,' he replied, obviously surprised by my question.

'Took them off?'

'We just swap 'em around. Only takes a few minutes.'

'You drag them off?'

'On rollers. Look.'

And he wasn't joking. Each fence and hurdle was built on a platform of giant roller skates. I felt as if I was backstage at *Starlight Express* waiting for the band to strike up the first number and Rusty to come steaming up the five-furlong straight.

Twenty minutes later, Derra Glen rolled into view, with Pertemps hard on his heels, while Red Emperor trailed more than twenty lengths behind. The leader was tiring fast in the leaden ground, while Pertemps looked full of running. Over the last, Tony McCoy went for the kill and drove his mount into a three-length lead, probably urged into action by my shouts of 'Get him in!' ringing in his ears. The form was holding up and I was about to end the visit with my hand in a bookmaker's wallet.

Unfortunately, the form book had failed to mention that Pertemps had been fitted with disc brakes, which he employs as soon as he hits the front. In less than a hundred yards, Derra Glen turned a three-length defeat into a comfortable two-length win. Favourite backers whooped as I wept. It was time to go.

I can see what Southwell's trying to do and there's no doubt they've made some real progress. On paper, function rooms, children's play areas, a small hotel and golf course all add up to a fairly appealing set-up. But I feel they've become so excited by the amenities that they may have forgotten their reason for living. It's a race-course, not a conference centre. Get rid of the all-weather, build a decent turf course and change your name to Newark. At least the public would know where you are. I doubt I will return until all these changes are made. Like my bathroom mirror first thing in the morning, I can only face it once. To paraphrase my friendly stewardess at Deurne airport, 'You are a baard adivert for British racing, I zink.'

CHAPTER FIFTY

STRATFORD-UPON-AVON

Act I, Scene I – A heath near Stratford-upon-Avon.

Man with notebook: 'Blow, winds and crack your cheeks! Rage! Blow!'

A foolish steward: 'Hail, sirrah! Enter here and rest thyself. Thou journeyed far on this bleak night? (*aside*) Me-thinks he plays the drowned rat.'

Man with notebook: 'I thank you, kind steward. From fairest Chester do I come. Whilst cataracts and hurricanes spout, to drown the cocks on every steeple. I am too tardy? Tell me I am not too late. Answer, fool! The clock turns upon the hour.'

Foolish steward: (*aside*) 'I'll grant to him some title . . . Aye, my lord. And you have missed all contest bar the two and they but measly affairs. But enter gratis and test thy skill against the bookie foe. There is a horse I have espied, which would fill the satchel for a gentleman of empty pocket. I give it here. Come, I shall whisper in your shell-like ear.'

Man with notebook: (*Now suspicious of this tipstaff*) 'How come you by this news? Does thou make fool of princes?'

Foolish steward: 'Upon my oath, sweet lord. If by my word you are undone, I'll sell my codpiece unto . . .'

Man with notebook: 'Unto?'

Foolish steward: 'Unto a nunnery, ere I should give deceipt.'

Man with notebook: 'There's no gain there, thou rogue!'

Foolish steward: 'Then gain upon my loss, my lord. If you do gain, then losses have I none. But losses to a prince may subject his subject to a loss he can ne'er regain, unless he thrives on a maiden's pleasure.'

Man with notebook: 'Away, fool! Talk not in riddles to a prince.'

Foolish steward: 'Away I cannot, sirrah. The gate remains companion on this windswept night. If you away and here I stay, then I will away as you will go.'

Act I, Scene II

Man with notebook (*against the rails*): 'Come sweet, Shaboor! Rise above thy hurdle. Stretch every sinew. Let blood seethe in every vein. You owe me subscription, though I am in your debt. Here I stand, a sorry punter at your mercy. A face drenched by nature's storms – I have a mask. More grinned against than grinning. To the line! To the line! Muster all reserve. And give me victory over Chester's cruel defeat. Shaboor! Shaboor! The battle's won!'

(*enter foolish steward*)

Foolish steward: 'Thy satchel's full, my lord?'

Man with notebook: 'As a king's stomach, fool.'

Foolish steward: 'Thou shouldst make a poet one day.'

Man with notebook: 'I thank you, fool.'

Foolish steward: 'Thank me for but one day. I see no more.'

Man with notebook: 'Take thy riddles, fool. You have no losses made.'

Foolish steward: ''Tis true. And I shall lay abed with friends this night. Adieu!'

Act II, Scene I (some days later)

I made my return to Stratford after only two weeks. My first attempt had been sabotaged by an ill-timed journey from Chester, which normally takes about two hours. Despite the sun setting at 8.30 p.m., the skies had blackened by 5 p.m., the rains so heavy that visibility was down to no more than thirty yards. Four and a half hours after joining the M6, I arrived at Stratford, the third race already well underway. My first visit, therefore, became more of a pit-stop and a chance to stretch my legs before battling with the M40, which had now become a raging river.

Seeing my plight, the kindly steward allowed me in for free and suggested that Shaboor in the fourth race might be a good each-way bet. As chance would have it, this colt, owned by the wonderfully titled Sir Evelyn de Rothschild, strolled in by five lengths and paid a handsome 25-1 on the Tote. As my only bet of the night, the fifteen-minute stay at Stratford netted a handsome £53 profit from a £4 stake. I left quickly, but with an eagerness to return. Two weeks later and on a sun-filled evening, I entered once again – stage left. If you're expecting an idyllic setting surrounded by Elizabethan thatched cottages full of playwrights, you're in for a major disappointment. The course lies about two miles outside the town centre, the only Shakespearean reference being a sign for Anne Hathaway's cottage about a mile before you turn into the car park. Despite hammering on her door for five minutes, there was no reply and I assumed she must have popped out to the bookies for a small wager.

As it turned out, I was in for another profitable evening and you may well expect me to be biased in my appraisal. Not a bit of it. Did you ever hear Clement Freud sing the praises of a one-star restaurant? Though obviously popular with the locals, Stratford seems to lack the character that stirs a punter's soul. Like *Measure For Measure*, it enjoys all the component parts of good theatre but lacks the passion of a *Hamlet* or *King Lear*.

To give the course some credit, they have made a real effort to spruce up the place. Sadly, I felt they'd had about as much success as the effort I once made to become a concert violinist. As hard as I tried, I never got beyond an excruciatingly painful rendition of 'Three Blind Mice' (in E flat minor, no less). I sense the architects of change at Stratford possibly had the same problem.

The first building you encounter on entering the course is a restaurant that appears to have been built in a bunker below the Garrick Bar. Small windows look out over the passing crowd, with no sight of racecourse or paddock. Diners must feel an urge to escape well before the pudding hits the plate. In almost all other racecourse restaurants, designers have made the logical decision to make the dining area part of the racing experience. Not at Stratford they haven't.

At £14, the Club badge isn't really worth bothering with. (The magnificent Goodwood was only £17.) The badge is a crudely printed and an unimaginative pink, oblong piece of card. Apart from the members' stand there is little if no advantage in paying the extra fee, as viewing from Tattersalls is equally good. At the heart of Stratford's modernization lies the new Grandstand, a curious construction, which resembles the mouth of a large sperm whale about to feed on plankton. Large plate glass windows drop towards the ground at an alarmingly acute angle, patrons looking as if they are all about to topple out onto the main concourse.

Inside the mouth of the whale, the design is even more extraordinary. Rows of raked seats are placed between a series of rails, the clients apparently readying themselves to be catapulted down a fairground big dipper. And the front row is no place for the more demure female punter. The design of the enormous glass windows means that lady members cannot display their normal discretion. Not since I inadvertently wandered into a rather suspicious suburb of Amsterdam have I witnessed such an array of female flesh in windows. I must stress that this is not an admission of a leering voyeur. If I hadn't noticed course bookies fighting for the front row of pitches which faced directly onto the Grandstand, it would probably never have come to my attention.

It was on leaving this stand that I bumped into my old school chum, Michael Ingdom, a boy who had first introduced me to the delights of Rigby & Sons, Turf Accountants. In a brief conversation, it soon became apparent that he had learnt less about racing than I had forgotten, his rather threadbare shoes a testament to his inability to read form.

'Heard any whispers?' I asked.

'Miss Bertaine in the second looks a good thing,' he answered in a rather over-earnest manner.

Turning to the racecard, I immediately drew a line through Miss Bertaine's name. It had no form on firm ground and was carrying a 6 lb penalty for its recent win. The outsider, Apachee Flower, looked far more enticing.

Apart from having a nicer name, it was one of the only hurdlers to have won over the distance and was sure to handle the ground, especially with Stormin' Norman Williamson on its back.

A well-known punter and raconteur planted a seed of doubt in my strategy. Clement Freud, a man who, without effort, could impersonate a depressed bloodhound, appeared to be favouring William Hill's with some serious folding money. When he spoke, he had such an economy of facial movement that he must have been a lip-reader's nightmare. What was certain, however, is that the words Apachee Flower did not pass his lips.

I had first encountered him making a gastronomic inspection of the seafood bar. He had already sniffed the hog roast with disapproval and was now casting his bulbous eyes over the whelks.

'What can I get you, Mr Freud?' asked a rather nervous waiter, dreading the reaction to his one-star display.

'A smoked salmon sandwich, please. Brown bread,' answered Clement, revealing his tendency to back safe winners.

Ten minutes later and as an act of celebration, I was chewing a similar sandwich. Apachee Flower strolled home at a delightful 33-1, Miss Bertaine having been pulled up a mile from home. I was beginning to enjoy Stratford.

But two losers later I had regained my objectivity and was still searching for Stratford's soul. Nothing about the course really fires the imagination, even the paddock and winners' enclosure lacking any real sparkle. The course itself is flat and nondescript, the short straight being the only part of the one-mile, two-furlong circuit which offers any real view of the racing. Even from the bustling centre course enclosure, the contest seems distant, the unkempt scrubland doing little to add anything to this rather plain racecourse. Admittedly, it does seem popular, the crowd, even at a late spring evening meeting being big enough to supply a hint of atmosphere. But it's all a bit tame and suggests that punters throng to Stratford simply, rather like scaling a mountain peak, because it's there. By the third race I felt it had little more to offer and decided to head for home while I was still in front.

Leaving the course I passed the restaurant once again, the tables creaking with abandoned puddings. A late-comer approached me as I headed through the car park.

'Where's the best place to eat, mate?'

'Well . . .' I hesitated in response.

'Got any good tips?' laughed his friend.

'Well, not sure.'

It was too hard to resist and I called them back.

'I'm not really sure,' I added with a smile, 'but I know who could help you.'

'Yeah?'

'Couple of old friends on the course.'

''Oo's that then?'

'Well, Clement Freud for the food.'

'And a horse? A horse?'

'Mike Ingdom for a horse.'

'O'right, mate. Cheers.'

I wonder how they got on.

CHAPTER FIFTY-ONE

TAUNTON

I wonder if Bertrand Russell ever went racing? The old philosopher certainly had the dishevelled look of a crushed punter. Whatever the case, I think he'd have liked Taunton. There's something mystical about this whole area of west Somerset, which makes you think there might be more to life than backing a 10-1 winner. Well, maybe not.

Having left home, to the news that the owner of my local racing stable had just been arrested for drug smuggling, the sight of signs for Glastonbury suddenly took on a new meaning. Even driving down the inside lane of the M5 at 80mph (it's a racecourse), you can feel your stress levels dropping and I arrived at Taunton some three hours before the off.

If this should happen, take a quick stroll round the sleepy market town of Taunton. It has some fine cobbled streets and a Saxon castle, where Judge Jeffreys used to amuse himself by burning the odd Somerset heretic. He was probably just a misunderstood old softie once you got to know him. No doubt he used to pop into the local church to say sorry. St Mary Magdalene is definitely worth a detour, a building which dates back to the 13th century and has a stained-glass window that, on a sunny day, could burn out your corneas. It was a sunny day. I drove out of the town like an accident waiting to happen.

There are three free car parks at Taunton racecourse. Don't go to number three. You'll be taken up a farm track with no passing space and then asked to park your car on a grassed incline as steep as the Cresta Run. I finally plumped for number two, as it sits along the rail and gives you a view over the course. It seemed to be a favoured spot for local bookies, who appeared to greet each other with the words 'O'right, mi' dear?' without the slightest hint of embarrassment. I bet they wouldn't try that with a bunch of Scousers at Haydock Park.

I was soon joined by a glistening Bentley. A few months before visiting Taunton, a few members of the Animal Liberation Front (probably all from Glastonbury and high on a stable owner's drugs) had managed to release thousands of mink into the south of England. Some were caught, some shot, but a great many were never seen again. I now know where they went. One of the women in this sleek motorcar had obviously decided to liberate the escapees from their overcoats. I've seen less fur on a pack of huskies. And it wasn't the only animal skin that dripped off her body. The boots looked like they'd previously been circling round a South American river looking for their next meal. It wasn't what I'd expected at Taunton.

Neither was the music. If you associate country racing with the sound of songbirds and the gentle ripple of a flowing river, think again. Somerset folk obviously like a bit of razzmatazz on their day off from the farm. The tannoy was loud enough to disturb the wildlife in nearby Lyme Regis and pumped out the pop music of an unknown chanteuse, with enough power to rattle my car windows. The first song I heard was entitled 'Life, Oh Life' – a phrase which constituted 90 per cent of the lyric. I approached the paddock with a strange desire to read my recent purchase of *Socrates Made Simple*.

The word 'compact' sums up Taunton extremely well. Walking is minimal – the stands, paddock and course all within a few strides of one another. The viewing areas are adequate, though it's worth paying the day member's badge (£11), if only to enjoy the mugs of tea in the Portman Stand. No long-life cartons here. No struggle with impenetrable sealed plastic containers that cover you in their contents at one hint of trying to prise them open. It's all fresh Somerset milk and white porcelain in the Portman Stand. Pity they don't adopt the same colour for the outside.

There seems to be an obsession with beige paint on British racecourses, and Taunton's no exception. Put it together with grey concrete steps and the stand is more reminiscent of a motorway service station than a race-course facility. It was opened by the mayor of Taunton in 1968 and he must have been very pleased to get back to his 16th-century municipal offices – another highlight if you visit the town. Its saving grace is the dramatic view you can get over the distant Blackdown Hills, which provide a wonderful backdrop to the racing.

At best, you could describe the various bars and cafeterias as functional, though they do have one major asset at this racecourse. If, like me, you find the smell of cheap hamburgers as appealing as an old dog's breath, go racing at Taunton. There's not a fast food caravan to be seen. Bliss. The bars provide all you need, from fish and chips to homemade cottage pie and fresh baked Cornish pasties. My decision was made with ease. The next day I planned to go racing in Devon and had decided to undertake a comparative study between the merits of Somerset and Devonian pasties (see Newton Abbot chapter for startling result).

Picking winners at Taunton isn't easy, as I found to my cost. The course itself has been described as sausage-shaped, though I'd suggest you'd be better thinking of a taut rubber band. This gives you a better impression of the bends at each end of the course, which demand that all horses must list over like a racing dinghy in a force eight gale. I saw two occasions when horses were comfortably in touch only to spin away from the rails as they tried to keep their feet on the hazardous turn. The commentator shifted his opinion from 'steady progress' to 'tailed off' in a matter of seconds. If you happen to own a horse with both right legs slightly shorter than the left – run it at Taunton on a regular basis and back it heavily every time.

The one-mile, two-furlong circuit is a flat galloper and probably suits a horse with a bit of stamina, who doesn't mind an early good pace. Get up there and stay there, seems the best advice. If you see your jockey playing a waiting game and giving the leader a ten-length start, don't be afraid to hurl abuse at him as he passes on the first circuit. This can best be achieved at Taunton by sampling the delights of the centre course enclosure, which provides nothing more than an old wooden teabar and small Tote office. The only highlight is a delightful stewards box with a wrought-iron spiral staircase and the look of a giant dovecote.

But the real advantage is in the narrowness of the course, allowing the punters to get close up views of fences on both sides of the course. Admittedly, this does involve running from one side of the course to the other, immediately after the front runners have taken the fence.

Three or four days in the gymnasium before race day should be enough to equip you with the necessary stamina. Not knowing if you can actually make it in time provides an excellent adrenalin rush, especially for those of you who may be involved in tedious occupations.

It is at this fence, on the far side of the course, that I had the pleasure of observing Doctor P. Pritchard. Before the start of the third race, the jockeys introduced their mounts to the first fence, letting them sniff the brushwood and convince them that it's a lot easier to jump over than go through the obstacles. One amateur jockey approached slowly and commented to no-one in particular, 'God! This is a big bugger.'

A hardened old pro shuffled up next to him and declared: 'Wait till you see the others.'

The amateur's face drained of colour and he began to sweat heavily. Stay in the stand and you'd miss all this banter and fear. It might even stop you hurling insults at the jockeys when they're catapulted off the last leg of your Yankee.

Fascinated by the jockey's name, I kept a close eye on the progress of Royal Sweep, a 100-1 shot who had about as much chance of winning as I have of personally reclaiming Hong Kong back from the Chinese. For the first circuit he seemed to be handling the testing conditions fairly well. Unfortunately, his previous form of PPFOP suggested that things were about to change. And it did. At the first fence in the back straight, Royal Sweep hurled himself at the fence like a high jumper wearing concrete shoes. Dr P. Pritchard sailed past me in an elegant arc, hitting the turf with a thud which suggested that the doctor was about to need a doctor.

'All right?' I enquired. He smiled philosophically, as you would at Taunton. He was (and presumably still is) a man who believes in the adage 'physician, heal thyself'. Rubbing his shoulder vigorously, he took two deep breaths, dismissed the attention of the ambulance crew and remounted Royal Sweep without even asking for a leg up. I was impressed. 'I'm impressed,' I murmured in his general direction.

He didn't seem impressed at all. Doctor Pritchard trotted off down the woodchip trail which crosses the course, patting his horse as if he'd just gone past the winning post. Seconds later, I was running across the inner course just in time to see Dunwoody's hot favourite being turned over by a well-backed North Kilkenny. The race-card suggested this 100-30 shot needed to improve to have any chance. It must have read the comments.

The parade ring and winners' enclosure is quite a feature at Taunton. It's a simple enough oval and lacking in raked stands, but the turfed centre is circled by winter heathers, which were displaying their full purple bloom. Nice touch that, and proving that you don't have to spend a fortune to add a little glamour to an otherwise unfussy racecourse.

'Mind your backs!' came a call from behind. Royal Sweep, carrying Dr P. Pritchard, had finally arrived and was greeted by his connections.

'No luck then?' asked one.

'He'd rather lie down than stand up,' answered the good doctor, walking quickly to the weighing room.

'That jockey's completely mad,' laughed the man, left holding a bemused Royal Sweep. 'Completely mad.'

I suppose he summed it up really. I've encountered a lot of jump jockeys over the years and not yet met one who could be categorized as rational. You need a touch of insanity to jump a few hundredweight of horseflesh over a fence at 30mph.

I decided to linger by the paddock and wait for the next race. A small group of men shuffled towards the entrance, busily discussing their joint-ownership of what could only be described as a well-bred donkey. But their enthusiasm was infectious and they sounded like potential winners of the national lottery. The prize money was £1,749 – but it made no difference. It might just be their day. The favourite might fall. The ground might open up and swallow the rest of the field. Elvis might be found alive and singing in a Torquay hotel. It's fantasy. Just fantasy. And all the better for it. One member of this hopeful band declared that when he first stood in the paddock as an owner, it was the proudest moment of his life. Better than sex? Better than marriage? Better than the birth of your first child? 'You bet!' would be his certain answer.

Naturally, I had a small mug's bet on the animal that was about to make him happy. It performed well for about a hundred yards and tailed off after six furlongs. It won't stop him dreaming.

My own dream was still alive. I'd had four small bets producing only one second place. My placepot, however, was still intact, having backed all the favourites to struggle into the frame. As usual I left it to fate and headed off to find a bed for the night. It had been fun, a pleasant winter's day with a touch of spring in the air. Perhaps the only thing that's lacking at Taunton is drama, the racing seemingly over before most horses get to the last flight and complete the short run to the line. But, like Bertrand Russell, Socrates and Dr P. Pritchard, you've got to be philosophical about these things. Next time I'm in Somerset, I'll give it another go.

CHAPTER FIFTY-TWO

THIRSK

They were voices that could have grated a slab of ageing Wensleydale.

'Are yer off tert races?'

'Nah. Never bin. Stay int' square and tha'll keep what tha's got.'

'Aye.'

In case I was in doubt, I was in the heart of the Yorkshire Dales – or as my Uncle Bert used to call it, the 'land that time forgot'. My two companions on the bench, in the middle of Thirsk's mediaeval cobbled square, revived my memory of the Yorkshire motto that 'you don't get owt fer nowt'. They were obviously men who had never landed a 50p each-way Yankee, but I didn't want to argue.

Before leaving home, I had done a quick straw poll of friends and relatives posing the simple question, 'Where is Thirsk?' Oddly, 90 per cent seemed to think it was somewhere in Scotland and it appears to share the anonymity of places like Fakenham, Market Rasen and Lingfield Park. Everyone's heard of them but no-one's got the faintest idea where they are.

Mention James Herriot, however, and even the most

geographically challenged punter can tell you where it is. He's the once celebrated vet who had the unusual ability to make sticking your arm up a cow's bottom sound like an enjoyable way to earn a living. Thirsk is Herriot country and you can buy anything in this small town from Herriot fudge to Herriot lubricated surgical gloves. Not surprisingly, as I soaked up the May sun in the town square, there wasn't a cow to be seen.

You can tell when it's race day as the local pubs seethe with optimistic punters, coach parties arrive in convoy and you have to fight your way into the local bakeries. There's a sense of carnival, not unlike the party spirit you'll find at Cartmel, on a bank holiday. With a long car journey home, I stayed out of the pubs but risked the scrimmage in the bakery. Oddly, the most ancient bread shop is called the Delicatessen – but I must give it a mention. It serves the finest custard slices I've eaten since I first discovered that sin is one of life's greatest pleasures. It was while consuming this cholesterol-filled oozing piece of nostalgia that I came across my two bench companions. They eyed me with some suspicion as, by my last mouthful, I had the appearance of a six-month-old baby who'd just done battle with its first solid meal. One of the ruddy-faced men caught my eye and I returned his glance through a hazy sea of dripping custard.

'Racin'?' he asked simply.

'Erbubletimorblunfph,' I answered incomprehensively.

'Save yer money,' he replied gruffly.

Never being able to resist a challenge, I decided it was time to do battle. I walked to the course as it was the sort of day when the spring sun had decided to come out of its winter retirement. The course itself lies only about a mile from Thirsk's main square and is, unusually, a real part of the town's everyday life. At first sight it is rather un-appealing, a collection of plain brick stands peering over some dilapidated wooden fencing. But don't be put off. Thirsk was to prove to hold a few surprises.

In an act of penny-pinching which could give Yorkshire a bad name, I had been offered a complimentary ticket limited to Tattersalls enclosure. This was about as useful as being allocated a cinema seat which had its back to the screen. Forced to pay the extra £5 to transfer to the Club enclosure, I approached the gate. 'You need a tie,' said the official. As he made his demands, he flicked my open-necked shirt with his wiry fingers, invading my body space with the élan of a Pernod-soaked Frenchman. 'In my pocket,' I responded, taking a step back and hurriedly knotting a half Windsor.

If you intend to treat yourself to a day member's badge don't forget to take a tie, as the last thing you want to do at Thirsk is to be limited to Tattersalls. It's very much an *us* and *them* racecourse and if you prefer to be an *us*, pack that necktie. If you don't mind being a *them*, wear some-thing that's resistant to beer stains and cigarette burns, as the drinkers in Thirsk town square really get down to business once they arrive in the Tatts enclosure.

And they're not short of encouragement. This cheaper enclosure offers an array of watering holes which are sadly bare, plastic and uninspiring. Even the newish Grimethorpe Hall is a large sterilized bar, which has as much in common with comfort as Grimethorpe now has with coal pits. The Riders' Bar, under the Tattersalls stand, has less character than my old school acquaintance, Freddie Brotherton – the bore of the upper fifth, who knew only one joke. It had a punchline that, within seconds, could turn a happy extrovert into a manic depressive. The Riders' Bar was in danger of turning me into a teetotaller and I headed for the stands as quickly as possible.

It was from this position that I suddenly felt my 220-mile journey had been worth the effort. When the course was first laid out in 1854, the architects must have had a very straightforward brief – 'make it simple and ensure that the punters can see the damned thing'. They succeeded on both counts, the one-mile, two-furlong left-handed oval providing one of the clearest views in British racing. The five- and six-furlong chute can be a little obscured but in any race over seven furlongs you won't miss a step.

Unlike at most Flat courses, racegoers are given a true sense of involvement and a real chance to watch the race develop. The centre of the course is made up of levelled pastureland and opposite the winning post the town's cricket ground and tennis courts – none of which impede your sight of the racing. The only unusual part of the course is to be seen at the furlong-pole. Rather than a level run into the line there's a large dip in the course which makes even the most ordinary horses look as if they've got the acceleration of Brigadier Gerard in his prime. It was to prove a profitable dip.

Eventually I beat a retreat for the club enclosure and paddock. The people of the Yorkshire Dales obviously appreciate value for money, as Tattersalls and the even cheaper Silver Ring were heaving with beer-enhanced punters. As I was the only person wearing an enforced tie, I was also beginning to stand out like a Lancastrian at a Headingly Test match. Not that I was the only person in bizarre clothing. During my travels I have noticed a growing tendency for men to attend race meetings in women's clothing. What is this new trend? Whatever it is, Thirsk appears to be the mecca for cross-dressing men, whose hobby is to jeer at (real) women leaving the nearest lavatory. It was all too much and straightening my tie, I slipped into the Club enclosure.

It was akin to a starving tramp finding a £50 note outside a good restaurant. Thanks to the rather ungenerous management it had cost me an extra fiver but proved well worth the extra outlay. What made it even better was that the Tatts bookmakers had contributed to this extra expense as that fine jockey Willy Ryan had driven Nooshman to the line at the unexpectedly generous odds of 4-1. With 300 yards to go, he looked dead and buried. Then he hit the dip. It was similar to a reluctant parent being given a coconut mat at the top of a helter-skelter. Nooshman hurtled through the field with such ferocity that even Willy Ryan passed the winning post with a shocked expression and the crowd roared approval. It just goes to prove the old adage that the race isn't over till the mat horseshoes cling – so don't give up hope if your nag is five lengths down at the furlong-pole.

There are two main differences between the Club enclosure and Tattersalls. Firstly the cross-dressing Yorkshiremen wear dresses and ties, and secondly you can enjoy the wide open spaces at the far end of the paddock, plus a fine view of the course from the members' stand. If you're looking for an air of tranquillity, this is where to find it.

The parade ring itself is truly picturesque – flower-bordered, button-seated and a natural grass bank which allows even eight-deep crowds to gain a fine view of the nervous owners and sweating contestants. Two single chestnuts (I think) stand proudly at its centre and give the whole area a classy feel. The management have even had the sense to leave in place an antiquated black and white odds board operated from behind by (I'd guess) an ex-Punch and Judy man. The delightful winners' enclosure (unusually for a small course) is separate from the main parade ring and very accessible even to the Tattersalls punters.

I had made a point of watching the winners come into this area for each of the first three races. If you happen to have an Aunty Climax, she was definitely there during my visit. The triumphant horses in these opening races were respectively owned by the Duke of Devonshire, Maktoum Al Maktoum and Sheikh Ahmed Al Maktoum. As far as I could see none of them had even bothered to turn up and prizes were quietly accepted by their representatives. You've probably witnessed a louder cheer at a funeral.

Things certainly changed in the Thirsk Hunt Cup. In an eighteen-horse field there seemed no outstanding candidate and I prayed for divine intervention. My second glance at the card delivered the goods. The trainer of Volontiers happened to have his stables only five minutes from my doorstep and, though short of any decent form, seemed to demand a wager. Volontiers cruised in at 15-2 and I raced back to the paddock to witness yet another subdued ceremony.

You could hear the hooting and cheering from a hundred yards. Someone was celebrating. Glancing once more at the racecard, it became apparent that the horse was owned by a syndicate called The Commoners. Arriving at the winners' enclosure I was met by a hugging and kissing group of owners who looked as if they'd just discovered a cure for middle age. The cup was lifted high above their heads like a triumphant team at the top of the Wembley steps. How they came together as a group I'll never know, as they appeared to contain a complete cross-section of the embedded British class system. Tweed rubbed shoulders with denim; hearty country cheeks embraced earring-studded faces; minor bureaucratic hands slapped the back of hardened businessmen's shoulders. If this is the future of British racing, it looks good to me.

Flushed with winnings, I indulged in my usual Mars Bar treat and wandered off for a final appraisal of the Thirsk facilities. On my way past the back of the main stands, I happened to notice the new Manton building, for club members only. It's a strange affair, tucked away at the back of the enclosures and offering a small restaurant and bar, with no view of the racecourse whatsoever. A narrow balcony looks no more than a pandering to corporate entertainment and it's got all the hallmarks of a missed opportunity.

The fact that it had taken me two hours to notice this edifice suggests that its positioning has predetermined its ambiguity. Far preferable are the two main stands, the central building boasting a very ornate beehive weather vane. The small bar on the first floor is fairly basic, though the windows are worth a look. The glass must have been put into position in the 19th century, as a glance through the gleaming panes distorts the view as only antique glass can do.

The prime spot, however, is the old wood and brick stand adjacent to the paddock and winning post. To be fair to the management this is equitably shared between members' and Tatts punters. Rows of idiosyncratic slatted benches are set at an angle to the course and cleverly provide both a side-on and head-on view of the racing. It was from here that I planned my final coup.

An old Yorkshire friend had told me to always back high draw numbers in the straight five- and six-furlong sprints. In a 24-horse field this gives you far too many options but I went to work on the form. Sadly there's not much value in the minimalist racecard, which had apparently been printed on an old Gestetner machine – if you remember them. They were the 1950s equivalent of Caxton's first printing press and left more ink on your hands than on the paper.

After some earnest searching, the horses drawn in stalls 21 and 23 seemed to be the only nags with any chance amongst the high draw numbers. The money went on and I sat back to watch them romp into first and second place. Two minutes later Sulu flashed past the post at a wonderful 20-1. It had been drawn in stall 22. It was time to go.

Fortunately I had left Thirsk with a useful if not wallet-bulging profit. I strode back to my car content with the day and a quietly warm feeling about Thirsk racecourse. It's no great shakes and has a few drawbacks. But overall I enjoyed its quirky welcome. I reached my car within ten minutes and prepared myself for the long trip home. Checking my mirrors, the sign 'Delicatessen' caught my eye. Could I face another custard slice? You bet I could.

CHAPTER FIFTY-THREE

TOWCESTER

OK, so I told my wife I was going shopping for Christmas presents. At least it was a half-truth, which is more than can be said of a politician's promise of help for the racing industry. And a trip to Towcester provides every opportunity of killing the proverbial two birds with one stone. The designer shops of Bicester village are only thirty minutes down the road, tempting you with the exotic names of Lacroix, Ralph Lauren, Paul Smith and enough lingerie shops to give Ann Summers a permanent headache.

I trawled through the various boutiques in under an hour, packing the cut-price trophies into the boot of my car, but with the usual sense of having been led like a lamb to the slaughter and fleeced at every turn. If you want to buy two pairs of ill-fitting trousers, a sweater with one arm longer than the other, and a jacket the colour of Dijon mustard, give me a call.

I headed to Towcester racecourse with the certainty of a greyhound chasing a stuffed rabbit. It was familiar territory. My home course in many ways and a place I've always enjoyed. They were in for a rough day. The desire for objectivity had sharpened my critical eye and I was determined that no stone would be left unturned, never mind being thrown at two unsuspecting birds in Bicester.

The perennial argument about how one should pronounce Towcester has become a bit of a cliché. The answer is that there isn't an answer. There are two answers. If you have a bad day and your fingers get burnt, then it's Toaster. If you have a good day, then it's Touster, as in soused herring – if you see what I mean. You say potato and I say patarto. Many years ago, and still unfamiliar with the area, I stopped a local and asked him the way to Toaster, with the best Northamptonshire accent I could muster. The reply was inevitable. 'Oh you mean Touster?' he replied. 'Wouldn't start from 'ere if I were you.'

But in all honesty, it's easy to find. If you're coming from the south, just sit on the A5 until you see the very grand portico which provides an entrance to the course and Lord Hesketh's estate. At this point, reverse your car immediately, go back about 400 yards and look out for a sign which misleadingly directs you to 'owners and trainers'. It's a bit like drawing a 'Go back to jail' card when you play Monopoly. If you happen to be carrying a telescope, you'll also notice minute writing at the bottom of the sign which informs you of free parking. Make the mistake of turning into the main entrance and you'll be five pounds lighter before you get your first whiff of manure. Useful if you're a jockey who spends his life in a sauna but not much good to the average, rotund punter on a limited budget.

It's always been a lucky course for me. Two years ago I scooped a 20-1 winner simply because I'd fallen instantly in love with the jockey as they paraded in the paddock. I hasten to add she was the only female jockey in the race and I'll swear she gave me a wave as she whipped her horse over the finishing line.

The wooden-clad entrance from the (free) rear car park is quaint and as English as an old threepenny bit. And my luck was in once more. As I approached the rather confused lady in the pay box, a voice at my side asked if I was going into the members' enclosure. He waved a rather smart blue pass in my face and explained that his friend had been unable to come and it was mine for a fiver. He who hesitates is lost. I hesitated. I lost.

I seem to have spent a lifetime being harangued by ticket touts at sporting events and I view every offer of such a nature as non-violent mugging. A pensioner of battered trilby and threadbare suit grabbed the ticket before you could say 'Ten Number Six and a box of matches'. I turned away, disguising my disappointment and handed over my £13 entrance fee to the lady behind the desk, who had reached an even higher state of confusion.

The paddock is accessible from members' and Tattersalls. It's a fine open area with what I thought might be a large beech tree at its centre. There aren't many leaves to aid the identification in mid-December but it still looked a picture on this crisp sunlit day. The whole area feels like an old overcoat – familiar, cosy, comforting. I had arrived only ten minutes before the start of the first race, the horses already mounted, their ears pricked in anticipation.

I cast my eye around for an attractive jockey, hoping that history might be repeated. Sadly, there was nothing to be seen other than gaunt male riders, their faces taut with cold. Quickly reverting to the form guide, I settled on a spring-heeled eight-year-old with a strong chest. Five lengths down going over the last it sneaked in by a short-head and paid 10-1 on the Tote. Good start.

I'm not the world's greatest punter by a long chalk but one certainty at Towcester is that it's best to ignore two-mile specialists in a hurdle race. Go for something that's been placed in a three-mile slog in heavy going. The finish at Towcester must be like trying to run up a staircase with a 40 lb rucksack on your back. I think even a butcher's dog might find it difficult.

Flush with early winnings, I headed off for a cele-bratory cup of tea. Since 1997 the Towcester authorities have presented the punters with a bit of a dilemma. In the old days there was no choice, but now the racecourse has entered the world of corporate entertainment by building the new Grace Stand – a grand yellow brick edifice built in the style of a Chinese lantern – or so the racecard says. Thankfully the directors had the acumen to leave the old stand as a welcome alternative and there's a sense that it's not simply rolled over and conceded defeat to its new opponent. The two contrasting buildings stand like two opposing chess pieces, puffing out their chests with brick and wood bravado.

Call me old fashioned (many people do) but there really isn't any contest. The old stand reeks of a history the Grace Stand won't start to absorb for another fifty years. From the top of the wooden stands, you have possibly the best view of the paddock and racecourse to be found anywhere in the country. Moss-covered grey slate roofs, shoe-worn steps and tiny 'spy' windows ooze the elation and tragedy which have been witnessed over the years by tweed-garbed punters. It's quite delicious – a description normally confined to food, but you can almost taste its past.

Not to be outdone by its new neighbour, this aged construction had been given a fresh lick of paint, the steps so white that the area would have been declared a black run at any decent ski resort. If you get to the course early, before muddied feet have trampled across the pristine banked viewing area, head for the various cafes and bars, which form part of the main building. Even they had not been ignored in the revamp, though the tendency to paint everything in green preservative did make me feel that someone had done a very good deal at the local garden centre.

Two losers later (and back to my usual form) I returned to the Grace Stand to reassess its attributes. The centre-piece is the new, light and airy restaurant which has superseded the old, dark and smoked-filled cafe, which used to look over the paddock. No need to say which I preferred. I've always had a soft spot for any eating place with steamed-up windows that smells like a Dublin pub on a Saturday night. But the new restaurant has a lot going for it. A respectable menu for around £20 per head, a view over the finishing straight and a wonderful opportunity to enjoy a great deal of fun if you're not one of those fortunate enough to afford the meal. The designers made two crucial errors in their plans.

Firstly, the stand in front of the panoramic restaurant windows is open to all members of the public. This affords the average punter the opportunity to gawk at the diners as they tuck into their lunch. This is best done by placing the nose firmly against the window and sucking the cheeks inward in order to give the impression of a starving tramp. The subsequent expressions of guilt on the red-faced restaurant clients are well worth the entrance fee. By standing in front of these windows just as the race is reaching its climax, it's possible to obliterate any view the diners might have hoped to enjoy. Childish perhaps, but a good wheeze all the same.

I had noticed many seasoned Towcesterians (?) with distinctive scars on their foreheads and until I approached the Grace Stand had put it down to a sign of membership of some mystic Northamptonshire secret society. Ten minutes later, having watched yet another of my selections tail off halfway up the finishing straight, I appeared to have involuntarily gained full membership. Leaving the stand in frustration, my head hit the cornice stone of the small brick pillar with an audible thud. I had come into contact with the designers' second crucial error. I am a man of fairly average height and the architects had conveniently placed the sharp-stoned cornice at average forehead height. Towcester's extremely safe for the vertically challenged but lethal for anyone over 5' 10" or extremely tall women with large busts. You have been warned.

Blood still trickling down my face, I headed towards the tranquillity of the centre course. It was so quiet I thought I'd walked into a library on a bank holiday. Four course bookmakers eked out a small trade on £2 bets outside the one-storey bungalow that doubled as a Tote office and cafe. The main excitement seemed to be guessing the contents of the baguettes which had been pre-prepared and pre-sealed. I politely asked for a ham salad baguette, which threw the staff into a froth of enthusiasm as they poked and prodded the long plastic packages in a vain attempt to identify the contents. The resultant decision proved to be a very palatable cheese and tomato – but I didn't like to complain and wandered out to take in the local scenery.

In the very centre of the course stand two large man-made lakes which apparently serve as irrigation when the ground is declared hard or firm. 'Cheaper than the old meter,' explained a gateman as I continued to chew at my baguette. These reservoirs are visible from every section of the course and banked so highly at one end that they would have provided a perfect training area for the Dambusters in 1943.

By the time of the fourth race the wind had put in a new set of teeth and it bit into my face with renewed vigour. A wee dram was called for and at Towcester there's only one place to head for. High on the second floor of the members' stand is a delightful bar, which sports wicker chairs (green, needless to say) that are so soporific you could wake up in the middle of the next meeting.

The whole atmosphere is that of a vicarage tea party attended by members of Alcoholics Anonymous. It's warm, it's friendly and full of some very serious drinkers who, on this occasion, had exchanged check cloth caps for festive paper hats without the slightest sign of embarrassment. Not really being a hat man myself, I hid in the corner and peered over the top of my *Racing Post*.

Rejuvenated by a fine malt, I stepped out to watch my final selection scrape a place in the Santa Clause Novice Hurdle. In a fourteen-horse field this felt like quite a good result. I raced to the Tote to collect my pittance and took a final glance back over the course. Like many courses, Towcester is an amphitheatre but I'd be surprised if there's a better view of racing in Britain and the two racecourse vets I overheard as I left the course confirmed this opinion.

'Used to put down at least five horses a season,' said one. 'Better class of horses now.'

It's a course on the way up and well worth the visit. It was then that I noticed the vets' clothing. The woman was in a jacket at least two sizes too small and the man in a pair of trousers that obviously belonged to a friend. Or maybe they'd both stopped off at Bicester village for a quick Christmas shop. Who knows?

Postscript I: Two weeks before this book was put to bed (as Jackie Collins might say), I found myself with an afternoon free and paid another visit to Towcester. I returned home in a state of shock.

I have spent a great deal of this piece eulogizing about the merits of the old wooden 1928 Grandstand – a structure of such charm that it was capable of selling National Hunt racing to an animal rights activist. Well, it's gone. Demolished. Dismantled. Destroyed – and replaced by an immense stretch of tarmac, which must have resulted in McAlpine's shares rising by 50p. Punters wandered around the course with dazed expressions and tear-filled eyes. Tweed-clad women sobbed openly as they leaned against the stark white rails. Towcester has always had a fairytale quality and I now felt like a child returning to Disney World only to find that Snow White had been murdered by the seven dwarfs. The next morning, I rang the chief executive. Surprisingly, I was put straight through.

'Now look here . . .' I began.

The holder of the great office turned out to be Peter Gaydon, an amiable and enthusiastic man, with the comforting voice of a psychotherapist. I lay on my couch and absorbed his response. It transpires that the former

1928 Grandstand had been condemned as unsafe for public use. Sticking plaster refurbishment had been estimated at almost a million pounds and the course authorities decided on major surgery.

'So what happens next?' I asked.

'Bespoke racing,' answered the chief executive. 'A unique concept in racecourse planning.'

Peter Gaydon spelled out their intentions. 'The plan is to consult Towcester racegoers as to what sort of structure should replace the old stand and present them with a made-to-measure facility.'

'So you want the opinions of your present patron punters?' I queried, with as much poetic alliteration as I could muster on a thundery Thursday morning.

'Absolutely!' came the fervent response.

He had released me from my dilemma. On first seeing the tarmac void, where the old Grandstand had once stood, I had seriously considered rewriting this whole piece. Two problems arose from this strategy. Firstly, there's a limited amount of excitement in the description of two acres of tarmacadam and, even more troublesome, I'd promised my wife that I'd paint the spare bedroom. But it was the promise of democratic bespoke building plans which finally brought me to the decision to leave the piece intact and add this postscript.

All right, Towcester. You want opinion on the design of the new stand, due for completion in 2003? Just read this report – especially the section on the delights of the old Grandstand. It will tell you all you need to know. I don't want to sound like Prince Charles – a man who considers there hasn't been a decent building constructed since 1753 – but what you MUST retain is that unique sense of true charm and fairytale magic. When I come back and inspect the made-to-measure Towcester, I expect to find Snow White alive and the seven dwarfs imprisoned for attempted murder. Don't let me down.

Postscript II: The long promised Empress Stand saw the light of day on 5 October 2005, a pale yellow edifice with a tower which suggests that the architect has recently had a short holiday in Thailand. Sadly, there is a touch of the corporate overkill in the finished product, the top two tiers being given over solely for the use of 'winers' and 'diners'. Everyday punters are confined to the bowels of the building, which feels uncomfortably claustrophobic and is inadequately served by two small Tote booths. It definitely seems like a reversion to an 'upstairs, down-stairs' social division. The outside raked standing area is completely open to the elements and, unless paying for one of the many 'packages', I couldn't find cover from the elements, anywhere on the course. On a bitter January day, you'll need to strap two hot water bottles around your private bits. (People who have followed this sound advice will be easily identified by the continual sound of sloshing water as they walk up the steps or celebrate a winning bet.)

Should you still attend? You bet you should. Entry is now free. Towcester still provides one of the friendliest venues and finest views of racing in the country. It shouldn't be missed.

CHAPTER FIFTY-FOUR

UTTOXETER

You can gain a great deal of wisdom travelling around the fleshpots of British racing. Like great generals, you gather experience in the rules of encounter, learn how to attack your bookmaker enemies, grasp the importance of mustering your defences. I am happy to pass on a small piece of advice, which will prove invaluable to all punters – never travel in an aeroplane ten days before Christmas.

Four days prior to my Uttoxeter visit, I enjoyed a day trip to Scotland. Unfortunately I appeared to share the flight with over a hundred volunteers in an influenza experiment. I've heard fewer people coughing in a smoke-hazed bookies and by the time we touched down I knew my fate had been sealed and that my defences lay in tatters.

My strategy for inspecting racecourses involves the simple procedure of sniffing my way around. At Uttoxeter, this became a literal description, as my body began to succumb to an army of little bugs who hadn't heard it was nearly Christmas. In my experience, it's a ten-day battle. In the first three days, you feel slightly warmer than a stiffening corpse; for the next six days, you're as much fun as a dentist with severe halitosis; and by the last day, you can just manage to hold down half a pint of bitter without falling over. By my calculation that took me to 26 December, when the party hats have hit the bin and all that's left are two cold sausages and a slice of dried-up turkey. I drove into Uttoxeter racecourse determined to blank Christmas from my mind. Sadly, this was not a great strategy.

Whoever rigged up the tannoy system at Uttoxeter must have confused the racecourse with Wembley Stadium. Despite parking my car near the road and some 400 yards from the main entrance, the sound of the carol 'Oh Come All Ye Faithful' was as clear as I'd have got if I had made my annual visit to church and hijacked the front pew. And, to add to my misery, I was met at the entrance by a rotund Father Christmas whose false beard had been blown around the back of his neck by the growing icy wind. I sneezed as I passed through the gate.

'Ho! Ho! Ho!' went Santa.

'What are you laughing at?' I mumbled ungraciously. 'Can't you see I've got a dose of flu?'

'Ho! Ho! Ho!' he continued without any hint of sympathy.

By the time I entered the main enclosure, the shrill tannoy was almost hurling me across the nearby paddock. 'Mary's Boy Child' was being blasted into the air with the cheesy sincerity only ever achieved by an American evangelical choir who make abject misery sound like a real stroke of luck. I strode hastily away, determined to find a quiet corner and a group of born again punters.

You may be wondering, justifiably, what this has to do with Uttoxeter racecourse. To be fair, it took me three days of flu-ridden delirium to realize its significance. Until the mid 1990s, Uttoxeter was considered to be a bit of a poor relation, a country course which knew its place and had about as much floral brashness as a shrinking violet. The former chairman, Sir Stanley Clarke, injected some much-needed cash, gave the place some self-belief and set Uttoxeter on course for some in your face racing. Apart from owning a previous Grand National winner (Lord Gyllene), Stanley Clarke was obviously recognized as a man who knew a thing or two about how to persuade punters to have a nice day.

Uttoxeter has now been stripped of English coyness and been replaced with American razzmatazz. From the moment you walk into the enclosures you'll know that Uttoxeter means business. Even travelling through the town there's no disguising the fact that the course has become a local celebrity. There are so many signs directing you towards the course that I'd defy a blindfolded idiot to get lost on his way to a meeting. (If you do get lost, don't ask for directions – demand to see a psychiatrist.)

And this theme continues inside the three enclosures. Despite being fairly compact, huge boards inform you of every facility, the bright green lettering on such a large scale that you feel obliged to follow every instruction without protest. Such was my willingness to obey orders that the first thirty minutes were spent in a frenzy of activity, bouncing between the plethora of restaurants, bars and cafes like a metal ball being catapulted around a pinball machine. Finally exhausted, I came to rest against the parade ring rail. Of the fifty racecourses I had so far visited, Uttoxeter picked up the paddock prize. I don't know if Stan Clarke was a member of Friends of the Earth but someone had developed an ecosystem of such efficiency that in late December the paddock was surrounded by yellow roses in full bloom. The trick is, like all good ideas, ridiculously simple. As the runners strut around the parade ring, the tension of entering the race has a natural loosening effect on their bowels. Rather than create a redundant steaming pile in the corner, staff have to do no more than shovel the offending droppings directly onto the flower beds. Hey presto! – roses in December.

But it's not only the flower display which makes this such an exquisite area. The triangular grassed surface is flanked by stark white rails, comfortable green bucket seats and a collection of old stable blocks converted into function rooms. Just to confirm its festive appeal, the end box had been hired by Mr Dash and Mr Poppet. Though I never saw them, I'm certain they were fat jolly chaps with mutton chop whiskers, who handed out whisky and mince pies and referred to everyone as 'My dear fellow!'

Yet it's the centrepiece which just edges Uttoxeter past the elegance of Newmarket and the surprising amphi-theatre of Newcastle. A topiary statue dominates the parade ring. The beautifully crafted horse and jockey press for the line in a driving finish. If I had a runner at Uttoxeter, I'd make my nag stop and look at this work of art for at least five minutes in the hope that it would mimic the performance.

Following the advice of my deceased Aunt Ethel ('feed a cold and starve a fever'), I headed for the hog roast cabin. Just above another sincerely shrieked carol from the American choir, I heard the even more piercing voice of a young woman dressed in little more than a silk handker-chief and a pair of high heels. 'Big ain't it!' she screeched. She was a perceptive punter. Despite having a compact feel, Uttoxeter is built on a surprisingly grand scale. The

Prince Edward Stand, opened by our much maligned movie mogul minor royal, was opened in 1994, yet still looks as if he's just cut the ribbon.

It dominates the enclosures and is surrounded by a host of bars, food outlets and betting halls all decked out in Uttoxeter's corporate green and white. It's so smart I instinctively wiped my feet before entering any of the facilities. The problem is that it's almost too smart for its own good, and they are in danger of creating a pastiche of a modern Butlin's holiday camp. Thankfully the course announcer resisted shouting 'Gooood morning, punters!' over the tannoy – but there remains a slightly clinical feel about the whole place.

If you're looking for a cosy corner, head for the far end of the Tattersalls enclosure and you'll find the John Kenny – an old bar, which seems to be Uttoxeter's only remaining piece of history. Constructed inside an old wooden Tote building, it shares the same appeal as the centre course shack at Carlisle and is probably better positioned. From the John Kenny, you can step out to gain a perfect view of the final fence and clamber up onto a small mounded stand to watch the runners all the way around the course and take on the final four fences from the top bend.

But if you don't make it to the John Kenny mound, it's possible to stand anywhere on the course (apart from the centre course) and gain a prime view. Despite being a flat one-mile, three-furlong oval, Uttoxeter must be one of the most visually accessible courses in the country. The hurdles course covers a fairly conventional path, yet the jumps course takes some real concentration as the majority of the chasing events begin on two diagonal chutes which cut across the centre of the course.

The three-mile start sends runners galloping towards

the stands, while the two-mile, four-furlong start catapults the field in the opposite direction. Even more peculiar is the chicane in the back straight – a kink in the course, of such severity that a horse comfortably hugging the rail will suddenly find itself exposed on the outside of the pack. If you've backed a horse which is a left-to-right specialist, it may be very confused when it enters Uttoxeter's little wrinkle.

I'm certain it was this geographical oddity which guaranteed my complete lack of success in finding a winner. Any chance of my wife receiving a decent Christmas present also appeared to be diminishing by the second. Even the wrapping paper looked as if it might have to be put on hold. It was beginning to look like a Scrooge sort of Christmas and I headed off to the bar even more determined to dismiss the festivities as a load of old humbug.

My search for a single malt took me back past the paddock, where the winner of the novice selling hurdle was being auctioned. Rio Real had run away with his race by over twenty lengths and had created a frenzy of interest from a number of prospective owners, who seemed hell bent on emptying their bank accounts. Sensing the madness, the auctioneer delivered his patter like Santa Claus on speed and with as much political correctness as a comic in a working men's club. 'Make a lovely Christmas present for the wife!' he cajoled. Thanks for reminding me, I thought. Little did he know that one member of his audience wasn't thinking much further than a box of chocolates and a new biro.

Unbelievably, Rio Real finally went for 9,200 guineas and was bought by an obviously over-enthusiastic punter who must have had a twitch in both eyes. The horse had won well but beaten no more than a bunch of no-hopers.

As far as I could see it had little to commend it, apart from having a leg in each corner. Now shivering uncontrollably and unable to avoid the constant references to Christmas, I laid my final bet and headed towards the centre course enclosure and a quick escape. Every stride took me through yet more sugar-coated carols. Father Christmas refused to stop laughing and corporate party revellers were beginning to hit the brandy. For a man with influenza and a pocketful of losing betting slips this was not good news. Luckily, I had saved just enough of my flagging wisdom to head straight for the car park and do battle with the fogbound M6.

And the verdict? The jury may still be out. Uttoxeter's become a strange mixture – caught somewhere between the grandeur of a Grade 1 course and the cosy familiarity of a small country course. For my liking, it's perhaps edged a little too far towards the corporate world and there's as much value to be gained from a Tattersalls ticket as there is from a member's badge. But on balance, it's one to mark on your card, a course which has made and is still making a real effort to entertain the small punter. They sure want you to have a nice day. Just ditch that bloody choir.

Postscript: My last bet proved successful, Billy Nomaite (S. Durack) coming in at 7-1. There was a box of chocolates, one biro AND a racing diary in my wife's Christmas stocking. My generosity knows no bounds.

CHAPTER FIFTY-FIVE

WARWICK

Only a quick flick up the M40 for this visit. It had been raining for days and a canal barge might have proved a better option for the journey. It's Junction 15 if you're coming from the south – don't succumb to the confusing signs for Warwick, which come much earlier.

Head for the castle, then look out for small brown signs which direct you to the racecourse. I felt like I'd just had an annual eye test by the time I turned right into Hampton Street. Specsavers ought to consider sponsoring a few races at Warwick.

It soon became obvious that the morning paper's forecast of good-to-soft was a highly optimistic call. By the state of the car park, the horses were likely to go into the ground faster than a worm that's just spotted a starving magpie. Having arrived early, I reversed out in order to avoid the inevitable quagmire and found a spot just across the road. I always feel a little apologetic about parking outside someone's house but the grey-haired figure in the window seemed immersed in her newspaper and paid me no attention at all.

You need to buy a member's badge at Warwick. The paddock, winners' enclosure, stands and betting ring are laid out in a long strip, so there's no chance of sneaking a view of proceedings if you opt for Tattersalls. The main entrance is unpretentious and the staff obliging. The man selling me the badge even asked, 'How are you?' I presumed I must have carried an air of depression. I had a bad feeling about Warwick. Sometimes you have a sense that you're unlikely to pick a winner in a one-horse race and it turned out to be not far from the truth.

Once inside the racecourse, I was immediately aware of a military presence. Uniformed men and women appeared around every corner, resplendent in dark blue regimental garb, their berets tilted at a jaunty angle. But this was no group of crack young paratroopers, more of a *Dad's Army* reunion. A glance at the racecard explained all. It was the Royal British Legion race day and there was a sea of poppies amongst the crowd. I sought refuge from the rain inside the nearest cafe. Ex-servicemen and women exchanged tales of derring-do and fallen comrades, while huddled groups of civilian punters exchanged hard luck betting stories.

Embarrassed by my own lack of service to Queen and country, I joined a small group of non-combatants at a nearby table. Their jackets steamed like the hard-ridden winner of a three-mile chase but through the haze I could make out the three characters. Two of them appeared so horsy they could have modelled for a Pony Club advert. The third member, by contrast, looked as if she'd just finished washing up for a family of fifteen.

How wrong can you be? The moment she opened her mouth, the soft Irish brogue revealed a woman who could probably write the *Racing Post* single-handed. She was also a master story teller, a list of racing narratives that would make Dick Francis look like an amateur. The tales were delivered in a continuous flow, voiced in a slow Celtic pace that had her audience hanging on every word. Her companions soaked in these anecdotes like children waiting to see if the princess would be saved from the dragon.

To be honest it was the highlight of my visit to Warwick. I might as well put my cards on the table, I didn't enjoy it too much. There's a rather cheerless feel, a sense that the whole place needs a good shake-up, a sense that the good times have passed them by. And there must have been good times at Warwick. The main stands (possibly Victorian) are a delight, a curious green and magnolia hotchpotch of winding wooden stairs, secret little rooms and a whole array of bars and cosy restaurants.

The members' bar wraps you in deep red walls and carpets, the Tattersalls' Council Room Bar relaxes you in green floral wallpaper. They feel like a couple of libraries in an old stately home. The whole thing is quirky and comfortable. It's Warwick's main selling point. And they were due shortly to knock it down. Demolishing it. Scrapping it. It's about as good a marketing strategy as Kellogg's giving up the cornflake.

It's the course that's the major problem. OK, the stands could do with a lick of paint and a bit of smartening up, but the racecourse needs major surgery. Wherever you stand at Warwick, you can see very little. It's as if you've paid good money to see a film at the local Odeon, only to find that they can only open the curtains halfway. The jumping course has the majority of fences hidden behind a hill at the back of the course enclosure. It takes so long for the horses to reappear that you'd swear they'd stopped for a breather and a quick chat about their chances of getting over the next obstacle. If I was a jockey, I'd probably miss a couple of fences out. I doubt if anyone would notice and your mount would be much fresher for its run to the line.

In desperation and between races, I crossed over to the course enclosure to check the view and the facilities of the advertised Farrell Brookshaw Stand. It really wasn't worth the walk, though the chips in the small bar were as good as I've tasted since I was last in Blackpool. The view, however, leaves a lot to be desired and you need a keen imagination to watch your selection stumble around the course. The stand contains raked concrete steps and, for some unknown reason, six small rows of plastic seating. There is a fine view if you enjoy looking across the course to the crowd in the main enclosure. If you strain your neck to one side, you may be fortunate to catch a glimpse of the final fence. The three bookmakers, huddling under their umbrellas, were equal in number to the punters occupying the stand.

I joined them for a few minutes and tried as hard as possible to imitate a crowd. As I approached, the three men shivered in the cold November wind and drank ice cold beer. They probably turn the central heating up in July. Hoping for a little inside information, I listened in to their exchange. The name Wormwood Scrubs seemed to play a central part in their conversation and I couldn't find the horse's name listed anywhere on the racecard. I left immediately, my hand firmly gripping the wallet in my back pocket.

Back in the relative comfort of the main enclosure, I began to explore further. I was, by now, flush with a 7-2 winner in the first race – but, like a schoolboy who finds he can answer the first question on an exam paper, it usually spells nothing but later trouble. Twenty-eight bookmakers had arranged their pitches in front of the Tattersalls stand. Twenty-eight bookmakers on a mid-week November afternoon? That's about as optimistic as me hoping to get a date with Helen Mirren and being asked back for coffee. There was less money being exchanged than at a church jumble sale. Where's a bookie's next full-length camel coat going to come from if he keeps pitching up at courses like Warwick?

But at least they were high-tech. Not quite in the league of Ascot and computerized betting tickets, but they did all have tape recorders attached to their stands. Having gone AWOL for the afternoon, this arrangement made me feel a little uneasy. I didn't fancy having my voice replayed as evidence when I was protesting to my clients that I'd had a puncture and couldn't make the business meeting. Just to cover my tracks, I had five bets during the afternoon, two with a German accent, one as a Frenchman and two others as an almost incomprehensible Old Etonian.

I was starting to chase my losses by the time of the fifth race, the Flanders' Field Claiming Hurdle. A British Legion band marched into the paddock, the music stuttering as rain soaked into their bagpipes. An elderly ex-sergeant major bellowed his instructions, using the high falsetto screeches of his youth. It was as if he'd never left the parade grounds of Aldershot and he performed his task with chest-bursting pride.

I had just come down from chatting to a barman in the deserted Castle Suite above the main stand. For some reason, even though he had no customers, he had built a fine coal fire. The chimney, however, appeared not to have been used since British and German troops fought at Ypres. The resultant smoke refused to go up the chimney and, instead, filled the whole room, drifted out onto the balcony and slowly swirled down into the paddock. Through the rain and smoke the pipers continued to play their lament. It could have been Flanders.

I backed Rock Scene (in a French accent) and took 25-1. Within minutes it was announced as a springer and shot down to 14-1. This promising six-year-old ran its heart out and would have won easily had the race been six furlongs shorter. Unfortunately it's hard to find a one-mile, two-furlong hurdle race these days. I followed the winner, a 5-6 favourite, into the winners' enclosure just to see if anyone had the audacity to make a £5,000 claim for a horse that was well past its best. No bids were made, though there was a stirring in the crowd when a punter who looked like a retired all-in wrestler decided to shout abuse at the jockey who had come in second.

As this was delivered with an extremely strong Birmingham accent, the delivery didn't seem to have the menace of the delivered words. But he was loud enough to put a megaphone company out of business and suggested that the jockey had stopped riding before being well beaten. Eyebrows were raised in the crowd and I even noticed mine twitching slightly. As far as I could remember, the winning horse was about eight lengths in front when he approached the last and entered the final straight. Apart from this, the third horse was at least fifteen lengths behind the second. 'He should be hanged or given twelve months in jail!' came the voice. It occurred to me that with such inconsistency in sentencing, this man had probably missed a vocation to become a high court judge.

By this time the hurdlers were beginning to be led away, past the oval paddock which stands close to the winners' enclosure. This is a must see area, as it's probably the only time you have chance to get a real sight of the horses. I stopped for a moment to view the chasers, who circled the paddock. It was like a world political convention. Clinton was followed by Reaganesque, with a rather haughty-looking I'm Maggy coming close behind.

A connection of Clinton puffed away on a large Havana cigar. It looked like easy money, but it was time to go. I promised myself to check the results on the way home.

Even though I'd left it on the street, my car was still intact. Only twenty yards from the exit, life continued as normal. Children scampered home from school, mothers bent against the wind and rain with bags of heavy shopping. It was as if nothing was really happening on their own doorstep and I think they may have been right. Warwick is fine – as far as it goes, but I have to admit it's dreary. I'm not sure replacing an old wooden stand with glass and concrete is really going to make a great deal of difference.

I looked towards the house with half an idea of apologizing to the owner for inconsiderate parking. She was still examining her paper, oblivious to my presence. Perhaps she's a slow reader. Or maybe it was a very fat paper.

Postscript I: Halfway down the M40, approaching Banbury. The radio crackles into life. 'Latest racing results. Warwick 3.40. First, number four, Clinton . . .' I changed channels immediately.

Postscript II: Great news! The old stand turned out to be a listed building and Warwick were forced into refurbishment rather than demolition. OK. It cost £2 million more but at least it kept the corporate mob at bay and has left the old stand as a public facility. It's tempting to give Warwick an extra Racing Symbol, if only for their retention of sanity. But I don't always give in to temptation. Maybe next time.

CHAPTER FIFTY-SIX

WETHERBY

It had been over a year since I'd been to a real northern racecourse. By 'northern', I mean north of Manchester and not ten yards past the Watford Gap Services. Having driven up, non-stop, from leafy Buckinghamshire, my car still retained the warm southern air and cold social culture. You could almost see the car park attendants recoil as I opened my door.

I had arrived very early, unsure how long it would take me to negotiate the A1, a road that always seems to have more cones than a Wall's ice cream factory. Three elderly men, wearing flat caps that probably hadn't left their heads in thirty years, waved me to one side.

'Bookie are yer?' enquired the first, in a Yorkshire brogue as flat as his cap.

'Just a punter,' I replied with a smile.

'Over 'ere, lad. Tha'll get stuck int' mud if tha parks theer.'

It felt like I had just been transported into a modern version of *Wuthering Heights* and I searched their faces for a sign of an ageing Heathcliff. Stepping out into the bitter east wind I suddenly felt warmer. I had been concerned that they might have spotted my Lancashire accent and sent me packing. But these were men who had long forgotten the Wars of the Roses and simply wanted to give me a good time – in the nicest sense of the word.

'Nishe car, ish it?' enquired one of the attendants, helping me on with my jacket. He was a delight. A man who had apparently been coming to Wetherby for over sixty years. Unfortunately, his contribution to the conversation was almost unintelligible, his speech impeded by a habit of chain-sucking Polo mints between a set of loose-fitting false teeth. From what I managed to comprehend, he owned a Lada which he had bought cheap from his cousin, Beryl. By the time I headed for the entrance, he had given me so much detail that I could have taken a job in a Czechoslovakian car factory.

Having already been mistaken for a bookie, I was now taken for a vicar by a group of gatemen. I had donned a yellow polo neck in anticipation of an easterly winter wind. It's a favourite bit of kit, which has now been washed down to a rather insipid white and tends to give me the look of a cleric.

'Thought we had the clergy in,' laughed the man behind the desk.

'Bless you,' I responded.

'Thanks,' came a stuttered and embarrassed reply.

I stepped onto the course and left them to their uncertainty.

I was met by a hole. A very serious hole. A hole big enough to qualify as an abyss. Approaching a friendly looking steward, I fired one of my more perceptive questions.

'What's that hole?' I asked.

'New stand,' he responded gruffly. He was a man of

few words, who in seconds had disproved my ability to judge human nature. So much for instinct.

Wetherby appears to be a course with ambitions. The plans for the new stand were displayed for public view and showed a brick and glass construction that was obviously meant to give its big brother at York a good run for its money. I just hope the architects know what they're doing. The roof looked like a sail taken off Captain Ahab's whaling ship. Given anything more than a force three wind, I felt the whole construction could end up in the middle of a Leeds shopping centre. But you've got to trust these professionals.

When a new baby joins a family, the elder children sometimes lose the attention they've so far enjoyed. The old stand falls into this category and was beginning to look a bit faded and unkempt. But I doubt they'll be able to better the view that you get from this position – a wonderful sight of a long finishing straight, with the jumpers coming at you head-on. Sadly, only one of my five selections actually managed to make it as far as the last two fences, but you can't have everything.

I decided to take tea – as vicars do. I was beginning to enjoy my new vocation and found myself adopting the characteristics of a bumbling priest from an old Ealing comedy. Regrettably, the catering services at Wetherby leave a lot to be desired. A quick pit-stop for a bag of chips proved only that the frying oil had been lightly flavoured with an old pair of hiker's socks. The barren Tea Room at the back of the stand showed no improvement. It serves a brew that could strip the lining off your stomach in thirty seconds. To its credit it did appear to be run by an extremely health conscious manager. 'No Smoking' signs covered the paint-peeling walls and were just visible through the smog created by 200 chain-smoking punters. Is there a literacy problem in Wetherby?

Seeking refuge, I raced over to the Paddock Bar – a single-storey building reminiscent of a Methodist chapel, which I felt would suit a man of the cloth. The manager turned out to provide more fun than hearing that Ladbrokes had just been hammered by a 50p roll-up. He was a man of middle age who had the sartorial elegance of an Oxfam mannequin. Green wellingtons were fetchingly topped by string-tied grey bags, a red and white striped apron and a shirt which was last washed before Persil was invented.

His main characteristic, however, was his voice – delivered at a volume which could act as an early warning system. He shouted at everything. At everybody. At anything. His request of 'Next, please!' put fear into every customer and his dealings with other members of staff must have resulted in at least four nervous breakdowns since the start of the season. At one point he spotted a waitress placing a sausage roll in the microwave.

'Gold,' he whispered in a shout.

'What?' she replied.

'Gold! On t'plate, luv. Gold. It'll explode.'

He repeated this five times, the stress on the word explode producing total silence in the bar. People began to shuffle towards the exit and I shuffled with them. Within thirty seconds the room had emptied. There was no explosion and all I could hear was his voice screaming, 'Next, please! Next, please! Next, please!' I peered back through the window. A lone figure sat contentedly munching his hot sausage roll, oblivious to the panic.

Still without a cup of tea, I wandered over to the paddock. It's an impressive grassed oval, highly contoured with a drop of about ten feet from the back to the front, giving people a fine view from either the rails or the banked concrete steps. The major disappointment is that the winners' enclosure forms a part of the main paddock and is only marked by four small posts attached to the main rail. If I was an owner who'd just won a three-mile chase, I'd expect a lot more than Wetherby has to offer. The runners seemed to be dismissed in a rather perfunctory manner, with very little chance for connections to enjoy their moment of glory in a setting with a degree more grandeur. Perhaps they've spent so much on the new weighing room there's nothing left in the pot.

I visited Wetherby on the day that the former IOC president, Juan Samaranch, was being castigated in the press for spending a very reasonable £5,000 per night on a private suite at the last Olympics. What's the problem? It's well known that Olympic athletes prefer to sleep in bunk beds and share their room with three complete strangers. But, by the look of it, Samaranch had also taken a part-time job as a consultant to Wetherby racecourse.

The first phase of modernization took place in 1995 with the building of the Wetherby Steeplechase Committee Office, a modern construction with (I was told) very deep pile carpets, a beautifully appointed stewards and weighing room (I was informed), and the finest view of the paddock on the racecourse (I think). Sounds wonderful – until you realize it was probably built by a bunch of people who think the advent of the Freedom of Information Act is a communist plot. It's a no-go area for the racegoer. To say it's unfriendly would be as inadequate as remembering Stalin as a friend of the people. There's not even a sign over the door, just an anonymous building which suggests that the average punter should stay well away. It reminded me of pictures I recently saw of the old KGB offices in Moscow – in your face and threatening. A not-very-great piece of PR for what is otherwise a very welcoming racecourse.

Adjacent to this committee office are the new saddling boxes, a practical breeze block and steel construction which has all the appeal of a vet's operating theatre. The horses being prepared for racing seemed frightened by their surroundings and appeared to be searching for one sign of the reassurance offered by their old wooden stables. I couldn't wait to escape back to the course to watch my next selection fail to make the last fence.

I wandered into the centre course just to confirm that a class system was still fully operative in Britain. I wasn't disappointed. For the princely sum of £3 the course authorities offer the punter a faded green Nissen hut, heated by seven toasters hanging from the metal beams in the roof. A hard concrete floor, scruffy tables and second-hand seats are offered as facilities. You'd probably enjoy more comfort in a Salvation Army soup kitchen and find cleaner toilets at a Third Division football ground. Viewing is aided by four stands, which rise no more than two feet off the ground and are constructed by what appeared to be builders' pallets. My old faithful dog would report me to the RSPCA if I treated him like that. I just hope the committee enjoy their deep pile carpets.

I passed an elderly woman having her usual £1 each-way on the rank outsider, William Of Orange. She took 100-1 from the course bookie with obvious gratitude. Having just passed a Tote screen, I'd noticed that their estimate for a £1 stake was £256.68. Perhaps she didn't fancy the upset of winning too much money but someone ought to give her a brief lesson in successful punting.

A real treat at Wetherby is to stay on the inner course and place yourself by the stands' hurdle, as you can get very close into the action. William Of Orange (carrying A. S. Smith and an old lady's £1 each-way) was going fairly well when he first approached this obstacle, only to hit the hurdle so hard that the jockey ended up with a very fine view of my trouser turn-ups. Meanwhile, R. Garritty had tucked his mount, Meadowbank, at the back of the pack and popped the hurdle only to have a close encounter with the now prostrate William Of Orange. Seconds later, Mr Garrity also lay at my feet.

'Afternoon,' I said, as sympathetically as possible.

'It's an effing game this is,' he replied, hurling his helmet onto the ground.

'Yep,' I answered shortly. He didn't look like a man who fancied a chat.

Two races later and still without a winner, I headed back to the car park, determined to return one day and take my revenge on the bookmakers. And I would go back, despite my whingeing. This fast galloping course is definitely worth a visit and the building work on the new stand is now fully completed.

The gate attendants were still huddled together in the warmth of their small cabin. Glancing sideways, I happened to catch the eye of the man who had mistaken me for a priest.

'Any winners, vicar?' he queried, with a certain reverence.

'Not even a sniff,' I replied.

'Never mind. Another day,' he answered kindly.

'If it's the Lord's wish,' I responded gravely and quickly turned towards my waiting car.

Postscript: The new stand is now complete and a real success. Despite its sail-like roof it appears to have remained intact. Since my visit I have been scanning the pages of *Yachting Weekly*. I half expected to read reports that Wetherby's Millennium Stand had been sighted rounding Cape Horn. Not yet . . . but it's only a matter of time.

CHAPTER FIFTY-SEVEN

WINCANTON

If you've ever attended the Open Golf Championship at St Andrews, you'll know that one of the prime viewing points is at the side of the seventh green. I would advise you to adopt similar tactics at Wincanton. This Somerset course, lying close to Bristol and Exeter, is built around a golf course – or maybe the golf course is built inside the racecourse. Whatever the case, if you want to see races develop along the back straight, get yourself into the centre, head for the seventh – but don't stand on the green.

My initial sight of Wincanton was a bit of a disappointment. The signs for the course are limited and you'll need to keep your eyes peeled. The course itself isn't even marked, the only indicator being an ambiguous car park sign and a fluttering Union Jack. I entered warily, fearful that I had stumbled on a meeting of the Somerset Anti-Euro Society. The large, grassed car park brings you in behind the three main stands, two of which are constructed in grey corrugated iron and look about as welcoming as a nightclub bouncer.

But like theatrical stage sets, many racecourses are only worth admiring from the auditorium and Wincanton is no exception. Though simply laid out, the course does have a certain confusion, as it is littered with a variety of bars, betting areas and cafes. Even if you're Irish, avoid the Guinness Bar in Tattersalls at all costs. It's the sort of room you'd find at a youth club social – all echo and no atmosphere. The Tanglefoot Bar at the back of the Grandstand ranks as OK, but has the air of an upmarket motorway service station. Of all the watering holes, the Stalbridge Bar at the back of the members' stand probably wins by a distance.

Uniquely, it's a no-smoking area and though I enjoy the occasional cheroot, it came as a real breath of fresh air. Apparently refurbished, the designers have gone for an interior painted in green and salmon pink, which turns even the most ruddy-faced punter into an anaemic invalid. And the highly patterned carpet doesn't help. It reminded me of my Aunt Enid's front room in 1959, which contained a Wilton of such complexity that her guests would regularly keel over.

But the Stalbridge Bar does have a lot going for it – not least the fact that they supply hot chocolate in mugs, TV screens and a bunch of staff who must have trained at a charm school. Around the walls are handpainted display boards revealing past Wincanton winners, and some fine black and white photos dating back over fifty years. Look out for a picture of Sign Post winning the Badger Chase in 1964. The jockey, O. McNally, reveals how riding styles have changed. His posture in the saddle and look of abject fear would have embarrassed a twelve-year-old girl in her local gymkhana. To be fair to McNally, the jockey on the runner-up looks as if he's just been issued with eight paternity suits – a mixture of pleasure and severe shock.

If you enjoy your history, pay a visit to the Seafood

Restaurant, where apart from enjoying the delicious fish pie, you can join Jenny Pitman in gloating over her success in 1993. The Jim Ford Challenge Cup has been won by some famous names but none more so than Cavvies Clown, a horse first trained by David Elsworth, who won the race twice. Obviously past its best, Elsworth handed over training to Jenny Pitman, who won the race with the same horse at the tender age of thirteen. If David Elsworth ever visits the Seafood Restaurant, I bet he always stands with his back to that display board.

The first race was a two-mile maiden hurdle with sixteen runners. Collectively, they had as much class as Alf Garnett and picking a winner seemed impossible. I wandered over to the saddling boxes, a rather dingy row of stables which lie adjacent to the equally shabby paddock. I had encountered the trainer Miss Venetia Williams earlier in the week, where I had unkindly likened her to a delicious boarding school head girl.

What I hadn't noticed was her eye for detail. If you ever get a chance to watch her saddle a horse, don't miss the opportunity. She examines the bridle, saddle and girth with the precision of a neurotic who checks the back door five times before going to bed. Even a speck of dust on the number cloth doesn't escape her inspection. If you're ever tempted to join a small racing syndicate, I'd give her a ring. You might not be guaranteed a winner but you'll have the smartest horse in the parade.

Unable to find one selection with any likely form, I opted for a mug's bet on Venetia Williams' Guido. Even if it lost, it was going to lose with style. As it happened, it just made the frame, at a respectable 16-1, the jockey Norman Williamson almost carrying him over the line. The owners seemed delighted.

'Any chance of lodging an objection?' asked one with a smile.

'Oh do shut up!' responded Venetia in head girl tones.

The jockey, Jimmy Tizzard, was having a useful after-noon. A good second in the opening race was followed by an easy win in the next. Unfortunately I had chosen this race to engage a Bristol man in conversation, asking for his opinion on the various merits of West Country race-courses. He was a genial fellow but a serious punter, who advised me that Tizzard's next mount, Laredo, couldn't be beaten. Naturally I ignored his advice, feeling that this particular jockey had used up all his luck. Instead I backed Oscar Wilde, on account of my love for his intellectual wit. Minutes later, Jimmy Tizzard drove Laredo over the line on a tight rein, Oscar Wilde coming a puffing but creditable second.

'There you go,' laughed my new-found acquaintance, kissing his winning ticket.

'Every time a friend succeeds, a little of me dies,' I replied. It may not have been accurate but it was the most Wildean thing I could muster.

Returning to the Tote to collect my place money pittance, I noticed a small crowd gathered around a waste bin. The race had been slightly delayed by the second-favourite, Montroe, showing no inclination to slog his way round two miles, five furlongs and eighteen fences. So reluctant was this seven-year-old stallion that he never came under orders and it was announced that all bets were refundable with a small reduction for tax.

One unfortunate punter had missed this information and in anger had hurled his £50 betting slip into the waste bin. He was a respectable, tweeded and elderly man, who by now had forsaken any attempt at etiquette and was up to his elbows in betting slips and half-eaten burgers. To add to his ill luck, he was not a man of impressive height and seemed to be having trouble coming to terms with the fact that his arms were shorter than the depth of the bin. I can only watch a man suffer for so long and I hurried off to back my banker in the next race.

Apart from the golf course there are no centre course facilities at Wincanton but access is encouraged from all the stand enclosures. I headed off for the seventh green to keep a close eye on Naiysari and its inevitable victory. Another option would have been to remain in the stands, as the course management supply a wonderfully large TV screen, which allows you to watch every step of the race. As good as these screens are, I make a point of avoiding them at all costs. I've never seen the point in making the effort to go live racing, only to spend my time staring at a television. The problem with having the monitor facing the main grandstands is that, as hard as you try, it's impossible to ignore the broadcast images. It's quite likely that you'll stand by the winning post and be so consumed by the silent action on the screen that you'll view the sound of approaching hooves as an irritating interference. Thanks for the offer, but I'd rather take my racing in the raw.

Apart from avoiding the TV monitor, the main advantage of the centre course is that you can get close into the fences. It's here that Wincanton comes into its own. Despite being able to see three fences and two hurdles from the stands, you get no real impression of their difficulty. The brush fences are particularly testing and present genuine obstacles, even to the experienced chasers.

Unlike many courses, the finishing straight at Wincanton drops down towards the finish and horses approach these fences at a pace which often brings them into the jumps on the wrong stride. It guarantees many exciting finishes and isn't ideal for a punter's blood pressure. The wonderful Norman Williamson obviously had my health in mind as he popped Naiysari over the last, my shouts of 'Get him in, Norman!' ringing in his ears.

My celebration cup of tea was taken in the new Hatherleigh Stand, a red brick construction, built mainly to house private boxes. However, it also contains a very comfortable bar and raked seating, which looks over the course through wide, sun-drenched panoramic windows. You are so divorced from the racing in this area that apart from being a useful place to raise my spring seedlings, there appeared to be no point in watching my last race from this position. The £5 course enclosure seemed far more appealing.

As usual, course enclosure punters are kept well away from the paddock by high wire fences. Something tells me that the days of segregated racing are bound to be numbered and are soon likely to be as common as third-class railway carriages. In all truth, they're a bit of an antiquated nonsense and should be confined to history. But the facilities at Wincanton aren't too bad, a warm and cosy bar and a sizeable stand which looks directly over the penultimate fence. Unlike many course enclosures I've witnessed in my travels, the tannoy and race commentary is as clear as you'd enjoy in the members' section. The course bookies seemed to be doing a fair trade and the Tote building was adequate for the small crowd.

And it was here that I met George. To describe him as lascivious would be as inadequate as describing Martin Pipe as an inexperienced trainer. George was lecherous, obscene, smutty, crude and bawdy. George was also about 85 years of age. His opening line to the three red-coated

Tote ladies suggested he was a man with the subtlety of a comedian in a working men's club.

'Fancy three in a bed?'

Much giggling ensued.

'Who do you think would come off best?' he asked with a puff of his pipe and a leer that would unnerve a working girl.

'We would!' answered one of the ladies, quickly fastening the top button of her shirt.

'Bet you a tenner I could service you all,' he responded, his nose now pressed firmly against the glass partition.

'We only take bets on horses,' answered the more quick-witted of the three women, shaking her head in mock disapproval.

The rest of the punters in the room broke their silence and began to laugh, chiding George for overestimating his sexual prowess. You can learn a great deal by going racing. The next time I'm in a nightclub and spot three attractive women, I'm going to tell them I'm eighty-five and make some very suggestive comments.

I've got mixed feelings about Wincanton, though it probably deserves its accolade as the premier West Country course. The racing is impressive but the course is rather nondescript, though thankfully they've now spent some much needed money on that barren paddock (I hope they consulted Uttoxeter first). I was taking the following week off to enjoy Cheltenham and have a couple of rounds of golf at St Andrews. I suspected that I'd be thinking about Naiysari – and George – as soon as I stepped onto that manicured seventh green.

CHAPTER FIFTY-EIGHT

WINDSOR

An admission needs to be made. I came to bury Windsor, not to praise it. Back in 1992, I headed for one of the numerous Monday evening meetings – only to break down in the middle of the Slough rush hour traffic. Within seconds I had become the most unpopular man in Berkshire, as queues of over two miles built up behind me. How do I know it was two miles? Simple. One irate driver wound down his window and offered the following helpful information: 'Do you know there's an effing two-mile queue back there?'

Finally restarting my beloved Citroën 2CV, I arrived at Windsor, sweating heavily and covered in oil. Unfortunately the loss of one of my two spark plugs meant that my arrival was heralded by what fellow punters obviously took as heavy machine-gun fire. Women in fine summer outfits covered their heads and cowered in bushes while ex-military men appeared to be digging trenches. And things didn't get any better. Six straight losers followed. I ate a hog roast bun which the hog would have rejected and the facilities could best be described as dire. I swore I would never return.

Yet, nearly twelve years later I found myself on the same Slough high street, heading for Windsor racecourse – and in the same 2CV car. It's a summer luxury, which peeks out from under its covers for only four months of the year but is now transformed from the old French rust bucket of 1992 into a gleaming red, open-topped piece of motorized madness. I've had it refurbished. New roof, new bonnet, new chassis, new headlights. It's like New Labour on wheels: open to abuse, underpowered, often impractical, a bumpy ride – but just about gets to its destination.

The memories came flooding back and, as I entered the course along the tree-lined driveway, my pencil was as sharp as a surgeon's scalpel, ready to cut deep into the heart of Windsor. To make matters worse they had even scrapped jump racing in 1998 and I can't think of a more heinous crime. Revenge was well overdue.

If you're not familiar with this course, try to get there a little earlier than normal and ignore all signs leading to a free car park. From here it's quite a trek. Instead follow signs marked 'owners and trainers', as there's a little-publicized public car park right outside the Grandstand entrance. It'll cost you £2 but will make your escape much easier and is well worth the extra cost. From here, avoid all temptation to go into the racecourse. Rather than approaching the main gates, turn right and only fifty yards away you'll find the bank of the meandering and glittering Thames. Sounds over-poetic? On a fine July evening it provides a view that could make a *Sun* reader literate.

Two small jetties jut out into the bend of the river, rowing boats row, swans swan, geese geese (or is it geese goose?), while two gliding Victorian launches bring punters to the course from the nearby Windsor promenade. At only £3 return it's a cheap and unique way to go racing.

As often happens, my notebook gave a false impression of authority. Just as I was musing over the sleek lines of the *Windsor Sovereign*, I was approached by a confused father, a dishevelled mother and their three pubescent children.

'Could you help me?' he enquired.

'I'm not . . .' I stuttered.

'It's just that we haven't been racing before. Where's the best part of the course?'

Such was my dislike of Windsor that it was like enticing a child with a bag of sweets. I was sorely tempted to respond by telling him that there were no best parts and that he'd have a far better time window shopping in Slough. But I choked on the words and fluffed my first act of revenge. 'Try the Silver Ring. It's fun in there,' I lied. 'You can always transfer if you don't like it. At least it's cheap.' One mention of the word cheap seemed to have the same effect on this man as the sight of a mug punter has on a rails bookie. 'Gentleman says the Silver Ring's best,' said the father turning to his wife.

It was a slight over-elaboration but I sympathized with his motives. I never saw him again, which is probably a good thing, as the Silver Ring is truly awful. Its main attractions are an echoing cafe, which smells of deep fried chips and one small bar with a ten-deep tired queue. Views of the racing are limited to about 150 yards of the final furlong and even the obligatory big screen TV on the far side of the course is angled to favour the members' enclosure. There are no stands to remedy this restricted view and yet the place was heaving with punters unable to resist the £4 entrance fee. In the old days (when my 2CV was a wreck) most picnics were laid out in the centre of the course and barbecues could be seen at every turn. Sadly they are now banned, severe notices warning potential chefs that such practices are no longer allowed. At least you can smell the hog roast wafting over from the £10 Grandstand enclosure.

Those who do have a picnic really go to town and there were some mouthwatering feasts on display. And where else could you see a peroxide blonde wearing a diamante top with the words 'Universal Studios' emblazoned across her ample bosom? Just to complete the picture, she had set out two directors' chairs and was happily sipping Guinness out of a pink wine glass. Style. Pure style.

If (like the confused father by the river) you start in the Silver Ring and transfer your way up to the members' enclosure it will cost you an extra £11. As you enter, you will be met with a sea of blue and white, the course management having obviously given up their formative brown period and moved on to greater things. Since my last visit, the place suddenly looked less dog-eared with a far greater sense of order and a neatness in the presentation.

Just to maintain my resistance I made a note that the new blue and white Grandstand (1995) looked rather like Luton airport with a balcony. It also revealed the way that racing has given in to corporate entertaining. Only a ground floor bar and a small, open raked stand are open to the public. The rest of the building is made up of a large restaurant and private boxes. It's a matter of opinion but racing mustn't lose touch with its grass roots support. What worried me even more was that I could sense my critical pencil was being blunted by Windsor's new image.

It was then that panic set in. At one point I was a fairly regular visitor to Windsor and would always start the day by drinking at least five pints of water. This guaranteed that my lavatory calls would be regular, if not frequent. My concern was that, in all this modernization, they had removed Windsor's finest asset. I was running faster than an incontinent dog as I entered the Club Grandstand, receiving some suspicious and sympathetic glances, as I searched for the Gentlemen's cloakroom.

It might be £15 to get into the members' enclosure but it's worth it just to use these facilities. As I found out later, the interior of the club stand is subject to listing restrictions and thankfully it remains intact. It's reminiscent of a Victorian gentlemen's club: warm dark oak panels, creaking floorboards and a smell of old polish. Nowhere is this more evident than in the Gents (and more than likely in the Ladies). If the Royal family ever pays a visit, it's probably the only toilet in Britain that wouldn't need to change a thing.

This retention of the old in face of the new carries right through the whole building and the small Grandstand, though refurbished with sturdy wooden bench seating, has retained its distinct quality. Watching the first two races from this position unfortunately revealed Windsor's insoluble problem. As far as I know Windsor remains the only racecourse in Britain which is built on an island, the Thames weaving its way around the outer perimeter and limiting the available ground. In order to race at any distance over a mile, jockeys must steer their mounts around an elongated figure of eight. In many ways it's similar to Fontwell Park but completely flat and therefore far less accessible.

The effect is that even from the prime positions, such as the members' stand, viewing remains limited to only one loop of the course. As a consequence, most races take place in complete silence until the pack re-emerge at the two-furlong pole. Apart from draining the Thames, I'm not sure there's much that can be done other than compensating the public with good facilities and making a visit to the racecourse an all-round experience.

Ten years ago I'd have suggested saving your money, as you'd probably get more excitement from reading the obituary column in your local newspaper. But maybe it's time to praise the resurrection and admit that things have changed for the better. Nowhere is this more obvious than in the paddock area behind the grandstands. A forest of mature trees cast light and shade onto the lawns. I counted no less than twenty-three sycamores around the flower-circled parade ring, a setting perhaps only rivalled by Newmarket. Even on a busy summer evening, there was no sense of overcrowding. The new weighing room (sadly in blue and white Luton airport colours) and elegant winners' enclosure is set some way from the paddock and there is little difficulty in watching the post-race revelry, where successful owners kiss horses, trainers and anything that moves.

By some miracle or other I managed to land the winner of the first race and was able to join in the celebrations. I stood very still in case an amorous owner had any ideas. Jimmy Fortune decided to play catch me if you can on the short-priced Ameretto Flame. Holding a seven-length lead going into the far loop, the three-year-old novice appeared at the two-furlong pole with only two lengths to spare and fast running out of steam. But fortune was on my side and on my horse, the filly getting up with just over a length to spare. As you'd expect at Windsor, the opener was a selling stakes and much to the annoyance of the trainer someone in the ring forced the price up to

£5,400 before being bought in by the connections. (Watching owners' expressions move rapidly from elation to despair when someone tries to buy their horse has become a favourite pastime.) At a rough reckoning, the partnership walked off with no more than £800 in prize money – hardly enough to pay for two weeks' training costs. It's no wonder I gave up ownership more than five years ago. With prize money like that, the pleasure and status of winning are soon soured by a glance at your bank balance.

A couple of losers and two successful place bets later I headed for the car park and my refurbished 2CV. Like Windsor, I had almost lost interest and packed it off to the scrapyard. It would have been a bad decision. They've given Windsor racecourse a new roof, a new chassis, a new bonnet and new headlights. I was convinced it would fail its MOT – but it looks like it's back on the road and ready for a long journey.

Postscript I: If they want to drain the Thames – I know where the plug is.

Postscript II: They've brought back the jumps but for only four days a year. Hardly grasping the nettle. It's like expecting gratitude for offering a starving man a picture of a butcher's window.

CHAPTER FIFTY-NINE

WOLVERHAMPTON

It's an odd fact of life that, with a real commitment to parenting, you can encourage an adolescent to do their homework, avoid drugs, resist nose rings, extend their diet beyond a Big Mac and fries, and even do the occasional bit of washing up. With a bit of luck these are attainable goals. But have you ever tried to get a teenager to switch off a light? It would be easier to persuade George Bush to join the Communist Party. Any household that has survived the trauma of guiding children towards adulthood will be aware that between the ages of twelve and eighteen the electricity bill rises faster than my Aunt Bertha's sponge cake. (She was a woman famed for her liberal attitude to baking powder.)

Treat a teenager to an evening at Wolverhampton and they'll think they've entered paradise. There are so many lights burning at these events that the national grid must go onto red alert every time they hold a meeting. Is electricity free to residents of the West Midlands? If it is, I'm moving there tomorrow.

On a dark and rain-filled October evening, I headed for the racecourse with no preconceptions. Like many punters, I think of racing as a daytime activity, yet Wolverhampton provides at least twenty evening meetings a year, many of which take place under floodlights. Whatever conclusions you might reach about this Midlands course, it retains a unique quality, providing a style of racing found nowhere else in Britain. (At least until Kempton Park flicks its own switches.)

Whether it's your cup of tea or not is a matter of personal opinion. Arnold Bax (*Farewell My Youth,* 1943) suggested that we should try everything in life at least once – excepting incest and folk dancing. He made no mention of an evening at Wolverhampton – and I was willing to give it a go.

To be fair to this racecourse, I could have chosen from an additional number of daytime contests spread throughout the year but Saturday night floodlit racing is its speciality. It's the Midlands answer to *Saturday Night Fever* and I was expecting the stewards to be dressed in white linen suits and bell-bottom trousers. Access for the majority of punters will be from the M54 – a spur of the M6 which runs up as far as Telford, the supposed birthplace of the Industrial Revolution. Wolverhampton may well prove to be the birthplace of a racing revolution – only time will tell.

Like many of the new football stadia, the racecourse appears to prefer the policy of 'we've built it – you find it'. Apart from the usual small, galloping horse symbol you need some insider knowledge to locate the racecourse. Wolverhampton racecourse is at Dunstall Park and you're expected to know this before you arrive. And again, like many of its football counterparts, the course appears to have been dumped on a bit of spare ground, where the only access is through a small housing estate whose occupants obviously thrive on large doses of carbon monoxide.

Oddly, even when you arrive, you don't know you're there. What you are faced with is a huge hotel complex in the middle of an industrial building site. Getting a room with a sea view would be a major problem. Even stranger is that, if you intend to treat yourself to a day (night?) member's badge, entrance is gained through the hotel lobby. Thankfully the authorities have created a simple two-tier ticket system and entrance to Tattersalls is through a rather smart brick built gatehouse which takes you into the hotel courtyard. At least you'll be expecting a courtyard. Think again.

What you walk into is, in fact, the paddock – a rather barren yet well laid out oval, decked in finest AstroTurf and lit by a bank of lights attached to the top of the stands and the adjacent hotel. It's a subdued rather than stark illumination, giving the impression that dusk has just fallen. It's the sort of glow that theatres employ just before the curtain goes up, a light that heightens the anticipation.

And it was in that moment that I discovered Wolverhampton's secret. This is not racing; this is theatre. Pure and unadulterated drama, with six acts and a cast of unknown actors. For entrances, read 'foyer'. For the stands, read 'auditorium'. For the course, read 'stage'. For the floodlights, read 'spotlights'. For stewards, read 'directors'. For trainers, read 'actor managers'. My only concern was that successful owners might congratulate their jockeys by screaming across the winners' enclosure, 'You were simply wonderful, darling!' My first sight of the course only confirmed this theatrical impression.

As in any play, the audience must suspend belief. Since 1993, the one-mile oval circuit has been laid with an all-weather (make believe?) surface and has less undulations than my local skating rink. Any race over seven furlongs requires the runners to negotiate two tight bends and at least two short straights. Riding a thoroughbred around Wolverhampton must be akin to crossing a tight-rope with no pole. As subsequent races proved, position and balance are everything and there's little point in a jockey trying to come off the pace. Unfortunately, I only discovered this simple fact once I was battling back home through scenic Walsall.

At a guess, the only punters with any chance of land-ing winners at Wolverhampton are the locals. Strangers from the South, like myself, must approach bookmakers with 'SUCKER' tattooed on their forehead. I'm not the greatest reader of form in the world but have occasionally landed some long odds when the going has suddenly changed from firm to good-to-soft. Empty the contents of a reservoir onto an all-weather course and it seems to make no difference at all.

I selected Brief Call in the first race (Act I) for no better reason than I had arrived rather late and it seemed to have the nicest name. The six-furlong contest started in a small shoot in the far right-hand corner of the course. Brief Call lived up to its name and made a brief challenge only to fade away faster than a one-hit pop star. But I did see every step of its magnificent failure. Not an inch of the course lay in darkness and the open expanse of the centre course allows totally unrestricted views of the developing race. The brightly coloured racing silks shimmer in the artificial light, allowing you to identify your rider with as great an ease as I've found on any racecourse. Yet Wolverhampton has more surprises in store. Each act of the evening's play has its own grand finale.

As the pack hit the two-furlong marker, a giant bank of lights are snapped into action, illuminating the finishing line with enough bulbs to satisfy a Hollywood Oscar winner. If, like myself, you have not witnessed high theatre on a racecourse before, you may well be truly stunned. I know this to be a fact as, at the moment the winner passed the winning post, I muttered to myself: 'I am truly stunned.' Sadly, by the end of the evening, I had been stunned into silence, my four bets resulting in nothing better than third in a field of six runners. All-weather form was proving as much of a mystery as a Geordie phrasebook might be to a Latvian shepherd. Even if the evening had been spent watching sheep racing, I doubt if it would have mattered. As my later inspections revealed, Wolverhampton has little to do with equine battles as these remain only as support players to the real star turn. Close your ears to the local accents and you could be in Chicago – brash, glitzy and customer-oriented. Even the staff are trained to say 'Have a nice night, sir' – thankfully without any attempt to patronize. Wolverhampton's got a brash modern product and they're determined to sell it with a big toothy smile.

Despite my ingrained British reserve and genetic mistrust of sincerity, it's hard not to succumb to the Wolverhampton package. The place is littered with food outlets, bars and betting areas – all rather functional but clean, tidy and geared to some fairly hefty evening crowds. Although I only stayed for just over two hours, I've rarely seen so much alcohol consumed in such a short time. The benefits of evening racing is that drinkers go into evening drinking mode rather than the more refined and careful sipping which occurs during the day. After three races it was plain that the judgement of many punters was being blurred by Mr Booze. Not that they became unruly. Behaviour was exemplary but I did note that large wads of folding money were being placed on some obvious donkeys. I have rarely seen a more contented bunch of bookmakers gladly burying the bets in the depths of their bulging satchels.

But if the racing isn't the main attraction, what is? I would direct you to no less than the Zongalero restaurant – the epitome of downtown Wolverhampton night life. Viewed from the racecourse, the occupants appear to be stacked on top of one another like a triple filling in a gargantuan layered sponge cake. I wanted a closer look. Asking for directions on a lower floor, I was advised that entrance was not possible unless I had booked a table. But curiosity got the better of me, especially as a young receptionist in the hotel lobby had informed me that the Zongalero enjoyed views over the racecourse through windows which magnified the course and made punters feel as if they were riding the horses.

Fortunately attired in my smart but casual, I entered the restaurant with a lean and hungry but confident look, only to find myself muttering once again: 'I am truly stunned.' It was showtime. It was time to get it on. I've been fortunate to eat in restaurants all over the world but this was undoubtedly the biggest trough I've ever encountered. Apparently it can seat up to 400 people, though it looked more like the feeding of the five thousand. What's more, there wasn't a seat to be had. On the basis that a bad restaurant is an empty restaurant, the Zongalero must be doing something right.

The gigantic windows (which don't magnify – that girl urgently needs to see an optician) give a bird's eye view of the whole course and a clear sight from every position. Parties of between two and eight diners munch their way through an excellent menu, while a private TV for each table supplies betting information and relays the live race direct to the customers. Tote ladies flit between tables, their portable machines churning out tickets faster than a pay and display car park. Get your backside on a Zongalero dining chair and you needn't move for the rest of the evening. This is racing American style – good food, reasonable prices, fast service and responsive staff. Even when the racing has finished, the management provides a live band and dance floor, allowing punters to stamp rhythmically on their losing betting slips.

If you're tempted to go to Wolverhampton, this is the way to do it. There are at least four other restaurants on site, all offering packages including entrance and a four-course meal. Apart from the Zongalero, the Ringside restaurant provides the most bizarre experience. Set on the ground floor with a limited view of the paddock, the Ringside is equipped with three giant screens which relay the race to the 400 diners. If you've ever attended a race night at your local village hall, you'll be familiar with this set-up – the only difference being that the racing is live.

By chance I happened to attend the racecourse on Halloween, which provided the management with the opportunity to deck the facilities with paper spiders and ghoulish masks. But in the Ringside restaurant there was an extra treat in the form of an itinerant hypnotist of little-known fame. I've no idea how successful this retired cigarette lighter salesman turned out to be. A little later, however, I noted a number of respectable ladies trotting around the paddock on all fours and demanding to be mounted by a startled bunch of diminutive jockeys. I left hurriedly, praying that the hypnotist's hands weren't so cold that he couldn't snap his fingers in time to save the women from public humiliation.

As I strode back towards my car, I turned briefly back towards the racecourse. The giant lights reflected on my glasses as I reflected on the experience. There's no doubt that, in racing terms, Wolverhampton is unique, a brash oasis in the industrial desert of the West Midlands. But would I return? To be honest, it's not really my kind of racing. Perhaps it's just my aversion to pumpkin pie, New York bagels and anyone in a baseball cap who tells me to 'have a nice day'.

CHAPTER SIXTY

WORCESTER

Taking a car to Worcester is about as useful as wearing snow skis in the Gobi desert. It's gridlock city, with enough traffic lights to provide more illumination than Blackpool's Golden Mile. I don't know the physical capabilities of the local Worcester folk but the lights take so long to change that a slug could get across a zebra crossing without any risk of danger. The course is very close to the city centre, yet despite arriving in Worcester at 12.30 p.m., I entered the course car park only minutes before the 2.00 maiden hurdle. To make matters worse, it's another 'find it yerself' racecourse, the only token gesture to directing new visitors being a couple of minuscule brown signs bearing an equine symbol. For all I knew they could have been advertising the local rocking horse factory.

Like the biblical three kings, I had approached from the east, passing through the delightfully named hamlets of North Piddle and Upton Snodsbury. The Cotswold countryside is very nice, a description which, while obviously inadequate, sums up my feelings for this part of England. It's so damned nice it could have come off a Milk

Tray selection box. I'd describe myself as a wimp with rugged preferences. You know the sort of thing – craggy mountains, windswept coastlines and raging rivers. The Cotswolds have always struck me as being about as adrenalin-inducing as a bottle of tranquillizers – but we all have our opinions.

Fortunately, if you've got three days to spare, enjoy painting old tin pots and have a penchant for morris dancing, you can leave your car at home. Running alongside the racecourse is the non-raging River Severn, a stretch of water which regularly invades Worcester racecourse, even after a small shower. Moor your narrow boat at the back of the main stand and you could be filling a bookie's pockets within thirty seconds. As luck would have it, the day of my visit coincided with the annual Waterways Festival. The river was littered with over seventy gleaming barges, their poetic names reflecting in the still but murky water. *Maudelayne, Pegasus* and *Kippin Three* nestled together, while *Straw Bear* displayed the finest washing line of alluring lingerie I've seen since I took the wrong turn in my local Marks and Spencer.

Sadly, this boating intrusion also included a tented village in the centre of the course, which took up half the available parking. As a result, and being without my narrow boat, I was forced to moor my car amongst the organized chaos of a small area inside the course. By the time I made it onto the course, the starter was calling the first race into line. A quick glance at the paper in the morning revealed a horse I had seen put up a creditable performance on the testing course of Towcester back in May. With only seconds to spare, I went for a £5 each-way bet with the Tote and raced off to the rail to watch the pack go past the stands.

Miracle Island seemed to struggle from the start, clipped the first three hurdles and didn't appear to be enjoying the unusually heavy ground. But with two furlongs to go, Paul Holley (always a favourite) put him in contention and finally brought his mount home by a clear four lengths. The starting-price was 4-1 and the Tote paid 6-1. All was right with the world and Worcester couldn't fail to impress. But if you think that a replenished wallet might colour my opinion – think again. This was the 32nd course I had visited in my travels and to date probably the worst arena I had so far encountered. I was dry, I was warm, I was in profit. But I wasn't impressed. The Gentlemen's lavatory set the tone.

As often happens after a fairly lengthy journey, nature takes its course. Hurrying into the Tattersalls convenience, pre-flushed by my 6-1 winner, I was met with a small box-like room, which had been constructed out of materials obviously rejected by the local B&Q superstore. Graffiti adorned the walls, while hurriedly scrawled notices announced 'Out of Order' to desperate customers. It would have made a Salvation Army hostel look like the Ritz.

The nearby cafeteria and bar proved no better. This dark depressing cavern, decorated in faded emulsion and displaying the obligatory green carpet tiles, enjoyed the tempting aroma of my local fish and chip shop after a busy Saturday night. The deep fried furniture offered little relief, while the pink plastic tablecloths heaved with grease congealed, uncollected cutlery. Braving the tea bar, I ordered a hot drink, waiting at least five minutes to be acknowledged by four members of staff, more intent on discussing their latest romances than responding to their customers. Collectively they had about as much interpersonal skill as a dead vulture. The woman who eventually served me obviously reserved eye contact for her daily dose of TV.

My late Aunt Bertha (famed in Southport for her success with 5p each-way Yankees) would have called the place 'tatty'. I'd call it shabby and exhausted. Behind the tea-stained counter lay empty cartons, the floor strewn with discarded chips and uneaten slices of hog roast. Staff trampled amongst this debris, blissfully unaware of the message transmitted by this culinary shambles. They may as well have displayed a sign reading 'WORCESTER RACECOURSE – WE'VE LOST THE PLOT'.

Even the flagship facility of the members' restaurant fared little better. Tucked at the back of the stand it has no view over the course and proved little better than the Little Chef restaurant which had served me breakfast earlier in the day. The main stand (and only stand) perhaps signalled the decline of Worcester racecourse. Built in 1975, the management displayed their ineptitude by constructing the edifice at the wrong angle, resulting in Joe Public having no sight of the turn beyond the winning post. It was quite bizarre to observe a crowd fall into complete silence while the pack disappeared out of sight. You can lean forward as far as you like and you won't catch a glimpse of a horse's rear end. Experienced Worcester punters simply stared ahead with blank expressions, patiently waiting for the leaders to reappear in the back straight. In contrast, new visitors to Worcester contorted their bodies in unison as if engaging in a communal yoga display.

It was from this newly acquired lotus position that I first caught sight of the blackening sky. A blanket of rain was fast approaching and officials shuffled uneasily, glancing over their shoulders at the ever-rising River Severn. By the time I had left the dilapidated stand, the storm had broken, thunder rumbling in the far distance and sheets of rain sending punters hurrying for cover. Undaunted, yet dressed only for a summer's day, I pressed on with my tour.

The layout of the public areas is in the form of a long strip, extending from the stand down to the paddock and pre-parade ring. The Paddock Lawn, as it is rather grandly called, is no more than a rather scrubby bit of turf on which sit eight plastic tables and five fast-food outlets. The paddock itself is bare and uninspiring, not a seat, flower bed or stand in sight. If there is any saving grace it is the quaint weighing room which, in its green and white decor, was reminiscent of a giant Bournemouth beach hut.

Unfortunately I can think of little else to commend. Having recently visited the delights of Pontefract, Worcester seemed to have as much in common with this fine Yorkshire course as Manchester United have with the Conference League. By the time of the third race, and having drawn a blank in the second, I took refuge in the stand. Torrents of rain beat against the roof, the barges noticeably rising on the swelling river. In only twenty minutes the going had gone from good to heavy – and punters, including myself, were frantically hunting their form guides for soft ground specialists. Despite not having run for 130 days and with form of 40P5P, Paparazzo looked a certainty, even at early odds of 6-1.

Adopting the cobra position suggested by the Yogi Bhagavad Gita, I managed to follow most of the race. Sadly, for most of the crowd, the far end of the course was now so dark that it was impossible to make out their selection's progress. By sheer chance I had recently visited the optician, who managed to supply me with the wrong prescription for my glasses. Though I was unable to read any text less than twenty feet away, my long sight was now remarkable and akin to having a pair of binoculars strapped to my forehead.

Paparazzo jumped like a stag, taking at least three lengths out of the favourite at every fence. Unfortunately the final obstacle proved a fence too far and Paparazzo hit the top so hard that Carl Llewellyn remained attached to his mount by only one stirrup and a rein which must have had as much grip as a wet chamois leather. Despite my audible groan (enhanced by the excruciating pain of the cobra position), the jockey did well to stay on board and land the place money.

Having followed every step of the race, it became apparent that I had been fed some wrong information. I had read that Worcester abandoned Flat meetings in 1966, yet what I had just witnessed was not a steeplechase but a two-mile, four-furlong Flat race, with a few obstructions thrown in to liven up the contest. The level one-mile, five-furlong oval course is fairly undemanding and provides little more than a nursery for inexperienced maidens. I'm sure there are a few jockeys who've hit the deck at Worcester who might well protest at this claim. But from a punter's viewpoint there's little sign of tension, no evidence of horses being given a true test of their ability. In many ways the hurdles and jumps seem incidental to the racecourse and fail to set the heart thumping. Real jumping should make you feel like a lovelorn adolescent with a racing pulse and sweaty palms. On this visit, I doubt my blood pressure went any higher than that of a meditating Buddhist monk.

If nothing else, the day was profitable. The fourth race

produced another second place, thanks to some fine riding by Mick Fitzgerald. Wet and bedraggled, I hurried back to the car park, stirring myself for the city traffic lights. A gate steward viewed me with pity as I made my early exit.

'No luck then?' he asked kindly.

'One winner and two seconds,' I smiled in reply.

'Not bad,' he responded.

It was then that he gave me the only sign of hope for Worcester racecourse. He'd heard on the grapevine that the racecourse was about to be sold to private investors. Unlike the majority of courses, Worcester is apparently council-owned – and it shows. The setting is fine, lying as it does bordering the River Severn, with the magnificent cathedral dominating the skyline. But it's like a grand Victorian hotel which has seen better days and needs an injection of money – and, more than anything, a good dose of imagination.

Perhaps by the time you read this report, things will have begun to change for the better – as it couldn't get any worse. If developers do move in, a large bulldozer must be their first acquisition. It's time the council gave up any interest in racing as they appear to be having as much success as a one-armed archer at Agincourt. They should stick to shoring up the river bank and snarling up the city centre traffic. It's always better to stick with what you know. At the moment, I wouldn't touch Worcester with a bargepole.

Postscript I: Just as I left the course, I glanced back to the Grandstand. The bow of a narrow boat could just be seen peeking over the iron railings. Things looked ominous.

Postscript II: The council have finally relinquished control and handed over to private business. I hope the new owners possess a very fat wallet, know a few demolition contractors and an imaginative architect. I'm informed the company also owns, amongst others, Lingfield, Wolverhampton, Southwell and Folkestone. Not a great 'track record'.

CHAPTER SIXTY-ONE

YORK

I never carry a flintlock pistol, never wear a mask, never sport a three-cornered hat. But I do have one thing in common with the late Dick Turpin – we both came to grief at York racecourse. Many years after the infamous highwayman was swinging in the breeze to the cheers of a baying crowd, a young man entered York with his parents, hands clutched tightly around his first wage packet. It was the start of a career as a big punter. Three hours later, and a week's earnings sitting in a bookie's satchel, he was transformed into the small punter he is today.

If I'd never met the wonderful Mrs Dede Scott-Brown, I probably wouldn't have given it a second thought. As it transpired, my day at York proved to be a close encounter with an early racing history as successful as Dick Turpin's ambition to reach middle-age with a short neck.

I don't care where you live; approach York from the south. Only from this direction will you get the chance to wind through country lanes which leave you doubting your sense of direction. But suddenly, as if reaching a mountain top, the racecourse presents itself in all its glory, the lush six-furlong straight firing off into the distance, the gigantic stands looming against the horizon. There is nothing small about this ancient Roman course. This is racing on a grand scale and, like New York, its American namesake, big is considered beautiful.

Even the car parks (once you find them – they're poorly marked) are gargantuan. The main entrance seems to have more pillars than the Coliseum, the new Knavesmire Stand wouldn't look out of place in Manhattan, and the paddock is big enough for an arable farmer to make a decent living. Even the old Terry's chocolate factory, which stands adjacent to the main entrance, is more like a giant Victorian asylum for patients driven insane by trying to find the soft centres in a nut selection.

It had been thirty years since I last visited this course and I felt like a stranger in the city. This wasn't helped by the authorities failing to put up any notices telling the public what time the doors opened. Irate punters tapped on windows and shuffled up and down in growing annoyance. A seething hack hammered on the door.

'This is no way to treat customers!' he shrieked.

'I've got a press conference at 11.15 a.m. Let me in! Let me in NOW!'

He was met with no more than a blank stare from a security officer who had obviously come straight from an *NYPD Blues* lookalike competition. Despite his dark blue reefer jacket and badge-emblazoned baseball cap, he looked about as frightening as an angry jelly. The crowd grew even more restless but to no avail. Not until 11 a.m., and another exchange of window hammering and dead-pan staring, did the doors swing open. A simple sign could have lowered some very high blood pressures.

It would take a novel the size of *War and Peace* to describe the various facilities. Put simply, you can choose between the big and casual Silver Ring, the even bigger and casual Tattersalls enclosure, or the gigantic and smart County enclosure. I made my usual inspection of all these areas, starting in the rather dour Silver Ring, whose adequate stands look over the one-furlong pole. In order to view all areas I had taken the precaution to wear the required jacket and tie. Unfortunately the wearing of such an outfit causes great confusion in the Silver Ring. Within seconds of entry I was viewed with great suspicion.

'You sure you want to come in here?' queried the gateman.

'Can we bring our dog in here?' asked a young couple, mysteriously swinging an empty lead and carrying a bowl of murky water.

Retreating quickly to Tattersalls, I dived for cover in the new Knavesmire Stand. This construction (which the locals call the Ebor) could easily double as a modern multiplex cinema, its rooms so cavernous that each one would make a decent-sized theatre. It's the only time I've ever suffered agoraphobia inside a building. I'd have felt more confined if I'd been standing in the middle of the Sahara desert. By sheer chance, I had an old compass in my pocket and made it back onto the main concourse before my water supply ran out.

The Grandstand lying adjacent to the Knavesmire offers no refuge for a confused punter. This dreary, grey-clad building, reminiscent of a 1960s polytechnic, has an interior laid out with about as much logic as a square circle. Stairs, lifts and escalators appear to go in every direction, delivering the public into bars and restaurants they had no intention of visiting. Two hours in this building would give you enough training to get through the Hampton Court maze in under three minutes. If you've got a sure-fire winner lined up for the 3.30, it would be advisable to make your way to the betting ring no later than 2 p.m.

Having now exchanged agoraphobia for claustrophobia, I hurried back onto the concourse. A small jazz band thumped out the old standards to an unresponsive audience whose heads remained buried in their *Racing Posts*. I stopped just long enough to make sure the singer saw me tapping my foot in time with the music. We all need some recognition and he beamed with a smile like a tramp who'd just been given a bottle of sweet sherry.

But if you prefer French bubbly, the champagne and seafood bar, which lies behind the paddock, is the place to be seen. Personally, I've always regarded champagne as only slightly more palatable than a dental mouthwash – but each to their own. The setting, however, is a match for a Henley regatta. A flower bordered terrace fronts the long open air bar, the fashionable Yorkshire set guffawing their way through enough lobsters, mussels and oysters to ensure that by the next morning they'd all be in direct line to the throne.

A cheese sandwich seemed a far safer bet for my sensitive stomach, and reluctant to re-enter the brash Knavesmire Stand or the bleak York Polytechnic, I approached a steward for advice.

'Melrose Stand? Toffs and trainers only.' He made it quite obvious that he considered I failed to qualify for either social category. 'Try the Old County Stand – lovely spot up there.'

It was like being given a tip for a 50-1 winner. In their rush to provide modern facilities, the course authorities have had the sense to retain the 'pearl' of York. From the rear, this small squat building looks fairly nondescript and is dwarfed by the New York skyline of its neighbours. But look back from the rail on the course side and you're in for a real treat.

Despite the city's ancient Roman origins, this stand suggests that its designer favoured Venice rather than Florence or Naples. The magnificent slated roof is held up by twenty-four supports, which look as if they've just been festooned in red, white and blue ribbons by a group of racegoing maypole dancers. The ornate, wrought iron architraves are a work of real craftsmanship, each one studded with a series of white Yorkshire roses. As a dyed-in-the-wool Lancastrian, I usually get as much pleasure out of a white rose as Dracula does out of a clove of garlic, but on this occasion I put my natural animosity to one side.

The standing areas in the Old County Stand enjoy a fine view over the two-mile horseshoe course and the deep seated, white Victorian benches are as cosy as an old pair of slippers. Even better, a large sign makes it quite plain that these seats 'cannot be reserved' – a real slap in the face to the more commonplace elitism. York was beginning to win me over.

A step inside confirmed my growing optimism. Sweeping staircases with polished mahogany balustrades only add to the feeling of pleasure at finding this desert oasis. The whole building is more *My Fair Lady* than . . . well, *My Fair Lady*. As I was in the heart of Yorkshire, I heard no-one declare 'The royne in Spoyne loyes moynley on tha' ployne' – though I did overhear one woman suggest that, 'I've just 'eard it's pissin' down in't Costa.' Who needs Eliza Doolittle when you can meet Doris Boycott on a works outing from Barnsley?

I watched the first three races from the Old County

Stand, my losing run continuing all the way to and including the Dante Stakes, with a prize fund of £135,000. Revealing an extremely low IQ, I backed Mensa, a three-year-old colt who would obviously enjoy the one-mile, two-furlong trip and appeared to act on the soft ground. Unfortunately, after completely missing the break, Mensa seemed to be having about as much fun as I get out of rodding a blocked cesspit. My betting slip had hit the floor well before they reached the three-furlong pole.

It was at this point I suddenly thought of Galosh and, as it transpired, was only minutes away from meeting the indomitable Mrs Dede Scott-Brown. As I hinted earlier, York has always proved itself to be a financial graveyard for my wallet. For many years I have been haunted by the fact that one sunny October afternoon I had to suffer the indignity of leaving York races with no more than a sixpenny piece to last me until my next payday.

What I failed to relate is that in my deep subconscious I had buried the fact that on the very same day my now deceased mother had picked up a small fortune on Galosh, one of the biggest-priced winners ever seen at York races. For a woman whose ability to read form was only matched by my own skill in reading Mandarin Chinese, this was a highly unexpected result. Was it all a figment of my imagination? Some Freudian complex which was now surfacing as history took its cruel revenge? I was determined to face the ghosts of Knavesmire past.

Tucked away on the fourth floor of the York Polytechnic Grandstand is a small museum bursting with racing memorabilia and curiosities. Faded oil paintings decorate the walls, the early artists portraying their subjects as flattened greyhounds being ridden by giant jockeys with longer legs than a catwalk model.

Most peculiar of all is a display cabinet devoted to the famous race of 1851 between Voltigeur and The Flying Dutchman. Though Voltigeur lost this contest he has, for some reason, always remained the more famous of the two contestants. Perhaps it's the case that he was the only three-legged horse to run in a Group One race? In a rather macabre fashion, the visiting public are treated to one small glass cabinet displaying a leg (just the one) of this losing hero.

The notice informed me that it was presented by H. Dobson-Peacock and formerly owned by Lord Zetland. Was there a dispute between these two men? Did Lord Zetland leave this blood-soaked amputation in Dobson-Peacock's bed? Was there a 19th century Yorkshire mafia? We may never know.

Whatever the case, I had greater things on my mind. The doorman directed me to the curator's office which lies in the corner of the museum. 'Leave the door,' commanded Mrs Scott-Brown, leaving no room for debate. 'I'm on my own.' A small mirror hung on the wall close to the door and I glanced quickly towards it. As far as I could see I didn't possess the leer of a maniac, though I did have a small tea stain on my tie and her request was probably a very sensible precaution.

'Galosh? Goloosh? Galash?' she queried.

'I'm sure it was Galosh,' I answered meekly.

'Date?'

'Er . . . not sure . . . '63, '64? Maybe later.'

'Much later?'

'No later than 1970. Don't worry if it's difficult.'

'Love a challenge. Nothing better. Not been beaten yet.'

I got the impression that this woman wouldn't have been beaten by a full battalion of paratroopers. Seconds later and in a flurry of activity, reference books were scanned, dismissed, revisited and cross-referenced. This was no amateur curator. I was watching a true professional at work and minutes later she had sensed victory.

'Got it! Got it!' she exclaimed. '1968. Galosh. Trainer W. Elsey. Soft ground specialist over ten furlongs. October. Awarded race after stewards' inquiry. Winner relegated to last place.'

I stood for a second in stunned silence, my response choked by the awful truth.

'So it's true,' I spluttered.

'Absolutely.'

'Awarded race after stewards' inquiry? Does it give the starting-price?'

'Fifty-to-one. I shouldn't think anyone backed that one,' she smiled in triumph.

'You never met my mother,' I answered, a small bead of sweat appearing on my brow.

I hope she's still there when you visit York. Forget the new stands, the champagne bars and packed restaurants. You could spend a delightful afternoon just talking to the wonderful Dede Scott-Brown. I just hope they never decide to put one of her legs in a display cabinet.

My visit to York ended as it had begun, hovering around the sumptuous paddock watching other punters cheer in the winners I had failed to select. The curse of York was still upon me. At least I headed home with more than sixpence in my pocket, though there had been one fleeting moment when I was tempted to entertain the crowd from the centre of the course. I can do a very realistic impression of Dick Turpin's last moments after I've just backed five losers. Luckily for me, there wasn't a tree in sight and the tow rope was still in the boot of my car.

Postscript I: York? Too big. Too brazen. Too American. But fun all the same. Big is best? Not really. You've probably guessed. In my book, small is beautiful.

Postscript II: All right. Credit where credit's due. They've made even more changes at York. The new Ebor Stand has replaced much of the escalator ridden, claustrophobic 1960s grandstand. Thankfully they've left much of the wonderful old facade intact which suggests that somebody's still got their head screwed on. I think they've finally recognized that modernism has its limits. In 2005 they were granted the 'Royal' summer meeting, transferred from deepest Berkshire whilst Ascot underwent its all-singing, all-dancing facelift. Sadly they were 'persuaded' to call the meeting 'Royal Ascot at York'. Despite conditions which would have tested the resilience of an Arctic explorer, and a road system which appeared to be designed for horse-drawn carriages, the York authorities did a fine job – less pomp, more appropriate circumstance, and easier to get around. When the meeting returns south, they should demand that it's called 'Royal York at Ascot'. Fat chance.

Betting record on all 61 racecourses. Maximum stake fund at each track £30.

Course	Winners	Places	Losers	Profit	Loss
Plumpton	0	2	4		£25.20
Fakenham	2	1	3	£13.40	
Cheltenham	1	1	4	£22.80	
Warwick	1	1	4		£18.40
Newbury	2	1	3	£31.50	
Towcester	1	1	3	£13.80	
Huntingdon	1	0	4		£30.00
Wetherby	0	0	5		£30.00
Leicester	2	2	0	£126.90	
Taunton	1	0	3		£28.70
Newton Abbot	2	0	1	£24.50	
Sandown	0	0	6		£30.00
Folkestone	0	2	2		£28.96
Ludlow	1	1	2	£2.12	
Fontwell	2	0	2	£4.84	
Wincanton	1	2	0	£37.50	
Lingfield	0	2	2		£7.38
Aintree	1	3	2	£37.50	
Chepstow	0	0	3		£29.80
Brighton	0	2	4		£24.30
Chester	0	0	5		£24.60
Stratford	2	1	2	£229.00	
York	0	0	5		£26.00
Goodwood	0	2	2		£21.90
Great Yarmouth	0	0	3		£30.00
Epsom	0	0	4		£30.00
Salisbury	1	2	1	£22.20	
Ascot	0	0	4		£30.00
Bath	0	2	2		£25.20
Newmarket	0	0	5		£30.00
Windsor	1	2	2		£16.20
Beverley	0	2	3	£10.40	
Pontefract	0	1	4		£25.40

Betting record on all 61 racecourses. Maximum stake fund at each track £30.

Course	Winners	Places	Losers	Profit	Loss
Worcester	1	2	1	£47.50	
Doncaster	0	1	3		£19.50
Southwell	0	2	2	£6.75	
Exeter	0	0	4		£30.00
Sedgefield	3	1	1	£75.20	
Redcar	0	0	4		£30.00
Nottingham	1	2	2	£106.20	
Bangor-on-Dee	3	0	1	£56.90	
Wolverhampton	0	0	4		£30.00
Kempton	3	1	1	£97.45	
Carlisle	2	2	0	£105.50	
Kelso	0	2	2		£26.10
Newcastle	2	1	2	£7.40	
Hexham	2	1	2	£37.40	
Market Rasen	2	1	3	£0.75	
Musselburgh	1	3	2	£34.20	
Uttoxeter	1	1	3	£9.60	
Catterick	0	3	1		£7.20
Hereford	0	0	3		£25.40
Haydock	1	1	3		£22.40
Ripon	1	3	3	£87.40	
Ayr	3	2	1	£22.50	
Thirsk	2	2	2	£32.50	
Hamilton	1	1	3		£20.80
Perth	2	1	3	£5.55	
Cartmel	0	1	5		£26.10
Ffos Las	2	1	3	£3.25	
Totals	55	68	163	£1,312.51	£749.54

Total profit: £562.97
Average profit per racecourse to a £30 maximum outlay: £9.23
Average profit minus Mars Bars, Cornish pasties, single malts: nil